Running Against the Grain

The Story of Philadelphia Eagle and Movie Star Timmy Brown

RUNNING AGAINST THE GRAIN

THE STORY OF PHILADELPHIA EAGLE AND MOVIE STAR

TIMMY BROWN

ROY WEAVER, DAVID SULLIVAN,
AND SHAWN SRIVER

EAGLE22 LLC

ISBN 979-8-9868201-1-8

Published by Eagle 22 LLC, Muncie, Ind.

Book design by Amy Junod

Cover image:
Timmy Brown wearing No. 22 in Eagles green in a photo from the 1967 season, his last with the team. *BETTMAN ARCHIVE / GETTY IMAGES*

The authors used multiple sources of information – interviews, books, periodicals, documents, videos, and social media – to ensure the accuracy of this book. Every effort was made to locate any copyright owners of the photos used. The authors regret any inadvertent omission or error.

FOREWORD

By Merrill Reese

You could say I was born an Eagles fan. Almost. By the time I was 3 years old, my parents had plopped me down next to the big console radio in our living room, and I was transfixed by Eagles football. The golden voice of Byrum Saam was music to my ears beginning in the mid-1940s. He painted vivid pictures, brought players to life, and gave me my first Eagles hero. I envisioned Steve Van Buren running over, around, and through people as the Birds (they were always "the Birds") usually emerged victorious.

Steve Van, the Moving Van, was the first of the Eagles running backs who created a stir each time he touched the football. He was special. In my years as the Eagles' play-by-play voice, beginning in 1977, there have been three – Wilbert Montgomery, Brian Westbrook, and LeSean "Shady" McCoy.

But as a fan in the post-Van Buren years, there was only one – Timmy Brown, beginning in 1960. He was the Eagles' gift from the Green Bay Packers, who drafted him in the 27th round of the 1959 draft. Can you imagine 27 rounds? That's 20 more than they have today. Vince Lombardi is certainly on the Mount Rushmore of NFL coaches, but did he ever make a mistake. He went hot and cold on Brown and finally cut him after one game.

As a birthday present, my mother gave me season tickets to Franklin Field for the 1960 season. They were $35 for seven games – total!

The Eagles had signed Brown after watching him play against them in a preseason game. I remember the first time I saw him. Even in pregame warmups, he stood out. He moved with grace. He didn't play a lot that season – 11 kickoff returns, 10 punt returns, 9 carries, and 9 receptions – but he did score twice as a ball carrier and twice as a receiver. He was part of the Eagles' 1960 championship team. They beat the Green Bay Packers by 17-13 – the only playoff loss ever for Vince Lombardi. How ironic.

A few years later, a friend from college had gotten a job in the public relations department of the Eagles. He asked if I wanted to meet him at the studios of WCAU-TV, Channel 10, not far from my home. He was escorting Timmy Brown and Irv Cross to the station to record a public service spot. I was thrilled for the opportunity. We met in the lobby and I was star-struck. Both men were friendly and immediately put me at ease. Both were well-dressed. Timmy looked like a Hollywood star. Irv had more the look of a young attorney or executive. I was hardly surprised when Timmy got involved as a singer and actor. Irv became part of the "NFL Today" pregame show with Brent Musberger, Phyllis George (later Jayne Kennedy), and Jimmy "the Greek" Snyder. Irv also headed a management and investment firm.

Roy Weaver, David Sullivan, and Shawn Sriver did extensive research to bring us "Running Against the Grain: The Story of

Philadelphia Eagle and Movie Star Timmy Brown." For those of us who were electrified by the Eagles' dazzling No. 22, it's a fascinating rags-to-riches account. For those who are too young to remember this brilliant athlete and complex human being, it's a revealing look into a piece of NFL history.

Merrill Reese has been the radio voice of the Philadelphia Eagles since 1977.

CONTENTS

PREFACE

It had never been accomplished before in the National Football League. It would be decades before it happened again.

On Nov. 6, 1966, at age 29, he was wearing Philadelphia Eagles green, a running back in the middle of a gridiron career that would lead him to the team's hall of fame.

His life's journey had not been easy. He began it as one of six children growing up in a small city east of Indianapolis, but his family fell apart and he was sent to a home for orphans and at-risk children. He faced the racial restrictions and attitudes enforced on all African Americans before the civil rights era. Perseverance led him to college, but still, his world had consisted only of the flat plains of East Central Indiana. His dreams ran wider.

At Ball State, his talents started to jell. He did well in many sports, but also started to find his voice as a singer. While he often struggled academically, he excelled in football. He left college in 1959 before finishing his degree to join the Green Bay Packers in Vince Lombardi's first season there. His confident, sometimes brash demeanor did not sit well with Lombardi's no-nonsense style. But his quick departure was a blessing, as he soon joined the Eagles. In Philadelphia, he found himself as a player and entertainer.

By 1966, he had established himself as one of the best offensive weapons in the NFL. He had finally obtained his college diploma. He was a regionally popular singer, booked into nightclubs, and a friend – and sometimes boyfriend – of top recording stars such as Chubby Checker and Diana Ross. Helped by his team's proximity to New York, he found professional training not only as a singer, but as an actor – his next dream. He had appeared in summer stock theater in the Philadelphia area. He was beginning to talk of retirement from football, although from time to time he intimated that a trade to the Los Angeles Rams, to allow him to focus more on acting, would be of interest.

But his screen career – including roles in two iconic films of the 1970s and one of the most beloved TV series of all time – was well in the future. And his pursuit of work in entertainment was not always sitting well with coaches, teammates, sportswriters, and fans, who thought it distracted him from the only future they cared about – providing excitement and victories on the football field for as long as he was able.

In November 1966, Timmy Brown – everyone knew him this way, although his given name was Thomas – had established himself as a solid and versatile back who could catch passes and was one of the most effective kick returners in the league. He had studied how to play the position, and said he "ran against the grain of the blocking and tackling," sometimes faking to the right, then breaking quickly to the left. But as he walked onto Franklin Field on this Sunday afternoon, with temperatures in the mid-40s and a slight wind, his only focus was to keep Philadelphia in the hunt for a playoff berth. His 4-4 Eagles were in a must-win situation if they wanted to get back into contention against the division-leading Dallas Cowboys. The Cowboys were seeking their first trip to the playoffs since joining the league in 1960. The Eagles were also hungry for revenge for a game a month earlier, in which Dallas, led by quarterback Don Meredith's 394 passing yards and five touchdown passes, had crushed the Eagles by 56-7. In that game, Timmy had only been able to manage 8 rushing yards on eight carries, although he did have five receptions for 62 yards.

The 1 p.m. game got off to a bad start for the Eagles. Dan Reeves, the Cowboys' running back – his 135 total yards of offense would eclipse the Eagles' team total for the day by 55 yards – scored a 2-yard touchdown to put the Cowboys up by 7-0. The Eagles knew that the Cowboys were on the verge of taking the crowd out of the game and, in essence, ending their season. It was time for some big plays.

Timmy took his usual place near the end zone and watched Danny Villanueva's perfect kick fly toward him. As the ball landed in his hands, he saw an opening — one that would land him in the NFL record book.

As he ran toward the end zone, Timmy also was sprinting toward the end of his football career – which would come with a different team in the third Super Bowl. He was moving toward an acting career that would keep him in the Hollywood game for about a decade, but would largely lead to years of frustration. Philadelphia fans knew Timmy as one of the swiftest men on the field, a moody person not afraid to speak of and show his feelings, a football player who also wanted to be an entertainer (or perhaps an entertainer who also wanted to be a football player). Today, reaching any height seemed possible. Timmy was at the top of his game. It would not have seemed likely that this aspiring Renaissance man would nearly always fall short of his dreams. He lived his life running against the grain – making decisions that would often be unanticipated and surprising to those who knew him best, and that did not always work out as he intended.

Still, Nov. 6, 1966, would not be like that. It would be an unforgettable day. And this day belonged to Timmy Brown.

RICHMOND

CHAPTER ONE

The Birth of Tiny Tim

Thomas Allen Brown was born on May 24, 1937, in Richmond, Ind. In the 1930s, if you were Black, Indiana might not have been high on the list of places to be born, if you could have chosen. Just a decade before, the Ku Klux Klan in Indiana had been one of the largest and strongest Klans in the nation, and to a degree controlled the state government, at a time when nearly a third of native-born white males in Indiana were members. The Klan's statewide leader, D.C. Stephenson, once said, "I am the law in Indiana." By the middle of the 1920s, there were more Klan members than Methodists, the state's largest denomination. One of the last confirmed lynchings in the northern United States occurred in Marion, Ind., on Aug. 7, 1930, when two teenagers were hanged in the city center, having allegedly killed a white factory worker and raping his companion. The allegations were never proven.

Still, if one was going to be born Black in Indiana, Richmond was one of the better places. In the 1800s, Quakers had moved to the area, on the state's eastern border. They were fleeing communities in the South that supported slavery, and were looking for cheap but fertile land to work. In Wayne County, they built a town where differences among people were respected, at least by the standards of their time. The Quakers believed in social justice and equality. They supported education, founding a boarding school that became Earlham College.

The Quakers were active in the Underground Railroad. Newport (now Fountain City), about nine miles north of Richmond, was home to Levi Coffin, sometimes referred to its president. During the two decades that he and his wife, Catharine, lived there, they helped more than 2,000 enslaved people. Slaves crossed the Ohio River from Kentucky and made their way to the Coffins'. There they would stay for days or weeks, until they were strong enough to move farther north, sometimes as far as Canada.

By the 1920s, Richmond, now home to about 30,000 people, had also become a place where Black singers, songwriters, and musicians could find success. Gennett Records was a division of the Starr Piano Co., which was founded as the Trayser Piano Co. in 1872 and had grown to occupy several buildings, becoming a major local employer. Gennett recorded jazz and blues artists in the 1920s, when other large record companies refused to do so. It produced records by Louis Armstrong, Duke Ellington, Jelly Roll Morton, Fats Waller, and many others. Richmond became known as the "cradle of recorded jazz."

While Richmond was not legally segregated, most of its Black residents lived "across the tracks" from much of the city – north of a main east-west line of the Pennsylvania Railroad. Among them were John and Juanita Brown, who brought their newborn second son home from the hospital to a small, two-story white bungalow at 824 N. 11th St. Waiting for their new brother, while being watched by a family member, were John Brown Jr., born a little more than a year earlier, and three daughters – 6-year-old Anita Joan, 5-year-old Norma Delores, and 3-year-old Betty Alma. The couple's last child, Della Yvonne, would arrive about a year and a half later.

It was the Browns' custom to give their children nicknames. Anita was "Polly"; Norma, "Trixie"; Betty, "Betts"; John Jr., "Buddy." When Della came along, she would be "Buggs." And in 1937, the new baby became "Tiny Tim." In an August 1973 interview in Black Sports magazine, Timmy Brown said, "My name was Thomas Allen Brown, but it's always been Tiny Tim, since I was a baby, because I was the tiniest baby that any of my relatives had ever seen." Over his life, he would use Timmy, Timmie, Tim, and Timothy as his first name, although he never had it legally changed. He would be best known, however, as Timmy Brown.

During his first few weeks at home, Timmy slept in a crib close to a potbelly stove, near his parents' bedroom. The four other children slept upstairs; Timmy and Buggs would join them as they got older.

Bedtime was quiet time, with little talk, laughter, or play. When they were instructed to go to bed at night, typically around 8 p.m., the children obediently climbed the steep, narrow stairs. Timmy and Buddy slept in one bedroom, with Buggs, Polly, Trixie, and Betts in the other. No lights, no talking. Before bed, all the children would get onto their knees, fold their hands, and recite the Lord's Prayer. Both parents worked, and they expected quiet, as sleep was important to them. John was a porter at the Greyhound bus station; on the side, he hung wallpaper. Juanita made beds and cleaned rooms at a hotel.

The first years of Timmy's life were filled with times and events he remembered fondly. He said later that he could recall feeling the heat of that stove, though he was just a baby wrapped in a warm blanket and lying in his crib. "I'm too close to the hot stove," he imagined himself thinking. "I need to be moved further away." Shortly afterward, he felt wet. "I need to be changed, too," he thought. It was a memory he often shared when he was young, but he stopped talking about it later because others made fun of him. No one believed that he could remember an experience from that early in life. But Timmy didn't care what they thought. He knew he could remember it, and was amazed that he could go back that far in time.

The Browns were far from wealthy, but neither were they poor, and they knew how to find joy in life. Music filled the household daily. The popular singers of the late 1930s and the 1940s blared from the radio –

Frank Sinatra, Bing Crosby, Peggy Lee, Billie Holiday, Nat King Cole, the Mills Brothers, Ella Fitzgerald, and the Ink Spots were among the most popular. The entire family sang along, but Timmy was particularly enthusiastic. From the age of 8, he began to aspire to be a singer. He learned that he had a knack for quickly learning songs, imitating the lyrics and sounds, and singing on pitch. It just came naturally to him.

He never recalled a day when he went hungry, though at times there was not much to eat. But this was no problem for him, as he was "never a big eater." Fried tomatoes and eggs were a staple. Every Sunday there was fried chicken, a favorite.

Playing with his brother and sisters brought joy as well. Teasing, bantering, and harmless pushing and punching were routine. On one occasion, after he had teased Betts repeatedly, she grabbed the poker from beside the stove and chased him up the stairs. When she caught up with him, she lightly jabbed him with it. "You branded me," Timmy screamed. They broke into laughter. But although he laughed, he could feel a stinging, burning feeling. The hot poker had indeed left a mark.

Timmy was closest to his youngest sister, Buggs, and as an older brother he felt responsible for her. One day, he noticed that Buggs was in the alley and older children had started throwing rocks at her. He rushed to her aid. Trying to defend her, he threw rocks back. As he leaned down to get more rocks, he saw one of the boys take aim at her. He didn't realize how large the rock was that the boy was about to launch. He jumped in front of her and was hit above the right eye. The knot stayed with him for a long time and left a permanent indentation. But he remembered most that as painful as being hit was, he did not cry. He realized then, he said, that he had a high threshold for pain.

Timmy liked rhubarb. Across the alley, some neighbors had planted a rhubarb patch and built an electrified wire fence around it. Timmy eyed the rhubarb for several days once it began to ripen. One day, when a couple of his friends were at his house, the temptation became too strong. Because of his thin frame, Timmy was chosen to try to reach through the fence. As his friends stood as lookouts, he slowly stretched his hand and arm through the fence. But his arm touched the wire and he got a sharp jolt. He yanked his arm out, jumped up and down, and shouted – more from surprise than the electric shock itself. Frightened, the three friends ran quickly to his house, where, safe, they laughed.

One warm, humid summer evening, when he was 6, he, his brother, and four of his brother's friends walked several blocks south, into an industrial area near the railroad tracks. Timmy looked up to the group, which he later likened to Spanky's gang from the movies. He wasn't invited to go along with the older boys often, but when they needed his help, they included him.

They made faces, played tag, punched each other, told jokes, laughed, and walked fast, "looking for something to do." After some time, they came upon a warehouse. Timmy recalled that one of the boys said, "They have tires in there."

"Let's get some and roll them," another shouted. "Good idea," a third said.

But first they had to get in. After about a minute of discussion, one boy hoisted Timmy onto his shoulders. Timmy, small and willowy, was known as one of the best tree-climbers in the neighborhood. He could wiggle through a small window and drop into the loft. He climbed to the floor and opened the latch to a door. The others rushed in and grabbed a tire. As Timmy recalled it, he had no intention of stealing. But an older boy quickly pushed a tire toward him and said firmly, "Roll this for me." Timmy knew this wasn't a request but a command, so he rolled it out of the building with the others.

For what seemed like nearly an hour, the boys raced the tires and pushed them at one another like playing dodge ball, winding in and out of streets and alleys. Even though he had stolen the tire, rolling tires was one of the coolest things to do, Timmy thought. At times like this, he felt accepted, part of the gang. As the fun wore off, the boys simply left the tires along the way and drifted off to their homes.

The next morning, Timmy was sitting on his porch when a police car pulled up. He could see two of the boys he had played with in the back. He turned to the screen door and called for his mother to bring him some saltine crackers. She didn't see the police until she came out with them. She gave them to Timmy and asked the officers what they wanted.

One officer told her that the boys had said Timmy had opened the door to the tire warehouse the night before. The officer said several tires had been stolen, but had been recovered.

His mother asked Timmy if he knew anything about it. He didn't respond for a few seconds, then shook his head. Having stuffed several crackers into his mouth helped keep him from talking, but it also calmed him. He had thought he would be taken to jail, but the officers returned to the car and drove away. They had made their point with a warning, and the fear he felt would make him think twice in the future.

School was another source of joy for Timmy. In September 1943, at age 6, he entered kindergarten at Nicholson Elementary School. He looked forward to packing a lunch his mother made in the morning and walking the four blocks with his sisters and brother. Music was his favorite subject, and he always looked forward to running and blowing off steam at recess. The girls found him handsome and fun to be around. He had a magnetic smile and warm manner. They found it easy to talk with him, which was unusual, because other boys tended to ignore them. "Because girls liked me, it made boys angry," he recalled. "After school, two or three guys waited for me outside the entrance. I would hear them say, 'Here he is. Coming down here.' They saw me walking toward them, so I would rush down a hallway and out another door. They would chase me home. That's when I became a runner. I was quick, and they never caught me. I was running for my life, with three or four guys running after me. After a time, they gave up. I could never figure out why they were chasing me. I wasn't bothering them."

The next year, when he was 7 and his brother 8, their father decided it was time they began to learn a trade. As often as he could, he took them on wallpapering jobs. He asked them to help as he painted, stripped paper, filled cracks, and sanded. They handed him tools when asked and watched, but they didn't really get it. He was trying to be a good dad, but they were too young to understand what he was teaching them.

John Brown Sr. didn't believe that education led to anything in life, particularly for Black people. He wanted his sons to have a trade that would give them enough money to live on. Of school, he repeatedly said, "You're wasting your time. The man ain't going to let you get nowhere." His views reflected his own experience. Indiana was fertile ground for racial discrimination and hatred. It had shaped John Brown Sr., and he would try to prepare his children for it.

As he grew older, Timmy felt that his father favored his brother. He wondered if it was because Buddy was the elder son, or that Buddy had been named John Jr., or that Buddy was darker skinned. The feeling would linger for years. Nonetheless, he idolized Buddy, who he thought was a better athlete and smarter.

Around this time, his childhood began to unravel. His father enlisted in the Army on July 6, 1944, and entered service at Fort Benjamin Harrison in Indianapolis, joining the 629th Ordnance Ammunition Company. For nine months while in the Army, he was stationed in the Asiatic-Pacific Theater of Operations and was a cook for military personnel.

While his father was in the service, Timmy said, his mother would get a babysitter to watch the children when she went out. He said that on one occasion he found himself alone with the babysitter. "That's when I lost my virginity," he said with a smile. Of course, he was 8 years old when this allegedly happened.

After his father returned home on Jan. 7, 1946, the relationship between the parents quickly deteriorated. John Sr. expected to resume his role as head of the family, but for 18 months Juanita had been managing without him. Also, John became aware that while he was gone, she had found someone else. John and Juanita constantly argued and fought. John's habits of a fifth of bourbon and two packs of cigarettes a day – which he bragged about starting when he was 13 – were a major source of the discontent, Timmy thought: "He was that kind of alcoholic that knew how to turn it on and off, and he could. That broke the family up when he went off to war and left her with six kids. He didn't have to do that. If you had that many kids, you didn't have to go to war. There were exemptions. But he was gone quick. Irresponsible. I had a lot of inner thoughts." He thought his mother had been asked to do more than could have been expected.

Increasingly, the arguments became more volatile and physical. Timmy was told by his brother that his father had hit his mother. He didn't know why, nor did he care. He didn't believe a man should hit a woman under any circumstances. But while he didn't like what his father was doing, he still loved him.

On Feb. 14, 1946, just a few weeks after his father's return home, his parents divorced. Timmy did not know at the time that the divorce was granted on the ground that his mother had committed adultery. Juanita then left town. Timmy recalled, "Mom split town with a guy to Detroit." While Timmy had felt that his father should not have gone to war, Buggs now believed that it was unreasonable for her father to have to care for six children, and she could never understand why their mother had left. She had fond memories of taking the train to Virginia with her mother to see her father when he was posted there in the Army. And she remembered him bringing the girls wooden shoes and a mother-of-pearl heart with their name for each one. The heart she kept for life as a treasure.

With their mother gone, all six children became wards of the Wayne County Department of Public Welfare by order of Juvenile Court. They were taken from their home to the Wayne County Jail downtown. Separated from their parents, they were frightened, and worried about their future. They felt that somehow the divorce was their fault, and that being in jail would be part of their permanent record. They felt like criminals.

The divorce scarred Timmy deeply. He believed he had done something to cause it. "I was always sensitive," Timmy said. "I kept everything within myself. I never said anything. My brother – he was always the smartest, plus being the best athlete – did all the talking. He was like my lawyer.... I wanted my family because I was a little boy that needed a family. So did my brother, but he was a little man ... and I was a little boy."

After two days at the jail, they were moved to the home of their grandfather Everett Goens. He was an imposing figure. He had worked as a butler and accumulated sufficient wealth to own a spacious two-story home on South 12th Street. After the death of his first wife, Della, in 1931, and a brief second marriage, he married Doris Gonzales, who had been born in the British West Indies. The children called her Auntie Doris.

Timmy recalled her as caring, supportive, light-skinned, outgoing, and beautiful. It was through her that Timmy had his first formal experience with singing, acting, and manners. He, Buddy, and Buggs participated in the Wee Dramatics Club, a neighborhood group Auntie Doris organized. Among the other members was Paul Davis, who was the same age as Timmy, and lived eight or nine blocks south of him. He remembered her in the same way as Timmy.

Timmy sang "Sleigh Bells Ring," his first solo, in a Christmas program. At Easter, Doris took the Wee Dramatics members to Cincinnati, about 70 miles away, to appear on the popular "50-50 Club," a 90-minute daily variety show hosted by Ruth Lyons on the regionally dominant WLW radio station. They sang "I Wuv a Wabbit," written by Mickey Katz and made famous by Spike Jones. Nearly 70 years later, Timmy could still sing the song:

I wuv a wabbit, a cwazy, cwazy wabbit.
Hop hop, bunny, bunny, hop hop, bunny, bunny,

Hop hop, oh oh, hop hop.

He don't like cawwots, I'm cwazy over cawwots
Chew, chew, bunny, bunny,
chew, chew, bunny, bunny,
Chew chew, oh oh, chew chew

He cuddles up in beddy-by
I kiss him, he kisses I . . .

In contrast to Auntie Doris, Everett Goens was intimidating, mean-spirited, and controlling. He was verbally and physically abusive to his wife, Timmy, and the other children. Buggs recalled the most memorable incident of abuse and its consequences: "It was my responsibility to make the beds and empty the trash before going to school. I could not do this and get to school on time, and had to stay late at school as punishment. When I returned home late, my grandfather whipped me with a belt. After repeated beatings, I left school one day and went to my father's home." Goens called the police and claimed that John Brown had kidnapped her, but she told the police what had really happened. Thereafter she lived sometimes with her father, but mostly in a cottage with Polly and her husband, Buddy Hayes, at Earlham, which both were attending. Buggs said she could never figure out why Everett was so mean to her; later in life, all she could think of was that he disliked her because her given name, Della, was the same as Everett's first wife's.

And there was a deeper darkness to Everett Goens. Timmy indicated that on two occasions, Goens tried to force Timmy to perform oral sex on him. "He threatened to put us out if I didn't. I don't know how he was with the others, but he tried to molest me," Timmy recalled. "I avoided it by saying I had to go to the bathroom and leaving my bedroom." He found the thought of what Goens wanted demeaning and disgusting.

Not long after the second incident involving Timmy, all of the children but Trixie had moved to other homes, in part with the aid of members of Bethel African Methodist Episcopal Church. Betts went to live with her Aunt Kate's parents in nearby Rushville. Trixie remained with the Goenses for two years, until she graduated from Richmond High School on her 16th birthday; on the same day, she married Clarence Dixon. By then, Buggs had already left to live with her father or the already married Polly. And Timmy and Buddy moved into the home of Richard and Katie Bennett at 333 S. Ninth St.

Living with the Bennetts, Timmy said, was the most positive part of his childhood: "In a way, the breakup of the family was a good thing, in that we ended up living with the Bennetts." Katie, an ordained A.M.E. evangelist, and Richard, a factory worker, emphasized religion, discipline, education, and manners. The Bennetts made certain that the boys were dressed and ready for school each day, and had a packed lunch. For the first few months of spring 1947, Buddy and Timmy both attended Warner Elementary School, a short walk from their new home. A year later, Buddy entered Hibbard School for junior high. For Timmy, life at Warner was the same as school life had been before, except that the school was more integrated. He would jump on and off the merry-go-round, and slide through a metal tube during fire drills. Girls were still attracted to him. Boys were still jealous and would chase him home from school. But the Bennetts emphasized education more than his parents or grandfather had: "They were very disciplined, and made sure we studied and did our homework. They wanted us to do everything right." In a July 1964 Sport Magazine article, Berry Stainback wrote that the Bennetts noted that "all the children took the family breakup badly, but Timmy took it worst."

Every Sunday, Buddy, Timmy, and the Bennetts walked about a half-mile to Bethel A.M.E. Church at 200 S. Sixth St. Katie made sure that Timmy and Buddy were dressed appropriately. A handkerchief was tucked neatly into his back pants pocket. "Aunt Katie," as he and Buddy lovingly called her, had told them that they needed to dress nicely and carry a handkerchief when with ladies. And she commanded them to change their socks and underwear daily.

The church became an important part of Timmy's life, and he was baptized and considered becoming a minister. He learned about the church's history. Bethel "was organized Sept. 23, 1836, 25 years before the Civil War, by Rev. William Paul Quinn, a traveling evangelist and missionary of the A.M.E. church," Florence Lawson wrote in a 1976 article in the Richmond Palladium-Item. "At that time," she wrote, "Richmond was a struggling village with a population of about 1,200 persons, and fewer than 50 Black adults in the community. Most of these had come north from Virginia and North Carolina to escape the laws enacted by these states against Black people. Richmond, with its Quaker population, was like a 'city of refuge.' Here the Blacks could live in safety, enjoy religious freedom and make some progress." The church's second floor had been used as a school, where Quaker men and women served as teachers.

Timmy studied the Bible daily. One of his favorite verses was Genesis 1:24-25, which in the Revised Standard Version reads: "And God said, 'Let the earth bring forth living creatures of every kind: cattle and creeping things and beasts of the earth according to their kinds.' And it was so. And God made the beasts of the earth according to their kinds, and the cattle according to their kinds, and everything that creeps upon the ground according to its kind. And God saw that it was good." The passage had a profound impact on him: "I still am aware of not stepping on an ant or any of those things. I've always been very sensitive that way about killing. I even take dragonflies out of the pool, to save their lives." While he was becoming more religious, he also was superstitious. He avoided stepping on cracks on sidewalks, thinking it might bring bad luck, a belief that would stay with him throughout life.

He also enjoyed playing in a church basketball league, where he reconnected with Paul Davis, whom he had met in Wee Dramatics. Davis remembered playing for a year with him and how impressed he was with Timmy's speed.

Timmy worked for Bethel's pastor, the Rev. William D. Shannon, cleaning the parsonage yard nearly every week from spring to fall. Impressed by the pastor's performance in the pulpit on Sunday and the respect accorded him, he looked forward to the brief visits that came from his work. He was taken by how handsome, intelligent, and charismatic Shannon was.

As he worked, he noticed that one of the pastor's responsibilities was counseling parishioners. He understood that church members had problems that the pastor was expected to help solve. In his observation, most of the parishioners taking their woes to Shannon appeared to be women. And one day, he noticed that a woman was with the pastor for an unusually long time. Not long after that, there were accusations of improper behavior. As he thought about all this, he questioned the idea of pursuing the ministry. Meeting with someone in private, he thought, was dangerous, in that the person you met with could make up stories. He imagined not only the damage to one's reputation, but ending up in court or jail, accused of actions that could not be proved or disproved.

What he saw at church picnics also bothered him. He enjoyed the food and playing with friends at the park where the picnics were held. But as dusk approached, he saw couples walking off into the woods – some, he knew, not married to each other. What he imagined happening was distasteful to him. All this led to the end of his desire to become a minister.

While living with the Bennetts, Timmy met three boys who were to become longtime friends and go on to successful lives of their own: George Walker, Harold Jones, and Dave Chapman. Walker, whose father was a barber and mother was a homemaker, became a golf equipment salesman. Jones' father was a maintenance worker at Perfect Circle Corp., the piston-ring manufacturer, and a custodian at Dennis School, and his mother was a homemaker. Jones eventually left Richmond for the American Conservatory of Music in Chicago to study percussion. He became a world-renowned jazz drummer, working with Count Basie, Natalie Cole, Ray Charles, and others. Later in his career, he worked mainly with Tony Bennett. Chapman, a white boy whose father, Glenn, had played with the Brooklyn Dodgers, became a physical education teacher at Monta Vista High School in Cupertino.

In the alley behind the Bennett home, Timmy, Buddy, Harold, George, and Dave spent hours of free time doing the kinds of things boys do, like shooting marbles and playing basketball. Jones said in 2022 that they would play their own kind of horseshoes – they would put a can on the ground and throw washers at the can. Paul Flately, who would play football at Northwestern University and was rookie of the year as a wide receiver for the Minnesota Vikings in 1963, was a few years younger and an occasional participant.

Sometimes the boys played at one of their homes. Timmy recalled a time when they were taking turns swinging each other in a hammock. One of them wrapped the hammock around his body, and the others swung it as rapidly as possible, until the person could no longer hang on and would fly out. When it was Timmy's turn, he crashed to the ground and broke his right leg. For the next several weeks, his leg was in a cast. As a result of that experience, he said, "I have avoided hammocks."

In the summer of 1947, Katie Bennett had a nervous breakdown. Her condition, coupled with the fact that Richard worked full-time at Perfect Circle, meant that someone else had to be found to care for Timmy and Buddy. Katie was aware that fellow Bethel members Charles and Mae Ladd owned a 13-acre farm at the corner of U.S. Highway 40 and Pennville Road, about 13 miles west of Richmond. Charles "Bud" Ladd was a stocky, 5-foot-8 man who drove a grader in highway construction and farmed. He was considered friendly, outgoing, and talkative. Mae, light-skinned, 5-foot-2, and heavy-set, was known as a great cook who was crazy about children. Because they were respected church members, had no children, and owned a farm, Katie felt they were excellent candidates for becoming foster parents for Timmy and Buddy.

The Ladds agreed. In the fall of 1948, Timmy and Buddy moved to the farm. The first few days were filled with exploration, adventure, and learning to do chores. Moving from a small house in the city to a large two-story home on 13 acres expanded their world.

When school began, they rode a bus – Timmy to Pershing Elementary School, a little over a mile away, and Buddy about two miles to attend junior high at Lincoln High School in Cambridge City, the largest town in the western part of Wayne County. Gathering each morning at the Ladd farm to board the school bus were Timmy, Buddy, and neighbors Max Blose, a ninth grader at Lincoln who lived across the road from the farm on the southwest corner of U.S. 40 and Jacksonville Road; Chuck Swallow, also a ninth grader, who lived a quarter of a mile toward Richmond on the other side of U.S. 40; Pete Richardson, another ninth grader, who lived about a mile east of the Blose farm on the south side of U.S. 40; and the Colvin children – Julia, an eighth grader, and younger brothers Johnny and Jay – who lived across the road from the Blose barnyard. On the way home, the bus stopped to let them out at the Blose farm.

One day when he was 11, Timmy was late and the bus left without him, but with Buddy on it. Timmy ran to school that day. He found the race to be challenging and fun. Over time, Timmy deliberately waited to come out for the bus. He hid beside a shed, where the driver could not see him. At first, the driver waited patiently, expecting Timmy to eventually appear for the short ride to school. After a few times waiting, the driver simply drove away once Buddy stepped into the bus and sat down. Timmy learned that if he wanted to ride, he had better get on when Buddy did. But he enjoyed running to school. Two or three times a week, he raced the bus.

"I was fair. I let them get a head start, getting 50 or 100 yards away, where they couldn't see me," he recalled. "Then I would take off." He lost a few times early on, when he let the bus get too far down U.S. 40. He eventually figured out that if he gave the bus a 25- or 40-yard head start, far enough away that he couldn't be seen coming out from behind the shed, he could still win. He enjoyed catching up to the bus and waving to his classmates as they yelled and waved at him. Given that the bus had to make several stops and maneuver through the streets to the school building while he could run a direct route, cutting through yards, Timmy typically won the race.

Buddy was one of only a few Black students in the Cambridge City school, and Timmy was the only one at Pershing. On the first day of school, his color was an instant curiosity to his white classmates. Girls hovered around him, wanting to be close to him and talk. Boys kept a distance, yet stared at him. Mrs. Graber, who taught grades 4 through 6 in the two-classroom school, quickly got the students to their seats and welcomed Timmy to the class. She moved to get the students engaged in the day's activities and made sure that their attention was on the subjects being taught, not on Timmy. Her efforts made Timmy feel more at ease.

Nonetheless, early on, he thought the boys in class were out to get him. He said he always wondered, "Why are they after me?" On occasion, at recess and after school, a few of the boys would start circling him, and then one would accuse him of looking at their girlfriends. He didn't respond, staying cool – looking fearless and stoic – and watching to see who might be the first to go at him. For their part, the boys were looking at each other to try to figure out the same thing. As they sized each other up, Timmy would say, "Well, I got to go, the bus is here," and start walking away. It wasn't that he could not or would not fight if he had to. After all, he thought, "I'm quicker and smarter than they are." But he didn't like fighting and thought avoiding a fight was the wise choice. As he walked away, he knew that if he got a yard's head start, no one could catch him.

Such situations were short-lived. In time, Timmy was accepted.

Kay Knipp, a Pershing classmate, recalled that everyone liked him and played with him. His color didn't matter, she said. She recalled eating lunch with him and the others, outside during good weather and inside the classroom when they could not go out. There was no cafeteria. Everyone brought lunch in a paper bag or metal lunch box. A small stage and the principal's office were the only other rooms in the school building. Toilets were outside. Being active and athletic, Timmy enjoyed the swings and merry-go-round on the playground and playing softball on the grass field or basketball on the gravel court.

Around this time, Timmy honed his ability to remember the words and music to songs almost instantly. The magazine Hit Parader served as his biggest inspiration and provided an important hobby. Hit Parader began publishing in 1942 and lasted until 2009, though it had evolved into a focus on heavy metal and hard rock by then. When Timmy was young, though, it published features on popular artists of the era and ranked the top singles for each week. It also printed lyrics to some of the most popular songs at a time when they were not printed on album covers and most people bought singles anyway.

"I used to collect them all the time," he said later in life of the magazine. "I learned all the songs in there.... If I hear a song, I knew the music in my head. It's just a matter of doing the words. Once I write the words down, I know them. It's like typing it in your head or writing it in your head. It's so easy to learn when you write it down." Timmy never lost his ability to remember a song. "I can go back, and somebody will say something, and it will remind me of some song. So if I had to do it [perform] in a club, or if I had to do it at all, I could look it over real quick and I would have it. It wouldn't take more than one or two times to read it."

Timmy and Buddy quickly made friends with neighbors who rode the school bus with them. Max Blose recalled that he, Timmy, and Buddy, along with Johnny Colvin and sometimes Chuck Swallow, played touch football. More often, they played basketball on the Blose farm

– almost every day during the basketball season and often throughout the year.

A neighbor, David Skates – who lived about three houses west on the side of the road from the Blose farm, almost directly across from the popular Coffee Pot restaurant, noted for a giant coffee pot on its roof – built and flew U-control (today called Control Line) airplanes. While Timmy and Buddy were not as interested in watching Skates build the planes, or as involved in flying them as Blose – who eventually was named to the Academy of Model Aeronautics Hall of Fame – they did participate on occasion. They flew the planes on a vacated lot that Skates had plowed and then flattened so it was smooth.

Timmy and Buddy found Mae to be a loving and caring foster mother, though she could be very direct, argumentative, and stubborn. But Bud Ladd was not whom they had hoped he was. For reasons Timmy could never understand, the relationship between himself and Bud became increasingly troublesome. Part of the tension came from the difference in treatment of the two boys. Timmy was given the more difficult, messier chores. He waded through the glue-like mud in the pig sties, feeding the animals slop made from cornmeal and water, and shoveling manure every day. Twice a day he made sure that the chickens had scratch grains to eat and occasionally crumbs left over from a meal. Every three to four weeks, he scrubbed the chicken coops. The smell of rotten eggs and chicken feces made his eyes water and forced him to step outside regularly for fresh air. In contrast, his brother cared for the cows, bringing them in from the pasture in the morning, feeding them, and milking them. Afterward, he walked them back to the pasture.

And it wasn't just that Buddy got the easier work. When Bud Ladd was dissatisfied with the work or behavior of the two brothers, he tended to take out his anger on Timmy, calling him "pretty boy" or, worse, saying, "You look like a girl!" The sharp words hurt: "You know, when you are a kid, a boy, and someone calls you that. I just clammed up. Discipline, anything that I had to do, I never questioned."

When challenged about whether he had done something wrong, if he had not, Timmy said, he would not change his story to satisfy his accuser and avoid discipline. "I would say I didn't do it if I had not.... If they asked again, I would say, 'No, I didn't.' If they asked me 10 more times, I would not say a word. I had told them. And I didn't lie. I would just get quiet."

In contrast, he noted, "my brother probably would have. He was the little lawyer. The brains. He would speak up. I would take the blame for a lot of things he did."

On occasion, Bud Ladd's anger moved from verbal to physical abuse. There were numerous times when he took a strap to Timmy's back, causing welts and sores. Recalling the abuse, Timmy reflected, "I never showed any emotion. I just got quiet. And I wouldn't eat a couple of days after." He did eat, but not with the family. A few nuggets of Kellogg's Gro Pup dog food and water sustained him, he said.

In 1949, Freddie Stark, a 17-year-old, came to live with the Ladds. From November to May, his parents went with their employer, Leora Teetor, to her winter home in Fort Lauderdale, Fla., leaving Freddie to attend school in Cambridge City. Teetor's husband, Charles, had co-founded Perfect Circle and served as its president from 1928 to 1937. Stark joined Timmy and Buddy in helping with the chores. They enjoyed having Freddie on the farm for a couple of reasons. One was that another hand to help with chores reduced the amount they had to do. More important, they looked up to him, because he was one of the few Blacks in school, and was considered a good student and athlete at Cambridge City High. Freddie was a starter on the basketball team and a runner in track, and boxed in a Golden Gloves tournament in nearby Hagerstown.

Because of his parents' relationship with Leora Teeter, Freddie Stark had worked odd jobs at the Teetor estate on Turnpike Road near Hagerstown, and had been given a key to the house. But about a year earlier, according to an April 25, 1950, article in the Richmond Palladium-Item, he had been dismissed by John Senn, assistant advertising manager of Perfect Circle, who lived at the estate when Leora Teeter was in Florida. The article noted that "Stark had been surprised earlier in an unauthorized party for some of his boy friends when Mrs. Teetor was away. Senn was reported to have had some difficulty with Stark only a few weeks ago but Perfect Circle officials did not have any details."

About 7:45 p.m. on Monday, April 24, 1950, Senn was returning from a dinner with Lothair Teetor, chairman of the Perfect Circle board and Leona Teetor's son. He opened the front door and was struck by three .22-caliber bullets, one in his chin and two in his neck. As he turned to reach for the light, he was struck by two more bullets in the back.

Although badly wounded, he was able to walk to the home of Homer Isaacs at 55 Tidewater Rd. to get help. He was taken to the hospital in New Castle, where he eventually recovered. And he was able to identify his assailant, who had run off, as Freddie Stark. A statewide search was begun for Stark and was extended into nearby Ohio. Early Wednesday morning, Bud Ladd called the police and told them that Stark was at his farm. According to Max Blose, Buddy had been collecting eggs that morning and was frightened when Stark, who had been hiding in the barn, whispered to him. He went to the house and told Bud. At 6:50 a.m., Wayne County Sheriff Ora Wilson, Deputy Ryland Jones, and Indiana State Trooper Cecil Melvin surrounded Stark in an oat field on the Ladd farm. Blose recalled that he, Timmy, Buddy, the Colvin siblings, Swallow, and Richardson heard shots as they were getting ready to board the bus to school.

About two hours later, Freddie Stark died at Reid Memorial Hospital in Richmond. What happened is disputed. The official report said that Melvin and Jones fired warning shots after Stark fired twice at them. Seeing no escape route, it said, Stark pointed the rifle at his head and pulled the trigger. The April 27 Palladium-Item headline read, "Shooting Suspect Commits Suicide," with a subhead of "Fred Stark, Cambridge City Athlete, Ends Life After Firing at Pursuers." Another view was that as he climbed over a fence, he accidentally shot himself. A third view, largely held in the Black community, was that one of the shots fired by either Melvin or Jones was not intended as a warning – that there was no effort to capture him.

This incident, coupled with the abuse that Timmy got from Bud Ladd, led to the brothers moving back to their father's home for a few months. As Timmy recalled: "My brother, in fact, did complain, finally. He felt guilty about it. I told him not to cause any trouble. But he told my dad one time when he came to see us. He told my dad that the guy was beating me, and my dad wanted to see my back."

John Brown Sr. reported the treatment to the Wayne County Department of Welfare. As a result, the boys were moved from the farm and, after a brief time at their father's house, were enrolled at the Soldiers' and Sailors' Home in Knightstown in the fall of 1950.

KNIGHTSTOWN

CHAPTER TWO

A New Home at the Home

On Sept. 14, 1950, Timmy and Buddy arrived at the Indiana Soldiers' and Sailors' Children's Home, about a mile south of Knightstown, a town of about 2,500 people 34 miles west of Richmond on U.S. 40. Like most Hoosier towns its size, it had an assortment of businesses and institutions, and had left its small marks in history.

Charles A. Beard, one of the most respected American historians of the early 20th century, was born nearby. Forrest Lewis, an actor who appeared on "The Andy Griffith Show" and "Gomer Pyle, U.S.M.C," and in the Disney "Flubber" movies, was a native, as was Clifford M. Hardin, secretary of agriculture under President Richard M. Nixon.

In recent times, Knightstown has been most known for its high-school gym, the home court for the Hickory Huskers in the 1986 movie "Hoosiers." Yet the Home overshadowed everything. It was the largest employer in the area for decades until 2009, when its last graduating class marked its closure.

The Home had been the vision of Indiana's Civil War governor, Oliver P. Morton, who wanted a place for disabled soldiers and sailors to live. It opened in June 1867 after the state bought a failed spa and hotel on 54 acres known as Knightstown Spring. Over time, its purpose expanded to include the children of veterans who were no longer able to maintain their families – the circumstance in which John Brown Sr. had found himself.

By the time the Brown brothers arrived, the Home had expanded to 377 acres and more than 30 buildings, some dating from the 1880s and in the Romanesque Revival style. Many survive today. The 3½-story Administration Building, with 18 window bays on its ground floor, had opened in 1888 on a gentle rolling hill facing the drive entering the campus. The same year, the Town Hall had opened; in 1919, a gymnasium was added. In the early 1890s, Lincoln Chapel was constructed. It contained a two-story auditorium and wooden balcony with a vaulted ceiling and theater-style seats. Nearby, a tall chain-link fence surrounded a cemetery. With enrollment growing toward 600 students in the 1920s and '30s, buildings such as the bakery and laundry were added.

In 1925, the Home was admitted to the Indiana High School Athletic Association. Two years later, a two-story brick school – Morton Memorial, named after the governor – opened. In 1936, wings were added to the east and west sides, more than doubling its size.

A number of storage and maintenance buildings dotted the campus, including the Grounds Building, Paint Building and Shop, Power House, Water Tower, and Gas Pump Building. A couple of years after the Browns arrived, more buildings were added. A redbrick, V-shape, 50-bed hospital with second-floor living spaces for nurses and doctors opened, and a one-story Tramp Shed was constructed for housing the dairy cattle. A vast network of tunnels connected the buildings, which made passage between them more tolerable during the winter. The tunnels were a favorite place for play during the winter as well.

The youths lived in duplex cottages called "Divisions," with two divisions containing from 10 to 20 students. On the first floor of each division, near the entrance, was a private living room for the house parents, as well as a student living area with stuffed chairs, couches, and tables for studying, visiting, or playing games. Shelves were stocked with books, and a black-and-white television was available for entertainment. There also were a restroom and a locker room; each student had a locker. The second floor had dormitory-style bunk beds. The house parents also had a bedroom upstairs. The house parents were responsible for overseeing up to eight males and eight females. The division had two-mirror living units, open porches, and a projecting sunroom.

When Timmy and Buddy arrived, the races were segregated, with Black males and females living on one side of a lake near the white males, and the white females on the other side of the lake. Until Timmy's senior year, the Black males lived in Division 10 and the Black females in Division 11, which abutted Division 10 but had no common entrances. Division 10 and 11 were sandwiched between divisions where white males lived. The races were integrated during Timmy's senior year in 1955, as a result of the "Brown v. Board of Education" ruling. Timmy moved to Division 27, where his white friend Earl Lambert also lived. Lambert described the move as normal, noting that he and Timmy shared lockers and clothes.

Before integration, Blacks sat separately in the dining hall, with the girls at one long table alongside the boys at another. The races also sat separately at Movie Night on Fridays as well. All that changed in 1955, but there still was no interracial dating. Talking with a white girl, or even looking at one, could be problematic. It was the first time that Timmy felt segregation so strongly, and it made him uncomfortable. He later reflected, "People tried to make you think you were different,. Segregation was an irritable thing, because I always felt equal. But I didn't dwell on it. I didn't really feel any animosity."

Timmy seemingly was admired by everyone and earned the nickname "Big Tim." He was a talented entertainer and an outstanding athlete, was friendly with others, and was outspoken. At the Home, everyone had a responsibility. Until junior high, children had chores. They set up tables in the dining hall, peeled potatoes in the kitchen, scrubbed toilets and showers in the bathrooms, and swept the floors and polished furniture in the living areas. In junior high, everyone was assigned a trade. Boys usually worked in the shoe shop, paint shop, greenhouse, pipe shop, or tire plant, or collected garbage. Girls worked in the laundry and bakery, and also cooked for the employees, who had their own dining hall.

Earl Lambert had volunteered to work at the dairy farm. He got up at 5:30 to round up the cows, and then he and another classmate milked them with automatic milkers. Timmy worked in the shoe shop, so he didn't have to rise until an hour later than Lambert. They were awakened each morning by a shrill whistle blown from the Power House. Fixing shoes was called the "lazy man's job," according to Timmy. For periods of time, there wasn't much to do, so Timmy and others working in the shoe shop practiced shooting baskets, using a lidless small tin can and a tennis ball. On occasion, the shoe shop supervisor, who had beehives at his home, would bring honey to spread on fresh-baked bread brought over from the bakery, across from the shoe shop.

Breakfast was served at 7:30 a.m. and school began an hour later. Dinner was at 5 p.m. While Timmy was free until Town Hall, which lasted each evening from 7 to 8, Lambert had to milk the cows again at 6. Bedtime was 9:30 p.m. A movie was shown each Friday night for the older students and on Saturday afternoon for the younger ones.

Saturday was free time, except for Lambert and the others who milked cows. On Sunday, everyone was required to attend Sunday school and church. For milking cows, Lambert earned $5 a month. Everyone else at the secondary school level who worked made 75 cents a month. Until seventh grade, they earned 45 cents.

Most of the students spent the money they earned, or the tickets obtained through good behavior, on ice cream, soda pop, and candy and other snacks, or on toothpaste, toothbrushes, combs, and other personal items. These could be purchased at a store in the school. It was run by the older girls, although an adult managed and supervised it. For a few students, the goal was to save enough money to buy shoes that were different than the standard-issue black ones. Finding a way to show one's uniqueness was prized, but difficult to attain.

On occasion, one of the boys would collect money from others, sneak off the grounds, and walk one mile to and from a gas station at the edge of Knightstown to get cigarettes. While Timmy never made the "Fag Run," Lambert did. As he recalled, "I would put a pillow in the bed and cover it, making it appear that I was asleep. I hid under the bed and waited until the governess closed her door and turned off her lights. Then I watched for the night watchman. When he was out of sight, I moved quickly off the grounds and stayed off the highway. I ran across the Blue River bridge to a little store." He returned with packs of cigarettes and distributed them. There was a rush that came from the possibility of being caught. And there was a hero-like feeling from the success of getting the cigarettes and giving them out.

Besides the modest allowance that came from working, Timmy was issued a couple of pairs of blue jeans and prison-blue shirts, as well as the black shoes. This was the attire that he wore for the entire time he lived at the Home, and was the only clothing he took with him to college in the fall of 1955.

The Home was run like a military academy. Historically, a former officer, often a major, was hired to organize the males into platoons, with sergeants as squad leaders, and to run them through drills three times a day. The drills varied from calisthenics to marching. Until the late 1940s, the males wore cadet uniforms daily to class. After that, uniforms were worn only on special occasions, such as Memorial Day, by the Color Guard. Responding to adults with "Yes, sir" or "Yes, ma'm" was expected. Being on time to work, class, chapel, or Town Hall was equally important. Failure resulted in punishment. A mild punishment might be not being able to attend the Friday night movie. Lambert, after being caught by the night watchman attempting the "Fag Run" one night, found himself exiled that week. Sometimes there was a paddling, such as Timmy's younger friend Jim "Jug" Hart received for sledding on the lake one winter day. The most severe punishment was being forced to sit on a chair for up to two or three days, except for using the bathroom, eating, sleeping, or classes. That punishment was reserved largely for runaways.

Jug Hart entered the Home at age 5, along with two sisters, Betty and Barbara Ann, and a brother, Dave. Being Black, he lived and ate in the same area as Timmy. While he was a couple of years younger than Timmy, they were teammates in football, basketball, and track. Hart also played volleyball. When Hart graduated, he was recognized for having played in all four sports from his freshman through senior years – one of only two students in the school who had done so. In the spring of 1957, East Central Indiana Conference basketball coaches selected him for the all-star starting five. That same spring, he set school records in both the 100-yard dash and the broad jump. Because of his success, he was named the outstanding senior athlete.

Not everyone at the Home wanted to be there. As Timmy recalled, "Kids were always trying to run away. Sometimes they would get caught in Muncie, halfway to Richmond, or wherever they were running to. Most often, they didn't get further than Knightstown. A couple in our dorm was running away every chance they got. They would go back to their neighborhood, where they had freedom to run the streets. Their parents didn't care what they did. They didn't care about them. But their folks would send them back. [The students] didn't like the organization. They didn't like being told what to do."

Timmy's sisters Betts and Buggs were at first perplexed by their brothers' having gone to the Home. On their first couple of visits, Buggs recalled, she thought that they were going to bring them back to Richmond to live: "Why are we leaving them here? Why aren't they coming with us?" Eventually both asked their father why they couldn't join their brothers. According to Buggs, John Sr. had tried to enroll Betts but was told that she was too old. And he told the younger Buggs that he didn't want her to be there alone after Buddy and Timmy left. The sisters tried to stay close to their brothers. Once, Buggs asked her father for lunch money that she didn't need, and gave the $2 to Timmy.

During the summers, most students left the Home and stayed with family or friends. Lambert returned to Shelbyville and stayed at his aunt and uncle's home, as his stepfather refused to let him stay with him. Earl's aunt got him a job in a factory that made paper bags.

For their part, Timmy and Buddy returned to Richmond each summer and got jobs. They stayed with the Bennetts. One summer, Timmy worked at a car wash, cleaning the whitewall tires that were then popular. "I always made work a game that would help my mind or body in some way," Timmy recalled. "I always wanted the toughest jobs, because I figured one day I would be on my own, and I had to be prepared to work, not knowing how education might go. Besides, scrubbing tires was a great way to build up my muscles." He also built up his strength by striding across the railroad ties, spaced 19½ inches apart on the tracks running through the north end of town. George Walker, his neighbor and friend, recalled watching Timmy run fast forward and backward without missing a tie.

When fall came and the brothers went back to the Home, there was always something to do. Much of the time from Monday through Friday, from 5:30 a.m. to 9:30 p.m., students' time was occupied with meals, work, and school. At the Friday night movies, boys and girls could get permission to sit together, but no hugging or kissing was allowed. As Lambert recalled, "As soon as the movie was over, we would run as fast as possible across the lake. There, as quickly as possible, we would get in some hugging and kissing." An officer would round them up and get them to their dormitories.

Special events were scattered throughout the year. Everyone's birthday was celebrated with a cake, gift, and party. At Christmas, the Home became aglow with brightly lit trees and astir with carols and songs. Each child could choose three gifts off a list. On Halloween, everyone wore costumes and prizes were given, and a hayride through Knightstown, followed by a horror movie, ended the night.

The first Sunday and Monday after Labor Day were Legion Days. Cars packed the parking lot and snaked down the road as the grounds were transformed into a small carnival. There were rides, food booths, and games, like ring toss and basketball, with accompanying prizes. The students' dance band and choir performed. The American Legion was a strong supporter of the Home for years, providing funds for Christmas gifts and for picnics, camping, and other outings.

Monte Blue Day was held annually in honor of one famous graduate. Gerard Montgomery Blue (some sources give his last name as Bluefeather) was one of five children, and after his father died, his mother could no longer care for all of them at her home in Indianapolis. He and one of his brothers, Morris, went to the Home in the late 1800s. After graduation, he went to Purdue University and eventually made his way to California, where he worked as a laborer at the movie studio of the famed director D.W. Griffith and took the stage name Monte Blue. He had small parts in movies by Griffith, including "The Birth of a Nation" and "Intolerance," and, later, ones directed by Cecil B. DeMille. His break came in "Orphans of the Storm," in which he co-starred with Lillian and Dorothy Gish. He would go on to star with Clara Bow and Gloria Swanson in other silent movies, and made the transition to talkies. In one of his later films, he played the sheriff in "Key Largo," starring Humphrey Bogart and Lauren Bacall. He continued to appear in movies until the mid-1950s and was recognized with a star on the Hollywood Walk of Fame.

Movies and entertainment had already become one of Timmy's interests and possible paths in life. Back in Richmond, when not working, he and Buddy hung out with friends Dave Chapman, George Walker, and Harold Jones. Whenever they could scrape together 50 cents, they would walk down Ninth Street to go to the Tivoli Theater downtown. On occasion, they watched three movies in a day. The Tivoli was a large theater, with about 1,200 seats.

Two of Timmy's favorite movies were released in 1951, "Jim Thorpe – All-American" in August and "Saturday's Hero" in September. In the first, Burt Lancaster starred as the American Indian athlete. The movie includes both Thorpe's high points – success as a student-athlete at the Carlisle Indian School in Pennsylvania under coach Glenn "Pop" Warner; marriage to his college sweetheart; and stardom at the 1912 Olympic Games – and the lows – his inability to get a coaching job because of his race, the loss of his Olympic medals because he had played semi-pro baseball in college, the end of his marriage, his fall into poverty.

In "Saturday's Hero, " John Derek portrays an innocent high school football star who attends a Southern college with hopes of being a good athlete and student. His innocence unravels under pressure from a corrupt and influential alumnus who views college football as a business, an overly demanding coach and unscrupulous teammates. As he loses his self-respect, is injured, and is apparently finished, his girlfriend, played by Donna Reed, comes to his aid.

In 1953, "The Joe Louis Story" was released. Louis scored 71 bouts between 1934 and 1951, winning 68 – 54 by knockouts – and defended his title 25 times. In 1938, he became a national hero when he defeated the German Max Schmeling in a rematch for the heavyweight title. The fight was pitched by media as a battle between Nazism and democracy, even though Schmeling was not a Nazi. While he enjoyed the story, what intrigued Timmy most was one of the training techniques that Louis used. He learned that Louis caught flies – the insects, not baseballs – to improve his reflexes. It was a strategy that Timmy adopted. Over time, he became good at it. He enjoyed catching and releasing the flies, and he tried never to kill them. Friends and others who watched him were amazed and entertained. Some tried to catch them, too, but to no avail.

Timmy's favorite teacher at the Home was Almeda Garriott, who taught typing, shorthand, and bookkeeping. Timmy kept for the rest of his life an eighth-grade paper in which she had asked the students to think about three things they would like to do with their lives. Timmy prophetically wrote that he wanted to be a singer, football player, and teacher. Four years later, in his senior yearbook, Timmy reaffirmed his commitment to football. In the Retrospect, students were asked about their favorite subject and their ambition. While most students claimed an area of study, such as agriculture, chemistry, or art, as a favorite subject, Timmy identified football. Similarly, when asked about ambition, he declared: "Play pro football."

While Timmy idolized his brother, thinking him a better athlete and smarter, the feeling apparently went only one way. Buddy had told him when they first went to the Home, "You don't know me," and stayed cold to him thereafter. At the Home, Buddy completed the "academic track," while Timmy finished the "commercial track." In subjects that he enjoyed, Timmy did well. He consistently received grades of A and B in physical education, home economics, choir, chorus, and piano. He struggled with English, mathematics, science, and history. The notable difference between the tracks was the number of general business courses taken and some extracurriculars. Timmy took bookkeeping, typing, office practice, and shorthand. Buddy took more academic courses.

Both brothers sang in the mixed choir for four years. Timmy sang in the boys' choir for four years, while Buddy did so during his last two years at the Home. As he had as a young child, Timmy continued to learn his favorite songs, mostly rhythm and blues, and loved performing them for his fellow students. He quickly turned his attention to mimicking the songs and moves of Elvis Presley after the 1954 Sun Records release of "That's All Right."

Timmy participated with the dance club from his sophomore to senior year, while Buddy did so in his last two years as well. Timmy said his dancing was most inspired by the 1952 movie "Singin' in the Rain." In his sophomore and junior years, Timmy was in the Color Guard, and as a senior he was on the Firing Squad. He worked on the yearbook staff his senior year. For his part, Buddy served on the newspaper staff his sophomore and junior years, was in Drill Corps as a freshman and sophomore and in band his last three years, and spent four years in student government.

Driver Education proved a challenge for Timmy – "I drove off into a gully and back up. I had never driven before," he recalled. Pete Stepanoevich, driver education teacher and football coach, chided, "Quit playing with me," to which Timmy said, "I wasn't. I have never driven a car. I'm going to run or walk wherever I am going. I don't want to get out there with cars." But he did learn to drive, although it was a challenge for many years.

One of Timmy's most significant high school memories was acting in the senior play, Thornton Wilder's "Our Town." He played the leading role of the Stage Manager, who serves as a narrator. Acting in the play sparked his interest in theater, which he would pursue later in life.

Timmy and Buddy both excelled in athletics. Every year, from August to May, they moved through football to basketball and ended with track. Little is known about their individual performances during their first year at the Home, 1950-51, other than that Buddy played on undefeated freshman football and basketball teams, and ran the 100- and 220-yard dashes and the low hurdles.

During the 1951-52 football season, William Lynch coached the varsity team, which went 5-3. The Tigers were a high-scoring unit, averaging 25 points a game, and three times winning with more than 40 points. Timmy played on the freshman team that year. He recalled his initial uncertainty about playing football, as it was a much rougher game than he had thought. Timmy attributed his interest in playing football to his brother, but wasn't sure he wanted to pursue it after his first play. "I remember the first time I ever got hit," Timmy recounted. "I said, the hell with this, I can give this up. I was ready to cry. It didn't hurt that bad. It was just the idea of getting hit and not being able to do anything about it ... guys piling and a lot of unnecessary stuff."

He went on to say, "I didn't quit. But I got up. I went back, and the next time I was on the 'hamburger squad.' We were playing the varsity. The next couple of times I carried I [tried to go] all the way, because I didn't want to get hit. Well, I got caught both times, in fact, about two yards from the goal line. My brother caught me, because he wasn't going to let me excel over him."

In an early game of the season, with his father watching, he remembered being hit hard and lying on the ground, faking injury for what seemed like an eternity. "I think I did it to get attention," Timmy reflected. His father climbed from the stands, leaped over the fence, and ran onto the field, yelling: "You're not hurt, boy. Get up!" He didn't know if his father was inspired by alcohol, embarrassment, or both. But for the rest of his career in sports, he would never lie on the field with his feelings more bruised than his body.

As for Buddy, he had an exceptional sophomore year. He scored a touchdown in six of seven games; in four of those games, he scored twice.

In his junior year, 1952-53, playing for a different head coach – Stepanoevich, also the driver-ed teacher – Buddy again set the pace for the brothers, scoring three touchdowns in a victory over Cambridge City, and rushing for 160 yards and a touchdown in a Tigers loss to Sacred Heart. As for Timmy, the yearbook photo shows him on the team, but there is no record of how he did.

The 1953-54 season was the Brown brothers' last as teammates, and the Tigers ended the year undefeated, 6-0-1. Both Buddy and Timmy were instrumental in the undefeated season – Timmy, in fact, kept the loss column empty by scoring the tying touchdown in the opening game, a 7-7 tie. He also showed his speed with a 65-yard punt return for a touchdown against Hagerstown, and the winning TD against Royerton. For his part, Buddy regularly crossed the goal line, including five touchdowns in one 73-0 Tigers victory.

Before the 1954-55 season began, Stepanoevich was involved in a car accident. From the hospital, he called Bill Brewer, the assistant football coach, who had just joined the faculty at the Home. Brewer had started at Union College and completed an outstanding basketball career at Texas Western, and was to be head coach of the basketball team. Given the small staff at the Home, the coaches helped one another by serving as assistants. Stepanoevich told Brewer he was going to have to take over football. Brewer was reluctant, admitting, "I don't know anything about football." To which Stepanoevich said: "Well, talk to Timmy. Timmy will tell you who does what and how." Brewer called Timmy into his office, and they went over the players, the positions they played, and some of the plays. Given what Stepanoevich had said, Brewer assumed that Timmy led the team and asked: "You going to play quarterback?" Timmy laughed and said: "No, no, no, I'm not a thrower. I don't have a thrower's arm. I mean, I probably could, but I'm a running back."

Timmy had wanted to follow his brother at left halfback to see how well he could do in comparison, but now "Buddy was gone, so I wasn't really competing with him," he said. Before and after each game, Brewer and Timmy would review the game plan and the results. "In a way, he treated me like I was a coach," Timmy recalled. "He respected what I had to say. We got to know each other really well that way."

With Brewer and Timmy consulting throughout the season, the Tigers recorded five wins and three losses. Timmy led the team in scoring with 115 points – more than half of the squad's total. He rushed for five touchdowns in one 40-0 shutout, and in another game not only caught a touchdown pass, but also kicked two extra points. The season, and Timmy's high school football career, ended with another conference title for the Tigers.

During the winters, Timmy and Buddy competed in basketball. Al Miller coached the Morton Tigers through 1954. In addition to coaching, Miller taught biology and chemistry. In Timmy's senior year, Brewer taught physical education and general science in addition to coaching.

In 1951-52, Timmy played on the freshman team, which went 10-

6; Buddy played sparingly on the varsity. In 1952-53, Miller's best year as coach, the team went 23-3 and won the Henry County tournament. Timmy was a starter for the junior varsity and also played in 10 games with the varsity team, scoring 17 points. And both he and Buddy were there for one of the most controversial games in Indiana high school basketball history.

THE Game in Indiana high school basketball history, the one that nearly all hoops and movie fans can recall instantly, is the one on which the film "Hoosiers," with Gene Hackman and Dennis Hopper, was based – the 1954 state championship match between Muncie Central (2,200 students and four state championships, the most recent in 1952) and Milan (161 students and no state crowns). And nearly as many know the pivotal moment of that game, when, with the score tied at 30, Bobby Plump hit a 14-foot jumper in the final seconds. That basket, forever known as Plump's Last Shot, gave the little school from far southeastern Indiana the state title.

But for most Morton players and fans of that era, a different game involving Milan is THE Game. In 1953, Morton and Milan (pronounced, in Indiana, MY-lun) faced off in the regional final, which neither had ever won. At the end of the first quarter, favored Milan led by 14-9. But by the half, the Tigers had edged ahead, 27-26, and kept that advantage at the end of the third quarter, 35-34. With just over two minutes left, the Tigers had built what appeared to be an insurmountable lead, 45-36. But it was not insurmountable, thanks to two Milan surprises.

One came from an unexpected full-court double-teaming press – a style of play almost unheard of at that time. The other resulted from a clock that failed to run. Apparently, a plug was knocked out of its socket and about 20 seconds elapsed before it was noticed. Tigers fans and coaches were enraged, shouting and screaming at the officials. When the clock was restarted, it showed 1:35 left – the same time that it had showed before it went dark for 20 seconds. The Tigers had only a four-point lead, 45-41. The teams exchanged baskets and free throws on two occasions, making the score 49-45 with less than a minute remaining. With two free throws, Milan cut the lead to 49-47. So, with 25 seconds left, all the Morton players needed to do to win was to hold on to the ball. They did not. Milan stole it, and the game ended tied at 49. The first overtime also ended in a tie at 51-51. That, according to IHSAA rules at the time, meant the second overtime would be sudden death, with the first team to score two points winning. Milan got the tip and held the ball for 1:45, until a player was fouled. He hit both free throws, and that was it. One writer described the victory as a result of a "full-court press, mental toughness, cool shooting, and a little bit of extraordinary luck." (Milan, though, did not win the state tourney this time.)

Timmy watched the game from the bench; Buddy scored only five points. But it would rank among the most memorable games they were involved in. Timmy recalled that while Morton fans and the team members and coaches were in a frenzy, he stood motionless and quiet, believing that nothing would change.

For Timmy, 1954-55 was a breakout season. He set the county scoring record for that year with 398 points in 23 games for a 17.3 average. But the season contained its share of personal pain as well. His father occasionally watched him play, and at one game became the center of attention – and a source of embarrassment for Timmy – when he was escorted, drunk, from the gym. And this was not the only time during this school year that Timmy's personal and athletic lives would cross and create tension.

One Sunday after chapel early in 1955, he was approached by a white girl, a cheerleader who had broken up with one of his basketball teammates. She thought he might be able to get them back together. It was a role he played, he said, "because everyone was always coming to me talking about so and so, and asking for my help." He was seen as a mediator. But "a teacher saw me talking to her and reported that I had been 'messing with her.' I guess he imagined that I must have been kissing her or even having sex with her."

"I got called to the office. The director said, 'So and so said you were messing with this girl.'"

"'Messing with her'; what do you mean, messing with her?" Timmy said he responded.

"So, what were you talking about?" the director asked.

Timmy bristled and shot back: "Oh, is that 'messing with her'?" He remembered getting mad when cornered. If there is nothing there, if I didn't do anything, I'm not going to sit there and be an idiot, he thought.

Bill Brewer, the first-year basketball coach, was brought in. He wasn't much older than Timmy, and they had worked together closely on the football team. Timmy could tell that Brewer didn't like what was happening and didn't want to be there, but he had no choice. Timmy recalled, "It wasn't him. It was the system."

Brewer told Timmy, "All you have to do is to tell the head man here that you are going to stop seeing her. You need to apologize."

"Stop seeing her? Apologize for what?" Timmy countered. "I haven't been seeing her. I haven't done anything wrong. She stopped to talk to me. She told me that she and her boyfriend had broken up. She asked me if I could talk to him and help them get back together. That was the first time I had talked to her. I told her, sure, I would talk to him."

"Well, I was just told I had to take you off the team, and tell you that you couldn't see or talk to her again," Brewer said.

"That ain't going to happen," Timmy replied.

"What am I supposed to do, Timmy? They tell me that I have to do it."

"Well, I'm sorry, you go back and tell them I'm not going to stop seeing her" – even though he had never been seeing her.

Timmy was suspended for two games in late January 1955, but the public never knew the reason. The Knightstown Banner reported that he "was out of the line-up due to an injury sustained in the ... Rush County tourney." The Tigers lost both games, 55-53 to New Salem and 52-51 to Morristown. With Timmy on the bench, they lost their highest scorer, the leader in assists, and floor general. Brewer had built the team around him. For her part, the girl felt bad about it. She didn't mean to get him in trouble.

"I wasn't allowed to dress for the games, but I sat on the bench with the team," Timmy recalled. "I would look over at her, smile, and wave. I knew they were watching me. I was trying to piss them off. I did it in such a way that I made sure Coach Brewer saw me. I knew it irritated him."

The tension with the coach didn't end after the suspension. "My first game back was away from home. I didn't start. So, I sat at the far end of the bench. When Coach called for me to go into the game, I acted like I didn't hear him. I played dumb. I wanted to make him come to the end of the bench to ask me to go in. A couple of the players next to me kept punching me, saying, 'Coach is calling you.' I told them, 'I know.' Brewer marched to the end of the bench and shouted, 'Get in the game, will you!'"

Timmy calmly looked up and said, "Oh, sorry, I didn't hear you, Coach." He slowly got up, walked to the timekeeper's bench, and entered the game. "I figured it was payback for the way I had been treated. I never forgot. And I became a rebel." He went in just before halftime and scored 18 points in a 63-40 victory over Brookville.

Another form of payback came as he made up his mind to "go after" the cheerleader. "I followed through, and saw her a few times after that. I would sneak across the lake to the girls' side. We kissed a couple of times. Nothing serious. That was enough for me. It would hold me for a month. I felt bad for the other guy, since he was on my team and he wasn't guilty of anything. I just wanted them to know that they couldn't tell me what to do. I was a human being like anyone else. But they ended up marrying anyway, and had three or four kids."

Other incidents showed hope for change in breaking down traditional racial attitudes. When Timmy moved into Division 27, the previously all-white dormitory, he was readily accepted. He became closer friends with Lambert, who had always openly associated with him in the classroom and on athletic teams. It was a friendship he always remembered.

Another illustration of change came during a return trip from a football game. According to Lambert, "We were coming home and stopped at a place to eat. The manager of the restaurant wouldn't let Timmy come in. Of course, we all got back on the bus and ate somewhere else."

Each spring, Timmy and Buddy ran track. The coach, Ralph "Curly" Eder, was the oldest of the coaches at Morton; he taught industrial arts and coached track for the entire time that Timmy and Buddy were at the Home.

Again, the brothers drew attention to their excellence on a squad that won the conference title every year that Timmy was in high school. Timmy was on the varsity as a freshman, while sophomore Buddy set a school record in the 100-yard dash. The next year, Buddy improved that time by a tenth of a second, while Timmy also ran the 100 and the high hurdles, and was a broad jumper. By his senior year, Timmy's most consistent event in track and field was the broad jump, usually finishing first.

Timmy continued to idolize the athletic ability of his brother, an honorable mention Associated Press all-state football player in 1953 and 1954, and state finalist in the 100-yard dash. "He was a faster, stronger football player and track star than me," he said. In the August 1973 interview in Black Sports magazine, he recalled a time when the track coach asked Buddy to do the long jump in a meet. Timmy said, "I had broad jumped 21.2 [feet] or something like that, and I thought I had won it. [Buddy had] never broad jumped at all. He came over and took one jump and went 21.5, and then walked off with first, took my ribbon from me, but just to show he could do it. That's how good he was." Timmy said of Buddy's football talent, "I used to love to sit on the bench and watch my brother run the ball. He had more moves than Carter's got liver pills." People would say, "Boy, you're fast; you've really got a lot of moves," to which Timmy responded: "Man, you should see my brother."

Timmy likened his brother to Buddy Young, a 5-foot-4, 172-pound All-American running back at the University of Illinois in the mid-1940s, who as a freshman tied Red Grange's school record for touchdowns in a season with 13, and ultimately was inducted into the Pro Football Hall of Fame. For his part, Buddy Brown graduated from Morton Memorial in 1954 and went to Butler University in Indianapolis.

By the spring of 1955, Timmy's time at the Home also was about to come to an end. For his senior yearbook, he had written in the "Last Will" style common in schools then: "I, Tim Brown, being of unusual talents do hereby will my lockers and possessions to Donny Boy [Jug Hart]. My athletic ability I leave to Lorenzo; may he work harder than I. To my coaches my many thanks and the best of luck to your future teams." The yearbook noted that his nickname was "Big Tim"; that he liked sports and disliked bad food; that his favorite saying was "What's hap'ning"; and that his ambition was to "play pro ball." It listed his favorite sports as football, basketball, and track, and also called football his favorite subject. And as for his favorite song, it was "If I Didn't Care" by the Ink Spots.

Timmy had decided to attend Ball State Teachers College, just a half-hour or so away in Muncie. In the Black Sports interview, he said, "I had about 15 basketball scholarship offers, and a few for track, and, ironically, only one for football [to Michigan State] ... because my high school coach went to school with one of the assistant coaches there" and "was trying to get me in there." But he never seriously considered any place other than Ball State. Brewer had talked with Jim Hinga, the Ball State Cardinals' basketball coach, about Timmy's talent and convinced him that he would be an asset to the team. Given his close bond with Brewer, Timmy said, he never questioned the chance to play at the nearby school.

But that was not known to two Ball State football players, Ernie Butler and Sonny Grady, who went to Richmond one spring day to encourage Timmy to attend. They chose to connect at Melody Skateland at 1501 S. Ninth St. because they all enjoyed skating. Butler, a member of a family that would play a large role in Timmy's life going forward, recalled that there was a bit of tension between Timmy and Grady, because Grady was a running back – the position that Timmy would compete for if he enrolled. "Sonny wasn't mean about it," Butler remembered, "but I could see that he wasn't excited about it. Timmy resented that Sonny was a bit condescending." Butler, however, felt good about their meeting, saying: "I liked him. There was just something about him."

Whether Timmy had made up his mind beforehand, or if Butler's and Grady's meeting made a difference, on April 16, Timmy attended Ball State's High School Senior Day, an orientation program for prospective students. The program focused on exploring degrees, scheduling courses, learning about campus and community life, and the cost of attending. It included a campus tour, a mixer, and a variety show. In his book, "One Sports Fan Left Behind," Timmy's college friend and classmate William J. "Bill" Butler, Ernie Butler's brother, wrote: "I do not know how many high school seniors were present for that Senior Day, but I know that only two of them were African American males. Naturally, I met the other one. Timmy Brown. He was from the Indiana Soldiers' and Sailors' Children's Home. We spent most of the day laughing and joking and assessing the crop of prospective incoming coeds."

Timmy and Bill Butler connected again in the summer, unplanned, at the Rushville Roller Rink on U.S. Highway 52, west of the nearby small city, to which Betts had moved with her aunt. John Casterlow, who played center on the Muncie Central team that had lost on Plump's Last Shot, was also there. Butler characterized Casterlow as "humorous without trying to be." The three of them were headed to Ball State the coming fall. "None of the three of us set foot on the skating rink, [though I] imagined Timmy could probably skate very well, [but wasn't] sure about Casterlow. [We] were too busy boasting, signifying, and making fun of the skaters.

On May 24, his 18th birthday, Timmy graduated from Morton Memorial. In 1892, an alumni association had been formed. Each year it organized a Homecoming Day on campus to maintain connections among graduates and provide support for the Home. Returnees shared their successes with current students, offering career advice and future education. The Home Journal, a newsletter sponsored by the alumni association, was begun in 1906 to enable graduates to exchange ideas and stay in touch. Later in life, Timmy would return to the Home to share stories of his success and try to inspire and motivate others. It was a way to give back. Throughout life, he spoke fondly of the Home, once saying: "The habits that were formed there shaped my life in so many positive ways. The discipline, respect, courtesy, work ethic, and opportunities to participate in music and sports made a significant difference in what I was able to do in my life."

MUNCIE

CHAPTER THREE

Having a Ball with the Ball at Ball

Muncie, like Richmond, was a small city based around factories, in its case related primarily to the automotive and glass businesses. The Delaware County seat had been recognized internationally as a typical middle American city as a result of two studies by Columbia University sociologists Robert Staughton Lynd and Helen Merrill Lynd, "Middletown: A Study in Modern American Culture" (1929) and "Middletown in Transition: A Study in Cultural Conflicts" (1937). As those books, especially the latter, showed, the city was dominated by a small clique of industrialists, including the family that gave its university its name.

Ball State Teachers College was established in 1918 as Indiana State Normal School, Eastern Division, by the five Ball brothers – Lucius, William, Edmund, Frank, and George. The brothers had moved from Buffalo, N.Y., to Muncie in the 1880s to take advantage of a natural gas boom to expand their glass jar business. They prospered and put their stamp on civic institutions, including the hospital, the airport, a large Masonic Temple, and eventually the biggest department store in eastern Indiana. After a privately owned teachers' college in Muncie closed, they purchased its two buildings and 64.6 acres of land and gave them to the state, which at first operated it as a branch of the existing teacher's college in Terre Haute. In 1922, in honor of the Ball family's support, the Indiana General Assembly renamed the institution Ball Teachers College, and in 1929 Ball State Teachers College.

When Timmy arrived, the campus spread over about eight square blocks, bounded on the east side by McKinley Avenue and on the west by Tillotson Avenue. To the south was University Avenue and to the north Riverside Avenue, with the campus spilling across them for about a block in each direction. The heart of the campus was the administration building and the student center, facing each other across University Avenue. Classroom buildings and the library and gym spread out from there. There were four women's dormitories and two for men – perhaps reflecting the teaching profession's makeup at the time. The symbol of the campus was, as it remains today, the statue "Beneficence," a tribute to the generosity of the Ball family that was the last commissioned work of Daniel Chester French, sculptor of the statue in the Lincoln Memorial.

Timmy arrived amid a time of rapid expansion for Ball State and all of higher education, in the years after World War II and under the GI Bill. There were 4,177 students on campus when he arrived, 3,745 undergraduates and 432 graduate students. When he left four years later, the student population had grown to 5,266 undergraduates and 977 graduates.

John R. Emens, the sixth president of the institution, led this growth. Emens served for 23 years – 1945 to 1968, the longest term of any Ball State president – and when he retired there were over 13,000 students enrolled. Several residence halls, academic buildings, a student center, a football stadium, and Emens Auditorium – a 3,581-seat performance hall named in his honor – were constructed. He provided the leadership for Ball State to become a university in 1965.

Timmy's father arranged for him to ride the Greyhound bus running the 42-mile trip from Richmond to Muncie on Tuesday, Sept. 6, 1955. Timmy came to campus with one bag with his belongings – a couple of pairs of blue pants and blue shirts and shoes that he had worn at the Home, socks, underwear, a toothbrush, toothpaste, and deodorant. On that day, he reported to the Housing Office and was assigned to live in Elliott Hall Annex. The next day, he attended orientation for new students. On Thursday, he registered for classes, and declared a secondary-school teaching program with a major in Health, Physical, and Safety Education and Recreation, and a minor in Business Education. Courses began on Friday.

The school was on a quarter system, with three quarters during the academic year, each running 11 weeks, not including holiday breaks and final exams. Autumn Quarter was from early September to early December, Winter Quarter ran from early December to mid-March, and Spring Quarter was from mid-March to early June. There also were two five-week summer terms, as well as pre- and post-summer terms of 10 days each. A full academic load was 12 quarter hours, with a total of 192 quarter hours required for graduation.

During Timmy's first two years, students paid less than $1,000 per year for tuition, room, board, and books and supplies. Estimated costs were $37 for tuition per quarter ($101 for the year), $5 to $6.50 per week for room ($180 to $234 for the year), $10 to $14 per week for board ($360 to $504 for the year), and $25 to $35 for books and supplies per quarter ($75 to $105 for the year). For his last two years, tuition per quarter increased by $13 to $50 per quarter or $150 for the year.

Timmy had to work to cover his expenses. In 2009, Robert Linson, director of alumni relations when Timmy was at Ball State, indicated that "no scholarships were provided to athletes" in the 1950s, as was being done at the time of the interview. "Coaches would find jobs for them to do." Timmy worked five or six hours a day in Elliott Hall, which "earned ... $3 a day," he said in a July 1964 Sport magazine article by Berry Stainback. "I started at 60 cents an hour, went up to 80 cents after 200 hours, then up to a dollar."

Records of his work on campus are incomplete. Three documents showing his performance evaluation indicate that during his freshman year he worked in Dining Services, getting up at 5:30 a.m. to bus dishes in the cafeteria and at night, buffing the halls, mopping, scrubbing the toilets, and performing other tasks. When he worked, he said, he was always learning the words to songs. He loved the echo in the hallways and bathrooms. A favorite was "We Three – My Echo, My Shadow, and Me."

On weekends, he said, he often worked 10 hours a day cleaning toilets and buffing halls. One Dining Services Evaluation dated Nov. 10, 1955, for Fall Quarter, showed ratings of "average" for appearance, attitude, cooperative spirit, dependability, efficiency, initiative, and judgment, and "good" for knowledge of work, public manner, and punctuality. The other, dated April 30, 1956, for Spring Quarter, showed similar ratings except those two items that had been rated as "good" – public manner and knowledge of work – had dropped to "average." Two items received the highest ratings – dependability as "very reliable," moving up from "average," and punctuality, "always on time," moving up from "good." The only other evaluation available rated work he did with the Department of Physical Education during Winter Quarter 1958-59. It is not clear what that work was, however. The Jan. 30, 1959, evaluation rated his performance as "average" – attitude, cooperative spirit, dependability, initiative, and punctuality – and "good" – appearance, efficiency, judgment, knowledge of work, and public manner. He also worked with four or five other athletes cutting weeds on campus grounds during at least one summer. He recalled that one summer he cleaned the offices of a lawyer on Saturdays.

This was not what he had intended to do. Shortly after arriving on campus, he had walked a couple of blocks east from campus to the Village, a neighborhood shopping center, and went into the Varsity Barber Shop to see if he could get a haircut – and the job that was posted on a sign outside. He was not acknowledged, took a seat, and waited for 45 minutes. Eventually, one of the barbers – they were white, as were all the other customers – told him that they did not cut Blacks' hair and didn't know how to. Timmy asked about a job and was told they were not looking for help, despite the sign outside.

A couple of years later, after Timmy had become a football star at Ball State, fans regularly waited after games to talk to him, One Saturday, one man said, "Mr. Brown?"

"Just Tim," he responded.

"A couple of years ago," the man continued, "you came into our barber shop. We felt kind of bad about the way we acted and would like to have you come in and sweep for $25."

Timmy was indignant but remained polite. He told them he had a couple of jobs and didn't have any additional time. As he walked away, he felt a sickening feeling.

As the months rolled on, Timmy found balancing time among work, classes, athletics, and socializing – during the fall and spring quarters in particular – to be a challenge. He recalled spending no more than a couple of hours a day studying. His academic performance suffered as a result. As at the Home, he excelled in coursework that he enjoyed and found interesting. Athletes received grades for participating in sports, so he routinely got high marks in football and track each year. He received above-average grades in courses like voice, folk dancing, recreation, gymnastics, family relations, and secondary student teaching. In core general studies courses in literature and history, his grades ranged from average to slightly below.

In 1955-56 and 1958-59, Timmy lived in Elliott Hall Annex, a group of four former military barracks put up between Elliott Hall and Burris Laboratory School for use as residence halls to meet the influx of students after World War II. The barracks were part of the campus from 1947 to 1960, the year after Timmy left. In the other years, he lived in the home of Odell Dollison, a widowed domestic worker, at 1001 Kirby Ave. along with her sons, Bob and Clarence, and Bill Baird, a student from South Bend. The home was in a largely Black neighborhood east of downtown, recalled Anne Warren, who was born in Muncie and attended Ball State, graduating in 1961. "There were pockets of white families living in the area. There were numerous businesses serving primarily single-family, owner-occupied, well-kept homes." Some Black athletes and a few other Black students lived on campus, but most stayed in this neighborhood, called Industry.

Dollison's was a big old house with four bedrooms upstairs and one for her downstairs, according to Baird. He described her as "a mother figure, accommodating ... who prepared our evening meal every day – family-style meals."

Off-campus lodging for all students had to be registered by landlords with the Ball State housing office. However, there was no requirement that a landlord rent to any student. Segregated housing was the rule in Muncie, both off and on campus.

The Westwood neighborhood, next to the north and west sides of the campus and much closer to the school than Industry, reflected this. It was established in 1923, according to Bryan Preston in an academic paper, "'These Covenants Are to Run With the Land': The Hidden History of Housing Segregation in Muncie, Indiana." The author said, "Westwood was a new kind of exclusive residential development ... the first subdivision in Delaware County to include any plat restrictions at all. The restrictions consisted of two pages of pedantic legalese in tiny typewritten font." In part, they read: "No negro, mulatto, Chinese, Japanese or person of any race, or mixture of races, other than the pure White race, shall acquire title to any lot or building or part of lot or building in this addition...." Preston noted that "the description continues for 321 more words and provides one exception to the whites-only rule, as 'domestic servants' of any race were allowed."

Preston pointed out that "from 1923-1954, there were 137 new subdivisions in Delaware County which included restrictions of any kind. Two-thirds of these subdivisions included racial restrictions against non-white people. Between 1923 and 1950, that number [was] nine out of ten. About one out of every seven of Muncie's ... residences [in 2017 were] within a subdivision founded for white people only – many ... concentrated in the upper-income northwest area of the city west of Ball

State University." Thus, Black students tended to live in more distant areas of the city, such as Industry or Whitely.

To get from Industry to campus, some Black students used the city bus line, which did not run on Sundays, and was considered slow and undependable. Those who could car-pooled. Students who came from Calumet Region cities like Gary and East Chicago, who had families working in the well-paying steel industry, often came with cars. A few others walked; Baird, until he could get a car, did so. It took about an hour to walk to campus. He said it "seemed like everybody had four or five dogs to bite you." As a result, Black students' participation in campus activities was often limited. Warren reflected: "We often had lunch together at the Tally-Ho [the main student hangout] and made sure we had study tables at the library until it closed. Because we didn't stay on campus, we didn't participate in activities." "Between classes," Baird said, they would go to the Student Center – "get a sandwich, play cards, [ping pong], listen to the juke box. Quasi-segregated. People did their own thing. No friction. No racial things. Had our own area."

As at most campuses of that era, student life centered on the library and student union. The Ball State library was open from 7:45 a.m. to 9:30 p.m. Monday through Thursday; 7:45 a.m. to 5 p.m. on Friday; 8 a.m. to 4 p.m. on Saturday; and 2 to 4 p.m. on Sunday. During breaks, the library closed at noon on Saturday and was shut all day on Sunday, with other hours subject to change. Given the hours that Timmy worked and his commitment to football, he admitted that he didn't make it there often. The Student Center cafeteria was open weekdays from 7:30 to 8:30 a.m. for breakfast, 11:30 a.m. to 1:15 p.m. for lunch, and 5 to 7:30 p.m. for dinner. On Saturday, it was open from 7:30 to 8:30 a.m. for breakfast, 11:30 a.m. to 1 p.m. for lunch, and 5 to 6 p.m. for dinner. On Sunday it was open from 8 to 9 a.m. for breakfast and 11:30 a.m. to 1 p.m. for lunch. On occasion, Timmy would eat at this cafeteria when he was hanging out with friends at the Student Center, but more often he ate in the one in Elliott Hall where he worked.

Access to off-campus recreational activities became a hot issue in Muncie in the summer of 1956, the time period when A.B. Floyd, age 17, came to Ball State from Opelika, Ala. A graduate of segregated J.W. Darden High School, he had intended to attend the nearby Tuskegee Institute to study medicine. The sudden death of his sister's husband, Samuel Lovejoy, in Muncie from a heart attack changed his plans. His sister, Pearl, was left responsible for the care and support of three young girls – Constance, Brenda, and Debra, around ages 8, 7, and 4 respectively – and needed help. She asked Floyd if he could come live with her in Muncie. She told him that there was a teachers college in town and that she would enroll him, he could stay with her, and there was a job prospect at Ball Memorial Hospital.

Floyd took the bus ticket that his sister sent him and headed to Muncie. From Opelika to Bowling Green, Ky., he and the other Blacks rode in the back of the bus. In Bowling Green, he was told he could now sit wherever he wanted. "I had found the promised land," he thought. The night he arrived in Muncie, however, he had a different feeling. "They were fighting over the integration of the [Tuhey Park] pool. Somebody was shooting at people," he reflected. "Hell, we were shooting at people in Alabama, where I left for some of the same reasons. If this is the Land of Milk and Honey, where's that milk and honey, cause this ain't it!"

Tuhey Park is on the northwest edge of downtown Muncie, on the same side of White River as Ball State and the opposite side from the city's traditionally Black neighborhoods. According to longtime Muncie civic activist Hurley Goodall, writing in an unpublished manuscript, "Desegregation of Tuhey Swimming Pool," Tuhey "had always been off limits to Muncie's Negro youth, not by official directive but by custom they knew they were not welcome there so none tried to swim there." Over the years, Black people swam unsupervised in gravel pits and the river, which led to several drownings and increasing discontent in the Black community. This reached a crescendo in August 1942, when Guy Robert Ennis, 15, drowned in the Torrence gravel pit. Goodall, who was a classmate of Ennis', said Ennis was "destined to be an outstanding football, track, and baseball star at Muncie Central High School. Because of his athletic ability and high visibility in the community," Goodall wrote, "the funeral held at Antioch Baptist Church in Whitely was attended by almost everyone in Muncie's Negro community."

After the funeral, leaders of the Black community asked city officials to "provide a safe supervised swimming facility for Muncie's Negro youth." Nothing transpired until 1954, "after much agitation, confrontation, and conflict." The city purchased Phillips Lake on the east side near downtown to provide a public, supervised place to swim for Black residents, and renamed it "Municipal Pool." Goodall said this move was made to appease the white community, which resisted the desegregation of Tuhey.

The conflict came to a head on a hot, muggy Saturday in June 1956. Goodall noted, "This arrangement was challenged by four Negro youth accompanied by Roy C. Buley, Executive Director of the Madison Street Branch Y.M.C.A., and Mr. Levan Scott who appeared at the pool, purchased tickets, and were admitted into the pool. According to news accounts a large crowd of white boys gathered around the pool, and when police and park officials feared a racial outbreak was imminent the pool was cleared and closed...." On June 19, both Tuhey and Municipal were desegregated and reopened without incident. Municipal was closed in 1961 when "Prairie Creek Lake, a man-made reservoir designed to prevent future water shortage from occurring in Muncie, [became] a public park and beach" managed by the Muncie park department.

Like Floyd, Bill Baird experienced some consternation about life in Muncie in 1956 because of the Tuhey pool situation. He found coming "from South Bend to Muncie was a totally new experience. Black people couldn't go to A&W Root Beer stands. If a Black family went through, they got a paper cup, not a glass mug. Completely different from South Bend."

Race and color were issues for Timmy on campus, as they had been in his childhood and at the Home. He didn't fit in with most Blacks at

Ball State. One day when he walked through the Student Center and passed an area where Blacks tended to congregate, he remembered, a Black girl said, "You walk and talk like a white boy!" He retorted: "Jesus Christ, as you can see, I ain't white."

"Usually, you know, I never said anything," Timmy reflected, "but I was very quiet then and dressed like I was brought up. I didn't wear low pants. I guess that's the way a white guy dressed. I didn't curse or use slang. I walked like Charlie Chaplin." Having spent the years at the Home associating mostly with whites, he mirrored their habits of dress, hair, walk, and talk: "Blacks thought I was 'square.' Not hip." In the interview in Black Sports, he lamented: "I wasn't invited to anything until I started excelling in sports. So, I remained a loner, because I thought I should be accepted for me. Not because I excelled in sports – to anybody, white or Black. Whites didn't want me messing with them, because it was in Muncie, Ind., right next to Kentucky. Blacks didn't want me because I talked white and didn't know how to dance. To them I was trying to be white. But I wasn't. I was just me."

Ernie Butler, the football player who had been sent to help pull Timmy to Ball State, was now a senior and considered himself a big brother. He thought other Blacks were "jealous because Timmy was so handsome and Greek-god looking – T-shirt sleeves rolled up, like rockers." According to Butler, Blacks taunted Timmy into tap dancing in the Tally-Ho. Timmy "obliged and jumped on a coffee table and began to dance. I wasn't sure if he caught on that they were actually making fun of him. I remember a lot of times that I would try to tell him, 'Don't do those things [like] some of the black guys – that culture [that] makes fun of one another, like playing the dozens. Trying to be one up on somebody by insults and razzing.' My theory was that because he grew up in a [predominantly] white orphanage, he didn't know how to react to the cruel games of signifying and playing the dozens and the putdowns that were a part of black ideology during those times. So, he sometimes felt alienated. At that stage of our cultural development, tap dancing wasn't the coolest thing going. But on the other hand, his cockiness, which was often innocent and misunderstood, made some of the Black kids pissed at him."

Throughout his college career, he remained an enigma to many. To some students, he was a standoffish, arrogant, shy loner. To others, he was a handsome, charismatic star athlete. Don Mikesell, a white student from Culver, Ind., who entered Ball State a year after Timmy and ultimately became dean of students, remembered him as "extremely well-liked. Very popular. Very independent. He had a flair about him. He wasn't an ego guy. He wasn't arrogant. He was confident – cocky – knew he was good. He was an outgoing, fun kind of guy to be around." Linson recalled that Timmy was so popular that "lots of pretty white girls on campus were after him."

However, it wasn't a white girl from campus who captured his attention in freshman year, but rather a white 12th grade girl from Muncie Central. To Timmy, Sandra Kay Collins was the most beautiful girl he had ever seen. She had long black hair, dressed in tight-fitting clothes, wore lots of makeup, and walked with her chest out. Compared with other girls in high school or even on campus, she looked like a woman. "She was bad – a bad babe," Timmy said. "Miss Pepsi-Cola. A tough girl."

One of Timmy's Black female friends, who asked not to be identified, was less enamored of Collins, and said she and her friends found her repulsive. "My freshman year she would strut into the Student Center. We always spoke. We both knew who the other one was," she said. Racially mixed couples were rarely seen in public in those days, and Timmy's openly dating the girl hurt his acceptance among Blacks and whites. As Timmy's friend noted, "Blacks and whites didn't date back then, so any white girl that dated a Black guy didn't have a good reputation."

Timmy met Collins during a vacation period when he remained on campus to work. One evening, near closing time in a dining hall where he was working, she and a couple of her girlfriends approached. Timmy had his back to her, as he was looking at a playlist of songs on a jukebox. He saw her face in the glass, turned around, and said, "Oh, hi, how are you doing?"

"Are you Tim Brown?" she asked.

"Yeah," he responded. They talked for some time and agreed to meet again.

On occasion, they hung out in the Tally-Ho, listening to music and talking. Sometimes Timmy jumped on a table and swiveled his hips to an Elvis song. His performances always drew a crowd.

To spend time together privately, Collins often invited Timmy to come to a house about a mile from campus when she was baby-sitting. It was "an easy walk that took only about 20 minutes," Timmy recalled. "We dated for several months, but we weren't lovers. We kissed a few times. Nothing else."

Their relationship ended abruptly one Friday night. About a week before, Timmy told Collins that he had some laundry to do and wondered if he could bring it to the house where she was baby-sitting. She told him, "Bring it here and we can see each other, and I can do the laundry."

Timmy walked to the house, went up to ring the doorbell, looked through a space in the curtain, and saw Collins dancing with a male he recognized as a Muncie Central athlete. He started to knock, then thought again. Then the woman for whom Collins babysat walked into the room with another man.

"I guess she forgot I was coming. So I just turned around and took my laundry back to the dorm. I didn't sleep good that night, 'cause I realized that that was it.... I never ever said anything to her. She would call and ask, 'What's wrong?' I'd say, 'Nothing, nothing. I'm just busy.'"

While Timmy thought he had heard the last of Collins, a short time after the breakup college president Emens called Timmy to his office. He told him that Collins' mother had contacted him, saying, "One of the ballplayers on your squad, Tim Brown, is seeing my daughter and I want him to stop."

"You never told me you had a girlfriend," Emens said. Timmy feared that the mother was trying to get him in trouble and that somehow he would be asked to leave college.

Emens reassured him, "I'm on your side. Trust me, I don't think any girl is too good for you."

"Well, I appreciate it," Timmy said.

For a while, Collins continued to break hearts in Muncie. Larry McCabe, a longtime radio personality on Muncie's WERK and later in Phoenix, said in his 2018 book, "Lar' on the Air," that Collins was "his first great Love … a rare Muncie beauty." He added, "I made one big mistake. I drove her to Florida and she fell in love with the state. Sandy liked it so much, she moved there permanently." A photo of Collins in McCabe's book makes clear what a number of men saw in her.

After the Collins incident, Emens continued to show an interest in Timmy, and over time they became close. Timmy recalled getting notes from Emens on a weekly basis. If Emens saw Timmy walking across campus, he would approach him and talk. On one occasion, Emens commented, "I always see you walking around with your head down."

"I'm counting the ants. I just don't like stepping on bugs," Timmy said. He reflected years later, "I was very quiet and pretty much to myself a lot."

"If you need anything, anything at all, you just let me know," Emens said.

"No, I'm fine," Timmy replied.

"President Emens was my father figure," Timmy said later in life. "I would go to see him every other week. He was always looking out for me." Timmy recalled once wanting to borrow $50 to hold him over until getting paid the following Tuesday. He waited in line to ask a financial administrator for a short-term student loan. It was denied. He felt rejected and embarrassed. The decision came as a surprise because he had received a student loan on another occasion, when he needed $142 to cover room and board for Spring Quarter 1956. Richard and Katie Bennett had acted as security on the note through the Second National Bank of Richmond with Pastor M.A. Lowe and barber E.L. Walker, father of his friend George Walker, serving as references. The only other financial issues he could recall that might have affected the decision were so minor that he was perplexed by the decision. He had had to pay 50 cents once, after picking up a second college catalog on Feb. 13, 1956. He received a letter from registrar Leo M. Hauptman indicating that he had already picked up a catalog on July 26, 1955, that students were only allowed one, and that he either needed to return the second one or go to the Information Desk and pay 50 cents. That same spring, he had lost a pair of tennis shoes that he had been provided by the college, so he had to pay $1 to cover that cost. He didn't know why he was rejected: "I got by that week on 25 cents on candy bars and a lot of water."

Two or three weeks later, he got a note that Emens wanted to see him. When they met, he said: "I heard that you were asking for a loan. What happened?"

"I guess I wasn't qualified," Timmy said.

"That doesn't make sense," Emens replied. "Maybe you didn't know how to ask." He called the loan officer and had him come into his office to apologize. He told him: "Any time Mr. Brown ever comes in to ask for a loan, give it to him."

"I never went back. It was a matter of pride," Timmy reflected later in life.

"Rejection was always a big problem for me," Timmy said. The barber shop owner. The loan administrator. Sandy Collins. "I wouldn't go up and ask a girl to dance at a party or to ask a girl that I liked for a date, for fear of being turned down. If I'd ask a girl for a dance, and if she said no, I wouldn't ask another girl for a dance for a year. I think it came from my parents' divorce. It was like they rejected us. Put my brother and me in the Home. Sent my sisters to different families to live. Rejection always hurt deep inside and stayed with me for a long time."

He found some solace by returning home to Richmond on occasion, and in friendships he developed at Ball State. On several weekends in the summer until football season began, Timmy walked from the residence hall, after working in the morning, the 40-plus miles to the Richmond city limits dressed in a T-shirt, jeans, and sneakers with a sweater tied around his waist. He knew that no one would pick him up and give him a ride, because he was Black. He walked, jogged, and ran, leaving at 1 p.m. and arriving around 8:45 p.m. He did so, he said, because "I just wanted to see if I could do it. I was always competitive with myself, not the other guy." Once there, he stayed with Aunt Kate and Uncle Richard. Since his father worked at the bus station, he knew the drivers and was able to arrange a ride back to Muncie. During the summers, he lived in Richmond some years and Muncie others. In Richmond, he sometimes worked at a car wash, and exercised by running on the Pennsylvania Railroad tracks.

Timmy's connections with Bill and Ernie Butler grew in his freshman year, as they also lived in Elliott Hall Annex, the four barracks between Elliott Hall and Burris Laboratory School. Ernie and Bill lived in an end unit, and Timmy lived in an adjoining room. Neither Timmy nor Ernie could recall the name of Timmy's roommate that year. Ernie recalled that in 1952-53, his first year at Ball State, he lived in a room in Elliott Hall, not the annex. He indicated that he did stay in the annex that year, but just for the two weeks of football practice prior to the start of the fall quarter. This was a pattern followed until his senior year, when he moved full-time to the annex. The annex room had two beds and two desks, with a small vestibule that could be used to sit and chat or store one's bike. A small, shared bathroom had a couple of sinks and a shower. Ernie preferred the annex because it provided greater privacy.

At that time there were no coed residence halls, but because of construction, the women from Lucina Hall had to dine in Elliott with the men. In "One Sports Fan Left Behind," Bill recounted: "Three times a day, Tim and I would walk together to the dining hall and seat ourselves at a table among coeds. We would try to speak as properly as we knew how. We would exaggerate good table manners and made every effort to be overly polite. We had fun doing this, and the [women] seemed to be generally amused by our silly little show. Tim had the habit of counting the number of spoonfuls in a cup of tea. I found this to be generally amusing."

On occasion, Timmy spent the weekend with the Butlers at their home at 798 S. Eighth St. in Noblesville, a small town just northeast of Indianapolis. There he met the head of the family, the Rev. Dr. Ernest D. Butler – known as "The Rev" or simply "Rev." He was pastor of the First Baptist Church and was heavily engaged in district, state, and national Baptist activities. He served as a township trustee and was an activist in the civil rights movement. Mary Louise Jones Butler, his wife, managed what Bill described in his book as a "warm and welcoming environment" – a home that "was always open to everyone." Given his demanding schedule, "Rev" was in and out on weekends when Timmy visited. Of the eight children in order from oldest to youngest – Ernie, Bobby, Bill, Grayce, Bert, Florence, Mary Ann, and Jimmy – only Bobby was away when Timmy visited, attending Franklin College.

Grayce Butler would play a special role in Timmy's life. Before she first met Timmy, she had heard many stories about him from Bill and Ernie, both of whom who were enamored with him because of his personality, athletic and musical talent, popularity, and a growing friendship. She was aware of the breakup of his family and that Timmy and Buddy had been placed at the Home. "Even before I met him," Grayce recalled, "oh, my gosh. Protect yourself, protect your heart. Make sure you don't fall for him." She reflected, "I'm a very warm person and had a whole lot of love to give, because we had so much love in the family."

Grayce remembered a Noblesville High School home basketball game on a Friday night in 1955 as being the first time she saw Timmy. She was sitting with the pep club in the stands when he came to the game with Bill. He stayed the weekend, eating meals with the family, checking out the town, and attending church on Sunday. He came to be considered a part of the family. On Saturday night, Grayce was at a house party that Timmy and Bill attended. She was "taken to him. Girls were saying, oh, he's so fine. I was trying my best to be cool. My heart went out to him because of his background."

In May of her senior year, Timmy, now a sophomore, returned to Noblesville again for the weekend. A party was held at a lodge in Forest Park. Normally, Grayce recalled, mostly students from surrounding smaller towns would come – a few from Muncie. But in this instance, a girl from Ball State hosted the party, so more from Muncie came than usual. As Timmy dressed to go to the party, he got some honey on his sports jacket. Mary Louise got the honey out of it for him – a moment she relished sharing after Timmy became an NFL star. At the party, Grayce said: "Tim gave me a whole lot of attention. This was special. He could be charming."

When Grayce got to Ball State in 1957, she first lived in another old Army barracks, called North Hall. She had a Black roommate at the time, but that girl left after the first quarter, leaving her as the only Black student in the hall. She didn't get another roommate, and assumed the housing policy did not allow placing a white girl with a Black girl. "It was the first time in my life that I had a room to myself," she reflected.

While there, she worked the desk, answering the phone, letting girls know when their dates arrived. "I knew everyone in my dorm and knew their boyfriends. I've always been a very friendly person. I always thought [people] wanted to talk to me. If they didn't, I [made them]." The dormitories were very strict. Boys were not allowed in girls' rooms except during open houses – but girls couldn't sit on their beds while they were there unless their feet touched the floor.

Because the Elliott Annex and North Hall didn't have dining areas, Grayce and Timmy ate together at Lucina Hall on occasion during her freshman year. Often, afterward, at Timmy's request, she would stay and watch Timmy play ping-pong with Jack Clark, a white classmate who was also a freshman. She had attended Noblesville High with him, where he played football and basketball and ran track. "I hung out with Tim when I should have been studying," she recalled. "My grades suffered as a result.'

She described herself as a freshman as "young and silly." Like her brother Bill, she remembered Timmy's antics, such as drinking tea with a teaspoon to see how many teaspoons he could get from one teabag. "I thought he was retarded," she joked. She was the Kappa Alpha Psi Homecoming queen nominee in her first year and the Kappa Sweetheart not only that year, but the remaining three years as well.

In 1958, she moved into Lucina, where she remained until graduation in 1961. She dished up food and bused tables for those three years to help finance her education.

Timmy and Grayce's friendship led to a long-term on-again, off-again romantic relationship. She described it as erratic. "A lot of times," she said, "the two of us would go to a dance or a party [and] guys would try to hit on me. I wasn't trying to get them to notice me. Whenever we would break up, Timmy warned: 'Don't you dare date Carl Miller.' 'There he goes. He's angry again,'" she thought. Reflecting on Timmy's upbringing, their relationship, and her feelings, she wrote a paper for a class in which she asked whether a person who didn't know love as a child was capable of loving later. She also wondered if someone who didn't appear to trust women would be able to love a woman.

Carl Miller was a Muncie native and basketball player on the 1952 Muncie Central state championship team, and was older than Timmy or Grayce. After graduation from high school, he played basketball at Arizona State in 1953. He followed with a stint in the military before coming to Ball State. He earned the nickname "Goose" after the flamboyant Harlem Globetrotters player Reece "Goose" Tatum. Like Tatum, Miller was a free-spirited player known for his ability to make nearly magical passes to teammates. He studied Spanish with the hope of teaching it to elementary-age children. He enjoyed calypso and Latin American music, would call himself "Carlos," and often spoke Spanish among friends.

What caused Timmy to warn Grayce about Carl was not so much his magnetic personality and interests as his reputation. A classmate, who asked not to be identified, observed that "Carl liked the ladies and liked to spread his love around a lot." Grayce's older brother Ernie, who was protective of her, attributed Timmy's admonishment to his moodiness. "He *was* moody!" Ernie stressed. In the July 1964 Sport article, Stainback attributed that moodiness to having "been hurt by a youth he can't forget. A youth that left wounds so deep in his psyche they have refused to heal...." Stainback went on to say that during his conversation with Timmy, "it was as though he, subconsciously at least, wanted to provide insight into his moods. For he spoke of times past and jarred festered wounds, speaking quietly but with occasional shadings of bitterness toward those who had hurt him."

While looking out for his sister, Ernie continued to act as an "older brother" to Timmy. During Timmy's freshman year, Ernie took him to a dance. Ernie recalled that "they had dances at the armory in downtown Muncie on weekends – programs you couldn't find in Indy. We danced to Ray Charles, James Brown, and Duke Ellington. Duke performed on a hot July night – so hot and humid in the joint that all of the band members took off their coats first, then their shirts, sitting with their tank-top underwear shirts, except the Duke. After the break, Duke and the bassist came out in a fresh new suit.

"Tim really didn't have anything hip to wear, so I dressed him up in a nice gray suit with a pink shirt and black tie. Sonny Grady, who was a senior running back on the football team – a position for which Tim competed – Tim and I went 'cattin'.... Every brother and sister in town was there except my brother Bill, who went home on weekends to our mother's cooking. We went to the dance and there was a beautiful girl there. Sonny wasn't as nice looking, but he wasn't ugly. He was funny looking. His head was very thin. He had a nice body. Sonny was the boldest, so he went over to the girl and made a hit. Started dancing with her. Tim said, 'Oh, man, I wish.' I said, 'OK, look around here. Who is the prettiest woman in the house?' The girl Sonny was with, of course. "'K, who is the best-looking guy in the house? You. You all are the perfect match. As soon as Sonny is finished dancing with her, go over and ask her to dance. You don't have to say lines from the movies or sing a song,'" as he sometimes did, "'just tell her you would like to dance.' He liked to use words from the movies. Really corny. I don't think he went out with her, but he spent the rest of the night at the dance with her. All the way home, Tim was swooning about how fine she was. Sonny was a little bit pissed that Timmy had outdone him. Sonny was sour-graping that she wasn't all that fine, that the one he ended up hitting on was of much higher quality. 'Look at the greenhorn,' Sonny said. He was razzing Timmy for being so starstruck over this girl."

"After that, Tim and I were much tighter," Ernie said. Any friction that may have remained from their meeting at the skating rink in Richmond in the spring of 1955 was erased when Grady was injured early in the season of Timmy's freshman year. Because he was not at his best, there was never a comparison made between him and Timmy. "There was no antagonism between the two, but there wasn't a bond, either," Ernie said. "I became the mediator between the two. In the long run, I became much closer to Tim, as our relationship continued after Ball State, whereas I lost contact with Sonny after college."

In fall 1957, two freshmen enrolled at Ball State who would connect with Timmy as friends. One, Jim Hart, he already knew from the Home. The other, Dean Campbell, he met through athletics, and worked for when Campbell was head of a summer crew cutting weeds on campus.

"Jug" Hart came to Ball State and moved into Wagoner Hall. On his first day on campus, Hart recalled, Timmy saw him and shouted, "Hey, Butt," and ran across the lawn and hugged him. Hart viewed Timmy as a friend and mentor who showed him how to get student loans and the jobs that constituted a kind of "athletic scholarship." Hart worked in Wagoner buffing floors, and was a part of the crew clearing trees and brush on campus during the summer with Campbell and Timmy. With their first paycheck, Hart said, they bought a fifth of blended Black and White Scotch whisky. Thereafter, they reunited on and off the field, as Hart became a regular on the football team and continued to rely on Timmy's companionship and guidance.

Campbell was the third in his family to attend Ball State. The oldest, Larry, had graduated in 1955, and in the 1955-56 academic year was a graduate assistant while working on a master's degree in counseling psychology. He took a job as director of Elliott Hall and worked in the Counseling Center for the next year, but it was interrupted mid-year when he was drafted into the military. He wasn't around when Dean enrolled. The next oldest, Wayne, was a senior at the time, married, and living at 3121 Bethel Ave., north of campus. Dean, with brothers Dick, three years younger, and Rex, 12, resided at the family home at 1608 N. Riley Rd., about a mile from campus. In 1955, the family had moved there from a farm halfway between the small towns of Yorktown and Gaston. Their father, Francis, was "fed up" with farming, so sold the farm and worked for the Delaware County Farm Bureau Co-op delivering gas to farmers' tanks. Their mother, Mary, worked at a Kroger store.

Like both his older brothers, Dean played all four years on the baseball team and was recognized as an all-conference player. As freshmen, Larry and Wayne were able to play on the varsity. However, the year that Dean enrolled, a new conference rule prohibited freshmen from playing on the varsity. His brothers felt that was unfortunate, because they believed he was by far the most talented. Both Dean and Larry played basketball – Larry for two years before he decided it took too much time, and Dean for 1½ years, being cut at mid-year of the second season.

Timmy and Dean most likely met through their interest in basketball. Dean talked about playing one-on-one games with Timmy at Ball Gym in the evening. He was impressed by Timmy's prowess and admitted that whenever they played against one another, he "got his clock cleaned." On four or five occasions, Dean recalled, he invited Timmy over to his family's home – an easy 20-minute walk from campus – for dinner and to play ping pong in the basement. Rex, who was in junior high, wanted to hang out with them in the basement, but their mother was protective and felt Dean and Timmy should be left alone. A few minutes later, Timmy went upstairs and asked her if Rex could come down and be with them. Mary agreed and Rex was thrilled – a moment he never forgot. He was even more ecstatic on another occasion when Timmy, knowing that Rex was playing football, brought him an old-style leather helmet. Rex felt like he had been given a thousand dollars.

Timmy found great joy performing in musical groups on campus. In a 1959 article written by Van Young, features editor of the Ball State News, Timmy stated, "I've been singing as long as I can remember. Someday, I'd like to make it my career." Young wrote, "Tim's popularity on campus can be attributed to not only his athletic abilities, but his engraved smile, looks, manners, singing, and ability to quickly make friends with almost anyone. Tim began singing on campus at the Variety Show and the Orange Oyster Dance. His pleasant tenor voice has been heard around the county at some of the high school functions, too."

The Orange Oyster Dance was held in mid-April at the Student Center Ballroom and followed a nautical theme. Casual Bermuda and beachcomber attire was appropriate. Students danced on the ocean floor accompanied by music from a band seated in an underwater-cave set. The dance lasted from 8 to 11 p.m., with 50-cent admission per person.

On Feb. 13, 1959, Timmy sang with a group called the Nu-Tons at the Kappa Alpha Sigma Variety Show on campus. Other members were juniors Dorothy Washington from Muncie; Nat Pittman from Mishawaka, Ind; Joe Dinnell from Chicago; and A.B. Floyd, the student who had come up from Alabama to help his widowed sister. Floyd remembered "Tim [as] a big, friendly, good-looking jock, who possessed a good tenor/baritone voice and would perform Elvis Presley and other pop songs at the drop of a hat in the Ball State Student Center, where we all hung out and played Bid Whist between classes." Floyd pledged Kappa Alpha Psi and sang bass in a do-wop Kappa singing group that would also "break into song without provocation to serenade any coeds within earshot." He suspected that Dorothy, a classmate, most likely mentioned him to participate with the group on that occasion, as Floyd had a group of his own that included lead tenor Bernard White from South Bend; tenor Gene Thompkins from Muncie; and baritone Pittman.

Timmy also performed with a band called Timmy Brown and the Thunderbirds, with three white musicians – pianist, guitarist, and drummer. Upon hearing him singing while he worked in Elliott Hall, they asked him to join their band. Time erased the names of the other Thunderbirds from Timmy's memory, but he did remember that they were accomplished musicians and how unusual it was for an interracial band to perform in the 1950s. Timmy said he did some shows on campus and at high schools as well. "We used to work school proms, things like that," Timmy recalled in a 1966 article in the New York Times, in which he called his performances then "scat-singing and not real singing."

The band covered popular songs of the time, including Elvis' 1957 smash "(Let Me Be Your) Teddy Bear," one of Timmy's favorites. Timmy's ability to almost instantly remember the lyrics to hits meant that the band could perform without much rehearsal.

Although the band only played a handful of dances in the Muncie area, it gave Timmy his first taste of being the lead singer. It also was an early indicator that Timmy's performance on the gridiron could be the perfect advertising for Timmy the entertainer.

While music was close to his heart, in sports he found the greatest refuge from rejection – a shelter where he could get lost in the moment and feel exhilaration, success, and pride. While he had been recruited by Ball State to play basketball, Timmy liked football and decided to try out for the team his first fall on campus. He enjoyed the cat-and-mouse game of trying to avoid being caught by defensive players chasing him. There was a rush to the game he didn't feel in any other sport. Football practices and games were held at Ball State Field on University Avenue, located between the coal-burning heating plant and Ball Gym to the north, and Ball Memorial Hospital to the south. A cinder track around the football field and land nearby served track and field events. A baseball diamond and outfield occupied space west of the field. Next to the heating plant from the southwest, adjacent to Lucina Hall to the south and the Arts Building to the north, overlooking the Quad, Ball Gym, in addition to hosting basketball games, served as a physical education facility and offered other activities. Locker rooms there were used by athletes for all three sports.

Ball State participated in the Indiana Collegiate Conference (ICC), which was established in the 1950-51 academic year. Members included public colleges Ball State and Indiana State; smaller schools St. Joseph's (Catholic), Evansville (Methodist), and Valparaiso (Lutheran); and independent Butler and DePauw.

In 1955, unlike today, freshmen rarely saw any action in varsity games. Timmy is shown in photos with the varsity, however, and wore No. 39, also worn by his favorite NFL running back, Hugh McElhenny of the San Francisco 49ers. Two freshmen games were played that year. In the first, against Valparaiso, Ball State was shut out. In the second, against Butler, Ball State lost again, but did manage a touchdown, while missing the extra point. According to Bill Butler, the final score was "twenty something to six." Bill carried the ball for the lone score and joked with Timmy that he had tallied all of the points registered by the team for the entire season, and would probably be the only Ball State football player to ever do so.

Linson, who had been principal at Spiceland High School before coming to Ball State, had refereed track meets that included Morton Memorial teams. As a result, he was familiar with Timmy's skills upon his arrival. He was baffled by Timmy's treatment during his freshman season, saying, "Tim was a talent sitting on the bench that first year, when he should have been playing with the varsity."

Ernie Butler, who was playing on the varsity as a senior, had only a glimpse of Timmy's skills, given that he was a freshman and didn't get to practice much or play with the varsity. But he also noted that Timmy "was in the doghouse some. I wouldn't say he wouldn't take authority, but he didn't glom on it. He walked cocky, and he was a rookie."

Ernie recalled how impressed he was with Timmy's ability when Timmy got the opportunity to practice with the varsity. Timmy was assigned an end run. "My assignment was to go downfield blocking," Ernie said. "Ideally, he would swing around, and I would hit the defensive halfback and he could cut behind my block. I thought this was the perfect situation, and I went to throw the block, and I missed the guy and fell on the ground. I [saw] the guy hit Tim with his arms around him, but he didn't lock his tackle. Tim slipped one leg out and then the other, like he was ... tap-dancing [through the tackler's grasp]. He could stop and move so quickly. I thought, damn! Oh wow!"

George Serdula, who had played football at Muskingum College, was the varsity coach during Timmy's freshman year. He compiled a 14-9-1 record from 1953 to 1955, but after a 3-5 season he resigned to work on a doctorate at Indiana University. He later served as a professor of health sciences at St. Cloud State in Minnesota for many years.

Serdula was replaced in 1956 by Jim Freeman, who had been an All-Big Ten player at Indiana University and the 76th player drafted in 1938 by the Detroit Lions. Instead of trying out for the NFL, he coached at the high school and university levels for several years. He came from Bethlehem High School in Fredericktown, Pa., to become the Cardinals' coach for Timmy's sophomore through senior years. Freeman retired in 1961 with a record of 18 wins, 28 losses, and 2 ties.

Timmy and Bill Butler developed a "friendly competition in football" and "were very good friends." Butler, in his book "One Sports Fan Left Behind," told of where his rivalry with Timmy led: "During practice ... when it came time to hit him, I felt compelled to put a little something extra into it."

Shortly before the opener of the 1956 season, Timmy's first on the varsity, Bill had "injured the big toe on my right foot." While it was not very painful, he couldn't "drive off of that foot." Soon after that, he hurt his back. That meant he "could not make certain movements with my usual alacrity. The coach had a policy of moving injured players to the bottom of the depth chart. That player then had to work his way back up to his former status. It was while trying to fight through this ... that I had the greatest misfortune of my athletic life."

At the time, Bill "was playing linebacker. A would-be blocker was deftly disposed of, in order for me to get a good shot at Tim. My great toe injury would not allow me to drive through him. The back injury would not permit me to tackle him properly. In retrospect, I should have simply grabbed him and pulled him to the ground. But, no, this was Tim. I had to go all out."

While the competition between them was friendly, it was also "fierce." "The only thing to do," Bill thought, "was to arm tackle him. I knew this was poor technique. I had often heard coaches warn against it, but at that moment, it did not matter. Tim was a very quick, shifty, and elusive ball carrier, and difficult to hit. However, it was fairly easy to bring him down if you could ever get a good shot at him."

Butler said of the play: "With my right arm, I hit him just below the knees, as hard as I could. Tim went flying through the air, end over end, and landed in an ungraceful heap, several feet away from the point of initial contact. Everyone thought I had killed him. The trainer, coaches and players went running to him to see if he had survived."

"Meanwhile," Bill said, "I lay on the ground with a shattered radius (lateral bone of the forearm). In that brief, convulsive moment, I knew deep down that I would never be able to play football again." Bill was taken to Ball Memorial Hospital, across the street from the football field. "The radius was completely shattered, all the way through. The arm was placed in a cast without being *set*. Several weeks later, X-rays revealed that the arm was not healing properly. The radius was re-broken and placed in a new cast. That was painful. I wore a cast for 13 weeks."

In 1956, the team compiled a record of 4-4 (4-2 in the ICC). For the second game of the season, on Sept. 22, the Cardinals traveled to State Teachers College at Indiana, Pa., for a game that Ball State was not expected to win. In a surprising 26-0 victory, Timmy, who had played only briefly the preceding week against Hanover, exhibited his potential by scoring three touchdowns, accounting for 18 points, all in the second half. It was late in the third quarter when he took a handoff at the 9-yard line and ran 91 yards for a score. In a Dec. 4, 1969, Ball State Daily News article, Paul Berebitsk wrote that the handoff was the first time that Timmy had actually touched the ball. Running for a touchdown on his first carry, he wrote, garnered him the nickname "Scooting Bolt of Lightning." Timmy followed up with a run for 20 yards for his second touchdown, and midway through the fourth quarter scored from 15 yards out. Despite his outstanding performance, the official program for the next week's home game against DePauw noted: "Surprising as it may seem Tim still has a battle on his hands to win a starting position as both regular halfbacks, 'Pug' Hoover and Dave Kindt, have continued to shine as consistent ground gainers." Timmy was puzzled as to why he wasn't starting more often and playing more, a point that would lead to some discontent later.

Ernie Butler, who had graduated and was living in Indianapolis and teaching at School 29 there, came back to Muncie to see Timmy on Homecoming weekend, arriving on Friday evening, Oct. 12. He also came to see a "lady friend." Before the bonfire and pep rally that began at 7:45 p.m., he and Timmy "went into a store to get some beer. Tim was going to walk past the counter, but the girl stopped us, wanting us to pay. Tim stared at the girl and said, 'Don't you know who I am?'"

Surprised by Timmy's action, Ernie said, "Come on, Tim."

The girl responded, "No, I don't." There was a Muncie newspaper near the counter. Tim pointed to it and said, "Look on page so and so and you will see who I am." He was in part joking and burst out laughing. Ernie thought, "Man, he has really changed a lot. That guy's got guts. His confidence had grown."

They walked to West Quad to the bonfire and pep rally, where the team was introduced.

Afterward, they drank a couple of beers. Ernie stayed with his friend and went to the game the next day. Both teams came into the Oct. 13 game undefeated – Ball State with three wins and Butler with two. (Buddy had only played football for the Bulldogs for two years, so the brothers never played against each other.) The game drew an over-capacity crowd of approximately 11,000, leading to fans sitting on the ground close to the field. Butler scored twice in the first quarter to take a 14-0 lead. In the second quarter, the Cardinals responded twice to end the half just 2 points behind after missing both extra points. Timmy scored the first touchdown on a 23-yard run. Teammate Norm Helms recovered a fumble for the second. The Cardinals were held scoreless in the second half, while Butler scored two more touchdowns, winning 28-12.

For the season, Timmy led the team in rushing and scoring. Playing at halfback, he rushed 42 times for 355 yards, had five pass receptions for 120 yards, returned six kickoffs for 89 yards, and had three punt returns for 11 yards, and successfully kicked one of 2 points-after-touchdown, scoring 31 points. He also punted six times for 260 yards and a 43.3 average and played defense, and had one interception on defense.

So it was quite a shock to Ball State administrators and coaches when, at the end of Winter Quarter in March 1957, their star running back was given notice that he was "ineligible to further attendance for one year because of poor scholastic record."

Football coach Freeman wrote on March 13, 1957, to W.R. Renke, chair of the Admissions and Credits Committee, asking "for a revaluation and reconsideration for admission" based on Timmy's background, potential, and "lack of proper guidance and counsel." Freeman said he was "willing to take the responsibility of providing guidance and counseling in order to help him make the proper adjustments, which I believe has been the cause of his difficulties."

A day earlier, Linson had written to Renke, "It has come to my attention that Tim Brown has been disqualified for scholastic reasons." He referred to Timmy's attendance at "an orphanage of war veterans" and "putting himself through school." He suggested that Timmy be readmitted for Spring Quarter on probationary status. Linson concluded by saying he had talked with the president of the Teachers College Alumni Association, Vernon Craig, who coincidentally was school superintendent in Knightstown. Craig, he said, would "do everything possible to see that Tim brings his academic grades up." On Timmy's official transcript, below the list of courses, grades, and credits for Winter Quarter 1956, it reads: "Ineligible to further attendance for one year because of poor scholastic record." On the next line, it reads: "Readmitted March 12, 1957."

In a March 15, 1957, letter to Timmy, Hauptman, who in addition to being registrar was executive secretary of the Committee on Admissions and Credits, granted him readmission for Spring with the understanding that he "confer with Dr. Howard Johnsboy, Dean of Student Affairs, as early as possible" and "carry a full load of college work for each quarter ... enrolled." Hauptman noted that Timmy would be "disqualified at the close of any quarter ... at which time [his] cumulative scholastic ratio ... [fell] below 2.0." Doubtless everyone involved knew of president Emens' interest in this young man. In an Aug. 14, 2009, interview, Linson underscored the college's efforts to make sure that Timmy was successful, saying: "We worked pretty hard to put him in the right classes."

For his part, Timmy had not been unaware that his academic career was less than stellar. Looking back in 2008, he said, "I was always on time for class. I spent an hour at night studying because that's all the time that I had. I would be happy to get a C or C-minus."

Once he had been reinstated, Timmy continued his studies toward a physical education degree and at one point, according to the 1973 interview in Black Sports, aspired to open a school for typing and shorthand someday. He noted that he "was up to 85 words a minute in typing, 120 with the old shorthand." He had hoped to enroll in more courses in typing and shorthand but was unable to do so because there were no seats available. As a result, he took a course in interpretive reading and one in acting, both of which he said he "dug." These courses tweaked his interest in acting. He also wanted to coach after graduating.

All this activity cleared Timmy to play again in the 1957 season. And despite his injuries the preceding year, Bill Butler wanted to play again, too. But in his first contact, he got Timmy in what he considered an "unforgettable tackle." Again, he fractured his arm; this time it only healed around the perimeter. Now, he truly knew he would never play football again.

Timmy also was hurt that season. While the injury was not nearly as serious, it hampered his playing time for several games. In the fourth game of the season, on Oct. 12 at Evansville, he ran 63 yards for a touchdown in the first quarter. In the second quarter, he was hit hard by a defensive lineman and suffered a shoulder separation. His availability for the next game, against DePauw, was questioned in the official program: "Possibly out of the starting line-up will be Quarterback Ed Corazzi's right-hand man, Timmy Brown." He played sparingly in the next several games. (In addition to this injury, a December 1962 story in the Philadelphia Evening Bulletin said Timmy "admitted to [Philadelphia Eagles physician James] Dixon that when he was a junior at Ball State ... he was on crutches six weeks with a knee injury.")

The Cardinals had a disappointing 1957 record of 2-5-1 (2-3-1 in the ICC). Timmy started in five games and again led the team in rushing and scoring. He was named All-ICC first team despite being "hampered considerably ... with [the flu] and injuries ... [still managing] to impress opposing players, coaches, and spectators," according to the Ball

State News in a Nov. 13, 1957, article. He was fourth in ICC scoring with 27 points. At halfback again, he rushed 42 times for 419 yards, had five pass receptions for 71 yards, returned three kickoffs for 72 yards, had six punt returns for 38 yards, and successfully kicked three of six PATs, scoring a total of 33 points. He punted 18 times for 632 yards and a 34.8 average, and had one interception and made 13 tackles.

In the offseason before his senior year, Timmy had decided that he might not return to football again. He wasn't getting along with Freeman. Timmy said Freeman talked down to him and made him feel "like a piece of crap." He also believed that the best players weren't getting to play on the line to block for him. Timmy said, "It wasn't just giving me the ball, it's playing the right people in the right positions. Maybe players know better who is good and who is not. But I never took on that as being a coach.... It's just, you lose five games in a row ... [and] something's wrong when you [have] a pretty good team."

"[As] the running back," Timmy said, "I want the best blockers in there for me. I'm the one who was going to get hit." He felt there was prejudice, claiming "the guys we had that were Black were twice as good as the guys [Freeman] put up front."

The fact that he had come to Ball State to play for Serdula and "didn't care much for Freeman" played into his feelings. So did the fact that as the team leader in rushing and scoring in his sophomore and junior years, and coming off a three-touchdown, 158-yard performance in the second game of the 1956 season against Indiana of Pennsylvania, he was perplexed as to why Freeman hadn't started him in every game. In the July 1964 Sport article, he noted: "I didn't become a starter until my senior year, and this hurt. I knew it hurt them too when the coach didn't start me. I don't know, maybe there was a racial thing involved." In addition, he was not pleased that Freeman had brought along a quarterback from Fredericktown.

In 1957, Ed Corazzi replaced Timmy's "good buddy" Larry Koehl, who had been playing the position during the 1956 season when he was a junior and Timmy a sophomore. Timmy "liked [Corazzi] pretty well, but ... [he] thought Koehl was better" – built like 2017 NFL Hall of Fame inductee Kurt Warner, who played for the St. Louis Rams and the Arizona Cardinals, and who like Warner "had a great arm." Timmy was impressed by his all-round athletic ability, as Koehl also played guard in basketball and shortstop in baseball. He touted Koehl as a little guy (5-foot-9) "who could do it all." He said Koehl was "crazy," and was enamored by the fact that if you didn't know Koehl, you would think he was Black. "If you heard him talk, you would be convinced. He had swagger. Was cool." But Timmy hadn't anticipated that Koehl would be drafted by the Detroit Tigers and leave Ball State to play minor league baseball for five years.

In addition, Timmy didn't think he was going to be in football or any other sport after leaving Ball State. "I wasn't going back my senior year [to play]. I just figured, hell, I could put more time studying [to] get my degree. I [was] going to be a teacher."

Ray Louthen, then the assistant coach and later the head coach, learned that Timmy was thinking of not returning. The word was out among teammates, some of whom were the first to ask Timmy to return. Louthen got in touch with Timmy and said, "I've been watching films on you, and you have a chance to go pro." Timmy responded, "I understand you want me to come back. I'm not having fun," to which Louthen said: "Don't set it in your mind you're not going back."

Timmy respected and liked Louthen and felt "he was a good man." Timmy recalled Louthen's trying to talk him into returning several times during the summer. Finally, after one conversation, Timmy said he would return on one condition – that Louthen, not Freeman, communicate with him. "Look," he told Louthen, "if I go back out, [Freeman] can't say nothing to me. If he says something to me one time, I'm walking." Later, Louthen got back to Timmy and said, "OK, OK, I've talked with him. He said OK, he won't say anything [to you]. He will go through me."

And thus Timmy returned to his final year of collegiate football. In a practice before the season began, Timmy ran a play where he dipped into the line and out, trying to get around the defenders, but was stopped for a loss. Freeman shouted, "Oh, Tim, come here!" Louthen jumped in and said, "I'll talk to him." Timmy responded immediately to Louthen, saying calmly, "No, I heard it." All that Timmy could think of in that moment was that he had told him that if Freeman said one word to him, he would be gone, and that he had meant it. "That's it," he thought to himself. "I'm out of here." As he began walking off the field, he knew that the entire team had heard it and wondered what would happen. As he continued walking toward the dressing room in Ball Gym, Timmy thought that Freeman "messed up. He didn't believe me, did he?"

Louthen followed him into the dressing room and said, "Tim, now come on. Be reasonable."

"Ray," Timmy responded. "What did I say? I said, if he said anything to me at all. I don't want to deal with him." Louthen persuaded Timmy to give it another try, assuring him that he would be the one communicating with him throughout the season.

Timmy had also been concerned about Jug Hart's treatment. Like Timmy, Hart was given jobs on campus, and he and Timmy referred to the pay as their "athletic scholarship." Timmy believed that Hart was getting a bad deal, because he believed that "white players generally got more and were taken care of better." Timmy told athletic director Robert Primmer, "Just take my 'scholarship' and use it for him." Primmer didn't. Timmy held that against Ball State and his feelings toward Primmer soured. It was not that Timmy felt Primmer was prejudiced. But he thought that Primmer walked slow and acted cool so that Blacks would think he was cool. Timmy didn't feel it was sincere.

"I didn't have anything my last year," he said. "I wouldn't accept anything. I just worked. I had no problem with working. I was preparing myself for what life may be out there. So I just always took the toughest job they had." According to Linson, there was another source of income, but one not widely known. He said "a local accountant, Bob Hughes, would slip Tim $10 or $20 after a game." Robert L. Hughes was managing partner at R.J. Whitinger & Co., a large accounting firm in Muncie. Both he and the firm's founder, Ralph J. Whitinger, had attended Ball State, and Whitinger, a civic leader in Muncie, also was the founder of the Ball State University Foundation.

With Timmy's return, the team had its most successful season since his arrival at Ball State. Mikesell, a Theta Chi, and Don Hutson, a Sig Ep from Noblesville who was friends with Bill Butler, recalled watching Timmy play. Mikesell said that of the 120 Theta Chi brothers, 40 to 50 went to the games to support their brothers on the football team. They were among the 3,000 people who typically attended. He said, "Tim was a cut above. An outstanding and exciting running back. He was a special player." Hutson considered a 100-yard run Timmy made for a touchdown as "the best running return [he] ever saw. It seemed as if he ran 160 yards, horizontally back and forth across the field. He was shifty and difficult" to tackle.

Timmy was never sidelined during the 1958 season, and the team compiled a record of 6-2 (4-2 in the ICC). In the opening game of the season at Illinois State on Sept. 20, he had one of his best games, rushing for 236 yards in slightly more than 30 minutes of play and accounting for 25 of the team's 31 points. A highlight of the season was the only defeat of Butler University in Tim's four seasons, by a score of 14-7. It broke an 11-game winning streak by Butler and was only the third time in 22 games with Butler that Ball State had won. Though heavily favored, Butler left the field at halftime behind 6-0, the result of a 60-yard punt return by Timmy. The try for an extra point failed. In the third quarter, Butler scored a touchdown and converted the extra point to take the lead. Most of the rest of the game was a defensive duel, with Timmy and the Butler punter taking turns keeping the other team at bay. In the fourth quarter, quarterback Corazzi passed to Nat Pittman for a 12-6 lead. A fake kick and 2-point conversion made it 14-7 with only 2 minutes, 54 seconds left. The win put the Cards into a first-place tie in the ICC.

"The punt return helped preserve Freeman's job for three more years," according to Linson, "We were getting ready to fire him." It wasn't just because of coaching. "Freeman was bad news. Kids said in class he was a terrible teacher." Linson, who was close friends with Emens and could confide in him, shared this concern. But after their meeting, Linson consulted with Billy Williams, head of the physical education department, who countered that Freeman "was the best teacher he had."

In addition to repeating as the rushing and scoring leader, Timmy also led in pass receiving. He led the ICC in rushing and scoring, and was second in punting. He was selected as the ICC Outstanding Back and named to the All-ICC first team. He was selected to the Williamson's All-America Team (college division, second team). For these accomplishments he received the Ball State Most Valuable Player Award.

Finishing his career in his usual position at halfback, Timmy rushed 112 times for 551 yards, had 10 pass receptions – three for touchdowns – for 213 yards, returned five kickoffs for 132 yards, had 10 punt returns for 137 yards, had nine touchdowns, and successfully kicked 11 of 14 PATs, scoring 69 points. He punted 27 times for 975 yards for a 36.1 average, had one interception, and made 13 tackles.

By the end of his football career at Ball State, he had set six Cardinal records. In 1957, he set three: best rushing average in a single game (20.5 years in eight carries) and most net yards rushing in a game (164 yards) – both against Valparaiso – and best rushing average in a season (10-yard average). In 1958, he also set three records: most rushing attempts in a game, 21 against Wooster; most rushing attempts in a season, 112; and most points scored in a single game, 25 against Illinois State. Nearly 70 years later, he still stood as the leading scorer in a single game.

Whatever effect Timmy's refusal to talk with Freeman had on the coach, he was able to overcome it in a 1969 interview in the Ball State

Daily News. He called Timmy "one of the finest athletes he ever worked with" and said his accomplishments were even more remarkable given the types of teams he played on. One year, he said, there were only 29 football players, and in general it was not unusual to have 160-pound linemen. "As Tim went, so went the team," he said.

While Timmy had been recruited to play basketball for varsity coach Jim Hinga, he never did. During his freshman year, he played on a successful 8-1 team under coach A.L. "Pete" Phillips, who had been varsity coach from 1938 to 1948. No individual statistics have been found. In a photo, he is shown wearing No. 10 and a brace on his left knee, an injury from football. In a team photo, he is wearing No. 24 and has no brace. Timmy recalled dressing for the varsity team as well.

As his sophomore football season began, he was planning to forgo basketball because of the time required for transitioning from football – which uses different muscles – as well as financial pressures. Even so, he did go out for Hinga's varsity – for a day. At the first practice, he popped a couple of long ones, but didn't feel comfortable with his form or confidence. He imagined that Hinga would have "unrealistic expectations" for him to perform at the top of his game immediately, and would want him to "run the show." He never returned to practice. "I walked off. Went to my own little world. Hinga didn't give me a hard time. He was OK with my decision. We never talked again."

Timmy thought basketball might have been his best sport, and one that he could have played professionally much longer than football. It would have taken less of a toll on his body. "I had to give up basketball because I couldn't do everything I needed to do to make it," he said. "It was the longest season, so it had to go." But Linson shared another perspective, saying that university officials "wouldn't let him play basketball because he would have flunked out."

Timmy didn't give up basketball entirely. According to Paul Snyder, who came to Ball State from Mill Creek, a small school in LaPorte County, on a small basketball and baseball "scholarship" in 1956, Timmy and he competed in the intramural program and in pickup games. "We weren't friends," he said. "He was just one of the guys around the gym. Being jocks, we tried to get as many T-shirts that said 'Ball State Athletic Department' as we could and free of charge." Dean Campbell participated, too, going to Ball Gym in the evenings, where Timmy would "clean his clock." Those who played with him or against him, or watched him, said he was exceptionally talented.

During his junior and senior years, Timmy participated in track. Richard Stealey was the coach, and later was considered a legend for his 42 years of successful coaching and teaching physical education. In track, his teams won nine ICC and three titles in the Little State competition among 13 smaller Indiana colleges. He was nominated for ICC Track Coach of the Year in 1967. His cross-country teams won 40 of 58 dual meets, and four ICC titles and three Little State titles. He was named ICC Cross-Country Coach of the Year in 1966.

Timmy had little initial interest in track. He felt he was too busy working and was out of shape. But during his junior year, as the season approached, he relented after several requests. "They called me and kept on me," saying, "We really could use some points – anything you can get us." I told them, "I'll come out, but I don't know what I can do. I'll try." In an inter-squad meet preparing for the season, he was asked to run against two white boys in an event. "You can't outrun me, I'm Black," he chided. It didn't work. "I was overweight by 20 pounds. That was crazy. They killed me," he said with a laugh.

He claimed he never tried to get in shape or work out for track much. Still, he lettered in track in 1958 and 1959. In 1958, the team placed fifth in the Big State meet, first in the ICC, second in Little State, and first in the district meet of the National Association of Intercollegiate Athletics (NAIA), an association for small colleges and universities. Timmy finished fourth in the broad jump in the ICC. In 1959, the team tied for seventh in the Big State, first in the ICC, first in the NAIA, and second in the Little State meet. Timmy set an ICC record in the broad jump at 23 feet, 3 inches his senior year. He placed second in the 220-yard dash and third in the 100-yard dash. In the Little State meet, he placed fourth in the broad jump, fourth in the 220, and fifth in the 100. In the NAIA meet he placed first in the 220, second in the 100, and second in the broad jump. In the Big State, he was sixth in the broad jump.

In the National Football League off-season during Timmy's senior year, he met a man who would play a large part in his life on the field and off. Jim Brown, the 1957 Cleveland Browns' No. 1 draft pick, visited campus as part of his work for Pepsi-Cola. Jim Brown, who had been an All-America player at Syracuse, was already a national star. He was rookie of the year in 1957 and a unanimous pick for the NFL first team in his rookie season and in 1958. He was the league's leading rusher in his first two seasons, setting an NFL single-season rushing record in 1958 with 1,527 yards in a 12-game season. He was a Pro Bowl player both years.

Timmy recalled that "university people wanted Jim to meet their Tim Brown." Before Jim's speech, they met and spent some time playing basketball and talking. After his speech, according to Timmy, Jim brought him on stage to answer questions. Reflecting on their meeting, Timmy said, "We got tight that weekend." It was the beginning of a longtime friendship.

Timmy claimed in a 1966 Ball State News article that as the NFL draft day of Jan. 21, 1959, approached, he didn't think he would be selected. However, he had received letters in the fall of 1958 from Pittsburgh Steelers director of player personnel Daniel Rooney and Baltimore Colts director of personnel Keith Molesworth, both indicating they were contacting top college players about playing professional football, and asking him to complete a questionnaire and return it if interested. "I had about decided to play in Canada, but that would be like going to a small school again," he said. "I wanted to find out how good I was." Apparently, Timmy had indicated he would play for the BC Lions in

Vancouver. The day before the draft, Timmy received a letter from Lions general manager H.P. Capozzi, in which he said that "on the instructions of Coach [Wayne] Robinson I am pleased to enclose a cheque for $200 as an advance on your 1959 contract." It went on to say, "I was very pleased to learn from the Coach that you have signed with us for 1959 and will be looking forward to meeting you at training camp." Enclosed was a questionnaire and a request for a glossy photograph for publicity purposes. Capozzi said that a booklet and pamphlet about Vancouver were being sent under separate cover. He told Timmy that if he had any questions, he should not hesitate to get in touch. Timmy never returned the form or cashed the check.

As it turned out, the Steelers and Colts were not the only NFL teams interested in Timmy. In the frozen north of Wisconsin, a sad-sack squad looking for a new start had noticed him as well.

GREEN BAY

CHAPTER FOUR

Playing Isn't Everything

On Jan. 17, 1959, Timmy had received a telegram from the Green Bay Packers' personnel director, Jack Vainisi, indicating that the team was very interested in selecting him in the draft, and asking him to send back a wire, collect, if he planned to play pro ball and was interested in the Packers. This he did.

Timmy was selected in the 27th round, the 313th player chosen out of 360. (The first four rounds had been picked on Dec. 1, 1958; the remaining 26 rounds came on Jan. 21, 1959.) On Jan. 22, Vainisi sent a telegram to Ball State asking that pictures and biographical material on Timmy be sent to him immediately. He also sent a telegram to Timmy saying the Packers "were very pleased to have selected [him] ... [and] know this will be the beginning of a long and happy association."

The Green Bay Packers to which Timmy reported in 1959 were not the "Green Bay Packers" of modern football lore, the legends perennially fighting for championships on the frozen tundra of Lambeau Field. At this point, they were a perennial joke in the NFL, the last of a series of small-market teams that had helped to create and solidify the league in the 1920s, but that had been unable to compete with operations like the Chicago Bears and the New York Giants. Most of those small-market teams had brief lifespans – the Duluth Eskimos and the Canton Bulldogs were atypical in lasting as long as nearly a decade. Some, such as the Portsmouth Spartans, got a new lease on life by relocating to a larger city, in their case becoming the Detroit Lions.

But the Packers remained, decade after decade, because of their singular ownership structure. Most teams were the whim of a local entrepreneur; the Eskimos, for example, were the brainchild of a Duluth hardware store owner. When he ran out of money or interest, the team ran out of time. But the Packers were owned by 1,600 Green Bay-area residents who held shares of stock in the nonprofit team. When other small-market teams found their owner unwilling to part with more of his fortune, the Packers just sold more stock during hard times. During the Depression and World War II, every football team struggled and the Packers could claim some parity. But by the late 1940s, as John Eisenberg wrote in his book "That First Season," the Packers were no longer in the same league, in practical terms, as their foes: "Their opponents played in Yankee Stadium and the Los Angeles Coliseum, and they played at East High School." Home games in Green Bay would draw 10,000 rabid fans – but that was a Texas high-school crowd in terms of size, while big-city teams might pull in 70,000. As a result, the team and its players had to live cheaply, staying in low-cost motels and using second-rate equipment. The Packers became the league's Siberia. If another team's player needed to be threatened a bit, saying "We could trade you to Green Bay" often did the trick. And married players could find their wives less than willing to live in small-town northern Wisconsin.

In 1958, a 56-0 loss to Baltimore and a 1-10-1 season had laid bare the Packers' problems. The team was run by a 13-member board of directors, including many of the city's leaders – but knowing how to run the H.C. Prange department store or the Green Bay Press-Gazette didn't necessarily mean knowing how to run a football team. The directors had seen it differently. They kept their silence on game days, but afterward would interrogate the coach, who would have to explain to their satisfaction what he had done. In the days before the game, they offered him ideas on who should start. And some players would bypass the coach to speak directly to board members. This didn't attract to Green Bay coaches who wanted to do it their way – and that meant most top coaches.

After the 1958 season, with the NFL becoming more popular as a television sport, it was apparent things needed to change. Team president Dominic Olejniczak asked personnel director Vainisi to find out which NFL assistant coaches were ready to take a step up. Two from the Giants were mentioned prominently – defensive assistant Tom Landry and offensive assistant Vince Lombardi. Landry was 34 and clearly on the way up. At 45, Lombardi might have seemed to have missed his chance. But after he got backing from league leaders Bert Bell and George Halas, the Packers decided the former assistant at Fordham and West Point was their man.

While their decision on Timmy had come during the last few days of the tenure of Packers coach Ray "Scooter" McLean, Vainisi was largely responsible for the decisions made in the 1959 Packers' draft. At 31, he had eight years of experience with the Packers as personnel director, scouting prospects and managing draft selections. Eisenberg, in "That First Season," noted that "most NFL teams cared little about scouting; some just consulted Street & Smith's College Football guide before making picks. But Vainisi was consumed by the process...." In his book "When Pride Still Mattered: A Life of Vince Lombardi," David Maraniss said of Vainisi: "He worked the telephones and traveled relentlessly in search of his 'boys,' developing contacts with hundreds of high school and college coaches around the country, and was so engaging that competing pro coaches – his favorites were Paul Brown and George Halas – took his calls without fail and talked football talent with him. For his honeymoon in 1952 he persuaded his wife, Jackie, to escort him on a trip through Oklahoma, Texas, and Alabama, where he spent most of his time signing new players. He also developed a network of informal tipsters, many of them former Packers or friends from Notre Dame [which he had attended for one year in 1945 before going into the Army]. His scouting reports, in 18 thick blue-canvas, three-ringed notebooks, ranked and coded the statistics of nearly 4,000 players. He became known around the league as a boy wonder, lending Green Bay a measure of respect that it could not gain on the football field."

Green Bay announced its choice of Lombardi the week after the draft. Vainisi was not a stranger to Lombardi, and they had similar backgrounds. Maraniss noted: "Lombardi was his salvation, a paisano who understood what he had been doing. They had known each other for years through mutual friends, and they shared the same passion for football and a desire to make the Packers a first-class organization."

Lombardi's plan was based on a back-to-basics approach. As Eisenberg wrote, Lombardi believed that "football didn't need to be complicated. The best players were fit, disciplined and tough, willing to inflict and endure pain. They could win by mastering a small set of formations and plays, executing so crisply it didn't matter if the other team knew what was coming." Quarterback Bart Starr told Cliff Christl for his book "A Championship Team" that Lombardi "simplified the gobbledygook stuff. He reduced the terminology that was necessary to call plays. I think he felt if he could keep it as simple as possible, it would be much more appealing for the players."

Coaching Army had left a big impression on Lombardi. Soldiers were trained to not make mistakes, and he expected the same from football players. For the 1959 season he began to put together a team that could do what he wanted, and that meant doing away with the Packers culture of second-rate and what-did-you-expect. For example, he traded Billy Howton, a talented receiver and team stalwart who Lombardi felt was comfortable just getting by. Howton was a leader in the locker room and was used to being treated as a team star. However, Lombardi did retain as one of his quarterbacks Starr, perhaps not the most talented at the position, but a player who shared his love of excellence and had been frustrated by the Packers' penchant for losing. Lombardi was sending messages.

Lombardi wanted to send a message about race as well. He was a New Yorker; Green Bay was almost entirely white. He wanted the team to become more integrated, like the Giants; Green Bay residents seemed happy with one Black Packer. Lombardi was no revolutionary in race relations. He understood that the league in the late 1950s and early 1960s had a comfort level of three or four Black players per team, and he wasn't trying to push beyond that. But he also knew that he would be missing out on top-quality players if he couldn't attract more Black pros to a town that couldn't offer the off-duty life of a Philadelphia or Los Angeles, and to a team that held its training camp at a 950-student Catholic college about five miles away.

In a March 26 letter, Vainisi sent Timmy a copy of his 1959 contract, signed on Feb. 16 by Vainisi, Lombardi, and Timmy, and approved and signed on the 18th by NFL commissioner Bell. The contract took effect May 1 with a sum of $7,000, stipulating that 75 percent be paid in weekly installments beginning with the first regularly scheduled game and ending with the last regular game, with the balance also due at the end of the last regularly scheduled league game. Vainisi also asked Timmy to notify him when he had completed his remaining eligibility in track so that his signing could be announced. Given that the track season didn't conclude until the Little State meet at Wabash College on May 23, Timmy's signing didn't appear in newspapers until May 29. In a Ball State News article, Timmy extended praise to the Cardinals coaching staff, saying: "I appreciate all the good advice from Ball State coaches, especially Bob Primmer, Jim Freeman, and Ray Louthen. I will undoubtedly need more of the same advice in the future." This, of course, was the same Freeman whom Timmy had refused to speak to.

Around the same time, Timmy had received a letter dated March 19 from Frank "Pop" Ivy, the Chicago (later St. Louis) Cardinals' head coach, inviting him to a tryout camp at Lake Forest College, to begin the first week of July. It is not known why Ivy thought Timmy might be available.

Timmy then heard from Lombardi, who sent a May 4 letter outlining benefits unanimously adopted on April 23 by the NFL to include "life insurance, major medical protection and a retirement plan." He stressed, "They are in no way dependent upon membership in a Player Association [and] are being provided by the League at no cost to you." While the National League Football Players Association had been founded in 1956 and was supported by a majority of players, management would not recognize the union until 1968.

Then on May 15, Lombardi sent a letter notifying Timmy that all first-year players, centers, and quarterbacks had to report to Sensenbrenner Hall of St. Norbert College in West De Pere, Wis., on July 23. Veterans were expected on July 25. He firmly noted that late reporting would not be tolerated and that because he planned "to start hard and fast," players should report in excellent condition, emphasizing "their legs and feet." He stressed that "there is no place in this league for a fat man." He indicated that the Packers would supply game shoes and all other necessary equipment, but players would have to furnish their own practice shoes. A two-page player roster for training camp was enclosed.

When Timmy learned his reporting date to training camp, he contacted an adviser about taking Ball State courses in the summer. He enrolled in three – Economic Geography, Education in Play, and Family Relations – during the first summer term, from June 15 to July 17. While he was getting ready to leave for Green Bay, he ran into Linson at the Student Center and said, "Mr. Linson, I have moves the Packers have never seen!" A week after the first summer term ended, he was in Green Bay, with an NFL contract but no college diploma, because of Ball State's requirement of a double major to graduate.

Hometown friend George Walker drove him from Richmond to Dayton, where he caught a flight to Green Bay. After he arrived in Wisconsin, he picked up a copy of the Press-Gazette. An article discussed Packers players who in the writer's view shouldn't bother unpacking, and his name was among them. That was on his mind when he went to meet his new boss – who was not yet the Vince Lombardi of later legend, but simply a first-year coach taking over a not-very-successful team. The conversation, Eisenberg wrote, went like this:

LOMBARDI: So you're Brown.

BROWN: Yes, sir. [Timmy later said that he wanted to say "in more ways than one," but thankfully stopped himself.]

LOMBARDI: You don't look like a football player.

BROWN: Well, I'm not sure what you think a football player looks like. I'm not a big lineman. I'm a running back.

LOMBARDI: So you're a smart guy, eh?

BROWN: Well, sir, I did just graduate from college.

LOMBARDI: Go on, get out of here.

BROWN: You know what I'm going to do, sir? I'm going to go unpack.

Timmy's responses were not the sort Lombardi was looking for. For his part, Timmy said later, "I was being nice and I was being a gentleman until he started. Look, you don't know nothing about me, who I am or what I do. You're telling me I don't look big enough. It's crazy." He added, "I'm not going to be your fucking flunkie. If I'm going out like that, I ain't going out that way, 'Thanks for having me here.'" By the standards of his time and occupation Lombardi would not have been seen as prejudiced against Timmy because of his race, in fact the opposite. But this was 1959, he was a new head coach needing to impose his authority, and Timmy, who acted cocky despite being a low draft choice from an unknown college, might have drawn to his mind the word "uppity." Timmy was always able to mix his revulsion at the racist culture of the country and the sport with having grown up with many white friends, as he had a foot in both worlds. Talking to whites without too much deference was normal to him. Being cheeky was just his personality. Emlen Tunnell, a Black halfback who had played for Lombardi in New York, said Timmy came up to him on the day he reported and said, "Baby, I'm going to make this team." Timmy later said, "I thought I had to be cocky to hold my own. I wanted to make that team so bad."

During the camp, Timmy made friends with a white girl from the area and went to her family's house for dinner. Word got back to Lombardi from some displeased players. The next day, Lombardi gathered the team around him and said, "If I ever hear 'nigger' or 'dago' or anything like that, regardless of who you are, you're through here. You can't play for me if you have any kind of prejudice." So the players now knew not to go down that road with their new coach. But Lombardi still kept a close eye on Timmy. (Timmy believed teammate Jim Ringo was a racist and had told Lombardi about the girl.)

Being Black in the Green Bay area was a challenge by itself. For example, the institution of the Black barbershop was not to be found in DePere. Local barber Jim Gevers told Christl: "The first year Lombardi was here, Timmy Brown was a kid from Ball State who went on to play for Philadelphia. We got a call one day and [the caller] said, 'This is Mr. Lombardi.' We thought someone was putting us on. He said, 'Do you have a color line down there in your barbershop?' We said, 'No, no.' I had been in the service and had cut black guys' hair before and felt a little comfortable, not that I was expert at it. He said, 'All right, I'm sending Timmy Brown down at 12 o'clock.' We thought it was a joke.... All of a sudden, in walks this black kid, Timmy Brown. Of course, we had to take him even though there were a couple of guys sitting around. It was well received, but they were kidding us after."

On July 22, with training camp about to begin, Lombardi told Press-Gazette reporter Lee Remmel his view of the team. He said his "No. 1 objective will be to defeat the attitude of defeatism, which I know is here." Lombardi, whom Remmel described as an "impressively built Italian," said "a pretty fair football team will be forthcoming." He noted that Paul Hornung, the former Notre Dame Golden Boy, would move from fullback to halfback, and said he would be unlikely to get a "speed back" for his team.

Training camp opened on July 23 with 40 rookies, four quarterbacks, and about 25 veterans; others would trickle in over the next days. The rookies all lived two to a room on the second floor of the college's newest dormitory, the three-year-old Sensenbrenner Hall. Veterans lived on the first and second floors, as did assistant coaches; each night, one assistant was in charge of room checks at 11 p.m. Team meetings were held in the science building or the dorm's lecture hall. Some members of the college's Norbertine religious community also lived in Sensenbrenner. The camp was no picnic for the players, as Lombardi ran it tough. One drill had players running in place for 30 seconds, lifting their knees as high as they could. When Lombardi yelled, "Down!" the players threw themselves onto the ground; "Up!" brought them back to their feet and more running in place. Most teams would do this "grass drill" eight or 10 times at a practice to get players in shape; Lombardi would have his team do it 60 times, according to Glenn Swain's "The Story of Football's Oldest Rivalry: Packers vs. Bears." Morning sprints were followed by afternoon laps around the field if the coach felt they hadn't worked hard enough in the sprints. Lombardi had his pet phrases, such as "you don't just hit that man, you seal him." And he didn't allow star turns. One day, after breakfast in the student union cafeteria, Hornung wanted to drive his car to practice. Lombardi said, "If you get in the car, keep going and head south. We all get on the bus," according to Christl.

The rookies were getting careful looks. That Saturday, the new players had a 45-minute scrimmage that was carefully photographed – another Lombardi innovation, one that he picked up while coaching at West Point. The cameras had been placed on a 15-foot scaffold between the two practice fields. Among those drawing attention was Bill Butler, a 180-pound "swiftee" from the University of Chattanooga, who coincidentally shared a name with Timmy's college friend. Lombardi also noted "good speed" from Timmy as well as George Dixon from the University of Bridgeport. Timmy was having his own frustrations, though. Lombardi's system was like advanced mathematics compared to what Ball State taught him. In a later interview, Timmy said a back coming in new to any team has to learn "a whole thing of 200 plays and 50 audibles. It would be the whole season by the time you learned it all. That's why training camps are very important."

The rookies would go up against the first-string defense, and call a play from 10 yards back. "Nothing like letting them know what was coming," Timmy said. "So basically I would dip into the hole and dip out and reverse my thing. I have instincts. I run to daylight. So we did this about four or five times and he said, 'Brown, do you know how to run through a hole?' We were in a huddle and I said, 'Coach, I didn't see a hole.' I said [in the huddle], 'Well, hell, give me a hole. He wants me to run through that hole.' There's not one there. I dip out 'cause there ain't no hole there. So now I'm supposed to be afraid to get hit."

On another occasion, he said, Lombardi "is going to throw the ball to me and I am supposed to run straight at these two big linemen. 'Here's what we are going to do. You stay at the five-yard and don't go outside of that.... Why are you looking at me like that?' You going to give me all that room, I said. 'You're a smartass, Brown. I'm going to throw you the ball, you got to get by those guys, but you got to stay within that line.' He threw me the ball, I went really low, so now these guys got to come down, and just as they started to lunge, I leaped over them, rolled, and came up on my feet and said, Ta-da! Lombardi said I wasn't going to make this team if I acted this way, and we ran it again. But half the time I chuckled, because I had fun with football."

But there were times of camaraderie as well. Every day at 5 p.m., it was cocktail time, during which Lombardi would talk about events in the news and politics, not football. And it was a football tradition that after dinner, the veterans would order the rookies to stand and sing, and the rookies would croak out a version of some college song like "Hail to the Victors" or "On, Wisconsin." No one knew that Timmy had been a singer for years. He asked what his audience wanted to hear, then sang a well-known do-wop song the way a professional singer would. This did not amuse the veterans, although Lombardi generally enjoyed the singing-hazing sessions. And Green Bay remained Green Bay. While Lombardi was doing his best to raise the squad's professionalism, the Packers were still a small-town team. The first Packer Kickoff Dinner was to be held on Aug. 11, and while the $2 ticket would "cover the cost of the buffet style chicken dinner," the price didn't allow for entertainment. "The Packer band has been asked to play for the event, but because of the fee they ask for performing," they were ruled out, said dinner chairman John Martinkovic. So the call went out to the community – if you could play an instrument, come to the dinner and provide some musical accompaniment.

In the second week of camp, it seemed that perhaps Lombardi would find his "speed back" in Timmy. He was the fastest man in camp, running 40 yards in 4.75. For the Aug. 8 intra-squad game, Timmy was wearing No. 22 for the Blues. This was an offense vs. defense game, so the 30-member Blues had all four quarterbacks as well as Dixon and Timmy; Butler was on the defense's 24-player Whites squad. In this type of game, the offense kept playing, moving ahead on downs if it could; if it had to punt, the offense then resumed from where the ball was downed. A newspaper story noted that "Lombardi plans to make a big cut in personnel after watching the pictures of today's game. Thus, the athletes will be fighting for their jobs." By that standard, the offense's players looked to have secured their futures, winning by 28-7 in a type of game that generally favored the defense. The leading ground-gainer was Timmy, with 75 yards in four carries. But the longest run was by Butler, a 56-yard return of a punt for the defense's only score. Hornung missed three field goals but scored on all four extra points for the offense – as well as kicking one through the crossbars for the defense, which didn't have a kicker of its own. That game ended the weeks of twice-a-day drills for the squad; there would just be morning drills for the next week, leading up to the first exhibition game against Chicago. But that wouldn't matter to seven players; they were dismissed after the squad game. For the Aug. 10 practice, Lombardi put himself in at quarterback so he could assess the defense's weaknesses. The next day, he played in the defensive secondary. He concluded that the defensive team wasn't in top physical condition, and prescribed more runs.

In the late 1950s, the NFL was rapidly changing thanks to its sky-rocketing TV popularity. But it still carried traditions from the era when it was a clear second fiddle to the college game and was competing with boxing for the country's attention. The league thus began each year with a month of barnstorming, to try to promote the game in markets that didn't have a team. The exhibition season began in Milwaukee in late August with the annual Shrine game against the Bears – described as the Packers' oldest and bitterest rivals. Timmy, brought onto the field in the fourth quarter for his first pro appearance, gained 46 yards on a pitch from Starr and ended the contest as the game's top rusher with 61 yards on four carries. Chicago won by 19-16, but Lombardi was satisfied; his team had showed it could compete. Asked about Timmy, Lombardi said curtly, "We know what he can do." After the game, Lombardi became concerned about "dropitis" spreading throughout the Packers. "Catching a pass just takes a little effort, and if you want to stay around here we've got to have effort on every play," he said.

Next, in Portland, Ore., the Packers took on the Philadelphia Eagles, led by quarterback Norm Van Brocklin. Green Bay won by 45-28; Timmy was not a factor. The Eagles' only lead was after a 44-yard TD pass from Van Brocklin to Tommy McDonald; they would combine for another six points later in the game. That game appeared to be it for Bill Butler as a Packer, as he was put on waivers as part of reducing the squad to 46. The following week, the team met with the Packers' 13 directors – they were letting Lombardi do his thing, but still wanted to show they were in charge – and then flew on a chartered plane to Bangor to meet the Giants in the first (and only) professional football game ever played in Maine. Around 12,500 people went to Garland Street Field on Sept. 6 to watch New York win by 14-0. Why Bangor? The year 1959 was the city's 125th anniversary, and the steering committee had asked the NFL if it could come. Ballantine Beer was a sponsor of the Giants and saw a marketing opportunity Down East. But most of the fans at the game came from the Bangor area because, as organizer Gordon Clapp told the Bangor Daily News later, "people from the Portland area wouldn't come up, because Bangor was the host." That left about 5,000 seats unfilled, and their provincialism cost them a chance to see a game that included 12 future Hall of Fame players and two Hall of Fame coaches. (Meanwhile, back in that other small town, Green Bay, the Packers were looking for furnished apartments or houses for the players; anyone with space available was asked to call HEmlock 2-4873.)

Timmy's race again was a factor when the Packers rolled into the Triad region of North Carolina for their annual exhibition against Washington, the only team in the league whose owner prohibited Black players. Timmy and the other three Black Packers – Tunnell, Nate Borden, and A.D. Williams – could not stay with the team at Greensboro's Oaks Motel (air-conditioned to the mid-70s amid daytime temperatures as high as 95) and were sent to dorm rooms at nearby North Carolina A&T, a historically Black university. Timmy was not pleased. According to Eisenberg, he said, "This is bullshit. We're supposed to be a team and we can't even stay with our teammates?" Tunnell, who knew Lombardi well from the Giants, talked Timmy out of objecting, saying that the coach would make things right in the end but that objecting publicly might be the last straw for him. Timmy stayed quiet, got into the game, and ran with a pass from QB "Pineapple Joe" Francis for 22 yards to the Washington 3-yard line, setting up the winning touchdown. The Packers won the game, held in Winston-Salem, by 20-13, with all 20 points being scored by Hornung. Wearing a Giants uniform was the peripatetic Bill Butler. Dixon, another Packers "swiftee," was placed on waivers after the game.

The final exhibition, on Sept. 20 against the Steelers in Minneapolis, saw Timmy drop what could have been a TD pass; later, about two minutes into the fourth quarter, he fumbled a punt at midfield and Frank Varrichione of the Steelers recovered. But the game ended in Green Bay's favor when Hornung kicked a last-second field goal for a 13-10 win; once again, the Golden Boy was responsible for all the Packers' points. That ended the exhibition season 4-2 in Green Bay's favor.

"I had a great exhibition season," Timmy said later. "Like God was with me. But I was getting too much, doing too well, for, you know." Racial animosity had flared once when Timmy went to a bar after a game to hang out with the team. "So I go down there, I walk in and everybody turns around and looks. There's no Blacks in there. So I see Mitch Gale up at the bar and this guy, what's his name, next to him. I go in, Mitchy says, 'Hey, Tim, what's going on.' I said, 'I don't know, I thought I'd see the guys here.' And this guy says, 'What the fuck are you doing in here?' And he was big, about 6-6, you know. And he started to turn around in his chair and Ray Nitschke stopped him. I was going to knock him on his ass so fast, I was just ready for him to flinch because he was a big-ass slow guy. But anyway, Nitschke, he says, 'Hey, lay off. Forget it.' I say, 'No, I'm quite all right, comfortable with him.' But he was a bully, I could tell. He was a bully with every little person, always getting on some person. I was hoping one day he would do that shit with me 'cause I don't like bullies. And I'm quick, too quick for you, big guy."

With the real season about to start, things were tense and insecure. Longtime QB Babe Parilli, another local hero, had been cut. Starr, who at this point in his celebrated career was shy and lacked confidence, was even worrying that he would be cut. Timmy believed he would be, and was surprised when Lombardi said, "Congratulations, Brown. You're on the team. You had a hell of a camp," putting him on the final squad of

36 as one of six offensive backs, including Hornung. (This was an era without special teams; Hornung was the kicker of punts, field goals and extra points in addition to being an offensive back, and could also play quarterback.)

In the Press-Gazette on the Friday before the game – a "Beat the Bears" edition of expanded coverage, including reruns of stories from the 1921 matchup in Chicago of the Packers and the Decatur Staleys, as the Bears were known before moving to the Windy City – a two-page ad (sponsored by several local firms) introduced the 1959 Packers to the city. Timmy, wearing No. 25 in the Packers' new uniforms, was in the group sitting on the grass, third from right in the front row, and also was sitting down for a color team photo on the front of the Sports section – in an era when color photography was nearly impossible for newspapers to print. When the game came around, he was wearing No. 22. This was one of the few chances the Green Bay faithful would get to see their Packers at home. Only four home games were scheduled at City Stadium, with two more "home" dates in Milwaukee. After the first three weeks of the season, the Pack would be absent from Green Bay until Nov. 22, and would not return thereafter.

An editorial in the newspaper looked ahead to the season, as written in the formal style of journalism at the time: "This year there has been no thought of a National League championship. Emphasis has been on building for the future. This has been a healthy thing for the team, for the coaches and the fans. With this attitude there has been room for selection of players who may be great in two to three years but can scarcely be expected to be outstanding this season. Likewise, it has made it possible to drop some older players who are experienced and might help to win a game or two this year but probably will have little to offer in the years ahead." The editorial cautiously hoped that, following the 1-10-1 season a year earlier, the Packers "may win some football games – three or four, perhaps more." Clearly the culture of low expectations that Lombardi wanted to expunge was still alive and well in Green Bay. Probably based on uniform numbers, Timmy was fifth in the newspaper's list of "Your 1959 Packers," following Hornung and quarterbacks Starr, Lamar McHan, and Francis. All seemed well for him, although Timmy was not one of the 31 (out of 36) players to get a thumbnail profile in the section.

But the first game, before 32,000 fans, brought Timmy back to earth. In the fourth quarter, the Packers were on the Chicago 19 in a fourth-and-one situation. Lombardi called for a field goal and sent Timmy into the game for the first time, to hold the ball for Hornung. It was a rainy day, and Timmy dropped a perfect snap; while trying to right it, he was swarmed. (The Press-Gazette simply reported that "Hornung went for the field goal but the pass back was fumbled," apparently by an unknown player.) Later in the quarter, Timmy tried again, and this time did it right – but Hornung didn't, and the ball, kicked from the 14, sailed off to the left. Still, Green Bay won by 9-6, and the players made clear their belief that it was due to Lombardi's efforts. Starting off under a new coach with a victory over the hated Bears meant one thing in Packerland – the corner had been turned.

And the coach now decided it was time to pull the plug on Timmy Brown. He had been dropping the ball more, and blowing the Hornung hold did it for Lombardi. Training camp and the early exhibition games had showed promise; the later games and now the start of the season had showed weaknesses. A quote attributed, in one version or another, to Lombardi was: "There are trains, planes and buses leaving Green Bay every day, and you might be on one." It was Timmy's turn. He went back home to the Bennetts in Richmond. In an ironic moment, the player who replaced Timmy was the returning Bill Butler, the white man from Wisconsin who coincidentally had the same name as one of Timmy's Black teammates from Ball State. The Press-Gazette noted it in the Oct. 1 issue – "Billy Butler, the fiery freshman halfback from Chattanooga and Berlin, Wis., was placed on the active roster after practice Wednesday. Lombardi made room for Butler by placing Timmy Brown, the rookie back from Ball State, on waivers. Butler had been used mostly as a defensive back during the training season but was switched to offense yesterday."

In "When Pride Still Mattered," David Maraniss wrote that Butler was "a tenacious athlete" and said Lombardi had two assumptions "that he carried with him for the next decade: first, he preferred veterans to rookies ... and second, he wanted only a certain type of athlete who was willing to play for him, even if the player disliked him." Butler referred to Lombardi as "the biggest asshole I ever met in my life," according to Maraniss, but the coach didn't care; he saw Butler as a player who went all out every time. (Butler may have needed the money more than Timmy in any case; he had welcomed a son two weeks earlier.)

Timmy believed that it was an earlier dropped punt, during the next-to-last exhibition, that had ultimately cost him his job: "Lew Carpenter and I were back, and I started up for the ball and hesitated – the worst thing you can do. I misunderstood Carpenter's call. This is not an excuse, because I'd caught punts all my life, and I should've caught that one.... I knew I couldn't make a mistake as a rookie – not under Lombardi." But, he added, "I still thought it was unfair. If he'd cut me earlier I would've had a chance to catch on with another team.... But when Lombardi cut me it wasn't really unexpected. He ... said he was sorry but that I didn't fit into his system. He said he felt I could play somewhere in the league."

For his part, Lombardi wrote in Look magazine in 1967 that "my first year here, I had, as a rookie, Tim Brown. He was a good-looking back, with great speed and quickness, but we had five other running backs and were carrying him into the first week of the season, but then he dropped a punt against the Bears in our first league game, and my first as a head coach, and the next day, I let him go." Lombardi might have been keeping Timmy on the team to start the season so he could use him to send another message – that there was a price for failure. Perhaps Timmy's cheekiness did play a role. Lombardi added in the article:

"When we keep a ballplayer, he not only has an obligation to the Packers but we have an obligation to him. No ballplayer must ever stop trying out for this team, no matter how long he has been a member, and we must never stop trying to make him better." While Lombardi was not one to publicly regret his decisions, in the Look article he came close: "In spite of the never-ending effort you make to understand and evaluate every ballplayer you draft and coach, you can almost miss on some and actually miss on others." He had come to see what he had given up, as Timmy had gone on to set records for the Eagles.

Timmy said later of Lombardi that "I thought he was a very tough guy. I thought he was a damned good coach. He was very direct. He had preconceived ideas. His was a big-back attack." After one game at Franklin Field in Philadelphia, Timmy said, "Lombardi held up the Packer bus specifically to come over and speak to me. He was very gracious, said I had really made something of myself in the league and he was pleased for me. He didn't have to do that." He added with a smile, "He said he always knew I would do well. That's why you let me go?" But by that time, Vince Lombardi had become a legend in Green Bay – and Timmy Brown had become a true star in Philadelphia.

PHILADELPHIA

CHAPTER FIVE

The City of Brotherly Football and Music

In 1960, Philadelphia was a study in contrast and paradox. In many ways the country's most historic large city and the birthplace of the United States, it had been bypassed by the Pennsylvania Turnpike. Touted for decades as "the Workshop of the World," it depended for its economic health not on giant steel or automobile factories, but on an abundance of skilled-trades manufacturers – most of which were already economically threatened or were about to become so. Philadelphia was the home of Stetson Hats, but a bare-headed John F. Kennedy at his inauguration was about to deal a nearly fatal blow to the men's hat industry. It had pioneering firms in radio and television – such as Philco and Atwater Kent – that would prove unequal to products from new names such as Sony. It had one of the East Coast's largest ports, which was largely unable to handle containerized shipping and was miles farther inland from the ocean than harbors in New York or Baltimore. Fels Naptha, Jack Frost Sugar, Curtis Publishing, Quaker Lace … these household names for generations soon would become trivia questions. And near the west bank of the Schuylkill River rose the headquarters of the giant Pennsylvania Railroad, which had once held unassailable control over Pennsylvania politics but was soon to disappear into Conrail and Amtrak.

But while Philadelphia had begun sinking into economic lethargy, it had a certain hold on American culture, particularly on the music listened to by, as one local disc jockey called them, "yon teens." Above all, it was the home of "American Bandstand," which had started in the 1950s era of local television programming on Channel 6 and quickly rose to become a national phenomenon on ABC. "Bandstand" was the early stomping ground of the young Italian singers from South Philly street corners who made their mark in the years between "You Ain't Nothing But a Hound Dog" and "She Loves You (Yeah, Yeah, Yeah)" with a brand of lightweight pop that bedazzled teenyboppers but was scowled at by rock and soul fans eager for an edgier sound. They included Robert Ridarelli, better known as Bobby Rydell; Fabiano Forte, just Fabian to you; Francis Avallone, who became Frankie Avalon; and James Ercolani, who as James Darren romanced Gidget, went through the Time Tunnel, and later in life became the lounge-singer hologram Vic Fontaine on "Star Trek: Deep Space Nine."

Fabian's high school classmate Ernest Evans was twisting his way to fame as Chubby Checker. The Orlons, who recorded "The Wah-Watusi," hailed from Philly. About to develop the Philly Soul sound were producers Kenny Gamble and Leon Huff. The Dovells, with lead singer Len Barry, told the nation about a stomp that started in nearby Bristol, "at a teenage hop"; and speaking of hops, "At the Hop" was introduced (for Sha Na Na to hear and later perform at Woodstock) by Danny and the Juniors, from John Bartram High School. Top 40 music, of course, was just part of a Philly symphony, ranging from John Coltrane and Stan Getz to Marian Anderson and Eugene Ormandy. And the sound continued across the Delaware River into South Jersey, where top artists performed at the Latin Casino on Route 70 in Cherry Hill and near the lights of the boardwalks in Atlantic City and Wildwood, just an hour away on the Atlantic Ocean.

The area was a rich home for actors as well. The Shubert and Forrest Theaters offered both shows on their way to Broadway and national touring companies of those already there. The Bucks County Playhouse, an hour away in New Hope, was the first stage on which Neil Simon's "Barefoot in the Park" appeared; stars such as Helen Hayes, Philly's own Grace Kelly, Angela Lansbury, Dick Van Dyke and Robert Redford appeared there. Trenton's Ernie Kovacs first brought his absurdist comic talent to viewers on Channel 3. And for artists of all kinds, one of the best things about Philadelphia was that it was just a two-hour train trip to New York City.

The city also loved (and loudly booed) its performers in another field – athletics. The A's had recently decamped to Kansas City, and the Warriors would soon be on the road to San Francisco – but the Phillies, though often hapless, were here for good or ill. But the city's deepest love was for its football team. The Eagles had started as a replacement for the Yellow Jackets, a team from the Northeast Philly neighborhood of Frankford that began playing in the late 19th century and was in the NFL from 1924 to 1931. They got off to an ignominious start – losing by 56-0 to the Giants in October 1933. But in 1948 and 1949 they took the NFL championship. After that began a period of decline in which a few great players such as Sonny Jurgensen stood out from a series of mostly forgettable squads. But for the 1960 season, Buck Shaw, in his third season as head coach, fielded a squad that included star quarterback Norm Van Brocklin and the league's last 60-minute man, Chuck Bednarik – who that season would famously stand over a badly injured Frank Gifford in a pose many interpreted as triumphant.

A largely blue-collar city amid a period of industrial decline; a center for young musicians and actors; a metropolitan area that defined itself by grit and worshipped its gridiron team. Into this messy yet creative cauldron, after his brief stint with the Packers, fell the football player, singer, and aspiring actor Timmy Brown.

In January 1960, a two-paragraph story in the Philadelphia Inquirer introduced Timmy to his new home. But first it introduced as a new Eagles halfback Dick Christy, who had played high school ball at St. James' in nearby Chester. The story noted that this was free agent Christy's third attempt to break into the NFL since being named an all-American at North Carolina State. As a locally known player, he was the lead of the story. Christy, who like Timmy also had been drafted and dropped by Lombardi, played several seasons in the American Football League and then went back home to Chester; he was later killed in an auto accident. "Dick could do many things with a football I couldn't do," Timmy said. "He was a complete player."

The article went on to note that also signing with the Eagles as a free agent for the 1960 season, according to team general manager Vince McNally, was the 5-foot-11, 195-pound Timmy Brown. It noted that he had been released by the Packers after their first league game, in which, it said, he fumbled twice. The story gave Eagles fans little reason to expect much from Timmy Brown.

Timmy was playing for Philadelphia because McNally had liked what he saw of him in the Packers-Eagles exhibition game in 1959, and sent a telegram to him in Richmond after he was cut asking him to join the taxi squad – players under contract who could join in practice, but were ineligible for games. "The Packers were beating us something like 34-0," McNally later told sportswriter Hugh Brown, "when Lombardi put his rinky-dinks against us in the fourth period. One of them was Timmy.... I liked the way he moved, and put him and another Packer rookie halfback, George Dixon, in my memory book. When I heard that Lombardi had cut both of them ... I went after them. Dixon, however, had gone to Montreal, but Timmy was still at home." Dixon was another of the fast backs Lombardi had considered, so McNally was clearly looking for speed.

As it was, Timmy could have made his Eagles debut a bit earlier. The team had wanted him to play in the last game of 1959, on Dec. 13 against Jim Brown and the Cleveland Browns (who won, 28-21), but, Timmy said, "I didn't want to take a chance on fumbling or something where they wouldn't invite me back." And in a different scenario, Timmy might never have come to Philadelphia. When he was dropped by the Packers, an assistant told him that the Colts and Bears were interested in him, but he was gun-shy. (Also, he could have come to Philadelphia via a different sport, as he was selected in the eighth round of the NBA draft by the Warriors.) Timmy had been vacillating about returning to pro football, but Ball State president Emens kept on him to "give it another shot.... He was like a father figure to me at that time, and it meant a lot." Emens, he said, told him that "Cleveland has called and Philadelphia will be in Cleveland next week, and they would like for you to come up and meet them and be their guest at the game." Timmy said he responded, "I'm not interested in that now," but Emens talked him into meeting with the Eagles.

And in a what-might-have-been scenario, Timmy could have stayed with the Packers had the second-string United Football League been in operation at that time. The surging popularity of football in the late 1950s had led to expansion, most prominently the debut of the AFL for the 1960 season. The Midwest-centered UFL, with teams like the Wheeling Ironmen and the Toledo Tornadoes, operated between 1961 and 1964. Most UFL clubs had agreements with NFL or AFL teams, which could park players on the smaller circuit but stay in charge of their futures. Had there been a UFL in 1959, Lombardi could have sent him there on option. On the other hand, that might not have reinforced the message Lombardi had in mind.

After being cut by Lombardi, Timmy had re-enrolled at Ball State to try to finish his bachelor's degree. In winter quarter, he completed eight credit hours of student teaching and got an A. In spring quarter he took 12 credit hours, finishing his classwork on June 5 but not earning a degree, because the college demanded a double major for graduation. While back in Muncie, he lived with his childhood friend from Richmond Paul Davis, who had served in the military and was now a freshman. Davis helped Timmy pack for his move to Philly. (Timmy finally got his diploma in 1966 after the college changed its rule mandating a double major, but his decision not to play the one game for the Eagles in 1959 led to his losing a year of pension eligibility.)

Whatever the route to Philadelphia, the city was a draw to Timmy for reasons other than football. Philadelphia had a thriving night-club scene as well as recording studios and local record labels. The New Jersey Shore had a number of seasonal clubs. New York City was an easy train ride. Had Timmy been allowed to stay in Green Bay, Chicago might have offered him some possibilities to perform or record, but it was 175 miles away. And other than Chess Records, the home for rock and blues greats like Chuck Berry, Bo Diddley, and Muddy Waters, the Windy City did not have the pedigree of Philadelphia in producing popular music. Philadelphia seemed perfect to show off his talents on the field and on the stage, although he would meet with mixed results, disappointments, and resistance from Eagles coaches and Philadelphia sportswriters who feared entertainment deflected his focus from football.

While on the taxi squad, Timmy and Christy would sit on the bench in street clothes for home games; they could not go on trips to other cities. "Sitting home and watching the game on television," Timmy said, "I could feel every thud. I felt like a disenfranchised citizen."

The 1960 Eagles training camp would be held, as it had been since 1951 with one exception, in Hershey, Pa., a couple of hours west of Philadelphia and close to the state capital of Harrisburg. Hershey was a company town, built by chocolate manufacturer Milton S. Hershey to house his plant and employees. Because of that, it had more community institutions than the average small town. The Eagles didn't stay at the luxurious resort, the Hotel Hershey, but in the Community Building, which had a gymnasium, library, bowling alley, and theater in addition to the dorm rooms that housed the players. (Also unlike most small towns, the building was designed by a world-famous architect, Paul Philippe Cret.) Practices were held at Hersheypark Stadium, which opened in 1939 as part of what had been an amusement park for Hershey workers and now is a major attraction in central Pennsylvania.

Timmy got to camp through the Eagles' relationship with Capital Airlines, which flew to Philadelphia. Capital didn't serve Muncie, so Timmy got a letter from Capital district sales manager W.I. Gates enclosing a ticket – to be used at any time, a sign of how different air travel was in that era – for a Lake Central Airlines flight from Muncie's Johnson Field airport (which maintained scheduled service into the 1970s) to Harrisburg. Gates noted that if Timmy decided not to attend camp, he should send the ticket back to McNally, "as it is non-refundable." Gates also wrote as a P.S.: "Enclosed is $5 in case you get stuck for a meal or cab fare enroute. Just a reminder – you're due back to camp 7/25." Timmy also got a letter from coach Shaw that appears to be a form letter sent to all players. The letter said that "quite frankly, I feel it is my duty … to alert each one of you on the importance of reporting to training camp in good physical condition." It added, "Make up your mind here and now, that if you fail to make this team, it won't be because you failed to do everything possible to prepare yourself for the test ahead."

Camp began about three weeks before the first exhibition game, held on Aug. 13 against the host Los Angeles Rams. For the 1960 Eagles, Billy Ray Barnes was the starter at halfback, and the No. 1 draft choice was a local hero, Ted Dean. "Billy Ray was like a little bullet," Timmy said. "Tough guy." By the time the regular season began, Timmy was on the active roster, but while he did get into games, he was never a starter during the entire season. This didn't affect Timmy's view of Shaw: "You would run through a brick wall for him. I always felt that way for a coach that was honest and fair." Against Cleveland in the season opener, he had two kickoff returns for 49 yards and one punt return for 10 yards. And in the Oct. 9 contest against St. Louis, he provided "one of the day's big thrills," according to Inquirer sportswriter Herb Good, returning a kickoff 79 yards and paving the way for a field goal.

Shaw mainly used Timmy as a kickoff and punt returner, although in the Oct. 16 game against Detroit Timmy gained three yards rushing on two plays, and against Pittsburgh on Nov. 6 caught a pass for seven yards. But in the Nov. 13 contest with Washington, fullback Clarence Peaks, who had taken Timmy under his wing, was injured and Dean took his place, creating an opening in which Timmy's skill as a running halfback and receiver became clear. On Dec. 11, although the Eagles lost to the Steelers by 27-21 on a field covered by several inches of snow, the Eagles, according to the Inquirer, "discovered a cold weather quarterback in Sonny Jurgensen and another fine stormy weather player in Timmy Brown," who were brought in as reserves after the Eagles were outplayed in the first half. (Van Brocklin, the story noted, "as great as he is, apparently isn't an outstanding player in bad weather.") Jurgensen and Timmy combined for a 52-yard scoring play, where Timmy got the ball on the Steeler 40 and outran two defenders to the end zone. Then he again accounted for 52 yards when he caught a short pass and evaded all tacklers to put the ball on the 18-yard line, from which Tommy McDonald then scored. Timmy scored again on a six-yard end run. For the season he had nine rushes, nine receptions, and 21 returns.

By the Dec. 19 game, the Inquirer was making sure its readers knew who Timmy Brown was; the headline read "Brown, McDonald Star as Eagles Triumph" over Washington. Timmy and McDonald each scored two touchdowns, and Timmy was described as "the brightest star of all," as he scored on a 34-yard run and a five-yard end run following a 60-yard run after catching an 11-yard Jurgensen pass. He was the game's leading ground gainer with 25 yards on six carries. The Washington fans, none too happy, threw snowballs at the Eagles and the referees.

In a satisfying end to Timmy's first full year as a pro, the Eagles ended the season as champions of the Eastern Division. They then defeated the Packers for the league championship on Dec. 26 (a Monday game because of Christmas) by 17-13 on their home turf, the University of Pennsylvania's Franklin Field – the only loss Lombardi ever suffered in a title game while at Green Bay. On the field that day in addition to

Timmy were NFL stars such as Hornung, Starr, Van Brocklin, Bednarik, and Pete Retzlaff. Timmy ran the opening kickoff back for 22 yards, but that was the only time he touched the ball. Late in the game Dean ran a kickoff back to the Packer 39, using a play assistant coach Charley Gauer had come up with only a couple of days earlier. Gauer had seen that two players on the right side of the Packers kickoff team were fast while a third was slow. The Eagles used that knowledge to open up a chute for Dean, who waited for Timmy to block for him, then ran for 58 yards. Indianapolis Star sports editor Jep Cadou Jr. noted that until this, Timmy "had been noted more for his breakaway running skill and pass-catching than his blocking." Dean also scored on a five-yard run to seal the Eagles victory, making him the game's hero.

While the season ended on an up note, Timmy had faced many challenges during it. In one game, he said, he was sent in and quarterback Van Brocklin "waved me off the field. Van didn't have any confidence in me." Like many Eagles players, though, Timmy came around to become a fan of the player known as the Dutchman. Looking back at the championship season, he said, "There was a lot of luck involved.... Everything went our way. We had a good team, but I don't know what happened that year. It was just togetherness, because we weren't the best overall talent." He ended the regular season with 35 yards rushing on nine carries, including two touchdowns, and nine receptions for 247 yards and two more TDs. He also had 267 yards on kickoff returns and 47 on punt returns.

Togetherness had its limits. While many of the team members regularly hung out at a bar in Center City, the Philadelphia term for "downtown," the three Black players – Timmy, Dean, and Peaks – weren't among them. "It wasn't that we were told not to go," Peaks said, according to "The Eagles Encyclopedia" by Ray Didinger and Robert S. Lyons. "We just didn't feel it was a good idea. You've got to remember how things were in 1960." At that time there were fewer than 50 Black players in the league. Bob Gordon, in "The 1960 Philadelphia Eagles: The

Team That They Said Had Nothing but a Championship," said Timmy, Dean, and Peaks never really felt like part of the 1960 team.

Of the Eagles players in that game, Timmy was the lowest paid, at $7,500 a year, the minimum league salary. Van Brocklin got $25,000 as quarterback. Timmy was acutely aware at even the earliest stages of his career in the NFL that he needed to make money outside the game. In the early 1960s, the average NFL player salary was between $10,000 and $25,000. In comparison, the average in 2018 was $2.7 million. Current NFL players can afford to focus exclusively on football in the offseason, using the time to work out, but in the 1960s, most players had to work outside of football. In a 2010 article for the Cleveland Plain Dealer by Bill Lubinger, former Ohio State University linebacker Jim Houston remembered Browns head coach Paul Brown's first speech to the rookies, in which he said, "Gentlemen, you're going to be off Mondays and Tuesdays. Get a job."

Lubinger wrote, "Once the season ended, coaches didn't expect to see the players for another seven months." Houston recalled, "All of us tried to get jobs that would help sustain the off-season. You needed money, you had to work." Houston, who retired from football in 1972, recalled that he made more with an insurance and financial planning company than he did in football, and he was the eighth overall selection in the first round in the 1960 NFL draft. His rookie salary was $10,000 with a $1,000 signing bonus. By contrast, wide receiver Drake London from the University of Southern California, the eighth overall selection by the Atlanta Falcons in the 2022 NFL draft, signed a four-year contract for $21.5 million and a $5.4 million signing bonus.

One thing that hasn't changed is the average career length of an NFL player. In the 1960s and today, that career lasts for 3½ years. That is another reason that Timmy knew early on that he needed to be thinking about a second career in his new home town, the country's fourth-largest city. Philadelphia was a difficult transition for Timmy: "I mean, I had been to Indianapolis, but just one area that someone had drove me to. I was a kid, I didn't know. But to go to a city, it's kind of amazing in a sense, but I always remained what I was, a small-town guy." And for Timmy, with his aspirations toward entertainment, Philly was the best kind of city.

When Timmy arrived to play for the Eagles in 1960, Philadelphia's music scene was largely associated with Dick Clark, who had taken over the local "Bandstand" program and made it a national institution before moving it to Los Angeles in 1964. "American Bandstand" was one of the more popular examples of how rock and soul music were transforming America's pop culture landscape from the 1950s through the 1980s. And Philadelphia was among the cities leading the way, along with New York City, Los Angeles, Detroit, Memphis, New Orleans, and Nashville. Philadelphia's Cameo/Parkway Records was the home to local artists such as Chubby Checker, Dee Dee Sharp, the Orlons, the Tymes, and the Dovells, as well as musicians from elsewhere in the country, such as Michigan's ? and the Mysterians. Their songs were played on local Top 40 stations that had a national reputation, so stations across the country picked up what was being played in Philly. (That influence peaked in the late 1960s when former Camden disc jockey Kal Rudman created the newsletter "Friday Morning Quarterback," a national guide to incipient hits.) The Philadelphia area was also home to large clubs. The Latin Casino had moved from Center City across the Ben Franklin Bridge to highly traveled Route 70 in Delaware Township, N.J., home of the then-thriving Garden State Park thoroughbred track. The township became better known, as Cherry Hill after it renamed itself for a hotel that, like the Latin Casino, drew the racing crowd. Until then, post office addressing standards misleadingly indicated that the club actually was in Merchantville, a small and sedate borough about a mile away.

At the New Jersey Shore, while Atlantic City was declining as a resort, it still had a number of nightclubs, and there were performances at the Steel Pier. And those clubs could draw big crowds when the teen-idol Philly singers of the late 1950s and early 1960s appeared.

While Philly music was changing, the Eagles were changing as well. After the championship season, Van Brocklin retired as a player and Shaw retired as a coach, saying that at age 61, he "wanted to get out while I was ahead." Van Brocklin believed that the Eagles had agreed to offer him the head coaching job after Shaw retired, but the team instead turned to defensive coach Nick Skorich. A miffed Van Brocklin went on to coach the expansion Minnesota Vikings, where he compiled a losing record over six seasons and openly feuded with Hall of Fame quarterback Fran Tarkenton. Years later, Timmy said of Van Brocklin's personality, "I thought he didn't like me, and when we went back to the (1960 team) reunion his wife wanted me to sit by her, right in the middle of the front row.... I said, 'Are you sure you want me to sit with you? I don't think Dutch liked me that much.' She said, 'Oh, Dutch loved you.' I said, 'Really? He had a funny way of showing it.' She said he did that with everybody. And it was funny, because I heard her talking to Tommy McDonald and he was saying, 'I didn't think Dutch liked me.' I said, 'You were his favorite target.' He said, 'Yeah, but he never liked me.' And his wife said, 'He liked you too.'"

Timmy continued to impress in the 1961 training camp, when the "nimble-footed Little All-American from Ball State" had become well enough known for a takeout story in the Inquirer. Reporter Herb Good noted that Brown "is confronted with one of the biggest challenges among the Eagles, and he in turn is somewhat of a challenge to the coaches." It noted that he had "the potential to blossom into a star" but said that "with typical youthful impatience" (Timmy was now 24) he believed stardom might take too long. "I have so much energy that I can't wait until I'm 30 to let it loose," he said. Timmy was third in line for the left halfback position behind Barnes and Dean – Good said these three were the top left halfbacks in the entire league, and noted that Dean was not at the camp because he was detained at Fort Knox for military reserve duty. Timmy said blocking was his biggest challenge – "it's an art, something that you have to work upon." Good said Timmy was as "articulate as he is earnest."

In early August, the Eagles played the College All-Stars in an annual game held in Chicago. Timmy's play impressed Skorich as well as his former adversary Jim Freeman, the Ball State coach, who was on hand for the game, the first with Jurgensen as Philadelphia quarterback instead of Van Brocklin. By this time, Timmy also felt experienced enough to comment on life in the NFL. "Is that exhibition season a grind," he said to a Muncie reporter. "The guys are all trying to make the team, and they're tackling and blocking harder than ever. When the season starts, though, it's just routine stuff. At the first of the week we run through the offensive patterns using our next opponent's defense. During the latter part of the week we employ our defense against our opponent's offense.

"We normally, if we played on Sunday, have Monday off," he added. "I don't actually mean 'off,' but it isn't a normal practice day. What we do is study films of our last game and films of our upcoming foe.... You should see the files they keep on each team in the league. They have a complete rundown on each team and player." While coaches always wanted to put together the best team possible, racial divides and customs still limited what was possible. Timmy said that when he entered the NFL, there was a widely understood limit of three Black players per team. "We couldn't room together, white and Black, when I went in. Irv Cross and I roomed together a lot. I don't remember rooming with a white guy in my time. They gradually changed all that stuff." Cross became the first African American to appear on a pregame show when he joined CBS's "The NFL Today" in 1975 with Brent Musberger and Phyllis George.

Like Dean, Timmy was for many years a member of the 28th Division of the Pennsylvania National Guard; many NFL teams made it easy for their players to become Guardsmen, to serve the country and pick up some extra cash. The division did basic training at Fort Knox, where Timmy recalled crawling in the mud with people shooting over his head. He said he was stopped by Kentucky police once – "they saw four Black guys in a car. The guys told me to be quiet. I was raised in an environment that wasn't all Southern, had a hard time being talked down to. 'Where you boys going' – a Southern 'boy' way. I realized you could get into trouble." The fort was not segregated, though, and the "man running the camp was a football fan and would have me over." Timmy said one sergeant didn't like him, so he had to do kitchen duty. "A guy had trouble getting up a hill, so I would try to help him. I went through the [six weeks of] training easily, because I had just come from football. Then I stayed to teach. I taught all girls, 18 to 19 – plush job." Also in the unit were running backs Theron Sapp, Dean, and Barnes. This not-onerous duty would become part of Timmy's yearly routine, with eventual consequences.

While at Fort Knox, Timmy began going to Ball State to see Grayce Butler, the sister of his college teammates Bill and Ernie Butler – every weekend, according to Grayce. Timmy was driving a white Pontiac Bonneville convertible, although Grayce noted that he wasn't a great driver and would often have a friend drive him back from Kentucky. "Sometimes," she said, "I would fix up his buddy with one of my girlfriends." They would go to Indianapolis and visit Buddy and his wife, Marilyn, although Grayce said that she "never felt comfortable around him. I knew how he had been to Tim." Also, since Buddy had gone to Butler University, he saw the Butler brothers from Ball State as rivals. Grayce did, however, hit it off with Marilyn. They also went to Richmond so she could meet Timmy's mother, with whom he had reconciled after he turned pro, and the Bennetts. Grayce remembered how well she got along with Juanita, saying that they corresponded for a time after the visit.

Timmy came to Grayce's graduation at Ball State and drove her back to her family's home – now in Bloomington, where "the Rev" had been called to another church – giving her a big box of clothes and accessories as a graduation gift, for beginning her career as a kindergarten teacher in Cincinnati. "We'd date, then break up or not see him for some time, then he would show up again," she said. "I was madly in love with him." But an aunt from Connersville who knew Timmy's dad said, "You are too strong a woman for him," and brother Ernie added, "He's not the person I want to see you married to" – a sentiment to which her mother agreed.

The 1961 season opened on Sept. 17 before a sellout crowd – officially 60,671 fans – at Franklin Field, under new coach Skorich and new quarterback Jurgensen, who became one of Timmy's best football friends. According to the 1964 article in Sport magazine by Berry Stainback, as Timmy went onto the field to return the opening kickoff by Cleveland, teammates John Nocera and Ed Khayat told him he would go all the way with this one. And Timmy indeed returned the opening kickoff 105 yards for a touchdown, a move that one sportswriter said "convinced the Eagles that it had to be their day" and set a team record that stood until 2014, when Josh Huff ran the opening kickoff back 107 yards against Tennessee. (The league record is 109 yards by Cordarrelle Patterson of the Vikings in 2013.) The kick had bounced into the end zone; Timmy grabbed it and slanted to his left. He avoided every Cleveland player who went after him and went the last 35 yards with no one having a chance to stop him. Even so, victory was not a sure thing until Don Burroughs deflected a pass meant for Jim Brown (who gained 99 yards on 18 carries in the game), and Tom Brookshier then intercepted another Cleveland pass. The Eagles won by 27-20, and the fast-moving Timmy Brown had overnight become a fan favorite.

On Oct. 8, the Eagles faced the Steelers, and Timmy was on his game again, returning a kickoff 84 yards to set up the game-winning touchdown for the Eagles. But Timmy was only being used in spot roles and was "as usual" held for emergency duty in the backfield for the Oct. 15 game at St. Louis while concentrating on kickoff and punt returns. "I really believe the only reason Skorich gave me a chance to play was the fans at Franklin Field kept chanting, 'We want Brown,'" Timmy said later.

Wide receiver McDonald, a longtime friend of Timmy's, believed

Timmy's skill as an entertainer helped him be so quick on the field. "You talk about moves, he was fantastic," he said in a later interview. "And by him being able to dance so great, that helped him out on the football field. 'Cause you try and tackle that guy, he'd be in front of you, and boy, could he spin out or spin away from you or something like that when you're going down getting ready to hit him.... He'd spin right out of your arms 'cause he could twist right out of there." Childhood friend George Walker said that Timmy "liked to work out all the time. He didn't lift weights. He did a lot of swimming, basketball, and running. He used to run the steps at Franklin Field."

Grayce Butler had been asked to subscribe by mail to the Monday issues of the Inquirer so she could read about Timmy's game-day exploits. In one issue in the fall, Inquirer reporter Herb Good noted: "Many fans had hoped that Brown ... would be slated for more scrimmage action since he's been so successful at returning kicks, and apparently has the outside speed and shiftiness the team could use.... The fans also recall that Brown was outstanding as a pass receiver against the Steelers and Redskins last year in the only games in which he had a good chance to display his talents." Skorich responded, "I'm using Brown where I think he can do the most good." The reporter said this meant that Skorich believed his other backs were better blockers than Timmy – and that Timmy wasn't as good at finding the proper holes or picking up audibles.

For most of his Eagles career, Timmy lived with Ernestine and Alfred Grice at 6238 Pine St., a block from Cobbs Creek Park in West Philadelphia. Dean also stayed there for a time. Al Grice was an electrician for the Philadelphia School District and a former Long Island Rail Road porter, and "Ernie" ran a beauty salon. Timmy told in 2010 of how he ended up living there: "I met this girl and dated her for a little bit, and she wanted to go by her aunt's house. Her aunt had a beauty parlor.... [Ernestine] and Al, I learned a lot from them. One time some girl said I got her pregnant and I knew better, but I wasn't going to deny; I would support if I had to, you know. But she said she was like three months pregnant and it had been six months since I'd seen her, so I knew it wasn't me. Ernestine, she came home just before the girl left and said, 'You leave, Tim. I'm going to talk to her.'" Ernie, he said, made him aware of what to watch out for in the big city. "She had my back and Al did too.... They gave me their bedroom, and I wouldn't take it. I said I would take the one in the back room, down the hallway." Timmy said Dean had been living "with his mother in another part of town. So I talked them into taking him too."

Timmy made the basement into his pad: "I want a big sofa so the bed can open, and a whole music thing. Stereo, records, everything. It just cost me five thou." He didn't eat there, he said, for the first year and a half. "They always invited me, I'd say no thanks. I'd go out and get a sandwich. But they kept on and on, so I said OK. And Al would be, 'What do you want for dinner?'" Ernestine told Sport magazine that "the important thing he gets here is love. It's just like a little stray kid in the streets – all it needs is someone to put his arms around him. Timmy was so lonely when he came with us. He never came out of his room. He still doesn't go out much."

The couple enjoyed being surrogate parents to young football players and their basement became a site for team parties. "I had different dates coming in for the games, so everybody would always want to meet them," Timmy said. "And sometimes I would be so beat up that I just asked them to enjoy the party. I mean, people, they want to talk to you. I got to sit down, I got to stay down, I can't get on this leg or I can't get moving around. And I wasn't taking any pills. I didn't believe in pills, so pain I just dealt with most of the time."

At a post-game party in 1961, Tim said, he got to know Art and Vicki Silvers, who encouraged him to take voice and elocution lessons. The Silverses were involved in Philadelphia's music scene, and Vicki Silvers wrote and produced Frank Sinatra's "Learnin' the Blues," which hit No. 2 on Billboard's Hot 100 in 1955. Amid the musical whirl of the

1960s, the Silverses let Tim know that they thought he had potential as a recording star. Their encouragement motivated Tim to seek help from master teachers in New York City.

In October, Grayce flew to Philadelphia to visit Timmy. It was her first time flying. She went to a game and sat next to Irv Cross' wife. An Eagles group then went to Atlantic City to party, which made her feel uncomfortable as she didn't normally drink, so, she said, she nursed a sloe gin fizz for the entire night.

On Nov. 19, Cleveland hosted the Eagles for a 45-24 Browns victory. Ball State president Emens, still a fan of Timmy's, was among a group from Muncie that braved wintry weather to attend. They tried to drive to Cleveland, according to a Muncie Star article, but icy roads turned them back at Lima, Ohio. They then went to Fort Wayne's Baer Field and bought tickets to fly to Cleveland – in 1961, an easy thing to do on the spur of the moment. The college leaders saw Timmy fumble to set up a Cleveland touchdown, but make up for it later by scoring on a 39-yard pass reception.

When the Eagles again met the Steelers on Dec. 3, Timmy's touchdown on a 66-yard punt return gave Philadelphia a 35-24 win. Muncie Evening Press sports columnist Jerry Fennell called this "Tim's brightest day in the National Football League." For the 1961 season, he was averaging 6.8 yards per carry and had scored five TDs – one by rushing, one by punt return, two by receptions, and one by kickoff return. That made him only the fifth player at that time to score in all four categories during a single season. He led the league in number of kickoff returns (29) and yardage on kickoff returns (711) and carried the ball from scrimmage 50 times for 338 yards.

Later in life, Timmy said of returning kickoffs: "Nobody wanted to be on kickoffs, but I loved running kickoffs back. Eleven guys trying to get you. It was a challenge to me. I used to beg for that.... There's just something special about a kickoff return. Everybody's up on their feet. Especially with me in Philadelphia, it was like every time I would receive a kickoff, they would stand up. They expected me to go all the way, and I expected to go all the way, too."

Despite his successes, Timmy was uncertain about coming back for 1962. In the 1961 season, he said in the Sport interview, "I was still a spot player – specialist, they called me. They might as well have cussed me as call me that. They didn't think I could take the pounding." In another interview, he said, "I felt like I was wasting my time. I really thought about not coming back ... but [Ernie], she was like my mother, told me to give it another shot. She said things would break my way, and she was right."

That break turned out to be a literal break. Dean was lost for the season as a result of a foot fracture on Jan. 6, 1962, at the Playoff Bowl, a runner-up event held annually during the 1960s. Timmy said later that "when I finally got to show what I could do, their reaction was, 'Gee, what a surprise.' That's the price you pay for coming out of a small college and going late in the draft. You get labeled a fringe player."

When 1962's training camp began in July at Hershey, the "mercurial" Timmy was one of three players who hadn't signed contracts. He, Peaks, and Bobby Walston were described as "bitter pills" whom McNally was attempting to "make palatable." All came to terms with the team.

In the opening game of the 1962 season, with the Eagles hosting the Cardinals on Sept. 16, Timmy – who was now starting at halfback in place of Dean – returned a missed field goal 99 yards for a touchdown, tying an NFL record in a game the Eagles lost by 27-21. Against the Vikings on Oct. 28, he caught a Jurgensen pass for an 80-yard TD, but again it was a losing effort by the team, 31-21. By early November, with Dean still on crutches, Timmy had gained almost a third of the Eagles' total yardage. Skorich, though, still mainly saw Timmy as a returner. "With Dean to spell him, Brown would have been an even better runner and catcher this season," the coach said. "He has been our heavy-duty back because of sheer necessity. But I think that if he had been relieved now and then, his yardage on punt and kickoff returns would have been better." Timmy didn't agree, saying, "I haven't been tired. Sure, I still have sore ribs, but I don't run with my ribs." He was referring to being kicked in the ribs in the Vikings game of October after fighting a virus for three weeks.

Meanwhile, Grayce was continuing to visit Timmy. One weekend, she said she was coming to visit with her roommate in Cincinnati, Florence Vaughn, a nurse who had been a friend when Grayce was growing up in Connersville. The women drove to Philly and got a hotel room. Timmy was not very welcoming, she said, telling them he was busy that evening and would see them the next day. When they met up then, Vaughn was not impressed by Timmy, and the whole trip hurt Grayce's feelings. Sometime later, Grayce concluded that she should never call him, but she should wait for him to call her. "When I called," she thought, "I hung up disappointed, close to tears, and really down. He was in a mood."

During one 1960s visit, Grayce went with Timmy to a club. She said she was "probably 22, looked like I was 16." A couple of women came by and said, "Oh, Timmy, that's Timmy Brown," acting like she wasn't with him. One asked if she could kiss Timmy and Grayce said no. Timmy just laughed, which further irritated Grayce: "Why didn't you say something? They were disrespecting me." But Timmy was a natural in nightclubs, according to McDonald: "He would sometimes sing in the bar.... People would just absolutely have their mouth open saying, 'Ah, this guy's really good.'... He was an entertainer."

Timmy did not confine his interests around this time to Grayce. He also dated Georgia Malick, a graduate of Cherry Hill High School East who had been crowned as Miss Cherry Hill. At age 18, she was Miss New Jersey in the 1962 Miss America pageant at Atlantic City. Her talent act was to play on the piano "Deep Purple," the 1930s jazz standard that the next year became a hit for Nino Tempo and April Stevens. According to Gene Kilroy, who as an Eagles executive became a longtime friend of Timmy's, Timmy was in love with her, but their relationship fell apart. "She dumped him. He took it hard. He was a recluse for most of three months, largely staying in his house." Malick continued to compete in commercial pageants, such as the Miss Wool of America contest. In 1966, she wore the sash as "Miss Careful Handling" in a promotion for the Pennsylvania Railroad; the ostensible point was that the railroad handled freight carefully. She died in 2011.

Timmy scored twice against the Cowboys on Nov. 25 as part of a 28-14 win, crossing the goal line on a 22-yard run with four minutes left after earlier scoring on a 2-yard carry. This made up for the Eagles' loss to the Cowboys by 41-19 earlier in the season. By late November, Timmy had gained more than 1,000 yards rushing and receiving in nine games. He averaged 26.2 yards on kickoff returns and 13.5 yards on punt returns. Skorich, still not fully on the Brown bandwagon, said, "Tim has made fantastic progress in the pro league in the last two years.... He is devastating when he gets in the secondary, but unaccustomed as we are to blocking, he hasn't been there too often. He should be a great one for us; that is, unless he fumbles on the goal line like he did the other day." In that case, Skorich added (probably with a laugh), "he may have to do it in Canada."

Before the Dec. 9 game against Pittsburgh, Timmy tested his right knee, which had been sprained during the previous week's game with Washington, and pronounced it ready. In that Washington game he had scored three touchdowns, one on a 99-yard kickoff return. "I usually do better when something's wrong with me," he said. Skorich was more skeptical about the injury. The game was played in a blinding snowstorm that made it nearly impossible to see the players. Pittsburgh took advantage of four field goals to defeat the Eagles by 26-17 in what was the last home game for Bednarik. Skorich's skepticism was warranted, as Timmy spent much of the first half on the sidelines. He returned to play in the second half but clearly wasn't himself; even so, he gained the most ground yardage with 35 on nine carries. After the game, as Skorich left the locker room, he said, "How do you feel, Timmy?" "Fine, coach, I feel fine," Timmy responded. Once Skorich was out of earshot, he said,

"I feel terrible. But what's the use of complaining? Next week I won't hold anything back."

(In 2010, Timmy said that he was normally very quiet in the locker room, "and I had an attitude ... because when I first went there, the white guys had an attitude. 'Boy' mentality, boy this and boy that. I just told them I don't play that shit, so they got a little uptight and defensive. So I never said much in the locker room at all.... I would be the first one there and the first one out.")

McDonald, one of the last players, if not the last, to play without a face mask, said in an interview that he would want Timmy playing with him "as a halfback anytime. He not only gives you 100 percent, I think he gives you 200 percent effort. Any time he feels that ball in his arms or stomach, he's going to fight for yardage." He said he and Timmy were "almost like brothers – old No. 22 and No. 25." Timmy became used to McDonald's giving him overwhelming praise, saying in 2010, "I always remind him, 'Tommy, Tommy, Tommy, don't build me up so much.' 'Cause every time we'd meet somebody, Tommy said, 'You all see this guy, he's got more moves than....' Tommy's a crazy guy, he's always building me up."

In a December 1962 story, Inquirer reporter Good again enthused about Timmy, noting that the fan support "gave Brown his first real opportunity to prove that he belonged with the league's better backs." He wrote that Skorich had begun using Brown in plays from scrimmage, apparently "reluctantly, after he and the newspapers had been bombarded with fan letters asking why a player of Brown's ability was kept on the bench." (In a different article, Timmy said the Eagles had been "committed to a big-back offense with Dean and Peaks. I was blue. Then Dean got hurt and I had my chance, but I wasn't glad, because Dean was my roomie three years.") Timmy, Good noted, had "refuted every argument against him with a steady, solid all-round performance." His ability to block had improved as well. In the article, Timmy said that when he was with the Packers, "Vince Lombardi said I was a chronic fumbler. Actually, I did not get to play enough to be a chronic anything." This line would become a routine gag for Timmy, sometimes ending with his telling Lombardi, "You never let me carry the ball enough to see if I fumble." For his part, McDonald remembered, inaccurately, "I don't think he ever fumbled the ball."

The 1962 season was terrible for the Eagles, as they finished in last place in the Eastern Conference with a 45-35 loss to St. Louis. Their record was 3-10-1. Skorich noted: "Whatever might have caused what happened to this club this year is history now.... Maybe next year we'll be the team we expected to be this year." But it was a great year for Timmy, who ended the season leading the team in five categories. He gained 2,306 total yards and led the team in rushing (545), scoring (78 points), and punt and kickoff returns (912), and was second in receptions at 52 yards. He was second in pass receiving to McDonald. Timmy had 137 carries, 30 kickoff returns, and six punt returns. He twice ran 99 yards for a touchdown; once on the missed field goal against St. Louis, as well as the kickoff return against Washington. He played for more minutes than any other offensive back and gained more total yardage than Jim Brown for the season.

On Nov. 27, with three games to go, Timmy had been honored with the Harry Merrill Award (given as a watch) as the "Outstanding Eagle" by the Philadelphia Sports Writers Association Football Club for leading the team in total yards, rushing, kickoff returns, punt returns, and points. He also got a bust of Benjamin Franklin from the Poor Richard Club, made up of advertising people. His 99-yard return against Washington drew particular notice. Skorich said Timmy won the award with "hard work and desire." At a banquet in late January he received the "Outstanding Eagle" award from the full Philadelphia Sports Writers Association, which honored Mickey Mantle at the same event. Timmy also was honored with Riley Gunnels as the team MVPs by the Bakers Club at the Father and Son sports dinner.

Timmy initially didn't make the 1962 Pro Bowl team – McDonald was the only Bird when the squads were announced. "If you had a good season," Timmy said, "more players from your team make it. We didn't have a good year." He noted that the team had been afflicted by injuries, including ones to Retzlaff, Tommy Walton, Dean, Brookshier, and Dick Lucas. "You take the core from a team and it is lost," he said. In the end, though, Timmy made the Pro Bowl team, although he didn't play. While attending a banquet of the Philadelphia Big Brother Association, he found out that he had been picked to replace the Cardinals' John David Crow, who had been injured. He quickly flew to San Francisco but ended up sitting on the bench in street clothes after Crow proved able to play in the Jan.13 game.

Missing out on postseason action, though, may have been a help to Timmy's singing career. He was finding his voice during an interesting time in popular music. The initial excitement that Elvis Presley had generated waned after his 1958 induction into the Army, and the Beatles had yet to invade America. However, many classic records were released between 1960 and 1963. Among the rich array of songs emerging in this period were a number of dance-oriented records. Although Motown, in Detroit, was the most prolific label at releasing up-tempo records, Philadelphia produced some of the more popular sides of this era, including the Cameo/Parkway classics.

Since he was a boy, Timmy had dreamed of a career as an entertainer, viewing himself as as much a singer and dancer as an athlete. "Entertainment could have been the easiest thing for me," he said in 2010. "Acting, singing, I loved those. Football was a challenge." As with football, though, Timmy knew he needed coaching for a singing career as well. Although he took lessons from the brother of Bernie Lowe, the founder of Cameo Records (which became Cameo/Parkway), his most noted voice teacher was Carmine Gagliardi. Gagliardi was more prominent as a teacher for singers like Patti LuPone, but he was able to help Timmy build the power to sing on records and in live performances. Timmy had weekly lessons with Gagliardi on Mondays (which was his day off from the Eagles) for four years. The key part of the lessons was "to see if I could do anything to improve the breathing and how to use my breathing. I had the power, but you got to know how to do the breathing; otherwise, you get thrown off," Timmy remembered. Gagliardi told Associated Press reporter Jack Hand in October 1965 that "Tim Brown has a very soft, warm quality in his voice. He has a voice that reminds you of Perry Como. He is a very gentle man, completely different from the person you might think of as a pro football player."

In 1962, Timmy's recording of "I Got Nothin' But Time," backed by an 11-piece orchestra, was released by Imperial Records, the home of singers ranging from Fats Domino to Ricky Nelson. It was the B side of "Silly Rumors," but both songs were being promoted as potential hits. The specifics on how Timmy was able to secure a record contract with Imperial have disappeared, although it would be easy to surmise that producers saw at least a novelty act in a singing NFL star. It was announced that he had signed a six-year contract under which he would provide two records every year, although little came of this and the contract appears to have been short-lived. "I've got an upcoming appearance at the Steel Pier in Atlantic City and then some in New York.... My managers are handling all that," he said, noting that his management firm's clients included the then-hot Nelson.

Both "Silly Rumors" and "I Got Nothin' But Time" were written by a pair of notable musicians. Van McCoy was a producer and arranger whose hits included "Baby I'm Yours" by Barbara Lewis in 1965 and "Walk Away From Love" by David Ruffin, formerly of the Temptations, in 1976. McCoy, from Washington, is best known for "The Hustle," released under the name of Van McCoy and the Soul City Symphony. "The Hustle" was one of the biggest hits during the summer of 1975, reaching No. 1 on the Billboard Hot 100 on July 26. It also won a Grammy Award as best pop instrumental.

The other co-writer was Norman Meade, a pseudonym for Jerry Ragovoy, a producer and writer from Philadelphia perhaps best known for his authorship of the classic "Time Is on My Side," recorded by Irma Thomas as well as the Rolling Stones, and for "Piece of My Heart," recorded by Erma Franklin (Aretha's sister) and covered by Janis Joplin when she was with Big Brother and the Holding Company. Ragovoy also recorded the soul singer Howard Tate in 1967, including the splendid single "Ain't Nobody Home." Tate was a heavy drug user and faded from public view soon afterward, which led Ragovoy to say in the early 2000s that Tate was probably dead. But the "Sound of Philadelphia" producer Leon Huff had run into Tate in a Philadelphia grocery in 2000. After Ragovoy found out from Huff that Tate was alive, he worked with him on a comeback album called "Rediscovered" in 2003.

Having a producer like Ragovoy added credibility to Timmy's work. Upon hearing "Silly Rumors" again, he recalled, "I forgot how it sounded, because I wanted to do that one as the B side. They were pushing 'Silly Rumors,' and it was OK, but it was a silly song." Timmy had made an appearance in December 1962 at the John Wanamaker department store in Philadelphia to promote his record, and showed he understood the publicity game as well as he did football when he closed an interview by saying, "After all, I've got nothing but time."

Timmy's records drew him some fans in 1962 at a Cleveland high school, where Jim Sullivan, a former Muncie Central and Ball State basketball player, was teaching physical education. In April, Sullivan wrote to Timmy, "I got your record ... and I really like it. I'm going to play it for the fellows in a couple of days and not tell them who it is. I want to know what they think about it before knowing it is you. I like the side that they are pushing.... I don't think the other side is as good, Tim. How would you like to appear on our local TV show here to push your record? I could take your record uptown and see if they like it.... A lot of stars appear on this show." The show was "The Giant Tiger Amateur Hour" on Channel 5, hosted by Gene Carroll; it later became simply "The Gene Carroll Show" and was a Cleveland mainstay for 37 years.

The following week, "Sullie" again wrote to Timmy: "I played your record for approximately 400 teenagers and they just went wild. What do you think about that? All the boys and girls flipped. They want to know where they can buy this record.... I also played it for some adults and they also was crazy about it. The kids dig both sides.... They also want to start a fan club. Why don't you come down and spend a few days at my pad. Everything is on me. Some sharp women want to meet you.... So drop on down and spend time promoting your record. My wife and I got our hands in with a lot of influential people. She works around nothing but rich blood." Timmy also got a letter signed by 35 Cleveland high school girls saying, "Our Physical Education teacher is a well-known friend of yours by the name of Jim Sullivan. In Physical Education April 11th he played your latest record, we enjoyed it very much, and hope to have many more of them. Since this is your first record we would like to start a fan club in your name. We would like for you to send photographs and other items." Whether Timmy followed up on this can't be determined.

Record deals and public appearances were well enough, but Timmy and his Black Eagles teammates still had to endure the open discrimination of the years before the Civil Rights Act, where they could not stay in the same hotels as their white teammates in many cities. "We would stay in the Black part of town, in a motel," he said. "It was comfortable to the [Black] guys in a sense, but they still resented the fact that they separated us like that. It was still very obvious that they [the NFL and the Eagles] didn't fight enough for us. Or maybe they did and they couldn't get any other recourse; nobody was going to bend.... There was one place, I think Tommy and a couple of the other guys said they weren't going to stay if we didn't. That was cool. Most guys just went along with whatever, but they felt bad for us."

Still, Timmy was finding camaraderie not just with his teammates but with people in the record industry. Through his voice lessons with Bernie Lowe's brother, Timmy met Chubby Checker, who recorded for Cameo/Parkway and became a close friend. While most people now associate Checker just with "The Twist," between 1960 and 1963 he had eight top-10 singles, including "Let's Twist Again," "Popeye the Hitchhiker," "Limbo Rock," and "Pony Time," which hit No. 1. But "The Twist" became the only song to rise to No. 1 on two separate occasions (1960 and 1962) on Billboard's Hot 100. (Bing Crosby's "White Christmas" achieved the same feat but in an entirely different chart system.) Checker, who grew up as Ernest Evans in Philadelphia, knew of Timmy because of his football career, and Timmy knew about Checker because of his singing.

Timmy's favorite record by Checker was his duet with Dee Dee Sharp, "Slow Twisting," which peaked at No. 3. Sharp had a string of top 10 hits in the early 1960s and may be best known for "Mashed Potato Time." Checker introduced Sharp to Timmy in 1962, when she was 16 and he was 24. They were recording at Cameo/Parkway at the time. In 2021, she said Tim was "very handsome. Very polite. Always treated me with respect. I went gaga over him. I most definitely loved him: 'Oh, God, he's so gorgeous,' that's what I remember. I didn't care about Chubby; he was my friend. I was more interested in Tim. How could you not like him? You had no choice, unless you were Kenny Gamble."

Timmy was once Sharp's date for the Overbrook High School prom, held at the Hawaiian Cottage, a tiki-and-puu-puu restaurant in Cherry Hill. At Cameo/Parkway one day, she said, she burst into tears, and Timmy asked her what was wrong. She said she feared that no one would ask her to the prom, and he said he would. Ordinarily when she went out, she was accompanied by her brother, Roy, or a cousin, but her mother let her go without a chaperone this time. When they walked in, she said, "I was so happy. It was unbelievable. [The girls] were extremely jealous. They didn't talk to me for some time. They were disgusted with my butt. He was so handsome." Timmy, she said, "kept his private business private. I was always crazy about Tim, but he looked at me as a kid – as a sister, not as a love interest."

When Checker was around, she said, "Tim would be there and I would always be there. We were chums. Not clubbing, because I was too young. We went to lunch and dinners and laughed. I loved Tim's very hearty laugh. Probably ate at a fish restaurant, DiNardo's. I loved mussels." She also would have dinner with the Grices. She believed some of the women Timmy dated were just using him, and told him so. He also opened for her on a couple of occasions when she was playing at Palumbo's, a then-legendary South Philly venue for singers.

Timmy was a participant in Checker's wedding, just across the Delaware River from Philadelphia in April 1964. According to a Camden Courier-Post article on April 13, he was one of the four ushers and the best man was Checker's brother, Tracy Evans; however, Timmy always said he was best man, and Checker called him that in a 2020 text message. The bride was Catherina Lodders, a Dutch woman who had won the 1962 Miss World title. The wedding was controversial because it was interracial; New Jersey allowed interracial marriages, but it was not until 1967 that the U.S. Supreme Court, with the landmark decision in "Loving v. Virginia," banned laws that outlawed interracial marriage in the United States. While a majority of people said they supported the marriage, the couple received threats as the day approached. A number of churches had refused to marry the couple until Temple Lutheran Church in Pennsauken, N.J., and its pastor, George L. Garver, agreed to preside. Garver had been approached by Checker's manager, who also lived in the township, just outside Camden.

Even Checker's mother had concerns about the match. On the cover of the July 1965 issue of Photoplay magazine, one of the headlines was "I Didn't Want My Son to Marry a White Girl," with the "I" meaning Eartle Evans. As it turned out, she shouldn't have worried. The couple stayed married and had three children. And Checker always remembered the officiant; a Dec. 10, 2015, story in the Bradenton (Fla.) Herald noted that Checker and his wife were at an event celebrating the 100th birthday of Pastor Garver. Garver's church is still standing on Crescent Boulevard, but is now known as the Martin Luther Chapel.

The wedding reception was at the now-gone Cherry Hill Inn, the hotel for which Delaware Township renamed itself.

Timmy and Checker were roommates on several occasions when they were performing live. In some shows Timmy opened for Checker, at others Checker opened for him. Timmy told in 2010 of one show with the "Twist" star: "Chubby and I had two rooms together. He came to my show, but he left before I could do anything, I just introduced him. He had to go 10 blocks to his show, so I went over to his show when I was through. I didn't plan to sing or anything, I'm just going to support him. So I go in and he is in the middle of a number, and he starts, 'Ladies and gentlemen, Timmy Brown.' He finished his song and he says, 'Timmy, can you come up here and do a number with me?' … I got up there and he says, 'Do you know any Elvis Presley songs,' and he didn't know I knew every one. I said, 'Elvis, Elvis, Elvis – I never….' People started laughing, and he says, 'Why, I thought we'd do a little medley.' I said, 'Well, I probably have heard of him, so I'll try.' So he had his band take off with the music, and it was all in the same beat that we were going into these songs. He opened up with, 'You ain't nothing but a hound dog, crying all the time,' and he would point to me. 'Baby let me be, bop do wop, your teddy bear. Put a chain around my neck and lead me anywhere,' and then he would take it, and point to me and then I'd come in with another one. We could have gone all night." Timmy noted in 2010 that when he did club dates in Philadelphia, "I always did two or three Elvis songs."

The summer of 1963 found Grayce Butler only calling Timmy rarely, and sometimes when she did, "he didn't want to talk to me, he would just grunt." Then a group of Butlers drove to Philadelphia, where brother Bill had gotten a job as a mapmaker. Bill said that to celebrate his arrival, Timmy took him to the then-famous Old Original Bookbinder's restaurant for lunch. "Timmy had cultivated a taste for lobster," he said. "I would have ordered one too, but this old Hoosier would not have known how to eat it."

The plan was for Grayce to stay over a few extra days with Timmy before he went to camp. Also making the trip to Philadelphia were brother Ernie as well as brother Bert and his girlfriend, Marsha. Once brought back together, former teammates Ernie and Timmy started swapping football stories and then challenged each other to one-on-one basketball. Ernie had a great time, but the visit wasn't turning into fun for Grayce. In a later interview, she said Ernie had said to her, "Sweets, I was thinking, why don't you go back to Bloomington and I'll stay here with Tim." She agreed. "They were having so much fun. I know Tim. Tim might have been happy having me here that day, but then the next day he might not have been." Ernie later acknowledged that Grayce "wasn't too pleased when Tim spent more time playing basketball with me than he spent with her." Once, Timmy said, at 3 a.m. he "jumped out of bed and went into his room and said, 'Come on, I can get you now, baby.' I drove my car right up into the park over the curb, which you're not supposed to do, and threw the headlights on the court. I had him, 26-17, when the cops came and said, 'What're you doing in here making all that noise?' I said, 'How can you say we're making noise when there's only two of us here and I'm burning him?'" All this showed that as Ernestine Grice said of Timmy, "He's a boy."

The 1964 Sport interview said Ernie, whom Timmy called "Ernie the Head" because he was a teacher, was, along with Walker, Timmy's only close friend. "The first time he saw me," Timmy said, "he said, 'Man, are you square.' People who know me now can't picture that. Ernie the Head dressed me in his own clothes, gave me money."

Ernie said Timmy gave him a part in his club act. Timmy would say he was going to do a Sinatra song. Ernie then would jump onto the stage and say, "No, Timmy, you don't want to mess with Frank Sinatra. You want to do what you do best." Ernie then would throw him a football and Timmy would sing, "Go, Timmy, Go," to the music of Chuck Berry's "Johnnie B. Goode" as restructured by one of Checker's writers at Cameo/Parkway. "I would always come from the back" to the stage,

Timmy said, "and people would have to turn around and see me go up, and I would do a little spin and grab the mic, you know. 'Now when I'm on the field and I want to dance…,' then a pass from Ernie from the back and I'd catch it and they'd go crazy." Despite this brush with fame, Ernie said of Timmy's vocal style, "I was never impressed with his singing. It wasn't bad. But it was a little on the Bobby Rydell or Frankie Avalon side – like white singers of the time."

One time that summer, Timmy had a club date set in the Shore resort town of Wildwood, and Ernie went with him. Checker was playing in one hotel, and another stage bore the Cannonball Adderley Quintet, then including Yusef Lateef. Timmy was an early act, for when the clubs opened. Ernie, now feeling at home among the era's entertainment giants, said, "Chubby and I would go see his act, then the three of us would go to the jazz performance." One day Checker invited them to go deep sea fishing with him from Wildwood, leaving at 4:30 a.m., "but as none of us knew what we were doing and got a little seasick, we went [right] back to his place [hotel room] and started drinking the booze we had taken [for] the trip." They were horsing around when Checker broke an arm trying to show his football technique by dodging Timmy – he "slipped, and hit his arm against the counter," according to Ernie.

Timmy in 2010 remembered the incident this way: "I was in a hurry because I was running late. It was in the morning … so I was getting ready to go to the door and Chubby gets in front of the door, and he says, 'I think I can tackle you.' I said, 'Chubby, I ain't got time, I'm running late. Come on, get out of here.' He says, 'You can't get by me.' So I just sort of did a slow-motion jog up to him, and he goes down and I do a spin, and I'm at the door. 'Bye,' and he is going, 'Ouch.' I said, 'Yeah, right,' and I left. I didn't know I had hurt him. I just thought he was horsing around to delay me again." That night, Timmy went to Checker's show and was invited to sing a couple songs with him. When he went onstage, he noticed that Checker's arm was in a sling.

Later, Tim had Ernie attend Eagles training camp for a few days, as Ernie still hoped to play pro football. Ernie said he "smuggled some beer into the place" for Jurgensen and McDonald as well as Timmy: "The night before the game, I was at their practice. As soon as the coach blew the whistle for them to come in, the quarterback, Sonny Jurgensen, was at the back of the crowd of players. He's just easing away. Jumped into his convertible and took off. Later, because they had bed check, guys said we got to go out and get a couple of six-packs of beer. There was a fountain in the middle of this complex where they were staying in Hershey. They were trying to throw their beer cans into the fountain. And I'm thinking, 'The night before the game! Man! You all aren't taking this that seriously!'"

Ernie eventually returned to Munich, Germany, where he was working as a teacher. Looking back, he said, "Oh, man, we had fun that summer." For his part, Timmy said, "Those were the best three weeks of my life.... That's all Ernie the Head and I did here, drink beer and play one-on-one.... When Ernie was here, he was always challenging me. One afternoon we played five games of 30 points in the park and he burned me three out of five. Then we came home and drank beer all night." Ernestine Grice noted that after Ernie left, she and her husband found their basement full of empty German beer cans.

The experience, Ernie said, had changed his view of the professional athletes of the time: "I had this thing that when I was playing, you don't drink, you don't smoke. That's not even considered." He also attended an exhibition game that year against Baltimore. In 2021, he said, "One of the guys who had been the hero ... when they won the championship, he got hurt. Looked like it might be a season-ending injury. I went over to him and said, how bad is this? He looked at me like I was crazy and said, 'You think it's bad news. I'm not so sure it's bad. Still get paid and don't get hit.' So I changed my regard." In a 2010 interview, Timmy also indicated that the legend of the highly fit football athlete was partly myth in the 1960s: "I don't really recall ever being in shape in football. We didn't have the facilities or the stuff to do anything. It was like we were in high school or college. You just go work out; you don't do anything extra."

New cartographer Bill Butler stayed with Timmy and the Grices while looking for an apartment for himself. "Wherever we would go in Philadelphia, people would recognize Timmy and ask for his autograph," he wrote in his book. "Rich men would ask him for tickets. Fans would then ask me for my autograph, assuming that I was one of the Eagles." While living with Timmy, he said, he met Jim Brown and asked him the source of his greatness on the field. Jim Brown, he wrote, "placed his index finger about a quarter-inch from his thumb. With genuine humility, he said, 'I am really only that much better than the other players, but that little bit makes all the difference.'"

In 1963 Timmy, his deal with Imperial apparently gone to oblivion, signed with Mercury Records on the same day as Johnny Mathis, the singer best known for his smash hits "Chances Are," "Wonderful, Wonderful," and "Misty." The signings took place at a press event on one of the piers in Atlantic City. Mathis had recorded for Columbia since 1956, but in 1963 was lured to Mercury by producer Quincy Jones before returning to Columbia in 1967, dissatisfied with how Mercury was presenting his work. Another trait Mathis shared with Timmy was athletics. He was a high jumper at San Francisco State and had been invited to attend the 1956 Olympic trials, but passed in favor of a recording career. In addition, he, like Timmy, was from a large family; he was the fourth of seven children, and was not the only one to seek a career in music.

Timmy's contract with Mercury, signed on May 27, 1963, states that he would "record a minimum of four phonograph record sides during each year in which this agreement is in effect" and would receive royalties "computed upon the basis of 5% of the ninety (90%) per cent of the suggested retail list price." The contract was signed for a year. Mercury was granted the option of "extending this agreement for four (4) separate terms of one (1) year each."

Going into the 1963 season, Timmy, who had also signed his Eagles contract in May, was described as "a 1959 castoff but now a National Football League hero." As the season neared in August, he was called "the moody nightclub tenor and football virtuoso," a player who worried about his small size in a "land of behemoths." "At my size," Timmy said, "I can't last a whole lot longer ... and I've got to get recognition this year.... I still haven't arrived. I better hurry." He said that in 1962, he might have ended up riding the bench for the whole year because the team was "committed to a big-back offense," but he got his chance when Dean was injured. By now, Skorich had faith in Timmy, saying that "with more help in 1963, Brown can be even greater."

Timmy was described in the New York World-Telegram as "the only pro to come from Ball State Teachers ... an institution never charged with football overemphasis." At least one other well-known athlete of the time would come from the Cardinal sideline, however; Merv Rettenmund made his name in baseball after playing as a running back for Ball State in the mid-1960s. The Ball State background was always a bit of an albatross for Timmy. Longtime NFL referee Jim Tunney said in an interview, "You come out of Ball State, why, people say, what the devil is all of that about? I mean, did he come out of Notre Dame or Penn State or yeah? Ball State, I mean, that wasn't highly respected that way, in terms of a great football team."

In August, the Philadelphia Evening Bulletin's Sandy Grady wrote that the Eagles wanted Timmy to be part of a run-pass option play that was used in the 26-21 exhibition loss to Baltimore at Hershey on Aug. 10, the game Ernie Butler attended. The play worked like this: Timmy gets the ball from quarterback Jurgensen and moves to his right behind a screen of blockers. If he sees the defensive backs charging, he stops and passes the ball. The play had been very successful for Hornung and Gifford. Skorich said, "This was the bread-and-butter play for Green Bay when Hornung was running it. Even if the pass doesn't work, it worries the defensive backs into laying back, so that a good runner like

Tim gets an extra five, 10 yards the next time he runs." Grady said Timmy had become the team's "No. 1 offensive missile, discounting Sonny Jurgensen's arm."

The NFL was a different game then than it is today, according to Tunney. "The linebackers could grab guys, there was a lot of holding on going on downfield ... so you didn't have the breakaway runners like when O.J. [Simpson] set records.... Running backs were very, very powerful.... What happens with a guy like that is that it's a running game then. Today's game, it's the wide receivers and five wideouts, and you get as many people down there as you can to spread it out." But he noted that "if you have a good running back, that keeps the defense more honest, and Tim Brown could do that. He could play in today's game that way, but ... they used him more often as just 'three yards to a cloud of dust,' as they used to say." He added that "if Tim played in today's systems, he could be over 1,000 yards with the kind of ability he had."

Tunney noted that he didn't recall Timmy's ever saying "a bad word to an official or to an opponent. That was from a kind of class guy that I remember. He didn't trash talk. He was just not that type of guy. He played his game. You'd give him the ball. He'd run with the ball. Get up and do it again." Timmy said, looking back, that "I always threw the ball to the ref. When I scored a touchdown, I always knew where the ref was and I just, over my shoulder, tossed it right to him and never complained about, you know. They are doing their job and it ain't going to do me any good anyway."

On Sept. 22, in the second game of the season, the Eagles lost to the St. Louis Cardinals by 28-24. Timmy ran 100 yards for a go-ahead touchdown on the kickoff after a Cards touchdown – both of which came about because he had goofed on an earlier play. Jurgensen had passed out of the shotgun from behind his goal on what he said "was supposed to be a screen pass but, unfortunately, my screen never showed up." Timmy admitted that he "blew the play" by going in the wrong direction. Jurgensen found an alternate receiver, Retzlaff, who lost the ball when tackled by Jerry Stovall, and the Cardinals began an eight-play scoring drive. After his 100-yard run, Timmy was able to say, "I was able to tell Sonny I had made up for my goof" by putting the Eagles ahead by 24-21. But the Cardinals scored to win after a punt went off the side of the kicker's foot and out of bounds six yards past the line of scrimmage. Skorich said Timmy's run was the only really good offense the Eagles showed in the second half.

Timmy said of his propensity for the long run – he now had scored on marches of 105, 100, 99, and 99 yards over three seasons – that he had studied how players broke on kicking plays, and that he ran "against the grain of the blocking and tackling." "I was supposed to go up the middle," he said. "I said to the fellows, let's fake to the right – block like I am going to go to the right when I come out of the wedge. I'm going left." He said the previous week was "the hardest week of work I ever put in at practice, because I wasn't satisfied with my game last week." By late September, Timmy said he had noticed that his reputation as the Eagles' long-distance return specialist had made his work a bit harder: "What good is a reputation if the other team won't kick to you?"

At this time he also was promoting his new Mercury record, "Do the Crossfire," but was disappointed in early sales. "Do the Crossfire" – not to be confused with the Orlons' "Crossfire" – was written by Philly natives Johnny Madara and Dave White, who also were responsible for "You Don't Own Me" by Leslie Gore, as well as "At the Hop" by Danny and the Juniors, a Billboard No. 1 for seven weeks in 1957. Timmy recalled that his records often took less than a day to make: "Once I had the words, I was a quick study, and we would go through it a couple of times. Usually two or three takes so they got the best. I like to get it right the first time and not change, and just go with the feel. That was pretty good. We never had to do much more than two or three takes." He did not recall the names of the session players, but thought most came through Madara or White.

On Oct. 6, the Eagles beat the Cowboys by 24-21, with Timmy

scoring twice, once on an 80-yarder from QB King Hill and once on a run from the 2. On Oct. 27, Grayce Butler and her sister Florence went to Chicago to see the Eagles play the Bears. They went into the locker room and saw the players being taped up, and were teased by McDonald. When they got to their seats at Soldier Field, Grayce found her coat wasn't heavy enough to fight off the Lake Michigan chill. Jurgensen walked by, and Grayce asked the quarterback to get Timmy's coat for her to wear. He said he'd have it sent up to her after he finished an interview – and he did.

The Nov. 10 game against the Giants at Yankee Stadium had Bill Butler in attendance along with the Grices. "Timmy had the worst game of his career," Butler later wrote. "He gained very few yards on a meager five carries. In addition, Tim had taken a physical pounding." The next day, he wrote, the singer Dionne Warwick, who had dated Timmy off and on since she had done some background vocals for one of his records, came to Philadelphia from her home in North Jersey to appear on "The Mike Douglas Show," a nationally syndicated afternoon interview program. "That evening, she stopped by [the Grices'] to see Timmy," he later wrote. "He had gone into seclusion and was seeing no one.... It fell upon me to entertain Dionne Warwick.... Timmy had all of her record albums. Dionne and I spent the evening listening to them. She told me which songs she liked and which ones were particularly difficult to record. Dionne could recall how many takes each song required." Warwick, he said, didn't act like a star with him: "The only thing in the refrigerator was a small piece of meatloaf. It was big enough for only one good slice and a heel. She prepared two well-garnished sandwiches. Dionne Warwick took the meatloaf sandwich containing the heel and presented the one that contained the good slice to me. That was impressive." Timmy said later that with Warwick, "the person you see is really that. She's just a down-to-earth, real good person."

Warwick, who grew up in Northern New Jersey, said in 2022 that she and Timmy dated for about two years. She met him in New York

City, in "one of those little bars where apparently all the football players frequented." He introduced her to Frank Gifford. Timmy, she said, "was just one of those guys that was very, very difficult not to like. He was always a gentleman. Always fun. Always giving and caring. We had a wonderful relationship."

She went to several parties at the Grices' while they were dating. "We did all the normal things that youngsters of our age group did. Movies. A lot of cheesesteaks. He loved movies. I think he loved movies more for the popcorn than anything else." He also introduced her to football. "It was quite interesting how all of a sudden I loved football," she said. "I love football now so much that if I could play it, I probably would. He inducted me into knowledge of football and how to really enjoy the game itself." She would drive to Philadelphia the night before a game and stay with the Grices.

Warwick played a role in Timmy's almost two-year relationship with Diana Ross at the height of the Supremes' supremacy. Ross, Mary Wilson, and Florence Ballard (replaced by Cindy Birdsong in 1967) were one of the most successful groups of the era, notching 18 Top 10 singles, 12 of which reached No. 1 on Billboard's Hot 100 from 1964 through 1969, rivaling the Beatles and the Rolling Stones. After leaving the Supremes in 1969, Ross had 12 Top 10 hits as a solo artist from 1970 to 1984, including six that reached No. 1. Timmy's relationship with Ross started at the Latin Casino. Timmy said that typically, when he would go to a club in the Philadelphia area, "they usually got me seats in the front. Then they would sing a song to me … and everyone in the place would know.… I asked the guy, 'What you got? … I'll stand in the back.' He said, 'Tim, you know you're not going to stand in the back.'" Front-row seats were found, and "I went down and everybody's turning around because the Supremes had just come on, and so now everyone is looking at me."

Timmy told different versions of how he met Ross. One went, "And I look up at Diana, and I didn't know her, and Diana Ross is looking at me and coming down and getting on my seat. I'm being as humble as I can be. And so the owner comes over and says, 'Diana would like to meet you.'" After the show, he said, "I went backstage and she tried to grab me right there. She is very much a go-getter, and we just struck it off and the next thing you know, I'm having her to the team parties." The other version was that he and Warwick had gone together to see the Supremes, and "I went backstage with Dionne, she introduced me, and the next thing you know Diana had her arm through mine and we're walking off. She's leading me. I felt terrible about Dionne, but they were good friends, so I assumed, you know." Warwick did get jealous, Timmy said – "They kind of fell out a little bit.... We were very close and then Diana just – you know what I'm saying. But it's crazy.'"

In the book "The Supremes: A Saga of Motown Dreams, Success and Betrayal" by Mark Ribowsky, Ross is described as having "a brief, fiery fling with ... Timmy Brown" in an unsuccessful effort to make Berry Gordy Jr., founder of Motown Records, with whom she was in love, marry her. Jim Brown later said that he believed Ross and Gordy truly loved each other. He said Timmy once brought Ross by his house: "At the time we were all compulsive for chess and we invited Diana to play. First Timmy beat Diana, then I did. After the second game, Diana told Timmy she was going down the hill to get some cigarettes, would be right back. Diana left and never came back." For her part, Ross told Jet Magazine for the issue of Oct. 5, 1967, about how the Supremes were being reported on at the time, "I was supposed to have leukemia. And, let me see, I was supposed to be secretly married to Berry Gordy or Timmy Brown. And Florence was supposed to have been pregnant – for two years."

Timmy was Ross' guest at a number of the Supremes' 1960s concerts, including their two-week 1967 engagement at the Copacabana in New York City. Once, he invited his childhood friend George Walker to come from Richmond to New York, where front-row seats awaited him. Philadelphia Daily News columnist Charles Petzold wrote in a

1972 article, "The last time I saw Timmy Brown, he was backstage at the Latin Casino. He playfully tossed Diana Ross of the Supremes over his shoulder and back as easily as an acrobat doing a cartwheel. 'What are you doing?' screamed her manager. 'Put her down. If she gets hurt, we're out of business.'"

Timmy said in 2010 that Warwick had been more a friend than a girlfriend – "I wasn't going to bed with her or anything" – but then "I got a call once, and this was after three years.... It was Dionne's mother, and she said Dionne wanted to talk to me. I didn't know she had gotten married [to actor-drummer William Elliott in 1966]. She called and said she wanted to annul it, but would I marry her if she did? I said, Dionne, I can't do that. We're great friends and all, but we aren't at that kind of stage." Warwick did divorce Elliott in May 1967, but then remarried him a couple of months later.

Looking back, Timmy said, "I put women on a pedestal but I don't want them to overthink something, then I'm a bad guy. I dated a lot of entertainers, singers. I have a thing for singers." While he enjoyed the company of famous women, he said, he had no interest at that time in marriage, thinking that he was too young and not established in a lifelong career, and also that "I didn't want to be a Mr. Ross or Mr. Warwick, you know."

Within two weeks of the Eagles-Giants game, the light-heartedness of the early 1960s seemed out of place after the assassination of President John F. Kennedy in Dallas. While many high schools and colleges, as well as the American Football League, rushed to cancel games, NFL commissioner Pete Rozelle said the league would play on the Sunday after the assassination – the day when, as it turned out, Texas gangland figure Jack Ruby killed accused assassin Lee Oswald. Rozelle's decision meant the Eagles would host Washington as planned. As was their custom before home games, the Eagles spent Saturday night at the Sheraton Motor Inn in West Philadelphia, near Franklin Field. Somehow, what Retzlaff called "the emotion of the moment" spilled over, and defensive back Ben Scotti beat up defensive tackle John Mellekas so hard that Scotti sliced a tendon on one of Mellekas' teeth, according to a Sports Illustrated article. Exactly what happened is not clear, but Scotti, known as one of the league's tough guys, apparently took exception to a racial slur against Italians that was directed at Rozelle, who was not even of Italian background. Mellekas never got over it and the team was visibly tense. The Eagles lost to Washington by 13-10, but even more had been lost in the Eagles' clubhouse.

Still, life went on. Just a week after the assassination, Timmy's vocal cords were put to use in the Holiday Hootenanny concert at the Philadelphia Athletic Club on Nov. 28, where he performed along with now-forgotten folk artists the New Hope Singers, Doug Moore, and Sandi Lessin, an actress who had been a partner with retired Eagles lineman Harold Bradley in a coffeehouse in Rome. Bradley had since become an artist. The emcee was Frank X. Feller, one of the DJs at Top 40 powerhouse WIBG.

The Dec. 8 game in St. Louis found Grayce and her sister Florence again in attendance, along with their brother Bert and his girlfriend. It snowed hard during the game and people threw snowballs. Afterward they went to Tim's hotel room, had a meal, and spent time together. "He really liked me that year," Grayce said.

When the 1963 season ended, Timmy again led the Eagles in total offense with 2,428 yards, once more setting a league record. When added to his 2,306 of the year before, that also set a record as the highest yardage in two consecutive seasons. In addition, he again led the team in scoring with 66 points on 11 TDs. He also led in kickoff and punt returns. Timmy was one of three Eagles, along with Retzlaff and Max Baughan, named to the Pro Bowl team for the Jan. 12, 1964, game in Los Angeles. He was in the starting unit for the game, along with, of course, Jim Brown. (The top stars of the year were Giants QB Y.A. Tittle and Jim Brown.) In addition, his fellow players had voted him one of the six best runners in the game. "Jim Brown told me that was the ultimate honor, being picked by the guys you played against," he said.

Before the game, won by the West squad, 31-17, Timmy described himself as "moody, sensitive and temperamental." Of the past season, he said, "I dreamed of seeing us both at the top, Brown and Brown," in terms of rushing yards. He finished third, behind Jim Brown and Jim Taylor. But the Eagles had only won two games that season. "I'm not blaming any of the fellows, but it was a discontented ball club," he said, including the fight between Mellekas and Scotti. Timmy was thinking ahead to his singing career in the offseason, with a new record about to come out. "On one side is the standard 'If I Loved You,' sort of done like a Kansas City shuffle, with a 13-piece orchestra and five voices behind me. The other side is something called 'Running Late.' Neither is as smooth as I want to sing," he said, adding, "They want me to do everything with a big beat. Oh, well, I'm just a rookie." Mercury, he said, saw him more as a rock singer, while he wanted to sing ballads. He added, "It's all a matter of material. I can sing as well as any of them, but I'm getting lousy material." He noted that Mercury had artists such as Mathis and "Brook Benton, so naturally they get the best things.... I guess I'll always be a football player who's a frustrated singer." Timmy did call "If I Loved You" one of his favorite recordings. And he acknowledged his continuing self-doubt: "Michigan State wanted me to play football, but I went to Ball State because I didn't think I was good enough. I wanted to go into the Canadian league because I felt I wasn't good enough for the NFL."

Timmy took the scenic route getting to the Pro Bowl game, and on Dec. 20 visited the Home along with Ted Dean. While there, they engaged in one of Timmy's favorite ways to spend time, basketball. Timmy and then-current Home basketball coach Verle Foster apparently got the better of Dean and Bill Brewer, who had been coach when Timmy lived there. The story in the Home Journal noted that Timmy and Dean would tour the East as part of an Eagles basketball team, playing exhibition games against squads made up of other NFL players. After leaving Knightstown, Timmy and Dean moved on to Indianapolis, where Buddy was working toward a degree in history and political science at Butler University.

Timmy's regional star quality was recognized by the Society for Crippled Children and Adults, known as the Easter Seal Society, when it named him one of Philadelphia's 10 most eligible bachelors. The group was organized to escort the 1964 Easter Seal Child to a Valentine's Day lunch. Timmy was among the younger bachelors mentioned; others included Thomas M. Foglietta, a lawyer and member of City Council who later became a congressman and ambassador to Italy; J. Roffe Wike, who became CEO of an investment firm and a civic leader in Philadelphia; William J. Green III, who also was a congressman and was mayor of Philadelphia in the early 1980s; and Larry Ferrari, an organist who had a show on Channel 6 in Philadelphia from 1954 to 1997. Timmy said he was looking for an "old-fashioned type" who would let him be the man of the house: "I believe in being the dominant male and you can't have two dominant figures in a family." In nearby Wilmington, Del., the fact that Timmy was simply going to attend the Wilmington Sportswriters and Broadcasters Association banquet was worth a 10-paragraph story in a local newspaper.

In 1964, Timmy would return to an Eagles team dealing with major changes. In January, Jerry Wolman, a 37-year-old contractor from Washington, had spent $5.5 million to buy the Eagles. Since the 1949 season they had been owned by a group known as the "Happy Hundred," each of whom had paid $3,000 for a share of the team. The "Hundred" was down to 65 members when they sold out to Wolman. The next month, he dispensed with Skorich and hired Joe Kuharich, a past Notre Dame coach (and native of South Bend, Ind.) who had been the NFL's supervisor of officials in the 1963 season. Kuharich was a longtime friend of Rozelle's from when he was the coach at the University of San Francisco, and Rozelle was first a student publicist and then athletic news director. In that job, Rozelle drew national attention to the

Dons' undefeated 1951 team, which outscored opponents by 338-86. The Dons also drew attention for turning down an Orange Bowl offer that was contingent on the team's Black players not participating. Two days after the season ended, the university canceled its football program. Looking back in 2010, Timmy saw the hand of Rozelle not only in the hiring but in the sale, saying Rozelle allowed Wolman to buy the team on the condition that Kuharich would be the coach.

Longtime referee Tunney worked for Kuharich when he was supervisor of officials. "He was hardly an official," he said, "didn't know anything about rules. So they put an experienced official with him ... somebody who could help him understand the spirit and philosophy behind the rules. Most of the time he was there as a supervisor, he was looking at other teams that he could go and coach." Told of this in 2010, Timmy said with a laugh, "And they told me all these years I was wrong." Tunney called Kuharich "very intimidating." Kuharich was never a favorite in Philadelphia; the Evening Bulletin's Grady said he "couldn't sell iced tea to a Tasmanian at a dried-up watering hole." In "The Eagles Encyclopedia," the authors wrote that "players with strong personalities did not last long" when Kuharich was coach.

Because the 1963 Eagles had been wracked by an unhappy clubhouse, Kuharich was looking for "harmony, unity and cooperation" as he took over the club. "I interviewed some of the boys about what was the matter last year," he said. "Their answers were kind of vague." One issue, apparently, was Jurgensen's tendency to favor passing to McDonald, who was traded to Dallas in March. "You can't glorify and glamorize just one phase of the game," the coach said. McDonald and Jurgensen were among Timmy's all-time favorite teammates, along with Brookshier, Scotti, and Mike Ditka. Timmy said Jurgensen was "a natural" as a passer – "You see somebody like that, they're born with a ball in their hand. He was like that with ping-pong, anything with a ball. Couldn't run, couldn't jump, but he could pass that ball." He said that at a golf tournament years later, Jurgensen told him, "I just wanted to let you know, in case we don't see each other later, you were a great pleasure to play with." Timmy said in 1964 that "Jurgy had a lot of confidence in me.... I fought for Sonny because he went through a lot – more than he should. The fans were disgraceful the way they booed him. They don't know anything about the injured players he had to use. They're front-runners – phonies, and I don't dig phonies. And I've been classified as a phony myself. Because I'm sensitive and moody, sometimes I'm one way and sometimes another ... and there's nothing I can do about it because that's just the way I am."

On April 1, Washington swapped quarterback Norman Snead to the Eagles to get Jurgensen, setting off a furious round of trading. "Once Kuharich started talking around the league and put Jurgensen and the others on the market, everybody started saying to themselves, 'What can I get for mine for what I need?' .... Certainly never before have bigger names been dealt," according to a story by New York Post reporter Milton Gross. Wolman, described as a "fire-breathing superfan" who got into skirmishes with fans in the stands, had made a request of Kuharich after they had decided, according to Gross, that the "cellar-dwelling team had to be ripped apart and an attempt made to put it together again." Wolman, who was Jewish, had said, "If you're getting ready to trade Timmy Brown, please warn me so I can get in a plane and go to Israel. I don't want to be around when that one's made. It would be less dangerous facing the Arabs." Kuharich said he didn't think Wolman would have to make a quick escape on El Al, "but only because nobody's offered a Taylor or a Hornung along with a Kramer for Timmy. In that respect you could say that Timmy's untouchable and Jerry's safe."

Kuharich also said, "Half the time I've made some trades and only told him [Wolman] about them so that he'd know it before it got into the papers. The other half of the time I didn't even give that much to him. That's when he told me about Timmy Brown. What we're really trying to do here is to get all of them to start fresh." About the same time, Grayce Butler also was looking for a fresh start. She saw Timmy perform in a club in the spring of 1964, but whatever romance they had left was running out of steam and she would soon marry another man.

In May, the New York Giants offered what they considered a large deal for Timmy. Kuharich, who had worked for the Chicago Cardinals and the Washington team in addition to his college employment, said the offer wasn't large enough. The Giants had put a number of players on the table – at the time, some reports said three, some said six. Kuharich said that for him to consider trading Timmy, he would have to get a somewhat comparable replacement, two journeyman players, and a bonus – "a player capable of playing some key spot that [we're] weak at." Kuharich, who had called Timmy "one of the most electrifying runners in football," noted, "Everyone knows better than to ask for Timmy Brown, because they know the price is too high. We look for Timmy Brown to be an Eagle for many years to come, but time changes many things and you can't predict what will happen."

That spring, Timmy was doing a half-hour sports show a couple of times a week for WIBG-AM, known as "Wibbage," the Philadelphia area's main Top 40 outlet, "the station built on a foundation of hits." It had legendary disc jockeys such as Feller, "Rockin' Bird" Joe Niagara, and Don Cannon – in the first "Rocky" movie, his voice is heard on the radio as the Italian Stallion prepares for an early morning run with a glass of egg yolks – but perhaps the best known of them was Hy Lit, who often referred to himself on the air as "Hysky O'Rooney McVoudie O'Zoot." Lit could rack up as much as 71 percent of the total radio audience during his 6-to-10 p.m. shift, Time magazine once reported, and even into the 1980s he was such a force that another disc jockey tried to arrange a mob hit on him because he was a rival for oldies-night business. "He was a white guy but he played all the great music," Timmy said. "And he would get all the records and opened a lot of artists with them. He called me in because I would be right across the hall doing my sports show.... So I would listen to them and he'd say, 'What do you think'? [Once] I was opening in Wildwood, N.J., that weekend, and this was a

Thursday. And I said, 'Do you have an extra copy of that? Can I borrow it?' He said, 'No, you can have a couple of them.' So I got up there and they have a band for me. We don't have much of a rehearsal, we just have a couple of hours tonight and tomorrow we open, so we got to rehearse and do it now. I got my band, I said, 'This song, I'm going to play it for you. You guys can pick it up, if you can't I'll understand, it's not out yet.' So I put the record on, I played it again, and of course they could, they were very good.

"The night we opened with it, it was packed because it was Timmy Brown and it's Wildwood, N.J., so anything Philadelphia, it's packed. I liked to play with the crowd a little, flirt a little – 'Baby, where did our love go' – and I was playing with it, walking, singing, and looking at a girl and then looking over at her guy, anything to entertain them. Afterward, everybody was like, is that your next song, when's it coming out? I said, 'Well, it will be out next week, but it ain't mine. It's Diana Ross and the Supremes.'" "Where Did Our Love Go" was released on June 17, 1964, and rose to No. 1 on the Billboard Hot 100, the first of five Supremes songs in a row to do so.

Timmy started July as a headliner at the Steel Pier in Atlantic City. The Shore resort was the site of that year's Democratic National Convention, and its aging hotels drew such negative publicity from visiting political journalists that the town never really recovered. Timmy was promoting his record "I Got a Secret (Gonna Keep It to Myself)," which had drawn notice in the East and rose to the No. 35 chart position in Hit Parader magazine but attracted little attention elsewhere. It was released on Ember Records, indicating that Timmy's deal with Mercury had also come to an end. Timmy said that at first he didn't even like the song, but "it had a nice beat, and during that time of rock and roll it was, you know."

When Timmy arrived on July 27 for his first training camp under Kuharich, he found a locker room stunned by the deaths of two Chicago Bears players, Willie Gallimore and John Farrington, who had been killed in an auto accident in Indiana. He showed up for camp a week late after spending the previous week with the National Guard, where he had again been teaching WACs at Fort Knox. "The Eagles had helped me get into the National Guard," he said. "I had to report to summer camp for two weeks. As a result, I missed the first week of Eagles training camp. When I arrived at camp, they were acting as though I just hadn't reported, like an attitude thing. At our first team meeting, Joe Kuharich announced to the whole team, 'We're not going to have any stars on this team. Do you have any problems with that, Mr. Brown?' I could never let statements like that go by ... so I said, 'I can do that if you just don't give me the ball.' The guys laughed, but Joe Kuharich didn't." Timmy said in a 2008 interview that "it was war from then on."

The coaches, he said later, "tried to get me in shape in one day." Timmy said in 1964 that he tried to stay around 200 pounds year-round. "I have heavy legs and a big behind – that's where all my weight is." Turning jocular, he said, "I can't match Jim Brown, Bobby Mitchell, Clarence Peaks or Ted Dean" in the derriere department. "Those guys'll never forgive me, but they're all good runners and that's where the power comes from." In 2008, he acknowledged that he had reported to camp overweight – "the girls [at Fort Knox], they were always bringing me cookies and cake" – but said the coaches acted "like I was playing prima donna not playing the first week." He injured a hamstring, he said, and a defensive line coach was calling out to him, "Where are you going, Brown, get back here! You're not going anywhere." Timmy said he responded, "I'm sorry, what? Watch me." He then walked by the other coaches and "said something like, 'I hope you guys aren't as crazy as this guy.' So ... I guess I became a rebel then because they were all new coaches."

He said the assistant coaches tested Black players "in every way. They had this image of slaves, I guess, in their heads from the past, that would succumb to the master." While Timmy and Kuharich didn't get along well, theirs wasn't a racial issue. "A couple of assistant coaches, you know I knew they didn't like Black, and it was quite obvious," he said in 1973. "But basically, overall, Kuharich wasn't that way. For him to battle me so much, and me to battle him so much, you'd think he was anti-Black; you'd have thought I hated whites. But it was neither way." One antagonist on the team, as he had been at Green Bay, was Jim Ringo. "He didn't like me at all and for no reason. He was that way with Jim Brown at Syracuse, too.... That's what football was like at that time. There wasn't many Blacks and [white players] didn't like you taking another buddy of theirs' job, so their job was to get you out of there so their buddy can stay."

Timmy said in 2010 that Rozelle had said to him at that training camp, "You're never going to be in the Hall of Fame, so don't even think about it," apparently as a result of his conflicts with Kuharich: "I knew it was because of Kuharich being his buddy and me being my own man." Timmy recalled a teammate at the time, Ollie Matson, a 1952 Olympian, who had played for Kuharich at San Francisco. "He was an easygoing guy. He would just go along. Of course, they're going to give him the ball. And so Ollie would tell me, 'Tim, you got to really back off some.' I said, 'I'm not doing anything; I'm just responding. They got to back off, you know?' If I'm doing something wrong, then just tell me like normal, you know, but don't make it like I'm a bad dude."

He often found himself fined: "I might have been the first one there dressed and ready to go. And they go through the dressing room, they see who's there and who's ready and what. And I would wait until everybody got out. The rookies that were late, I'd say, 'Come on guys, get dressed, get ready.'... Then I would go down and be the last one on. 'That'll be $500, Brown.' I'd say, 'Right, there's a team party coming up.' Cause all my fines always went to team parties. I got to be known for that with the guys, Tim throws the parties.... We didn't make that much money anyway, so it wasn't like life or death. But then, I just wasn't getting the work and I didn't realize it.... They had me standing the sides and all, and then telling the papers they were saving me."

The team parties in the Grices' basement sometimes included celebrities, including Ross when she would fly in from Detroit to see a game. "The guys would give me more credit for being a ladies' man than I was," he said. "It was just because I knew people who were entertainers."

"I would have a stereo and everything set up down in the basement. I would be so beat up I would just go up to my room and relax, and the guys and their wives or dates would be down dancing. And Al would cook, and Ernie would carry it if I was messed up a little. And I would have Diana go down, because they would all be wanting to see Diana Ross, and I said, 'You're going to have to carry this, because I can't get up and move around a lot.' So it was really good and she enjoyed it. Then, when we had our all-team end of the year banquet, I would have Diana Ross or Timi Yuro." Timmy had dated Yuro, who had a brief run on Cameo/Parkway, including "What's a Matter Baby (Is It Hurting You)," which peaked at No. 12 in 1962. Her biggest hit was "Hurt," a Top 5 hit in 1961 and the original version of what may have been Elvis' last great single, in 1977. Timmy remembered her as a class act with a great voice that reminded him of Brenda Lee, another top performer at the time.

Another notable girlfriend was Tammi Terrell. Although Terrell recorded a number of solo records for Motown, she is most famous for her duets with Marvin Gaye, such as "Ain't No Mountain High Enough," "Ain't Nothin' Like the Real Thing," "Your Precious Love," and "If I Could Build My World Around You." She died at age 24 on March 16, 1970, after a 1967 diagnosis of a brain tumor. Timmy's voice broke when he recalled that she wanted him at her bedside near the time of her death at Graduate Hospital in Philadelphia. "And she died the next day.... She was a beautiful girl. She was such a great person. I don't say that about a lot of women. She was genuine. She was one of the good ones."

Sometimes, Timmy didn't go back to the Grices' immediately after a game. "I always took my time, relaxed going out, and it would be dark and this cabby would always come by and wait for me.... I'd go to someplace to have a beer afterward to get away. I didn't want to go to my place, because I was at Ernie and Al's at that point and the parties were at my place after the game." He said he would go to a bar by himself, "thinking about the things I fucked up on that day. 'I should have done this or that. Yeah, maybe I got seven, eight yards on it, but it should have been all the way.' I was very hard on myself."

Life with the Grices, though, gave Timmy a warm center to his life. The 1964 Sport article said that when they were together, "he has a fine sense of humor and he's always putting them on.... 'Ernie and Al really spoil me,' he said. 'I haven't been spoiled for so many years. But, I really give them a bad time.'" He would do things like put a rubber spider in her bed and wait to hear her scream. He enjoyed playing with their black poodle, Pepe. Ernestine said Timmy was a soft touch who gave away his $5,000 check for winning the NFL championship in two weeks. "I told him that had to stop, and he's all right now that he has a business manager," who was Ellis Elgart.

In early August 1964 Bulletin writer Hugh Brown told of a Timmy – who had pulled a muscle on the first day of training – who wasn't the "shy, bewildered small-town Hoosier boy he was" in 1960. Timmy said that since the end of the 1963 season, "all I had been exercising was my vocal cords. It's impossible to run in the day and sing all night." Brown said Timmy was "dazzling the onlookers with his incredible change-of-pace darting." For his part, Timmy expressed amazement at the play of yet another Brown – new right tackle Bob Brown, whom he saw as a potential rookie of the year. He noted that this other Brown "has that major asset of being confident of his own abilities. I lost that confidence when Green Bay cut me. It took me a couple years to regain it." (Timmy often said that he evaluated players based on how they walked.)

Of his entertainment career, he told Hugh Brown that "I try to lead a normal way of life even in the difficult atmosphere of the entertainment world. I return to the hotel after each show. If a patron asks me to have a drink with him, it's either a Coke or a sherry on the rocks, which I nurse for hours." He added, "It's taken three tough years, but I feel I'm on my way to becoming a pro. I'm no Sinatra or Chubby Checker, and nobody has offered me seventeen-five for a week at Vegas, but I think I'm moving up." The next month, he told an Inquirer reporter that "I've got to make it fast in singing," again saying that his small size would lead to a short time on the gridiron.

As an entertainer, Timmy was once described by Elgart as a combination of Sammy Davis Jr. and, of course, James Brown. Timmy recalled playing around 20 dates a year with a set that lasted around 30 minutes and included six or seven songs, both ones Timmy had recorded and covers including Elvis' "(Let Me Be Your) Teddy Bear," which he had performed since his college days. Another song that Timmy covered was "1-2-3," another Madara and White composition in collaboration with its singer, Dovells alumnus Len Barry. The song reached No. 2 on the Billboard chart in 1965. Timmy counted Barry as a good friend. The Dovells had followed up the 1961 "Bristol Stomp" with another Cameo/Parkway hit, "You Can't Sit Down," in 1963. "He had a unique voice for a white guy. He was very soulful. He had the looks like a movie guy," Timmy recalled of Barry.

In addition to the Latin Casino – perhaps best remembered today as where Jackie Wilson collapsed on stage from a massive heart attack in 1975 – Timmy would perform at clubs and venues such as Palisades Park across the Hudson from New York City (immortalized by Freddy "Boom Boom" Cannon's hit, which was written by "Dating Game" creator Chuck Barris), Sciolla's Supper Club in Philadelphia, the Steel Pier and the Hialeah Club in Atlantic City, and Wildwood's Rainbow Club, which was also known as "Little Las Vegas" or the "Las Vegas of the East." Often, Timmy would serve as the warmup act to performers such as Sam Cooke. "One year, I did the Palisades Park. I was second to Sam Cooke, Sam Cooke was the main. I did three numbers there at the Palisades Park show. I think he only did five." At the Rainbow, Timmy once appeared on the same bill as Link Wray and His Ray Men. Wray was one of the best instrumental guitarists of the rock era, best known for the instrumental singles "Rumble" and "Rawhide." At times, Timmy would headline. He knew that a good portion of his audience was attracted by the novelty of seeing a football star on stage. "I can pack a place being Timmy Brown, the football player, more than I could being Timmy Brown, the singer. They come because of Timmy Brown, the football player, to see for themselves.... Of course, I always like the challenge," he said of his performances.

Although reviews of his shows are rare, Gil Faggen, a writer for Billboard, did write about one at the Steel Pier, "The Showplace of the Nation," in the July 4, 1964, issue of the recording industry weekly. On June 26 and 27, Timmy opened for the comedian Totie Fields. Faggen wrote, "On stage Brown is every bit the pro he is on the gridiron. He has a friendly smile and exudes boyish charm that immediately disarms the audience." Faggen enthusiastically described how Timmy, wearing a tuxedo, opened with a nine-piece orchestra and a cover of Ray Charles' "What'd I Say." He went on to perform the Beatles' "Do You Want to Know a Secret" and a version of Woody Guthrie's "This Land Is Your Land" while the audience clapped and sang along.

The highlight, Faggen wrote, was "I Got a Secret," beginning with Timmy "in a crouching stance as he puts his powerful body into the driving beat. The audience swung with him all the way." In his conclusion, he wrote, "Tim is as fervently interested in working hard to make it big in the record field as he has for the past six years on the football field. Strikingly handsome, young (27), and a football hero to boot, are several important reasons – coupled with genuine vocal and performance talent – why Timmy Brown could very well be a new idol of the younger set in the world of records and nightclubs." But "could very well" never really happened.

Back on that football field, Timmy was a 1964 starter – an Inquirer story that year noted that "every team in pro football" had made offers to the Eagles to get him – but he was slowed by tendonitis in the first four games, although against the Giants on Sept. 14 he carried 17 times, caught two passes, returned two punts and two kickoffs, and blocked. On Oct. 4 he gained 116 yards rushing and caught two scoring passes, one for 87 yards, in a 21-7 win over the Steelers. "Part of my trouble was dehydration," he said of his slow start. "I'm taking medication. I think it was emotional." According to the New York Times, Timmy said that emotion stemmed from worry that Kuharich did not like him. "When I didn't play much the first few games," he said, "I felt maybe I wasn't needed."

Following a 35-20 loss against Washington on Oct. 11 in which he gained only four yards on three carries, Timmy underwent surgery on a bruised and hemorrhaging right thigh muscle and was to be out for at least three weeks. The team physician, James E. Nixon, said the surgery was "minor and corrective." This was added bad news for Kuharich, who had also found himself without injured star tight end Retzlaff (separated rib cartilage) and defensive halfback Glenn Glass for the Oct. 18 game with the Giants. Veteran Ollie Matson took Timmy's place, with the 34-year-old making his first start since 1959. The Eagles pulled out a 23-17 win, but the team had been so pressed for players that the third-string quarterback had been working out as a running back.

While Timmy was facing problems on the field, he also was trying to keep his career as a recording artist afloat. Ember Records worked with CBS to get Timmy an Oct. 26, 1964, appearance on the popular game show "I've Got a Secret," in which a panel of celebrities tried to guess something about a guest, such as a little-known fact. The show was hosted for many years by Garry Moore, who also had a CBS variety program that brought Carol Burnett to stardom, but Moore had retired from television a month earlier and Steve Allen had taken over. Guests on "Secret" over the years included chess champion Bobby Fischer before he became internationally known and Pete Best, the Beatles' drummer before Ringo Starr. There is no recording of the show on which

Timmy appeared, but an online guide to the program created by "Secret" enthusiast Richard Carson identifies the panel for that show as regulars Betsy Palmer, Bess Myerson, Bill Cullen, and Henry Morgan. The episode was sponsored by Dream Whip. Timmy's "secret" was that he was an NFL star who was "making a phonograph album." Adding to the secret was that his single "I Got a Secret" aligned with the show's name.

After the panel guessed Tim's secret, Tim performed the song. After his performance, Allen, a former "Tonight Show" host, gave the panelists homework. They were encouraged to pen their own songs, based on the name of the show, for performance on the Dec. 7, 1964, episode. The online guide notes: "Betsy, Bess, and Bill sing their own songs with vocal accompaniment. [Guest Robert Merrill, a Metropolitan Opera star,] sings Henry's song accompanied by the Canterbury Choral Society directed by Charles Dobsley Walker." Allen alluded to Timmy and the Oct. 26 broadcast as he set up the activity, but Timmy did not appear on the program. This episode was posted to YouTube.

Also on the episode with Timmy was the actor Ray Walston, who had developed a jack-o'-lantern that lit up based on the strength of audience applause. At the time, Walston was being seen every week on CBS as the alien visitor known as "Uncle Martin" in the high-rated sitcom "My Favorite Martian." Walston, later known for playing Harry Bone on the CBS drama "Picket Fences," was a character actor who appeared in films including "The Sting" and "Fast Times at Ridgemont High." Timmy had mixed memories of his appearance on the program, which coincided with an Eagles game against New York. "I had been booked a couple months ahead and I got a hamstring pull, so I couldn't play in the game. So I went up with the team and I went to the studio and did the show with Steve Allen. I kind of just had to stand there with a cane because I couldn't move around. I like to move around and entertain; give them a little bit more than just my voice. I never worried about my voice and I'm on key all the time, but I just never had the greatest voice."

The song "I Got a Secret" was one of the earliest written by Leon

Huff, who with Kenny Gamble went on to write and produce "Sound of Philadelphia" hits such as Jerry Butler's "Only the Strong Survive," the Intruders' "Cowboys to Girls," the Soul Survivors' "Expressway to Your Heart," the Three Degrees' "When Will I See You Again," Billy Paul's "Me and Mrs. Jones," and an extraordinary string of hits by the O'Jays ("Backstabbers," "Love Train," "For the Love of Money," "I Love Music," and "Useta Be My Girl") and Harold Melvin and the Blue Notes ("If You Don't Know Me by Now," "The Love I Lost," and "Wake Up Everybody"). "I Got a Secret" is Timmy's best single, with the feel of an early Motown or Cameo/Parkway 45. Timmy's vocals are strong and the backup band was tight.

Timmy also performed the song on "American Bandstand" in 1964 and at shows that Dick Clark would emcee at the Steel Pier and Starlight Ballroom in Atlantic City. Timmy recalled Clark as a good man with whom he had lunch several times. He appreciated the exposure he and the song got from Clark: "They gave me a great buildup. Of course, I got a great big hand because of the football, too. So I know that football was giving me [fame] around Philadelphia. I always wore either a tux or suit. So it was a different look to the people than on the football field with a helmet. They were always curious about what you look like, because they can't tell." Timmy also sang in the mid-1960s on "The Mike Douglas Show," "The Merv Griffin Show," "The Joey Bishop Show," and others.

But the height of the British Invasion wasn't the right time for him, and "I Got a Secret" would be Timmy's last real chance for fame as a singer. A complete chronology of his recording career cannot be determined, but five 45 singles were released under the name of Timmy Brown by several labels. "Silly Rumors"/"I Got Nothin' But Time" was released by Imperial as catalog number 5898 in 1962. "Gabba Gabba"/"I'm Gonna Prove Myself" was released in 1962 on Marashel Records (M-1002-A). Virtually nothing is known about Marashel or "Gabba Gabba" other than that it was written by Frank Brunson, a member of a funk band, People's Choice. Timmy's two Mercury singles were

"Do the Crossfire"/"Love, Love, Love" (72175) in 1963 and "Runnin' Late"/"If I Loved You" (72226) in January 1964. Timmy recalled "Runnin' Late" as an intentional allusion to his skill as a running back with the Eagles; "If I Loved You" was the Rodgers and Hammerstein standard from "Carousel."

"I Got a Secret (Gonna Keep It to Myself)"/ "Baby It's OK," Timmy's last known single, was released in 1964 as Ember catalog number 1106. Timmy later in life thought that Ember had been a subsidiary of Cameo/Parkway, but it actually was associated with Herald Records, a Black-artist-oriented label established in 1950 by Fred Mendelsohn, who had been associated with the Savoy label previously. The physical records were pressed by Al Silver, who eventually gained control of Ember and Herald. Ember's biggest hit was "Get a Job" by the Silhouettes in 1958. Silver's finances collapsed amid the payola investigations of 1959 to 1962, according to a web page in a list of celebrity biographies created by Dik de Heer. According to it, Ember stayed in business for two more years and then was liquidated. Timmy's record thus was among the last Ember produced. By then, the days when it had artists like the Five Satins ("In the Still of the Night") and the Zodiacs ("Stay") were long behind it.

In 2021, "Silly Rumors" and "If I Loved You" were the only songs of Timmy's that could be found on CD or through streaming services. Several of the 45s were available on collectable-records sites and had a price of about $40 each.

Timmy did not make any royalties off his records. "I don't know if they even got their money back," he said. "It didn't cost that much for them to do, really. They knew the studios and they knew the people." While none of his records made the Billboard Hot 100, several had success in the Philadelphia area. "Runnin' Late" peaked at No. 70 on WIBG's Top 99 Records of the Week on Feb. 10, 1964. "I Got a Secret" hit No. 44 on WIBG on July 13 of that year.

As 1964 ground on, Timmy was still in and out of action on the field. He had returned to play against Los Angeles on Nov. 8 but was hit again, slightly below and to the side of the fiberglass that was protection from the previous injury. That kept him out of the Nov. 15 game with Dallas, which the Eagles won by 17-14. But he was ready to come back for the Nov. 29 game against the Browns. Even though he had been effective only on returns in recent weeks, Inquirer reporter Good believed that Timmy would give the team an offense spark that had been missing.

For the season, Timmy scored 10 TDs, five running and five receiving. He gained 356 yards running, 244 yards as a receiver, and 96 as a punt returner. One of the receptions was for an 87-yard TD. "I want to play on this team," he said of the Eagles. "I've got four or five good years left and I hope they're in Philly." The Eagles won six games in the 1964 season, which was progress enough for Wolman, who gave Kuharich an unprecedented 15-year contract at $50,000 a year. "He has this team going in the right direction," Wolman said. Timmy believed that Rozelle was behind this deal as well – one that would not work out well for him.

CHAPTER SIX

Fly, Timmy, Fly

By early 1965, Timmy had settled into life on the East Coast. Hometown friend George Walker, who said he called Timmy every Monday at the Grices', drove to Philadelphia to see him and was told by Timmy, "We are going to go to New York City." This was Walker's first visit to Manhattan, and Timmy had to help him figure out how much to pay the cabbies. Timmy knew their hotel's manager and got a free suite. Frank Gifford came by for a visit, and Timmy and George went to the Copacabana, where the Supremes were opening. The show was sold out, Timmy said, but Ross told the club manager they weren't going on unless Timmy and his friend got a table up front. Then, Walker said, they went to Arthur, a club run by Sybil Christopher, former wife of Richard Burton. Walker got sick, but they still went backstage, where they met actors Martha Raye and Hugh O'Brien as well as Soraya Esfandiary-Bakhtiary, divorced wife of Mohammed Reza Pahlavi, the shah of Iran. Timmy seemed to be a successful figure in the world of entertainment.

But a story that year in the Philadelphia Daily News noted that Timmy's singing career had gone flat, rolled over by the new British sound. Timmy's singles failed to generate a national audience and had only middling regional success, so in succession his record labels dropped him. Also, no album ever appeared, despite Timmy's announcement of a "phonograph album" on his "I've Got a Secret" appearance. In a 1965 article, Timmy noted that "you don't make any money on records, just the night club dates that result from the records. The trouble is, there are just too many people to pay when you make a record." Timmy had not been alone in wanting to star as a singer in addition to having a football career. Around the same time, Los Angeles tackle Roosevelt Grier was trying to make it as a folk singer and guitarist, appearing on music shows like ABC's "Shindig." Grier had been drafted by the Giants in 1955 from Pennsylvania State University and was traded to the Rams in 1963; he finished his career with them in 1966. The two-time, 285-pound Pro Bowl tackle recorded a number of songs for various labels in the 1960s, but none of his records found national success, although "People Make the World" was a regional hit in 1968.

In a 1965 article, Timmy recalled with amusement how dangerous it was to be a rival of Grier's both on the field and in the studio. "He liked to kill me one day when he was with the Giants. He'd come at me when I was blocking for a punt and run over me. I was in the slot. He did it a couple times, and each time he'd say, 'How's the record going?' I'd be on my pants five yards back, and I began burning. After a couple of doses of that, I decided to surprise him, and meet him low at the line of scrimmage instead of sitting back and waiting for him. The next time we punted, I charged at him, and he let go with a forearm up under my chest. He knocked me skidding back on my pants and I surrendered. I said, 'C'mon now, Rosey, I haven't had any records out for a while now.'"

Grier also had a career in television and film that may be most remembered for appearing with the Oscar-winning actor Ray Milland in 1972's "The Thing With Two Heads," a laughable "horror" film known for its advertising tagline: "They transplanted a WHITE BIGOT'S HEAD onto a SOUL BROTHER'S BODY!" But Grier's most prominent role off the field may have been on June 5, 1968. He had been asked by Sen. Robert F. Kennedy to serve as a bodyguard for Kennedy's wife, Ethel, and thus was in position to take the gun away from Kennedy's assassin, Sirhan B. Sirhan, at the Ambassador Hotel in Los Angeles following Kennedy's victory speech in the California Democratic presidential primary.

By 1965, Timmy had despaired of making it as a singer, saying to Daily News reporter Bill Shefski, "I think I've wasted four years there.... I haven't worked at it." He noted that he didn't have a recording contract after working with different labels. Shefski wrote that Brown's songs had failed "mainly because his discs couldn't find any daylight in an opposing line consisting of the Beatles, the Beach Boys, et al." But Timmy was again revising his dreams, saying, "I plan to work at acting, though." He said he would play whatever part was offered him "unless they want me to play a runaway slave or something like that."

While screen stardom is a dream Timmy shared with many, it is attained by few, and it was especially elusive for minorities trying to break into the business prior to the 1970s. Opportunities for African Americans were as limited in reel life as they were in real life. In the 1940s and '50s, when Timmy was growing up, there were almost no positive African American role models in Hollywood productions. Most of the roles offered to Black actors were based on insulting stereotypes and did not portray the reality of African American life. In the late 1950s, actors like Sidney Poitier began to make breakthroughs, but it was not until 1966 that an African American was given a co-starring role in a television series, when Bill Cosby was paired with Robert Culp in NBC's "I Spy." And it was not until the early 1970s, with series like "Good Times" and "The Jeffersons," that African Americans began to be more widely seen in prominent roles on TV. Poitier was the first African American actor to win a competitive Oscar, for "Lilies of the Field" in 1963, but it would be 33 years before a Black actor would again be awarded an Oscar, when Denzel Washington won as best supporting actor for "Glory." It was against this challenging backdrop that Timmy decided to become an actor.

Being a sports star further complicated things, although a number of professional football players essayed acting careers. Most notable are Alex Karras ("Blazing Saddles" and "Victor/Victoria" along with the television sitcom "Webster"), Fred Dryer ("Hunter"), and, of course, Jim Brown ("100 Rifles," "The Dirty Dozen," "Ice Station Zebra"). But none of those athlete actors seemed to work as hard to hone his craft as Timmy.

Soon after Timmy began voice lessons in New York City, he decided to also attend acting school. He selected the prestigious HB Studio, founded by Herbert Berghof, and attended from 1962 to 1966. An incomplete alumni list for the studio reads like a Who's Who of Hollywood from as far back as 1948, when the school opened, with Oscar winners Anne Bancroft, Robert DeNiro, Faye Dunaway, Whoopi Goldberg, Jessica Lange, Jack Lemmon, Liza Minnelli, Al Pacino, Jason Robards Jr., and Barbra Streisand among them. Timmy attended each Monday, paying tuition of $150 a week. During the football season, Timmy would often take the train from Philadelphia to New York on Sunday evening, and attend singing lessons on Monday morning and acting lessons in the afternoon. He would return by train either Monday evening or Tuesday morning to be on time for practice. The singing lessons lasted an hour, but often the acting lessons would take all afternoon. Then, during the week, Timmy would practice both singing and voice techniques and work on different scenes.

He kept meticulous notes during his classes, often on index cards that he would use to practice. These notecards, which Timmy retained for life, include notes on subjects like "Building a Character," "Cold Reading," "Psychophysical Action," "Improvisation," and "Loosening-up Activities," and exercises such as "Will and Memory."

By 1965, Jim Brown had made his debut in Hollywood, appearing in the movie "Rio Conchos" with Richard Boone and Anthony Franciosa. "I want to start out in a small part, get some experience," Timmy, always his fan and rival, told the Philadelphia Daily News. "Then if there's something there, I'll take lessons during the season at night when I have the time." He began his acting career in the summer of 1965 at the Bucks County Playhouse in the artists' colony of New Hope, an hour northeast of Philadelphia and within an easy drive of New York City. He appeared with Dodie Goodman and Eddie Bracken, and played five roles in a summer stock version of "A Thurber Carnival." "I've always wanted to be an actor and if I could get started this summer and see how I handle it, who knows?" he said.

"A Thurber Carnival" ran from June 28 through July 10 at the playhouse, which at that time was a nationally prominent regional theater. The play is a revue written by Thurber from his stories and cartoons in the New Yorker and elsewhere. It had premiered in Greenwich Village in 1960 with stars including Tom Ewell and Peggy Cass, and was directed by Burgess Meredith. Also in that cast was Peter Turgeon, who directed the production in Bucks County.

A playhouse advertisement for "A Thurber Carnival" promised "a glorious world of meaningful nonsense – makes you laugh out loud." Both Playbill and the advertisement listed Bracken and Goodman as co-stars, and added "Guest Star: Timmy Brown." This was clearly a way to promote to the Philadelphia market that the Eagles football star would be in the cast. Most of the actors played multiple roles, and Timmy was given the opportunity to stretch by portraying a wolf, a policeman, an airplane pilot, and the narrator of one act. One role drew curiosity: He played a Confederate general, which the reviewer called "not the most natural part for a Negro to play."

"A Thurber Carnival" let Timmy work with some seasoned theater veterans. Bracken, a child actor in the "Our Gang" series, had been in a number of movies and Broadway productions. Goodman was a frequent guest on the television talk show circuit in addition to her Broadway roles. Also in the cast was Charles Braswell, a character actor in a number of television shows and a star on Broadway who had played many of Timmy's roles in "A Thurber Carnival" in New York. And there was a young David Doyle, later to become famous as Bosley in the initial version of "Charlie's Angels" in the 1970s. In an article by Frank Bilovsky of the Philadelphia Evening Bulletin, published soon after the play's run, Timmy recalled, "The whole crew is great. Look at David Doyle. He's the funniest man in the world. He could be a great comedian, but he doesn't want it. He'd rather act. It's like in football. I've got my own style of running. These guys have their own style of acting. They really get into the characters."

The play was a great learning experience for Timmy. "I never realized what an actor's life is like," he told Bilovsky in the June 29 article. "We put in eight-hour days, just like regular working guys." Like most actors, he thought he wasn't being used enough: "I have no butterflies tonight, but maybe that's because I have so few lines. If I had as much to do as Eddie Bracken and Dodie Goodman, I'd probably really be sweating. You know, it's strange. I remember watching Eddie Bracken when I was a kid. Now I'm working with him." But Timmy could also serve as his own harshest critic. "I find myself unable to let loose, whether I'm singing or acting. At home, I'm OK. I entertain very easily at home. The same thing when I'm with the team. The guys know what to expect of me. But when I get out there, I fight myself. I fight myself more than anyone could. That's my main trouble." Bilovsky closed his story by noting that Timmy had asked him to review the performance. Using the Thurber vernacular, he wrote: "For a rookie, Tim Brown done splendid."

But Timmy's path was not going to lead to the stage. He recalled appearing in summer stock productions for years, but few records remain other than a listing in his resume with a talent agency for an appearance at the Zephyr Theatre in Los Angeles in "You Can't Take It With You." It would have been difficult for Timmy to do much more on the stage because of demands on his time. He recalled, "They would rehearse for three weeks and then the play would run for about five weeks. I could not put that on because I have other stuff coming up. You miss a lot of things that way. That's the thing about acting. You have to pass on some things that you wish you would have been free to do because it's better than what you were working on."

So, in the mid-1960s, Timmy got the itch for Hollywood. But he would need a good agent, and he didn't know how to find one. After an Eagles game, though, his friendship with Gifford paid off. Often, when Timmy would go to New York for business or for acting or singing lessons, he would meet Gifford and his then-wife, Maxine, for dinner. At one of these dinners, Gifford indicated that Burt Lancaster wanted to meet him. Lancaster was at the peak of his career and earlier had been the star of "Jim Thorpe – All-American," a film that had made a great impression on Timmy when he was living at the Home. "He was a real hero of mine," said Timmy. Lancaster arrived at their table and said, "I just wanted to come over and say hello. I watched the [Eagles] game. You had a hell of a game today. I know your career." The conversation was pleasant, and Timmy told Lancaster that he wanted to get into acting. "He got me an agent out in Hollywood," said Timmy.

In July 1965, in addition to acting in New Hope, Timmy signed up for another year with the Eagles. Showing the wonders of 1960s technology, this season was the first in which the Eagles had a videotape recorder in the locker room so they could instantly play back the entire game. The season began with Kuharich trying to make Timmy a flanker back during training camp in what he called "the great experiment." The coach's stated motivation was that he was short of flankers for an exhibition game. Timmy made clear that he had no interest in playing the position, although he said he would do so wholeheartedly if that was what the team wanted. After the one exhibition game, the coach said Timmy would "stay at running back." Timmy said he wasn't being obstinate – "at flanker I feel like I'm on vacation," he said. "There isn't enough action. I have to feel sore, all beat up, or I don't feel I contributed anything." He said he viewed Kuharich's plan as "a compliment. He has faith, confidence in me to handle a position where we need help." Still, it wasn't for him – "I want the yardage. I've got to outgain that other guy named Brown. I can't do it as a flanker." The "great experiment" had an unsuccessful outcome, a 37-0 loss against Washington. In his first preseason game back at halfback, against the Lions, he gained 92 yards in nine carries and caught three passes for 33 yards. Of the ground yardage, 46 was gained in setting up a field goal – and had it not been for Detroit's Wayne Rasmussen, Timmy might have gone all the way. All Kuharich could manage to say was, "I thought he played fairly well today."

Before the season began, Timmy felt good about his recovery from the previous year's hemorrhaging thigh, and in the second game, a 16-14 home loss to the Giants on Sept. 26, he caught eight passes for 103 yards. The New York Times' William N. Wallace said it was a wonder, given Timmy's performance, that the Giants were able to win. Wallace, who seemed to have no love for Timmy as an entertainer – he mentioned his "phonograph records that some people actually buy" – did go into depth on how the Eagles used Timmy:

"Using a flood formation esoterically called 'trips right or left,' the Eagles isolate Brown against the weak-side linebacker. That is pro football's classic mismatch, the halfback versus the linebacker in a passing situation. There are four pass receivers set on or near the line of scrimmage and when the ball is snapped they go. Three are on the right or strong side – namely Pete Retzlaff, the tight end; Earl Gros, the fullback, and Ron Goodwin, the flanker. In covering these three potential receivers, the defensive secondary is notably burdened.

"On the weak side, Ray Poage, the split end, is covered by Dick Lynch, the Giant cornerback. When Brown comes out of the backfield, the only one left to cover him is [Jim] Carroll, the weak-side linebacker. Once past the line of scrimmage, Timmy has an option of continuing to his right – the 'inside' – or breaking his pass pattern to the outside. Carroll's choices are to knock Brown down, a risky business, or to cover him in either direction. The linebacker who hesitates is lost."

The following week, the ghost of Lombardi came back to haunt Timmy, who dropped a punt return, setting up a three minute, 41-second run in which the Cleveland Browns scored three touchdowns, winning by 35-17. (Jim Brown also fumbled during this game.) Kuharich was not in the least critical of Timmy, but the loss stung. In the following weeks Timmy made amends, scoring once in a win against the Cowboys on Oct. 10, and twice on Oct. 17 against the host Giants in a losing cause.

However, Timmy's right thigh was bothering him again as the Eagles prepared for their Halloween game against Washington. The previous week, against the Steelers (a 20-14 Eagles loss), he had been tackled by Willie Daniel in the second quarter and had to wear his thigh guard for the rest of the game. A doctor drained 300 ccs of blood from Timmy's thigh after the game and said, "Timmy has good flexion in his leg and very slight swelling.... The report is encouraging, let's put it that way." Even so, Timmy was listed as doubtful for the Washington game. "Some people have been saying I'm brittle," Timmy said. "That's not true. Nothing ever happened to me until last year." Timmy did play in the Washington game and carried the ball 12 times, but was thrown to only once. Kuharich said he was using Timmy as a decoy; Washington coach Bill McPeak crowed about how the team had neutralized Timmy, whom they feared more than Retzlaff. Whatever really happened, a toll was taken. In 2010, Timmy remembered the train ride back to Philadelphia: "I couldn't even see my knee. And the doc would pop needles here, one there, one there, and the blood would squirt out every time he hit one. Johnny Sample got me on a sweep coming around and cutting in, and he got me down there and the knee just went.... It was like that for two weeks. I thought it would never go down." On the morning after the game, "I woke up and looked at it and it was like twice the size. I got out of bed and it was very painful to boot. I got dressed, I don't know how, putting one foot in at a time."

The following week, though, Timmy shone again as the dueling Browns faced each other on the Municipal Stadium field in Cleveland. Jim Brown, leading the NFL in ground gains, rushed for 131 of his team's 187 yards and scored three times. Timmy, however, rushed for 186 yards, his best single-game performance yet and only one yard short of the opponents' entire ground game, and also scored a touchdown. "He did a fine job," Jim Brown said. "He's a fine football player and a nice guy." Timmy responded, "Jim had a good day. But Jim has a fair day every day. We take turns going over and congratulating each other.... Jim wants me to have a good day, but not that good that we win." Jim Brown got his wish, as the Eagles came up short, 38-34. In 2010, Timmy remembered this as a game that stood out because he wasn't given the ball in the second half. His questioner asked him, "The one where you had like 185 yards?" Timmy responded, "186, yeah. Don't take a yard away from me."

During the 1965 season (in which the Eagles had a winning 9-5 record, seeming to back up Wolman's decision to reward Kuharich), Timmy played more minutes than any other offensive back, 369½. He gained 2,425 yards – 841 rushing, 487 receiving, 945 on kickoff returns and 152 on punt returns. He led the league in average yards per rush (5.4) and caught more passes that season than any other player. For the third and final time he was named to the Pro Bowl squad, along with Eagles quarterback Snead and their teammates Retzlaff, Bob Brown, Ringo, Baughan, and Irv Cross. (Jim Brown was one of eight players from Cleveland at the game, the last time the two Browns would play in the same pro football game; both played on the Eastern Conference squad.) After the Pro Bowl, Timmy had surgery to repair a ruptured tendon in his right thumb, hurt during the season-ending game with the Lions. A tendon from Timmy's right wrist was used and the cast was to stay on for about a month.

Timmy kept making connections outside of football. He was co-chairman of the 1966 Christmas Seals campaign in Philadelphia and Montgomery Counties along with Elkins Wetherill, president of the local stock exchange and a scion of two of the city's most prominent families. Timmy also became a popular choice for companies seeking celebrity endorsements for advertising. In January he signed an agreement with the Jantzen clothing firm to promote its sweaters, sportswear, and swimwear. His ads were to debut in August. Jantzen had long used celebrity endorsements, including such stars as James Garner and Loretta Young. The Oregon-based company also was known for striking deals with studios to make sure actors wore Jantzen sportswear in their movies, notably Elizabeth Taylor in "A Place in the Sun," Elvis Presley in "Blue Hawaii," and Annette Funicello in "Beach Party." (Jantzen figured prominently in a 2010 episode of AMC's "Mad Men.")

Timmy appeared in ads with Don Meredith, the Dallas Cowboys star and future cohost of "Monday Night Football," and National Hockey League legend Bobby Hull. In addition to the extra money and exposure the athletes got, Jantzen would fly them to exotic locations. Tim recalled, "Sweaters were usually in Los Angeles. Swimwear was usually shot in some place like Hawaii, Rio de Janeiro, or Mexico." Locations in Spain and Puerto Rico were also used. The campaign also allowed Timmy to make friends with Hull and the other athletes.

Around this time, Jantzen began an ad campaign that pitched "Sportswear for Young Sportsmen." The campaign, focused on magazine ads, featured popular athletes prominently dressed in Jantzen sportswear or swimwear. The Jantzen models made up a group known as the "International Sports Club," whose "regulars" also included Celtics great Bob Cousy, Gifford, Hornung, NBA legend Jerry West, golfer Dave Marr, and surfer John Severson. It was noted that Timmy was the second bachelor to become part of the group, after Hornung. Timmy said he got the job because "it was between Jim Brown and I, and Frank and a couple of the guys knew me pretty well and we were a lot of fun. Jim was a little more serious. Sometimes he wore a little chip on his shoulder."

One of the ads shows him; West, of the Los Angeles Lakers; and Hornung all reading books while dressed in brown Jantzen sweaters. The text reads: "This is study hall, and the subject is 'Double Lok' Jantzen sweaters. How come Paul has his little black book, Jerry his hero story, Timmy his book of prophecy? They know all about Jantzen sweaters.

They know that these are new double-knits with a very springy feel – an exceptionally soft blend of three-fourths wool, one-fourth mohair that we call 'Double Lok.' Superb hand. Very rich look. Paul Hornung and Timmy Brown have on the cardigans, available in char burgundy, Lovat blue, char navy, butterscotch heather, bronze heather, about $20. Jerry West wears the V-neck pullover, which comes in colors listed above plus four more, about $17. Seek these sweaters at stores oriented to sportsmen."

The "club" members would go to "Palma de Mallorca, Spain, Rio de Janeiro; you name it, we went. And we were always treated really great wherever we went. We were celebrities to the people, and we would be there a week or two sometimes," Timmy said in 2010. They would "be modeling swimsuit wear one place and another time winter stuff, winter sweaters. We were treated like heroes everywhere we went. They built us up, I guess, in the papers before we would get there – you know, America's sports guys."

Of a trip to Mallorca, Timmy later said, "I was half-bombed. I'm over there talking to some table with a couple of girls; I hear my name, and I said, 'What was that?' And here comes Giff and Jerry, and they said, 'They are calling you on stage, man.' I said, 'I can't go up there. I might not even make it.' I go up and it's just a little stage to work with, where I like to move around a little bit. But I didn't worry about that. I did a couple of Ray Charles songs. I had to go with the band, they didn't speak English. I had somebody tell them, do they know this song and do they know that? But they knew American songs." His Jantzen gig lasted four or five years, and it "paid good."

In addition to Jantzen, Tim was prominently featured in magazine advertisements with another men's clothing company, Botany "500." The brand, manufactured by H. Daroff & Sons in Philadelphia, also had a tradition of celebrity endorsements and providing suits to actors for on-screen appearances. The credits for "The Dick Van Dyke Show" indicate that the actors' suits were provided by Botany "500." Likewise, Botany supplied Cary Grant's suits in the Alfred Hitchcock classic "North by Northwest." Botany featured stars like Van Dyke in a series of full-page magazine and newspaper ads with headlines like "Why Dick Van Dyke Wears Botany '500' Clothes to Work." Botany hired Timmy for a similar campaign, featuring tag lines like, "The Personal Touch to Suit Your Personal Taste. Timmy Brown Picks Botany '500.'"

Over the years, Timmy also appeared in advertisements in print, on television, or on radio at various times for Century 21 real estate; Buick and Ford automobiles; Budweiser, Miller High Life, and Coors beer; Pepsi and Shasta soft drinks; Dawn soap; the Bank of Detroit; McDonald's and Weinerschnitzel restaurants; Union 76 gasoline; and Freedent gum. Timmy was selective with the products he agreed to endorse, something he regretted later. "You know, I turned down some dumb stuff. I turned down a shaving endorsement because I used Magic Shave," a line from L'Oreal aimed at Black men with the intent of reducing skin inflammation and irritation. "I said, 'I can't do that because I don't use a razor,' and they said, 'No one will know.' I said, 'Well, the people that know me will know.' I was just being honest. I didn't know that it didn't matter and it was a commercial and all, and that would have been a big one. I should not have turned that down, but I just didn't feel I was being honest. I was naive enough to think that people who knew me would say, 'He never used that stuff.'... It cost me a lot of money and a lot of things, commercial-wise," he said in 2009. In a 2010 interview, he added, "I passed up big bucks. More than I probably would have made playing football."

In spring 1966, the AFL, barely seven years old, was for the first time looking to lure talent away from the dominant NFL – and while the emphasis was on quarterbacks, with seven of them jumping leagues, Timmy also was one of their targets. He said in May that he had gotten "lucrative offers" from two AFL clubs. Timmy, however, had already agreed on a new contract with the Eagles for more money. He said it was "one of the few times I've been completely satisfied." Irv Cross, described as the club's "unhappy defensive ace" and seeking a trade, also said he had an AFL feeler. Cross told Kuharich immediately that he had been approached; Timmy waited a few days. Inquirer sportswriter Good wrote, "Brown, tied up with singing engagements and drama lessons, didn't see any need for haste in notifying his boss since he had actually come to terms with Kuharich several weeks ago and was in no position to do any serious talking with the AFL." Still, Timmy said at the time that the AFL teams "talked of some vague three-year plan that was quite lucrative ... but I told them I was an NFL man and wasn't interested." He said the AFL had hoped he would play out his option with the Eagles and become a free agent, one of the tactics the smaller league was using. Timmy, who was preparing to go to Rio on a Jantzen gig, said, "Maybe it's pride or something, but I'd prefer to stay where I am." Sportswriter Shefski noted that "essential Eagles are being treated as such." Cross was not considered essential.

While neither Timmy nor Cross said at the time who had approached them, the Inquirer said one of the teams was the new Miami Dolphins. In 2010, Timmy said he had been contacted by the sitcom star Danny Thomas, then a co-owner of the Dolphins. "They sent me, Mike Ditka and John Brodie a check for $50,000.... They said you can keep this whether or not you accept ... we want to get you with the Miami Dolphins. Well, Ditka and Brodie, they kept it and still didn't go. But I couldn't do that, though. I was making $16,000 and the Eagles wanted to take that up to $18,000 and I had been All-Pro, broke the total yardage record in the NFL." Timmy eventually signed for $27,000, "but I would have gotten $50,000 if I had went with the Giants. They didn't tell me that the Giants had offered nine players for me." (A 1969 column in the Baltimore Evening Sun said Timmy was told by three Giants coaches that nine players, not six, had been offered.)

Cross and Timmy had different takes on the AFL's motivation. "There's a personnel problem in pro football today, especially with the Vietnam situation," Cross said. "There's a shortage of top-notch players and the problem can only get worse." Timmy just said he took the effort as "a threat to scare the NFL." In June, the NFL and AFL announced their merger, which had been under discussion for two months. This spring also was the end of Timmy's service in the Army Reserve; he received an Honorable Discharge on May 30.

Summer 1966 brought reports in the Inquirer that Timmy was at least peripherally involved in an alleged attempt to bribe a jury that convicted a man of burglary. Randolph Holmes was a "West Philadelphia real estate man" who had worked as a $125-a-week public relations man for Milton Shapp, Democratic candidate for Pennsylvania governor. Holmes, who was Black, told the newspaper that he acted as Shapp's liaison with Black ministers and athletes including Timmy and Wilt Chamberlain, as well as Sammy Davis Jr. Timmy and Chamberlain were allegedly paid undisclosed amounts for endorsing Shapp that were not reported by Shapp. Holmes was charged with several counts of bribery and other charges by then-Philadelphia District Attorney Arlen Specter, later the longtime senator from Pennsylvania. Shapp had run an outsider campaign and took the 1966 Democratic nomination away from the endorsed candidate, State Sen. Robert P. Casey.

Shapp had an enemy in Inquirer owner Walter H. Annenberg, who used the newspaper to try to destroy Shapp's political career, an action that contributed to Shapp's loss to Republican Raymond P. Shafer in the general election. Famously, a reporter for the newspaper once asked Shapp, "Have you ever been in a mental institution?" Shapp replied, "Well, no, I haven't." The next day's paper reported, "Shapp denies being in a mental institution." "That's the sort of journalism that was practiced" at the Inquirer before it was purchased by Knight Newspapers Inc. in 1969, according to retired deputy editor Gene C. Foreman, a national authority on media ethics.

According to an article in Philadelphia Magazine, Annenberg was friends with Stuart T. Saunders, president of the Pennsylvania Railroad, which had been trying to save itself through a merger with the New York

Central. Annenberg also was a major stockholder in the Pennsy. Shapp, a millionaire from the early days of cable television, invested himself heavily in the effort to stop the merger. While Shapp was partly looking for an issue to make a name for himself in politics, he did believe the merger would be a financial disaster. "Shapp attacked the Pennsylvania Railroad," Annenberg said, "and Saunders is a personal friend of mine." Saunders moved easily in Philadelphia social circles and smoothed the way for their greater acceptance of Annenberg, whose father, Moses, had owned the horse-racing wire and had gone to prison for tax evasion. Timmy testified in Dauphin County Court in Harrisburg that he was paid $450 by Holmes to pose with Shapp in a campaign photo with Chamberlain and Olympian Ira Davis. Timmy said that he considered it an honor to meet with a candidate for governor, and that he and Shapp had talked sports for an hour as well. Also, though, he said, "I don't get paid for every picture taken, but if someone wants to pay me, I take it." Nothing else came of the incident involving Timmy, and the case against Shapp was ultimately dismissed. Shapp finally won the governorship in 1970, after Annenberg had sold the Inquirer. And Shapp had been right; the merger was a financial disaster and the new Penn Central went into bankruptcy.

In July – a month after Jim Brown announced his retirement from football to concentrate on his movie career – Timmy was looking forward to his "greatest year." He said he was going to start the season at 205 pounds; the previous year he was at 188, and that was too light, he added. The extra weight, he said, gave him more power. When the season started, he needed only 114 total offensive yards to become the seventh NFL player to total 10,000. (Atop that list: Jim Brown, of course, with 15,459.) "People say Jim Brown may have to come back to playing football because he's just a football player trying to act, and he has the disadvantage of competing with people more competent in their field," Timmy said with a bit of snark. "It will be different with me" because of his acting lessons. "I'll be an actor among actors and will be judged as an actor, not a football player." Timmy had recently returned from a "lukewarm" time in Rio de Janeiro, where he had been posing in Jantzen ads. "The people were friendly, but you couldn't talk to them," he said. "They speak Portuguese and that's the hardest language to learn." He noted that "their 'God' down there is a soccer player, Pele. The kids called me the American Pele. Brazilians wouldn't make good football players. Too small."

Timmy's goal was to win the rushing and pass-receiving titles for the season. No one had ever done that in the NFL. "I don't want to be the new Jimmy Brown," he said. "I just want to be Timmy Brown. I want to be the best halfback in the history of the league." Perhaps catching himself sounding boastful, he added, "I don't want to sound like Cassius Clay. Please don't make it sound like that." (Clay had become Muhammad Ali two years earlier.) In 2010, looking back, he said, "There was competition for me, some very good players. But I had no fear that I wasn't better. Now I'm sure if I play with Jim Brown, I got to concede. He's better at fullback, I'm a halfback. But when I was in my best shape, I didn't figure anybody that way. I think there's nobody in the history of the game that I couldn't outplay."

Washington Post sportswriter William Gildea visited Timmy in his "pad" in the Grices' basement and found 2½ rooms filled with clothes – "25 suits, 25 sport coats, 75 dress shirts, 115 slacks and 56 pairs of shoes, including 20 of the finest alligator." The bill for all that: $1,500. The column noted that the Eagles a couple of years earlier had demanded that a Kelly green hopsack blazer be worn by all players when in town and on trips. Timmy by that time was modeling for Botany "500," wearing items like a cashmere hound's tooth sports coat and alligator boots. He said no to the team garb: "It was a lousy color, I couldn't match it up with anything." He instead wore a Botany jacket with the Eagles emblem, and each week was fined for not wearing team colors. By 1965 the team blazer idea had been tossed. "I finally got to them," Timmy said as a joke. Looking back in 2008, he said that "if I ever made money, I was going to get nice clothes. Carry yourself with some dignity. I was always representing the Black man in my mind." He added in a 2010 interview that he told the Eagles that he could get better jackets "tailor-made, we can get a discount and get the guys looking right. Nope, old classless Tim, what does he know? It wasn't about just me. It was our team, what we represent." In 1965, he said of his "spats" with management that the team "probably would have traded me if they could. I'm not the most genial player here. I'm moody, kind of arrogant at times."

On Aug. 19, he finally received his bachelor's degree. Ball State had changed its rule regarding a double major, and Timmy appears to have been the main reason. The process to enable Timmy to receive a degree took about four years. It began on Jan. 29, 1962, when Ben Ervin, director of curricular advising, wrote to dean Richard W. Burkhardt (who later became Ball State president) indicating that "Mr. Brown has satisfactorily completed 213 quarter hours ... with a scholastic ratio of 2.134. Mr. Brown's ratio in professional education is 2.857. His ratio in his comprehensive area is 2.37 and 2.5 in his special services area. Mr. Brown has more than met the certification in Indiana. In view of the above information, it is respectfully requested that the Committee on Admissions and Credits consider: 1. Accepting the second teaching area – Special Services area in Driver Education – as a second area or minor area applicable toward a baccalaureate degree. 2. Waiving the requirement of earning 93 quarter hours of credit after admission to upper division."

On Feb. 8, Burkhardt wrote to Joseph Hollis, chairman of the Committee on Admissions and Credits, indicating that Timmy came "closer to meeting the requirements for graduation than is normally the case and still fails to do so." Without revealing a specific motivation for the request, he said, "There are some reasons why it might be desirable to have him listed as a graduate of this institution." He concluded by saying that he, placement director Charles McNaughton, or Ervin would be happy to meet with the committee to share more information. However, they weren't invited to meet with the committee. Instead, Hollis wrote on Feb. 23 that Timmy had been told sometime earlier that he was to have submitted a written application to take nine hours of credit by correspondence in his senior year as a condition of the college's acceptance "that he graduate with 89 instead of 93 hours after admission to the upper division." Hollis stressed that neither the admissions officer nor the registrar had received a request from Timmy, and that as a result, they would not act on his behalf. He went on to say that the committee had "no power to act ... [because] the standards for graduation were not established by it." He concluded that the "request be submitted to the Council on Curriculum, who probably made the rule and therefore would have the rights to grant a deviation if they so desire." It appears that the matter was dropped for over three years; at least, there is no evidence that there was any follow-up to Hollis' response to Burkhardt.

In 1964, a Pepsi-Cola public relations official showed interest in Timmy for promotional purposes, until it was discovered that he did not have a degree. The opportunity for Timmy to have a national advertising sponsor, and the attention that could bring to the college, prompted Ball State president Emens to explore a policy change that would enable Timmy to graduate. Robert Linson, who had been director of alumni relations, said, "President Emens called me in and said my job was to get Timmy graduated." At that time, Linson said, graduates "needed two majors. He had physical education, but not business. He had to have an A in accounting." With Timmy playing pro football in Philadelphia, Linson surmised, "there was no way he was going to go to Villanova and get an A in accounting." Linson said of Emens, "He just thought it was good having an outstanding Black do something for Ball State. He followed the athletes and just thought Tim should have the degree."

In a letter dated May 13, 1965 – the year Ball State officially became a university and was no longer a teachers' college, which included revising the standards for graduation – Linson wrote that students who entered Ball State in 1955, the year that Timmy enrolled, should be able to meet the same standards as those who entered in 1965. Linson noted that the revised standards for graduating in 1965 would "make it possible to grant a diploma to Tim Brown" and said all students should be grandfathered under the new policy: "I feel that we ought not to exact different graduation standards on students who entered here in 1955."

There most likely was some communication directly to Timmy at some point, given that on May 5, 1966, Timmy wrote to Emens asking if there was a possibility of receiving a degree under the new requirements, which stipulated one major. Timmy noted that he had enough credit hours for graduation but lacked a second major. He concluded, "I would appreciate anything that you might be able to do in my behalf regarding this matter, as I am most anxious to receive my degree from Ball State University." Emens wrote back to Timmy on June 3, indicating that he had referred Timmy's letter to Victor Lawhead, dean of undergraduate programs, and had directed Lawhead to send a memorandum to the Admissions and Credits Committee "in the hopes that under the new process [he would] qualify for graduation by completing 15 hours in general education either by correspondence or transfer from another institution." Emens also indicated in his letter that "these additional hours might not be necessary."

On the same day, Lawhead wrote to the committee underscoring that he had been asked to "review the status of Thomas A. Brown and others" (there were 15) "whose original approval for graduation was denied for a lack of completion of a minor." He said, "Since the university no longer requires a minor for graduation on certain curricula, and has recently developed new departmental minors of lesser scope, it seems desirable to clarify our policy regarding requests from such former students to qualify under the revised standards for graduation." He then added, "It has been a practice to view the undergraduate program in totality, that is, the pattern and scope of specialization was balanced with the pattern and scope of general education. Students matriculating prior to September 1963 have been given the option of converting to new undergraduate specializations provided they meet the new requirements for general education. In other situations where requirements have been modified, retroactive application of rules has been made where the students were favored by such action."

He gave the committee three options: "It could evaluate the student's progress toward achieving a minor area and decide if he qualifies or meets the requirements of a departmental minor or lesser scope than the earlier pattern. It could evaluate the student's total aggregate of courses to determine if, through equivalences, his pattern of general education could satisfy current requirements. Since the new program represents considerably greater prescription of courses, the student's earlier course pattern probably should be evaluated with the degree of liberal interpretation necessary for transfer students." He concluded, "Should either or both of the foregoing alternatives be adopted as clarifying policies in these situations, it would only be necessary to apply them on an individual basis in the few cases where they are applicable."

On June 22, registrar Hauptman delivered to Timmy the news from the Committee on Admissions and Credits' June 17 meeting: "It was approved that you are considered to have met the requirements under the new regulations for graduation with a bachelor's degree. [The] proper office will provide information for graduation, diploma, and notification with reference to participation in commencement." A week later, Emens wrote, "We have been waiting a long time for the new regulations for graduation to be approved. Will you be able to come for the Aug. 19, 1966, Commencement? I am looking forward to seeing you." On July 1, senior adviser Robert Kress sent Timmy a graduation application to be completed and told him to contact Orvid T. Richardson, dean of instructional affairs, regarding the August Commencement. Kress indicated that Timmy was certified to graduate by July 15, the end of the first summer session, in the General Arts curriculum rather than a teaching curriculum, "since you will have only the one major of Health and Physical Education and no minor area."

Timmy's application for graduation was received on July 18. It was made clear on the form that he was graduating with a non-teaching bachelor of science degree, with a major in health and physical education and a special services area in driver education. Kress reaffirmed this in a letter dated a day later. Between a pre-season 31-17 loss to the Baltimore Colts on Aug. 13 and a 24-23 victory over the New York Giants on Aug. 27, Tim flew from Philadelphia to attend the Aug. 19 Commencement on the Ball State campus and receive his diploma. Emens, presumably, was smiling.

Timmy also was hoping to graduate, in a sense, in his acting career. He told the Sporting News in 1966, "I would like to try 'Golden Boy' or 'Bye, Bye Birdie,' but when the summer seasons are on, we're in training camp." But while Timmy looked for stardom on the stage or screen to follow stardom on the field, Kuharich was not a fan of gridiron luminaries. He believed that as the coach, he would decide how the game was to be played, and the players would execute. After the 1965 season he had traded Pro Bowlers Baughan and Cross to Los Angeles after they complained about the amount of blitzing required of them. "The Eagles don't need stars," he said. "We need players whose level of performance does not rise or fall like the stock market. Baughan and Cross are good players, but for one reason or another they were not consistent, and this hurt us." That was not a philosophy that would appeal to Timmy, who, now that Jim Brown had retired, was "the most versatile runner in the game," according to Sports Illustrated.

In 2010, Timmy looked back at his era of mixing football and entertainment, and said that the Eagles "didn't like it. It was dumb, why wouldn't you like? It's not affecting you. They were afraid that it was going to take me away from football, though. I had no intentions of leaving football for it, because I'd have to have a smash – and even then I'm going to play football.... I could have been offered $10 million to give it up and retire," but "I got to get it out of my system." In another interview he said, "Football was my best love, and I knew I only had a limited time to play it. So of course it was a priority, and in the off-season I was going to work on the music and work on the acting, but I was spreading myself too thin."

And injuries were coming Timmy's way more often as the 1966 season began. He had a nose injury in September, but it was not a break. In the first three games of the season, Timmy protected his injured hip with a hard shell placed over inflated rubber tubing. It cut down his movement, so for the Cardinals game in October he used a normal sponge again. The season started brutally, with the Eagles losing by 41-10 to the Cardinals and 56-7 to the Cowboys. The latter game had Timmy controlling tears outside the locker room after he was held to eight yards. He had played despite a hemorrhaging groin injury that took some wrapping. "I felt we had a chance to win" the title, he said. Of Kuharich he said before the Steelers game on Oct. 16, "I think he's a good man and a good coach.... Regardless of what is written or said, I respect Joe Kuharich and have never had a falling out with him. People just don't believe that when they read some of the things written in the press." He indicated that for him the fun was now gone from the game and that he was playing to earn money to continue his acting lessons, noting that a Broadway show with Leslie Uggams, a singer who had come to wide notice on Mitch Miller's TV show, was possible.

The game against the Steelers started out as a series of fumbles and misses for the Eagles. After halftime, they came out a different team, and "from the opening scrimmage play of the second half," columnist Frank Dolson wrote, "it was evident that Timmy Brown, the old Timmy Brown, had returned. Where had he been for 5½ ball games?" For his part, Timmy said his play in the first half had led him to question himself: "Maybe I've got to be more reckless. Maybe I've got to take more chances. I used to be that way." Dolson said that in this cross-state battle, "apparently, what inspired Timmy was personal pride, pure and simple."

On Oct. 23 against the Giants, the visiting Eagles came on strong in a 31-3 win. The hero of the game, according to the Times' William

N. Wallace, was "Thomas Allen (Tim) Brown, a halfback who runs with the football as though he were tiptoeing through the tulips." Using his "so-called stutter-step action," Timmy gained 100 yards in 21 rushes and set up all the Eagles scoring, including a TD of his own. Before the game, Timmy, who was well acquainted with the Big Apple, said, "This is New York and it's important what we do here."

In the wake of that game, another of Timmy's New York City teachers, Seth Riggs, was interviewed by the New York Times about the singing halfback. Riggs, a baritone with the New York City Opera, appeared on Broadway in productions such as a revival of "The King and I" in 1960, "Paint Your Wagon" in 1962, and "110 in the Shade" in 1963. During his career, Riggs taught an impressive list of artists, including Streisand, Stevie Wonder, Michael Jackson, Bette Midler, and Josh Groban. He told the Times that Timmy was "extremely musical. He has a good ear and a wonderful sense of rhythm. He's easy to teach. All you have to do is tell him the right thing and he can do it. Some students never learn. He learns quickly." The interview was done during a music lesson, and in the middle of the class Timmy expressed pain and apologized to Riggs, saying, "My ribs. They're sore and they catch me every now and then." He had been hurt the day before in the Giants game at Yankee Stadium.

Leading up to the Nov. 6 Dallas game, Timmy told a reporter that the Cowboys "couldn't stop me if I got the ball in my hands. If the Eagles let me run back kickoffs again, run the ball and catch the ball, Dallas couldn't stop me everywhere." In a 2008 interview, he said of this game, "Dallas came in thinking they could take us, because I was so old.... Dallas can't stop me. They may stop me on this play or that – not going to stop me on all four." The day before the game, "Kuharich ... came up to me and said, 'You're running back kickoffs tomorrow.' Up until then, I hadn't even practiced with the special teams. I think Joe was just hanging me out there." In 2010, he expanded on this point. He said he had told a Philadelphia reporter that Dallas couldn't stop him, "so now they are really going to play me because I put this in the paper. The only person that could stop me, I said, was Joe Kuharich.... I'm just not going to sit back and take any more. And so in the paper, of course, they read that. So on Saturday we are at a half-day meeting and at the end of it he says, "Oh, by the way, Brown, you'll be running back tomorrow. I said, 'Glory hallelujah,' and the guys all laughed, and he said, 'Shut up, that's not funny.'"

Whatever the reason, it ended up being a stroke of genius on Kuharich's part. The Dallas game at Franklin Field was perhaps the high point of Timmy's career, when in the space of 39 seconds on the game clock he ran back one kickoff for 93 yards for a score, and a second kickoff for 90 yards for another touchdown. A reporter noted that Timmy "always wanted people to remember him" and had achieved that goal – "Nobody else ever did that in one pro football game. Nobody might ever do it again." The Eagles were behind by 7-0 in the first quarter when Timmy received a kickoff from Danny Villanueva, then cut past Mike Johnson and ran down the sideline. For his second run, with the score now 17-7 Cowboys, Timmy took another Villanueva kickoff, got away from Warren Livingston, and did another sideline dash.

On Timmy's first run, he took a long angle so that his three pursuers would have to take a longer route, on which they never caught up. The 90-yard second run ended in spurts of speed alternating with moments in which Timmy seemed to falter. "My thighs tightened up," he said, blaming it in part on the cool weather. "I knew No. 11 [Villanueva] couldn't catch me, but I wanted to draw him over so he'd be in the other guy's way." Timmy ran at a bit less than full speed while Villanueva and Livingston drew near. Villaneuva went for the shoulders and Livingston got his hands on Timmy's hips. Timmy shrugged his shoulders, and that took care of Villanueva; he jerked his hips, and Livingston lost his hold. "They have been kicking off to their right and sending most of their men down the right side," Timmy said. "So I ran to the left." Timmy nearly broke a third kickoff return for a touchdown, but ran into one of his own blockers and was knocked down after a 21-yard run. In 2010, Timmy said that he was "so out of shape, that's when Kuharich came in and they weren't playing me. Then I go in, and they score quick and I'm right back on the field, and I tightened up. But they tightened up the same, chasing me, and it looked like slow motion.... I looked terrible, I could hardly lift my legs. But *you* go 100 yards like that, twice, back to back in 30 seconds when you're not in shape."

In preparing his book "Game of My Life, Philadelphia Eagles: Memorable Stories of Eagles Football," author Robert Gordon asked players to recount their top contest while in Eagles green. Timmy said this had to be the game for him, although it was a close call over the 105-yard return of 1961. He said of his first run against the Cowboys:

"When they kicked off, I was ready. I just saw them all rushing down the center of the field, so I started up the middle and then veered over to the sideline. I could run sideways pretty fast.... When I was in college, I was always making up little games to challenge myself. I used to run down the railroad tracks nearby. I'd try to run sideways and step on every other railroad tie."

One reporter wrote after the game that "when Brown's returning a kickoff, he moves rapidly through a world of whirling bodies, most of which are bigger than his. There is violence on all sides of him and running avenues open and close and shift, almost quicker than a man can think about them.... He just moves along." In 2010, Timmy said, "Every time I ever scored, I don't remember hearing anything. It's like the concentration of seeing everything. Colors, I go by colors. You know, white-and-blue jersey, or something like that, and we're wearing green and white, or whatever so you can tell the difference. So I see my guys coming in, what they're doing, because the colors are this way and I'm reacting to those behind them." On another occasion, Timmy told Washington Post columnist Shirley Povich that in such situations, "I run scared. I'm kind of in a panic, really." But in 1962 he had told Muncie Evening Press columnist Fennell, "I never go so good when I get in the open. I seem to tighten up. Seem to get scared. I like running in crowds, getting past all those tacklers. It gives me confidence."

Even with all of Timmy's heroics, the Eagles only won by one point, 24-23. A story noted that Kuharich had removed Timmy from the runback team in 1965 hoping to give him more speed as a halfback. Timmy had been unhappy, and the writer noted that "when Brown's unhappy, no ear within range goes unscathed." In October, Kuharich had agreed that Timmy could go back on the kickoff return squad. "My idea of a good day," Timmy said, "is to run the ball 50 or 60 times, catch passes, and play defense. You think Kuharich will listen to me?" Timmy would long remember this game. Unfortunately for him, Dallas and its coach, Tom Landry – the coach who didn't get the job at Green Bay in 1959 – would remember it as well.

Sportswriters tried for years to get into the mind of the always quotable Timmy. One said that Timmy could be "charming before a big game, reticent before a meaningless game.... He is a superstar with the temperament of a stage actor, which he is obsessed to become someday. He himself admits he hasn't discovered what makes Timmy run, or what makes Timmy moody." (In the 1964 Sport article, Timmy called himself "the world's moodiest person. I'm too sensitive, and I think about things too much. At the last count I had 107 different moods.")

In early November, Phil Pepe, a longtime New York sports journalist writing for the New York Herald Tribune Paris edition – by that point the only thing left of that storied newspaper – sought to look into Timmy's soul as well. "It is not unusual for a boy from a broken home to turn to sports or the theater," he wrote. "The cheers of the crowd or the applause of an audience are the love and affection he missed as a child and craves as an adult and Timmy Brown's craving is so deep, so boundless, neither is enough. He must have both. This need is what makes Timmy run on the football field every Sunday and this craving is what makes him study acting every Monday. Timmy Brown always wanted to be the best damn halfback in professional football and attaining that could not satisfy his desire. He tried singing and that wasn't enough. Now it is acting." Pepe mentioned that the Giants had sought Timmy in 1964 and concluded with, "You have to want someone very badly to offer six players for him and you have to want someone very badly to turn down six players for him and to Timmy Brown, who is still a rejected 7-year-old in a children's home, nothing is more important than that." For his part, Timmy, neither a 7-year-old nor living in a children's home, had simply told Pepe, "I was very flattered. I don't think any one man is worth six players." Looking into his own soul in 1968, he said, "I never hated anybody in my life and I'm not gonna start now. Anyway, before you hate you have to love. And I ain't in love with a whole lotta people, either." But he also admitted in another interview, "I was raised in a children's home, so all the love I could get helped."

The rest of the 1966 season did not go as well as the Nov. 6 Dallas game. On Nov. 20, against the host 49ers, Timmy was taken out in the second period because of the effects of a concussion, which caused "retrogressive amnesia." He had been hit on both sides by two large linebackers, Dave Wilcox and Ed Beard; he seemed to be dazed and collapsed. But he quickly recovered and stayed in the game. Shortly thereafter, he was hit hard again and the ball flew from his grasp. He was woozy on the sideline and was taken to the clubhouse. All this came in front of his mother and his sisters Trixie, Polly, and Buggs, who had gone to Kezar Stadium to see him play for the first time that season.

Also at the game were Timmy's childhood friend Dave Chapman, along with George Mendenhall, a classmate of Chapman's at Richmond High School. Chapman had moved to San Francisco in 1965 and was roommates with Mendenhall. He called Timmy to get tickets to the game, and they agreed to meet afterward. During the game, Chapman said, "Timmy got his bell rung. They took him out. Later, he came back in. After the game, we were standing outside the locker room waiting for him. He walked out, looked at us, and walked right by." Chapman called out, "Tim, it's Dave." Timmy, he said, looked back and said, "Oh."

Chapman said Timmy "could hardly remember who I was."

"That was tough," Timmy said in 2010 of the 49ers game. "I got caught between two guys going up for the pass and the thing about it that made it work like it did is, I got hit simultaneously, front and back, smashed my helmet, smashed my brain.... I went down and I held onto the ball. It was raining and there was water up to your ankles on the field. I came down and I went down face down, and they said I was laying there five, six, or seven seconds, until somebody said, somebody better get him up." According to news reports, by the next day his memory had returned, although Timmy later said he had problems for about a week and that they recurred later in life – "I woke up at 42 years old and wondered where I had been, a crazy, weird feeling. Probably ruined my acting career – I was too mellow. Went back to the way I was at the Home, quiet. Maybe I didn't give them what I had."

Nearing the season's end, Timmy broke a finger on his left hand while carrying the ball in the second period of the Dec. 11 game against the Browns and thus was not going to play against Washington on Dec. 18. During the season he had also suffered a hip pointer and a concussion. He said that while he was on the sidelines, he wanted to be the best cheerleader the Eagles had. But he was keeping Hollywood in mind: "They've talked to me about two movies. In one I'd be a Negro James Bond.... The other is a pirate picture. I bet you didn't know there were Negro pirates." In another article, Timmy said, "Football has conflicted with some offers I've had to be in 'Tarzan,' 'Felony Squad,' and some other Western types. One of the biggest producers in Hollywood told me I'd work if I was there." He continued, "I've been told I can't miss as an actor."

As with Tim's singing career, his taking acting lessons did not always go over well with his coaches, teammates, the media, and fans. However, Timmy believed he was able to separate the two. "The energy level — you know. I managed with that. I always give myself plenty of time to just rest. In football practice, I would just work on football and keep it on my mind and know what the game plan was," he said while in his 70s. If anything, he believed football slowed his growth as an actor. In an interview from the 1960s, he said, "I've missed some drama classes lately because when I have a scene to study, I find it hard to concentrate. I'll be trying to learn lines, but I'll be thinking about running an end sweep."

One offer he did take up was to appear on "The Wild, Wild West," the early steampunk series on CBS starring Robert Conrad as a 19th century secret agent. Timmy said the role came about while he was modeling for Jantzen: "My agent called me from Philadelphia and says, 'You be available.' I said [of the Jantzen work], 'We're going to finish shooting, and so I'll just stay there and see that everything is taken care of.' … She wanted me to audition for it, and it was only a couple blocks from this hotel we were staying at. So I was reading the thing and I was saying, 'Why am I in here?' The role, a big, 250-pound guy, mean-looking. I tried to go in looking mean…. The other people that were going in, I don't know if they were actors, because they didn't do very well. They liked my reading…. Then Bobby Conrad went with it, and he was a football fan too, so he was happy, so they were happy to get me into the show." Timmy was the guest star in the third season's premiere episode, "The Night of the Bubbling Death." (As with later shows like "Seinfeld," all episode titles of "Wild, Wild West" followed a format, in its case "The Night of….")

The episode did not offer Timmy many lines, but it did allow for some action sequences. Then the time came for Timmy, playing desperado Clint Cartwheel, to have a fight scene with Conrad. "We just get started and I'm back like this on him. I got him grabbed here and I'm like this, and they cut. OK, so we went to lunch, but my sombrero had gone off in that scene. And when they wanted to pick up where we had left off, he said, 'No, you have to put your hat on.' I said, 'Bobby, the hat was off.' He said, 'No, you have to put the hat on, I'm not going to do a close-up with you,' and I said, 'Why?' 'I'm just not going to do a close-up with you.' I never understood that, you know? So I had to put the hat back on and they just spliced it together, and figured people wouldn't notice that it went off. And that's how Hollywood is, everybody is afraid of everybody, and there's nothing to be afraid of. I said, 'Bobby, this is your show.' ... We hung together, we were great buddies, but when it came to close-ups.... He was the best-looking guy I had ever seen in the movies. When I first saw 'Wild, Wild West' at home, I said, 'Wow, that's a good-looking dude, and he's a bad boy.' But that's the ego of Hollywood. I liked Bobby, he was a good guy, but there are very insecure people that worry about things like that." Tim's appearance in a television series a mere nine days before the season opener certainly did not quiet the talk regarding his future.

Also, there was his knee. According to a 1987 Orlando Sentinel story, the Eagles told him in 1966 that surgery on it could wait until he retired. So he had the knee taped and Novocain shot into it so he could play. After retirement the knee was operated on – unsuccessfully, according to Timmy. He was told he would need a knee replacement within half a year and surgery on his other knee after then. The limp from the painful knee also had caused a degenerative spinal condition.

But while Timmy was facing many challenges, at least the Eagles ended 1966 with a winning season – and no one could know they would not have another for the next 11 years.

In 1967, Timmy continued to expand his world. On March 5, he appeared on the game show "Password" in a special competition between NFL players and skaters from the Shipstad & Johnson Ice Follies. Gifford captained the football squad, made up of Washington linebacker Sam Huff, Browns tackle Dick Shaffrath, and Timmy. (Leading the skaters' team was the actress Betty White, the wife of the show's host, Allen Ludden.) The next month, Timmy left the Grice home and moved into an apartment in Society Hill Towers, an urban redevelopment project designed by the architect I.M. Pei, who later designed the original World Trade Center. (The Grices' home was destroyed in the

May 1985 police bombing of the compound that was home to members of MOVE, often described as a Black back-to-nature group. Ernie Grice told the Inquirer in a story on May 19, 1985, that "if my house had been the only one standing (after the fire), I would have liked to have picked it up and put it in the middle of Park Avenue. To me, my house was worth $500 million.")

At Society Hill Towers, Timmy lived on the 28th floor – "big glass windows all around to see the whole city." The apartment complex had attracted affluent residents to a redeveloped neighborhood in a decade when most cities were losing their middle-class populations. His six-room apartment had views of Independence Hall and the Delaware River. The decor he favored was "modern with a heavy Spanish flavor." He said he had "a big bar built, movable," and spent thousands of dollars on the work. In April, he had friends over for a housewarming. Dee Dee Sharp said she was a visitor there, "like a little sister visiting a brother," before she married music producer Gamble and her relationship with Timmy and Chubby Checker changed.

Going into the 1967 season, Timmy's career record was 2,976 yards rushing, 176 passes caught for 2,773 yards, 54 punts returned for 514 yards, 136 kickoffs run back for 3,620 yards, and 52 touchdowns, making him "the greatest all-around offensive back in Eagles history." (A Times article said that covering Timmy in a race to the goal line was considered the ultimate test of a linebacker.) On July 12, Kuharich told Inquirer sportswriter Gordon Forbes that Timmy was modeling swim togs in Hawaii and that he assumed Timmy would not report to training camp on July 23. He said he would use Izzy Lang at halfback. "Until Timmy … clarifies his position, we're going under the assumption he won't be with us," the coach said. But Timmy had made it clear to reporters that he planned to play – although he wanted a $50,000 contract that would make him the best-paid Eagle ever. The year before, he had reportedly been paid $30,000. "There's no salary dispute," Kuharich said. Asked how much the Eagles would miss Timmy, Kuharich responded,

"Not much." But when training camp opened on July 23 in Hershey, Timmy was present, although he had not signed his contract – he did so later that month.

Timmy said Kuharich had called Forbes' report untrue and "I accepted his word." He noted, "If they don't want to pay me what I think I'm worth, I'll play for nothing. Well, almost for nothing." The unofficial word was that the player and the team settled for about $40,000. (In 2009, he said that his pay for his second season with the Eagles had been $9,000, for the third $12,000, for the fourth $17,500, but when he was offered $20,000 for the fifth season he asked for $27,000 and settled on $23,000.) As for people who looked askance at his entertainment career, he noted that some players worked as insurance agents during the off-season and asked, "Is it because acting and singing and television is in the public eye?"

On Aug. 19, the Eagles met their first-ever AFL foe, the Jets under Joe Namath, in a preseason game in Cincinnati. (The game was held in the Queen City of the Ohio to whet local interest in the sport, with an AFL team – the Bengals – set to begin play the following year.) Timmy, uncharacteristically, was involved in a fight. The Eagles' Izzy Lang was bumped out of bounds after catching a pass. Timmy jammed an elbow into Johnny Sample's back, Cornell Gordon of the Jets punched Ditka, and the Eagles' Gary Ballman hit Jim Hudson. Timmy and Ditka were ejected, but it didn't matter to the team in the end, as the Eagles prevailed, 34-19. Grayce, now Grayce Shadd, who lived in Cincinnati, attended the game with her husband and their son, Jimmy, and they talked to Timmy after the game. Also present was childhood friend Paul Davis from Richmond.

But midway through the snakebit 1967 regular season, Timmy had yet to see one minute of play because of a pulled hamstring in his left thigh resulting from an exhibition game against Buffalo. He had been out for seven games, and the story noted that "some people already have made snide remarks" about how Timmy could "dance so much on Saturday nights and then not even run a little bit on Sunday afternoon," and mentioned a team official's comment that perhaps he was recovering in slow motion. (Fellow Eagle Ballman had publicly accused Timmy of dogging it.)

Timmy responded to complaints about how badly he was injured by saying, "I realize they see me do things like walk up the stairs and dance, and they wonder how much could my thigh really be bothering me. What they don't realize is that I can run straight, all right, but I simply can't cut at all." He noted that a hamstring recovery generally took four weeks but added, "Last Sunday there was a knot on my thigh the size of half a baseball. The doctor stuck a needle in it and got blood out." Of sitting and not playing, the player described by one sportswriter as the Eagles' "No. 1 convalescent" said, "My friends used to kid me about it and it didn't bother me at first. The last couple of weeks, though, if they joked about it, I blew up."

The ever-enrageable Philadelphia fan base, he said, would "see me sitting on the sidelines in civvies and start hollering at me from the stands. They'd yell things like 'Hey, Pretty Boy' ... or 'Hey, Hollywood, when are you going to get off your backside and earn your money?' Now, I'm not that sensitive," Timmy said in a remark straining credulity, "but I just couldn't believe the fans' attitude.... You know they knock Richie Allen and they knock Wilt Chamberlain in Philadelphia, and maybe they do it with a little reason. But what I can't understand is why the people in Philadelphia keep knocking guys like that even when they're doing well." He said his "own teammates didn't know how to be with me. Suddenly they don't believe I'm hurt now, and they think I'm putting on."

Timmy's interest in a career as a professional actor was no secret to Eagles management, coaches, teammates, fans, and reporters. While the Eagles had not been fond of Timmy's music career, his appearances had been mostly in the Philadelphia area and his recordings were made there. His roles in summer stock had been in the off-season and were also in the region. But success as an actor in film or television could hardly be achieved in the Quaker City. The talk in the press about Timmy's Hollywood fixation began to take its toll. In an interview around this time, Timmy said, "I was so hurt. I couldn't believe that those were the same people that loved me when I played so well, that loved the excitement I gave them. I remember thinking to myself, 'If I had to do it all over again, I would never play football, because I was happier when I was a country boy and innocent." While Timmy's back-and-forth talk left the Eagles and their fans uncertain and angry, his own patience was getting very thin.

("Pretty Boy" was an insult that hurt Timmy deeply. In 1973, he told Black Sports magazine that when he was growing up, "I had complexes. People don't know what they do to kids' minds sometimes. They'd say, 'Oh, isn't he a pretty boy?' You're a boy or a girl. It's always this stuff and other kids that you've got to fight. You've got to fight, you know, because they call you pretty boy and they're going to be pushing you.")

One NFL official unconnected with the Eagles said of Timmy's being paid while not playing, "He has earned his money and then some from the Eagles – even if he never plays another game for them." Timmy was weighing acting vs. football seriously. "If I can get a regular part in a series, or a couple of movie deals, I'll sign. Right now I'm planning on two or three more seasons. But the challenge in acting is just as great as it is in pro football." He indicated on more than one occasion in 1967 that if the Eagles won another championship, he would probably retire. But as things stood, he said, he would keep playing: "I can't go out on a year like this. To ... have people look at you and say things like some of them have is pretty hard."

By this time, Timmy had hired a secretary to pick out things he needed and see that they were obtained; she also answered his fan mail. The woman, he said, wouldn't take any pay. She met him at a practice and said, "I want to be your secretary." "It was kind of crazy," he said, "but she was very good. She stayed with me for three years." (Through Timmy's club connections, she wound up dating Bobby Darin.) Timmy was now living the high life, according to the Inquirer's Gordon Forbes, with a cigarette lighter made to look like the barrel of a James Bond pistol; 20 suits; 125 pairs of slacks; and 200 shirts. He was driving a Lincoln Continental. He had been paid $1,000 for his role on "The Wild, Wild West," but had paid $1,500 in team fines. While it was well known that he had problems with Kuharich, he said, "I respect him even though he fines heavy. I rebelled the first couple of years, but not now. Life is cool and good." Still, in addition to giving up acting classes, he said he had become more of a loner than ever, spending most of his free time in his bedroom watching TV and singing along to records.

During the 1967 season, Timmy, along with Eagles teammates Snead, Floyd Peters, and John Meyers, filmed a short message urging respect for law and order, to be shown on the Philadelphia CBS affiliate. The shorts were prepared by CBS in cooperation with the Federal Bar Association National Law Observance Committee.

On Nov. 5, Timmy finally got back onto the field against New Orleans, gaining 37 yards rushing and 93 receiving in a 31-24 Eagles loss at Tulane Stadium. Looking forward to playing Los Angeles, he said he had "never realized how much he missed the game until [the Saints game].... That one game told me how much I love football." Of his injury, he added, "The last few weeks with that hamstring turned me into an irritable guy who had lost his humor. The first five or six weeks I had to fight it to remain a good guy and all that jazz. It was the same question every 30 seconds of every day. 'How's the leg? When you gonna play?' It just kept me on edge." Timmy said he hoped to play for several more years and to retire as an Eagle, but that depended on "the people I'm dealing with in my outside interests and the people I'm dealing with in my football career." Sportswriter Gordon Forbes said it was "common knowledge" that Timmy had been on the trading block at least twice in his career. Timmy said he had asked for 30 tickets for the L.A. game:

"My mother will be there, along with four sisters and their husbands, 13 nieces and nephews, and 20 or 30 other people I know from the 'Wild, Wild West' show."

On Nov. 24, in a story by Inquirer sportswriter Sandy Padwe, Timmy was talking like a man who wanted out of the game and out of the city, after being sidelined with the hamstring injury. "After those first five or six weeks of being out, I went through a mental change. I could not fake being happy anymore. It has all been building up. I'm on edge now. I'm touchy and have to be careful and control my temper. I don't seem to trust people. There has to be a reason for it. People make you what you are when you're in the limelight. Now the people are being nice to me. But only since I came back. People are fickle. Well, I'm getting fickle myself. I can't smile anymore. Now I'm fighting for something I didn't think I'd ever have to fight for again. Respect. From my teammates first. From the people second. I resent that I have to fight for it. I resent it very much. I gave up the classes in New York. Being out like that, I didn't want to give them any excuse to say anything about my being more serious about acting than football. That's one thing I can't understand. I considered my acting and the classes an investment in my future. These other guys work so they'll have a future when they stop playing football."

But Timmy kept playing, and the 1967 season was near its end when the Dec. 10 game solidified Philadelphia's hatred of the Dallas Cowboys. They were already disliked for beating the Eagles by 56-7 in the fourth game in 1966, after they had lost by 24-23 in the contest featuring Timmy's two touchdown runbacks. This time around, Timmy's second-half 23-yard pass reception from QB Snead put the Eagles into Cowboys territory for the first time and led to a touchdown. But the Eagles were outclassed by the Boys, and the game became a Dallas grudge match. Cowboys quarterback Meredith was knocked out of the game late when linebacker Mike Morgan broke his nose, and things went downhill from there. Snead was sacked seven times. Timmy and Tom

Woodeshick took the hardest physical punishment. In the second half, Clarence Peaks went out for a pass, but it was underthrown. Turning around, Timmy was hit in the face by linebacker Lee Roy Jordan – hit very, very hard. Timmy lost "three or four" teeth in addition to three false teeth (costing $1,100 each) that he already wore. "He looked more like a hockey player than a halfback," Inquirer sports columnist Dolson wrote. Teammate Ditka said, "Let's put it this way. I'm gonna count the days until we play Dallas again. I know about 20 other guys on this ball club who are gonna do the same thing. Then we'll see what happens." Snead added, "That wasn't a tackle. That was an elbow.... He didn't have to throw an elbow. He got penalized, didn't he? Look at Timmy's mouth." Dolson described Jordan's hit as acting on Timmy's teeth "the way a bowling ball knocks down a row of pins."

Moments after being hurt, Dolson noted, "Timmy had gone to the sidelines and cried. He wasn't crying over the pain ... or the lost teeth. He was crying because Timmy is an emotional man who had kept too much inside too long.... It's been the kind of year ... the average person would be in a crazy house," he said. Timmy had been upset because Kuharich had said the Eagles didn't need him; he believed the coach was wasting him as a decoy. "Every week I've been ready to explode," he said. "That little cry for me – well, that was my way of exploding."

Despite his injury, Timmy wanted to go back in the game. He was a fan of the movie "El Cid," which ends with the Spanish hero, played by Charlton Heston, being struck in the chest by an arrow. Doctors tell him that they can remove the arrow and save his life, but that he will be incapacitated for a long time. The Cid, unwilling to abandon his army, refuses the aid and dies. Then his allies place his corpse, dressed in armor and holding a banner, on a horse, and lead the horse into battle. The demoralized foes believe he has risen from the dead. "They'll think El Cid," Timmy said of Dallas, if he could get back onto the field. Timmy's connection with "El Cid" went back to Ernie the Head. When Ernie scored on Timmy, he would put up his arm to form an "L." Timmy adopted the sign: "You know, El Cid was bad. Every time I was going to throw the option pass in training camp, I gave 'em the El. 'The El is about to unleash,' I'd tell them."

But the injury was too severe for him to return to the game, and it was probably just as well. The 38-17 loss to Dallas, at the Cotton Bowl, saw the Eagles rushing for a total of 23 net yards, and in the third quarter they could only run five offensive plays. Woodeshick was gouged in the right eye by a fist and couldn't see well for the rest of the game. The game set a record for points scored by all opponents against the Eagles. The previous high, 381 in 1963, had cost Skorich his job. Jordan later said he hadn't taken a cheap shot. "Timmy swung out of the backfield on a little circle route.... I thought he was going to catch it, and you just don't let a runner like Timmy do things like that. We rammed together, and I actually thought I hit him in the chest. That's what I was trying to do." Timmy disagreed: of newspaper photos of the encounter, he said, "He sure isn't playing the ball, because I'm nowhere near the ball, and he's nowhere near the ball and all over me."

In 2010, Timmy said he had been called before the Dallas game by players on other teams warning him that something was going to happen on Dec. 10: "They've put a hit on you. Now 'Pretty Boy' is going to get his." The following year, Timmy told sportswriter Larry Merchant that "it was a pass 15 yards over my head. I had already started to peel back to the huddle when [Jordan] hit me with an elbow. All he got was 15 yards. If he had done that to Hornung or Unitas, the league would have taken action. If that's all the respect they have for me, the hell with them." In 2008, he said, "Pass incomplete. Whistle blew. I walked five yards – LeRoy Jordan's forearm across my helmet. Payback. Dallas had a contract that week."

The damage to his mouth consisted of a fracture of the upper left jaw; a tooth on the right side severed at the jaw line; two teeth on the left side knocked out of line; and part of a permanent bridge lost. "At least this will keep me quiet for three weeks," he said with a smile, realizing he wasn't being quiet. "What I ought to do, what I really should do, is go home and take a Darvon, get the dog taken care of, and then just sleep for three weeks." (In 1987, he was still feeling the effects of this injury: "They tell me I may lose all of my upper teeth, and I can't do anything about it." His acting career had been restricted, he said, because of resulting limits on how long he could sit and stand.)

Longtime referee Jim Tunney didn't remember Timmy's being hurt often, but he did recall that Dallas game. "The year that he had run two kickoffs back in one game for a touchdown, I think the next time they played him they broke his jaw or broke teeth out of his mouth.... There was a lot of animosity in those days between the Eagles and the Cowboys. I don't think Timmy ever got involved in any of that, but there was a breaking of the jaws. Maybe not intentionally, but it did happen."

Gene Kilroy was more definite, saying: "Tom Landry hated it [the double-runback game]. In the next game, he had players knock his teeth out. Tim wasn't even close to the play." Kilroy was assistant to the president of the Eagles from 1962 to 1968, overseeing the stadium, team travel, alumni, players' speaking engagements, outside ticketing, and meetings. He came to admire Timmy: "I used to watch him sit in the locker room. Players would be yelling. He didn't like loud, crude people. He would be quiet, relaxed." He was touched by Timmy's story of the breakup of his family and having to go to the Home. Kilroy once asked him how he felt about being sent there, to which Timmy simply said that his parents couldn't afford to keep him. "Timmy had no animosity," he said. "He paid for his parents to come to his games."

As with so many people Timmy met, they developed a lifetime friendship: "We always stayed close. He spent time with me. He was like my brother. I would be there for him if he needed anything, or I thought he needed anything. A good guy to be around. No enemies. Nice to people. Made everyone feel like he was their best friend."

Timmy missed the final game of the season against the Browns because his jaw had been set and wired, and the wiring had to stay in place for two to three weeks. He finished the season with his second-lowest total of yardage gained, 682. Even so, his yardage total reached 12,416, making him fifth all-time. For the six seasons prior to 1967, Tim had averaged 4.43 yards per rush and 14.49 yards per reception, but in 1967, he averaged only 3.4 yards per rush and 9.4 yards per reception. In addition, because of lingering injuries, he only had 53 rushing attempts and 22 receptions for 1967 after averaging 131 rushing attempts the previous six seasons. As a result of the Jordan hit, Timmy said, he was "existing on soft food. A typical meal consists of a glass of orange juice with a banana in it, a malt, and maybe some Jell-O. I've dropped 21 pounds and now weigh all of 179."

By this time, he was openly looking for a trade. He wanted the Eagles – he was the only player left from the 1960 championship team – to either make him their key running back in 1968 or send him elsewhere. "If I'm not going to be used, then I'd rather be traded," he said. "I'm a running back and I have to run." Washington coach Otto Graham hinted that he might want to look at Timmy. But, he said, "Timmy's no youngster. How long can he play? What about his acting career? These are things you've got to consider." Timmy didn't help things with the league or the fans by making clear that any move would have to be tied to his thespian aspirations. "Any place outside of New York and Los Angeles I consider obscure," he said. In another article, he added, "If they trade me some day, it's got to be L.A. or New York. Otherwise I'd quit."

Inquirer sportswriter Padwe, in a story published on Feb. 9, 1968, said Timmy had been a "broken man" in the last few games of 1967, and said Timmy had been 10 times more successful as a player as Kuharich was as a coach. Ed Snider, who had joined the Eagles management team under Wolman (his brother-in-law Ed Foreman had a partial interest in the team), said, "It's a travesty what Kuharich did to Timmy Brown. He beat him into the ground and then traded him for less than he was worth. Timmy Brown is not the kind of athlete who needs a pat on the back.... He's a temperamental man, but a great artist. After we had that

9-5 season [in 1966] he couldn't wait to start the next season.... Then he went to Hawaii, and when he's out there he picks up a paper and reads a story quoting Kuharich as saying he had made his plans for the coming season and Timmy wasn't included in them. This completely demoralized the guy. It all went back to Kuharich's first year with the club. Timmy showed up a week late for practice because of Army duty. Kuharich treated him like the rawest rookie."

"Ed Snider understood me," Timmy told Padwe. "I just hope people don't think we're two guys with grudges against the Eagles." (Snider and Wolman fell into a bitter estrangement in 1967, when a Wolman skyscraper project in Chicago encountered construction problems. Wolman needed cash, and Snider and Foreman rebuffed him. In response, Wolman fired them. Snider went on to fame as the owner of the Philadelphia Flyers and Spectacor.) Timmy said Kuharich's staff had taken the attitude that "they were breaking a wild horse and this was how it was going to be." Sportswriter Larry Merchant later wrote that "Kuharich may be deft with x's and o's but he is heavy-handed as King Kong when they turn into people.... Kuharich overreacted to [Timmy's] status as a star, trying to show he was the same as everybody else, a traditional coachly cop-out. Four years of that broke Brown's spirit." In another story, Timmy said Kuharich "simply forgets there is more to life than playing football."

In the 1973 interview with Black Sports magazine, Timmy said that "when there was a clash between Kuharich and me, the management would say, yeah, well, we know he's wrong, but we're still going to back him. Now, that doesn't even make sense, you know. I mean, you're telling the players, the guys that are out there getting their butts killed for you, that you're going to back the coach-general manager regardless of whether he's right or wrong."

Tommy McDonald said Timmy "was disappointed in Kuharich for a lot of reasons. He didn't feel like Kuharich really allowed him to touch the ball very much.... If you have an outstanding runner ... you got to give them that piece of leather, that little football, an awful lot. 'Cause if you don't give it to them, they can't do nothing." In the end, Timmy's feelings about Kuharich seemed to be conflicted. "I really liked Kuharich, because he was funny to me," he said in 2010. "He was always sitting on the sideline scratching this one spot. He's just not a good coach.... He didn't have the record to prove it in the end either." He added, "He failed in everything he did." But he also said, "I thought he was a good man, a good guy basically, but I thought he was influenced by other people." He believed that in particular, defensive line coach Dick Evans had influenced Kuharich against him: "He was a military guy and it was like, don't talk to me like that, you know."

Kuharich only lasted one more season in Philadelphia, a year in which the Eagles went 2-12. His final game, a 24-17 loss to Minnesota, provided the iconic Philly sports-fan image of a Santa Claus being pelted with snowballs during a halftime show. A year after his firing, Kuharich was diagnosed with cancer, and while he lived 10 more years, he never coached again. Rozelle gave the eulogy at his funeral. In the late 2000s, Timmy said that if he had tried to attend Kuharich's funeral, "they would have kicked me out."

In addition to hoping that for the 1968 season he would be a Giant or a Ram, Timmy wanted a three-year deal like Sonny Jurgensen had gotten from Washington. Instead, the Eagles traded him on Jan. 30 to Baltimore for Alvin Haymond, and the Colts were to pay him $85,000 for one year as a running back. Timmy ended his Eagles career as second in rushing yards with 3,703 yards, behind Steve Van Buren, and third in touchdowns with 29 on 805 carries. He held the team records at that time for kickoff returns (169), kickoff return yardage (4,483), and returns for touchdowns (five).

"I expected to be traded, but not this quickly," Timmy said after he found out. "I expected it a month or two after the draft. Now I'm undecided whether I want to play for the Colts or not." Timmy didn't openly badmouth Kuharich – throughout his life he tried not to criticize other people in public – but said, "There were habits formed both ways and they took hold over any friendship we might have had. If I could put a finger on it, our differences were in communication and understanding each other. We had a chance, but it never came about.... We just have different theories and this made me a rebel." He said the team had wanted to trade him for four years, which would be since Kuharich arrived. He called Haymond "a fine ballplayer" – in 1965 he had set the Colts record for punt returns in a season – but added, "My value must have dipped." (As it turned out, Haymond would play only one season with the Eagles.) Still, he hoped to continue to wear jersey No. 22 when playing for Baltimore. Colts coach Don Shula said Timmy "fits into our system perfectly.... He is great running the ball or coming out of the backfield to catch a pass."

In the spring of 1968, Timmy began to participate more actively in social causes. He was among a group of prominent Black athletes who met with Democratic presidential candidate Robert F. Kennedy before the Indiana primary in April. Leading the group was Oscar Robertson, the NBA star and Indianapolis native. Grier also took part. Despite an order from newspaper publisher Eugene C. Pulliam (who controlled papers in five Indiana cities, including Ball State's Muncie) to downplay Kennedy and emphasize the favorite-son candidacy of Gov. Roger Branigin, Kennedy won the primary and was widely credited with keeping Indianapolis calm on the night of the assassination of the Rev. Martin Luther King Jr., just two months before his own assassination. On a cold, windy evening on April 4, he spoke to an audience on Martindale Avenue that had not yet heard of King's death in Memphis just hours before. Among those next to him as he spoke was John F. Brown Jr.

At that time, Timmy's brother was associate director of the Urban League in Indianapolis. After taking some time off from college to serve in the military, Buddy Brown had gotten his bachelor's degree in history and political science from Butler in 1964, and had become an education activist in the Hoosier Capital, working with the Fletcher Place Community Center and Indianapolis Pre-School Inc. The following year, he would join the Center for Innovation in Teacher Education of Indiana University, and soon thereafter became interim chair of the new Department of Urban Education at IU. The Kennedy campaign had reached out to Buddy, considering him, according to Walter Sheridan, a campaign coordinator, "a moderate black school teacher ... who had a good rapport with the militants and the moderates ... and he became kind of our liaison man." The fact that he was the brother of a pro football player "gave him some stature," Sheridan said.

According to Sheridan, influential Black people in Indiana sought money from the Kennedy campaign. It was better if Buddy told them no, he said, "than for us to tell them no." He added, "Any money we did dispense, which was just for opening neighborhood headquarters and for expenses, went through John Brown. And he accounted for every penny of it and insisted it be that way, and insisted that he get receipts, and did get receipts for everything that was spent. So it was a happy solution on both sides." About two weeks after Kennedy's assassination in Los Angeles on the night of June 6, Timmy received a hand-written letter, dated June 6, from Karen Mayers, a staffer in Kennedy's Washington campaign office. She wrote, in part: "Thanks for all your efforts on Senator Kennedy's campaign. Mrs. Kennedy came to our office last week and asked us to please tell people like you how much she appreciated all you had done for him." The letter ended on a personal note: "We'll be looking at you this fall but rooting for the other team when you play the Redskins. Good luck this season – don't break any bones." She asked Timmy to share the letter with Buddy, because she didn't have his address. Timmy said that about six months later, Ethel Kennedy sent him a picture of her late husband. In 2010, he said, "I have it at my place, hanging on the wall. Bobby had promised to send it to me and I had forgotten all about it. I got this lovely letter" from Ethel Kennedy "saying, 'Bobby promised you he would send you a picture and you were one of his favorite players.' That was really nice." Also in

1968, Jim Brown noted in a Playboy interview that Timmy was one of the athletes who was participating in his National Negro Industrial and Economic Union. Jim Brown said the group's primary mission was to "help black people help themselves economically.... The job of sincere and committed blacks such as the athletes in my NNIEU – who may be the only kind of guys the toughest street cats will accept and listen to – is to work inside the ghetto to eliminate the effects of racial prejudice and discrimination by helping black people acquire the green power they need to make life, liberty and the pursuit of happiness a tangible reality." Bill Russell and Kareem Abdul-Jabbar were also part of the group, which later became known as the Black Economic Union. Carl Stokes, the onetime Cleveland mayor, was a neighbor of Brown's on Cleveland's East Side and served as the group's legal counsel. The group continues to operate in Kansas City.

Timmy had been so glad to get away from Kuharich that the city of Baltimore, while not an entertainment hub, initially looked good to him, but he wanted to be paid well if he was going to spend another year in football instead of acting. His paycheck from the Colts would be his highest ever in pro football, but was not what he thought he deserved. "I hate to put it that way, but it will take a lot to go over certain things I've got working," he said. By May, Timmy was having second thoughts about the Colts. He said he was "leaning" toward quitting football and going after an entertainment career full time. "It's not that I don't want to play football," he said. "It's just that I want the other thing too." During the preceding months he had worked for a Job Corps anti-poverty program in St. Louis and spoken at the annual Ball State sports banquet, at which Emens was recognized upon his retirement. He was also scheduled to model swimsuits for Jantzen. He was still seeing Ross off and on as well, and was seen jogging with her at Philadelphia's Franklin Field in mid-May. Baltimore was close enough to Philadelphia that he did not have to move from his Society Hill apartment. Philadelphia sportswriter George Kiseda, who worked for the Daily News and the Evening Bulletin, and who was once praised as "the model of what every sportswriter should be," came across them jogging and running up the steps. Ross told Kiseda that she had run high school track, whereupon he suggested a competitive 50-yard dash. The 24-year-old Ross won easily over the sportswriter, then in his 40s.

As the weeks passed, Timmy decided he was indeed ready to hang up his cleats, and in mid-July said he had played his last game and would move to L.A. to concentrate on acting. Philly sportswriter Merchant thought Timmy would have given the Colts a true halfback for this season. Jim Brown, he noted, had also retired after nine years in the NFL at age 31 to go into show business. But Timmy had "no guarantees, no contracts, no commitments other than a shot at 'Tarzan.'" Timmy sounded a bit surprised himself by his decision: "Me of all people, as insecure as I am, giving up security for insecurity.... I wracked my brain with this decision for five months. I decided football wasn't going to do any more for my future than it already has. Why go to Baltimore?" Shula said the ethical thing for the Eagles to do as a result of Timmy's retirement was to compensate the Colts, possibly with a high draft pick. Talks involving both teams followed.

While living in Southern California, Timmy often went to the Hollywood YMCA. He played in pickup basketball games there, but he was always prepared to play on the spur of the moment at any time, in any place. In the trunk of his car, he carried numerous pairs of shoes of different sizes, in the event he met others who wanted to play or boasted about how good they were but who said they couldn't play because they didn't have the right shoes with them. He made sure there was no excuse.

One day when he was playing at the Y, he met Rick Whitfield, a 16-year-old who attended Hollywood High School and was an outstanding athlete in basketball, baseball, and football – not at the level of Timmy, but close. Whitfield would go on to play football at Los Angeles Valley

College in Van Nuys, where in 1972 he made 45 receptions for 504 yards and one touchdown. He became the No. 2 junior college receiver in the nation, behind Jessie Roberts of Pasadena City College, with 59.

About a year before their meeting, Whitfield had lost his father, Robert Jordan Whitfield, an African American actor, musician, and comedian known as "Smoki." In the 1940s he had begun a career as a character actor. His father and mother were both signed to MGM. Over the decades, he amassed more than 50 on-screen credits, including 12 "Bomba, the Jungle Boy" movies, in which he played the role of Eli, a native guide for star Johnny Sheffield. He played the roles of an African chieftain, witch doctor, porter, servant, carpenter, taxi driver, truck driver, and maintenance man in numerous other movies and TV shows. From 1959 to 1961, he was Oscar in the Walt Disney TV miniseries "The Swamp Fox" with Leslie Nielsen, John Sutton, and Joy Page. His work as a singer included "Function at the Junction," which he wrote, and "Take the Hint," recorded with the Freddie Simon Orchestra on Crest Records. He was friends with Redd Foxx, known for his raunchy humor and for his role as Fred Sanford, who ran a salvage shop in South Central Los Angeles with his son, Lamont, in the NBC series "Sanford and Son" from 1972 to 1977. He also was friends with Mario Moreno, the Mexican comedian known as Cantinflas, who was called the Charlie Chaplin of Latin America. Cantinflas also played the role of Passepartout, Phileas Fogg's manservant, in the 1956 film "Around the World in 80 Days." It was his introduction to U.S. audiences and earned him a Golden Globe for Best Actor in a Musical or Comedy.

His mother, Harriet Eileen Whitfield, was white; he said she looked like Ava Gardner. An actress, she was known as Eileen Jackson. Whitfield said that she appeared in Arthur Miller's play "All My Sons" at the LaJolla Playhouse in the late 1940s as Gregory Peck's girlfriend and had a role in the 1947 movie "The Unfinished Dance," starring Cyd Charisse.

According to Whitfield, his parents had to go to Mexico to marry because at the time, mixed marriages were illegal in California. Smoki also was running a club in Mexico, where he was unfairly arrested as a drug dealer and all his money was confiscated," he said. "Smoki called Cantinflas, who bailed him out."

In the 1950s, Smoki worked as a manager and emcee at nightclubs in Hawaii. Eventually, the family moved to Laurel Canyon, a liberal haven in the Hollywood Hills, where Whitfield grew up. Whitfield said the diversity of the people and their thinking in Laurel Canyon made mixed marriages acceptable, as they had been in Mexico and Hawaii, and motivated his father to move there. Neighbors included the jazz saxophonist Stan Getz, tagged "The Sound" for his warm, lyrical tone, and known for such hits as "The Girl From Ipanema" and "Desafinado." Another neighbor was the singer-songwriter Joni Mitchell, known for "Big Yellow Taxi," "A Case of You," and "Help Me" as well as her tribute to the "Ladies of the Canyon." Alice Cooper, Chaka Khan, and members of the Byrds, the Eagles, and the Mamas and the Papas were among those who lived in the canyon.

One of Smoki's best friends, Larry Parks, also resided there and gained attention during the House Un-American Activities Committee hearings of the 1940s and 1950s. Parks was nominated for the Oscar for Best Actor in 1946 for his title role in "The Jolson Story." Other important roles followed, including the movies "Down to Earth" (1947), "The Gallant Blade" (1948), and "Jolson Sings Again" (1949). In his testimony on March 21, 1951, Parks admitted to having been a member of the Communist Party, and in a private session shared the names of other members. Even though he named names, he was nonetheless blacklisted. His movie career was effectively over.

In L.A., Smoki owned the Top Banana Club in Studio City and was part owner of the Universal Bar & Grill in North Hollywood, close to Universal Studios. "There was an outstanding debt on the liquor license at the Top Banana Club," Rick Whitfield said, "which restricted alcohol sales. People were also stealing from him. As a result, it was challenging to make much money. He was able to get by for a time because of the support of celebrity friends who came by, such as Marlon Brando and Lee Marvin. Without being able to pay off the debt on the liquor license, though, he eventually lost everything." In Whitfield's opinion, the stress, coupled with an auto accident, led to his father's fatal heart attack, with his son present, on Nov. 11, 1967. He said Marvin was the first to show up at the house after hearing of his death.

With their meeting so soon after his father's death, Whitfield said, Timmy became "like a father to me. I saw him all the time. He stood up for me." He was impressed by how health-conscious Timmy was, noting that he fasted and focused on stretching to keep in shape. Whitfield recalled watching him practice shooting before they played and recalled that he sank 30-footers effortlessly. "When we played, I never knew how to guard him," he said. "He could move to his left and to his right quickly and equally as well, and hit his shot."

In 2010, Timmy said that while he was living in California, the Colts "worked all summer trying to get me and I kept saying no. They said, 'Well, we know what went down in Philadelphia, it's not going to be that way here. Here we are going to give you the ball 18, 20 times because we know that was a conflict with you.' I was getting the ball six, seven times and I'm breaking records with doing that.... I guess it spread around pretty much that I was very unhappy. So I just decide it was time to go, and [Gifford] called me, Howard Cosell called me. Gif said, 'What are you going to do?'" Gifford and Cosell, who had become famous in the 1960s as an ABC sports reporter through his interviews with Muhammad Ali, met with Timmy to discuss his being part of a concept that ultimately became "Monday Night Football." Timmy said Cosell told him, "They're coming out with a show next year and we'd like for you to be with us." Timmy said he was more interested in acting, but they pursued him and met over drinks in New York City. In response, Timmy said, "You know, it sounds good, but I've got to take this chance to go out there [Hollywood] and see what I can do. I've been studying and working on it [acting] for 10 years." ABC's "Monday Night Football," of course, transformed both the sport and television. Timmy recalled in 2008, "I wish I had done it."

Timmy said that in 1969, he didn't need money immediately because he had deferred part of his income, "but I was getting bored" in California because of not getting acting parts – often, he said, because his skin wasn't seen as dark enough. Still, his focus seemed set on acting, so it may have been a surprise to many that by Aug. 20, Timmy was at the Colts training camp at the small Western Maryland College (now McDaniel College) in Westminster, Md. Timmy had been set to perform at the Playboy Club in Hollywood and was to meet with Sidney Poitier about a possible movie role. But while in California, he visited the Rams' and Cowboys' training camps. The players there said they envied what he was doing, but people would also come up to him and say, "Oh, so you're never gonna play football again, huh?" According to wire service reporter Milton Richman in a story at the time, Timmy was lying in bed in California, unable to sleep. He then made the decision to cancel his show business commitments. "I want to get back in football, that's why," he said, "because there's nothing else in the world I can't do without except respect." Shula, now no longer having to negotiate with the Eagles over Timmy's worth, said the team's chance for a championship was brighter with Timmy on board.

In 2010, Timmy said that "I went up there [to Maryland], and I knew my knee was bad. I didn't know how bad. I could fake it good ... and Shula, he was a great guy.... If I had played for him all my career, I would have been a bad boy. He would have given me the ball." Time had passed, and Timmy said to himself, "It's no fun anymore, I don't enjoy it, I'm not going to be in shape." But even so, he said, he reported anyway.

But in another 2010 interview, he told another tale of why he decided to put his cleats on again. "I retired when I could have gone with Baltimore, and the agent [in L.A.] was happy to get me out, and all of a sudden he quit sending me out [for casting], and I was not working. And I found out when it was over why he quit sending me out, because Carroll Rosenbloom [the Colts' owner] and Don Shula were calling.... Carroll Rosenbloom had some weight in Hollywood [he was a co-owner of Seven Arts Productions, which financed a number of movies], and my agent, they were telling him not to send me out. They would make excuses, and I was running low on money. Don Shula and Rosenbloom were taking turns calling about me coming back there. And they quit sending me out and I lost a lot of confidence, so I ended up going back."

At training camp in Maryland, the now-31-year-old Timmy had to learn a new football system for the first time in years. To the training camp in Westminster, he brought "maybe one-twentieth" of his clothes – specifying 95 pairs of shoes. Asked about whether he was trying to show Kuharich that he still had it as a Colt, Timmy said, "Kuharich isn't important enough for that.... Kuharich spent [years] knocking me. I want to be a champion, that's why I'm here. I've been a loser all my life." Of the four years with the Eagles in which he took acting lessons every Monday, he said, "There were repercussions. Maybe they wanted me to go out and get drunk like a lot of the guys did. My going to New York on Mondays was a big hangup in Philadelphia.... I guess they thought I was going to play football for the next 50 years. I'm not a rebel, but they thought I was. It's nice to be here where they treat you like a man, not like you're in second grade." Of his acting career, he said, "If I'm going to make it, I can make it next year."

The season began with uncertainty as quarterback Johnny Unitas was nursing a bad elbow at the end of the exhibition season, during which the Baltimore Sun forgot to give Timmy a first name in a game story, just mentioning "a 6-yard run by Brown." Backup QB Earl Morrall, at age 34 a veteran of 12 NFL seasons, was called into action for the season opener, a 27-10 win over the 49ers. Shula said he didn't use Timmy until late in the game because he wanted longtime player Tom Matte in the huddle to help Morrall out. "You know the terminology here still gets me," Morrall said. "Tom Matte corrected me several times in the huddle." Timmy did gain 15 yards rushing and 18 on a pass reception in the fourth quarter, plus 24 yards on kickoff returns. "It made me feel like the team was depending on me," Timmy said. "Like old times. Before Joe Kuharich at Philadelphia. It makes you feel like playing." Kuharich's scars had clearly made Timmy change his mind about avoiding public putdowns.

Timmy continued to see action, including a 2-yard touchdown run in a 41-7 win over the Steelers in late September, but Matte was piling up the bigger statistics. And by October, Timmy had soured on the city of Baltimore: "This city is not my bag. It's a lousy town. Thank God I'm only here for 4½ months. I don't enjoy one moment of it except when I'm playing ball." He was living in a downtown hotel with Bubba Smith as his roommate and hadn't yet dated a Baltimore girl. "I import them from New York and Philadelphia.... I don't go out much," he said. "Maybe if I did I'd find it swinging out there." He said later in life that he told one reporter, "I never saw a beautiful woman there yet," which did not help his cause with the residents of Charm City when they read it. But Baltimore was used to this sort of thing. "Baltimore," native son Mark Kram once wrote in Sports Illustrated, "is an anonymous city even to those who live there, a city that draws a laugh even from Philadelphia." Kram ended up working for the Philadelphia Daily News.

In Baltimore, Timmy did go out to a club to see Dee Dee Sharp perform. He had invited some Colts teammates to come along as well, and she was seated with him and some others at a table. Kenny Gamble, then her husband, was a jealous man, she said in 2021, and didn't like seeing Timmy there with her. After he confronted her, she said, Timmy told him that if he continued giving her a hard time, he would get the Colts players there with him to take care of things. "I was embarrassed by Gamble," she said. "We became closer friends after that situation. It was unnecessary. I wasn't doing anything. Tim was friends with Dionne Warwick and I didn't care. I knew he was friends with Diana Ross. A whole lot of people, but he was my friend." Sharp and Gamble divorced in 1980 and she later married Philadelphia attorney Bill Witherspoon.

The Oct. 14 game against the host 49ers saw Unitas return to play for the first time in the season. He took the field with eight minutes left in the fourth quarter and handed off to Timmy for a 2-yard run during a 21-point blitz. Sun sports editor Bob Maisel wrote that "Unitas and Timmy Brown might have formed the most famous substitute backfield in history." He said that while Timmy had been used sparingly, his work in the offensive backfield "and in running back kicks improves every week, and it looks as though both he and Unitas will be able to contribute more whenever they are needed." But the next week, Timmy was out because of an injured leg, spending a night in a hospital. He returned to action on Nov. 4 in a shutout of the Giants, but neither Timmy nor Unitas met Maisel's expectations. Morrall stayed in as quarterback and then split the duties with Unitas, and while Timmy continued to post solid numbers, he was playing backup to Matte, whom he had been told would back him up. "Nobody likes being second string," he said. "I wanted to go out as a winner, but not as a substitute. But if that's what they want…." He said he was "making great money, more money than I ever had before."

By the Dec. 1 game against Atlanta, which the Colts won by 44-0, he had 38 carries for 159 yards. The Colts became champions of the Coastal Division on Dec. 8, and the following week in a "meaningless" game the attention was focused on back Preston Pearson, a "star of the future." A hamstring issue then kept Timmy out of a couple ozf games, but he was ready for Super Bowl III in Miami on Jan. 12, where he had four punt returns and two kickoff returns as the highly favored Colts lost by 16-7 to the upstart New York Jets, led by Namath. Morrall threw three interceptions before being replaced by Unitas, who led the drive to the only Colts touchdown. Timmy had figured he wouldn't play because of the hamstring issue. So he was open to spending some time with Namath on the night before the big game. "I was very suspicious of that after that," he said. "I guess he was trying to see if I was going to play or not." He added, "I had a few drinks, I wasn't drunk or anything, but found out later he was drinking water with something and ordering mine, 'Bring him another one.' In the Super Bowl game, Timmy said he "finally talked Shula into letting me try." He added, "The first punt, I ended up fair catch. Second punt, I made the wrong cut. Went down with that hamstring. The knee was weak. It was already grinding a little. I don't know how I carried myself where it wouldn't show."

Before the game, he said, the Colts were "pretty overconfident. We thought it would be a cakewalk." After the game, he added, "it was embarrassing that the AFL beat us." Namath had famously predicted the win three days before the game, breaking from the usual reluctance of athletes to give their opponents motivation through their own braggadocio. His unblinkered confidence that the Jets would win gave his own team extra motivation. (In a coda to Timmy's pro career, Namath left the game temporarily in the third quarter after hurting his thumb. That brought in, for a few plays, Babe Parilli – the once-popular Green Bay quarterback whom Lombardi had axed before his first season.)

With the Super Bowl bonus, Timmy earned about $97,000 in his final year of play. After the season, "they wanted to give me a three-year contract. [Shula] kept calling me about it. I said, 'I'm not sure yet. Let me think about it.' He said, 'Well, we've got a deadline on this.' So I went in, had the [knee] operation. Still had plenty of time to get it right. 'Cause I thought it was just chips, a couple chips in there that kept catching on the knee. They didn't have arthroscopic surgery then. And they took out my whole interior, my leg bowed out like this; I was like a freak. I should have got it done before I went to the Colts and then see how I felt after that, working it out."

So that was it for football. During his career, Timmy had cracked ribs, separated shoulders, broken his nose twice, fractured an ankle, ripped loose his rib cartilage, and gotten infections on his shins. He estimated in 2010 that he had had about 15 surgeries on both of his knees, largely to get rid of bone chips.

Timmy was one of three players from the 1960 championship team to make the Eagles' all-time squad, along with McDonald and Bednarek. In his 10 years and 109 games of NFL play, he gained 12,684 yards total, which placed him fourth on the all-time list at that time – and he kept his top-10 placement until 1988. (Who was first? Jim Brown, of course.) He gained 3,862 rushing yards, for 4.3 per carry, and scored 31 rushing TDs. He caught 235 passes for 3,399 yards and 26 more touchdowns, and passed for one, and returned five kickoffs, one punt and one missed field goal for touchdowns. He was the best pass-receiving back of his time, averaging 14.5 yards per reception for his career. At the time of his death in 2020, he remained the Eagles' all-time leader in average yards per touch (6.52), kickoff returns (169), kickoff return yardage (4,483), and kickoff returns for touchdowns (five).

Even so, as John Maxymuk noted in "Eagles by the Numbers: Jersey Numbers and the Players Who Wore Them," Timmy "never averaged 20 touches per game, and his highest rushing total was 861 yards in 1965." He gave the following reasons: 1) Timmy was never a big man, and was plagued by muscle pulls and hamstring problems; 2) teams in that era split the running game between the fullback and the halfback; 3) Kuharich didn't like him. Maxymuk questioned whether Timmy could have passed the 1,000-yard milestone had he been used more often – or whether he simply would have been injured more often. In 2010, Pete Retzlaff – who served three years as the Eagles' general manager, though not very successfully – said of his former teammate: "Timmy was a Gale Sayers-type back. He was very quick with a knack for finding daylight. He would be sensational in today's pro game. Spread the offense, throw him the ball and watch him go."

"If Timmy played in Green Bay or Oakland, there's no telling what kind of numbers he would've put up," Ron Medved, a safety on those Eagles teams, told Philadelphia sportswriter Ray Didinger after Timmy's death. "He just didn't have the supporting cast in Philadelphia. It was a shame. There was no prettier, no shiftier or more versatile runner in the league. He put up great numbers in Philadelphia, but he would've set (NFL) records with a better team."

As Timmy looked back on his football career, on more than one occasion he said that in his own mind, he never had a good game: "I will probably die frustrated." Later in life, he came to regret leaving the Quaker City. "If I had to do it again, I wouldn't have gone. I would have stayed in Philadelphia and just studied there and did stuff around New York, and would have had a solid job making good money. Philadelphia was very kind and very good to me. If I had been married or had a kid, then I would have been a little more realistic."

After retiring, Timmy continued to have a public profile as a top athlete. In spring 1969, he received the Distinguished Alumnus award from Ball State – early, as usually the award was given at Homecoming. "Some persons are blessed with special talents," alumni association president Tom Wallace said. "When these physical talents are combined with other outstanding characteristics, the one possessing them cannot help but bring distinction to his university." The citation noted Timmy's involvement in a campaign to reduce school dropouts in the Philadelphia area and his annual visits to the Knightstown Home. In June of that year, District of Columbia Stadium was renamed for Robert F. Kennedy. Frank Gifford was emcee of the event, which aimed to bring the greatest names in sports together to show how many top athletes had supported Kennedy. Timmy was among the 100 or so at the event, which also featured Gayle Sayers, Jerry West, Bob Cousey, Paul Hornung, Don Meredith, and Bill Russell.

And there had been the ceremony in the 1960s – the exact year has been lost to history – in which players on the 1959 Green Bay team got together to honor Lombardi. "Jerry Kramer and Hornung called," Timmy said, "and said, 'You're coming back for our reunion?' I said, "What are you talking about, reunion with you guys? I was only there two games.' [It actually was one.] They said they wanted everybody on Lombardi's first-year '59 team back for a reunion.... I finally went back and they introduced us individually, standing up, and the park was full of people. They came to me and they said, "And of course you will remember Timmy Brown, who is now with the Philadelphia Eagles.' And the whole place went, 'Oops.' It was crazy."

But that was Timmy Brown the football player. By 1970, Timmy was still moving downfield, but in a different game – the Hollywood game.

Timmy Brown leaps as he catches a 42-yard pass from quarterback Norman Snead during the Philadelphia Eagles' game against the New Orleans Saints on Nov. 20, 1967. Saints defensive back Jimmy Heidel is moving in on Timmy. The Eagles won by 48-21 that day at Franklin Field; their season was not as successful, ending 6-7-1. BILL INGRAHAM / ASSOCIATED PRESS

Timmy never forgot his childhood friends from Richmond, Ind., even though he moved from town to a suburban farm in 1948 and then the Indiana Soldiers' and Sailors' Children's Home. In 2013, they got together for a golf outing in Palm Springs. With Timmy are (from right) Harold Jones, George Walker, and Dave Chapman. COURTESY DAVE CHAPMAN

Timmy didn't get along with Ball State football coach Jim Freeman (center), and worked out a deal where he would only keep playing as long as Freeman didn't talk to him. By the May 15, 1968, Ball State all-sports banquet, at least he and Freeman were able to pose for a photo with Wave Myers, Cardinals football coach from 1968 to 1970. BALL STATE UNIVERSITY ARCHIVES AND SPECIAL COLLECTIONS

Vince Lombardi and his wife, Marie, arrive at the Green Bay airport in 1959, his first year of coaching the Packers. Timmy's career in Wisconsin would be brief. GREEN BAY PACKERS

Timmy on Ball State Field in 1958, with the college's Lucina residence hall behind him. Ball State Field, on University Avenue, was where football games and practices were held before what is now called Scheumann Stadium was built in 1967. TIMMY BROWN PHOTO COLLECTION

The three youngest Brown children, Della (Buggs), John Jr. (Buddy), and Thomas (Timmy), in 1953. Timmy felt more separated by age from his three older sisters. TIMMY BROWN PHOTO COLLECTION

Timmy with his sister Norma, known as Trixie, and Buddy at Buddy's 1954 graduation from Morton Memorial High School at the Indiana Soldiers' and Sailors' Children's Home. Timmy always looked up to Buddy but felt Buddy tended to look down on him. TIMMY BROWN PHOTO COLLECTION

In 1955, it was Timmy's turn to graduate from Morton. For once, he did not have to wear the Home's standard garb of blue shirts and blue jeans. TIMMY BROWN PHOTO COLLECTION

The Morton Memorial basketball team of 1954-55. Timmy was wearing No. 35. He set the county scoring record for that year with 398 points in 23 games for a 17.3 average. Bill Brewer (right) was the first-year basketball coach. TIMMY BROWN PHOTO COLLECTION

Timmy (left) showing his early running prowess for Morton Memorial in 1954. That year, he led the team in scoring with 115 points – more than half of the squad's total. TIMMY BROWN PHOTO COLLECTION

Timmy had long dreamed of becoming known as a singer. While he released five singles and performed in the Philadelphia area, national hits eluded him. But through his efforts, he came to know top stars such as Chubby Checker and Dionne Warwick. TIMMY BROWN PHOTO COLLECTION

New York vocal teacher Carmine Gagliardi, known for working with singers such as Patti LuPone, gave Timmy weekly lessons for years, including this one on Oct. 21, 1965. Timmy's focus on an entertainment career in addition to football did not sit well with some coaches, teammates and fans. MARTY LEDERHANDLER / ASSOCIATED PRESS

A number of football players served in the reserves to make some money on the side. Timmy, as an Army reservist, would annually teach female service members at Fort Knox. Fulfilling the terms of his service created a rocky start for his relationship with coach Joe Kuharich. TIMMY BROWN PHOTO COLLECTION

In 1966, Timmy finally received his diploma from Ball State after the school changed its rule requiring a double major to graduate. Congratulating him at Commencement was John R. Emens, the longtime Ball State president, who was a big advocate for Timmy. BALL STATE UNIVERSITY ARCHIVES AND SPECIAL COLLECTIONS

The Supremes – (from left) Mary Wilson, Florence Ballard, and Diana Ross – shot to fame in 1964. Timmy became romantically involved with Ross after meeting her at a South Jersey club where the group was performing. In 1967, they played for two weeks at the Copacabana in New York City. Joe Namath became New York Jets quarterback in 1965. Timmy played against "Broadway Joe" of the AFL twice – once in a preseason game and again in Super Bowl III, his final game. Namath also went on to an acting career, and for a time dated Wilson. TIMMY BROWN PHOTO COLLECTION

On a 1970 episode of "The Mary Tyler Moore Show," Timmy played himself and met with newsroom boss Lou Grant (Edward Asner) long enough to shake his hand. He had sought a role as the sportscaster in the series, but it went to John Amos. TIMMY BROWN PHOTO COLLECTION

*Timmy, as Spearchucker Jones, was living in the Swamp with Hawk-eye and Trapper John on the first six episodes of the TV series "M*A*S*H." Then his role, which could have meant stardom, came to an end. Some sources said he was written out because the show just had too many characters.* TIMMY BROWN PHOTO COLLECTION

*Robert Duvall played Frank Burns in the movie "M*A*S*H." Why Timmy got the credit he did at the end of the film, given his small part in it, remains a mystery.* TIMMY BROWN PHOTO COLLECTION

*Timmy said he left "M*A*S*H" because his agent said he would have a bigger career in films. But most of his roles came in Blaxploitation movies such as 1972's "Black Gunn," starring his longtime friend and rival Jim Brown (left).* TIMMY BROWN PHOTO COLLECTION

Timmy's first real role as a TV and film actor, done while he was still playing football, was as desperado Clint Cartwheel in "The Wild, Wild West," starring Robert Conrad. The sombrero Timmy wore led to a strange interlude with Conrad after it was knocked off his head. TIMMY BROWN PHOTO COLLECTION

Mercury Records signed Timmy to a contract in 1963 and released this publicity photo of him. But like most of his efforts to become a singer, it led to very little. TIMMY BROWN PHOTO COLLECTION.

In 1987, Timmy received the volunteer of the year award from the Los Angeles County Probation Department. The emcee of the event was the Fonz himself, Henry Winkler (left). Timmy went on to work for the department. TIMMY BROWN PHOTO COLLECTION

Timmy was part of the "International Sports Club," a group of athletes paid to promote Jantzen clothing. Among its other members was his friend Frank Gifford. Photo shoots took the club to exotic locales, such as Rio de Janeiro. TIMMY BROWN PHOTO COLLECTION

Friends noticed how when they were together, Jim Brown and Timmy would compete almost compulsively, from chess games to betting on tossing things into a wastebasket – or, on this occasion, playing basketball. TIMMY BROWN PHOTO COLLECTION

In Robert Altman's "Nashville," Timmy portrayed Tommy Brown, a character derived from Grand Ole Opry star Charley Pride. The movie was Timmy's high water mark as an entertainer. TIMMY BROWN PHOTO COLLECTION

As well as bringing him modeling work, Timmy's good looks rarely failed to be noticed by people, women in particular. TIMMY BROWN PHOTO COLLECTION

In the autumn of 1984, Timmy met Debra Lee Hartley at a spa in California. He quickly decided that she was the woman of his dreams. They were married on March 24, 1985.
COURTESY LEE HARTLEY

Timmy first met Gene Kilroy (left) when both were associated with the Eagles organization. Kilroy then became the business manager for Muhammad Ali, whom Timmy met. COURTESY GENE KILROY

Lee had grown up in a devout Christian family in the South, learning to sing as part of a family troupe at church events. By the time she was in her early 20s, she had performed on cruise ships and was hanging out with jazz musicians in New York City. COURTESY LEE HARTLEY

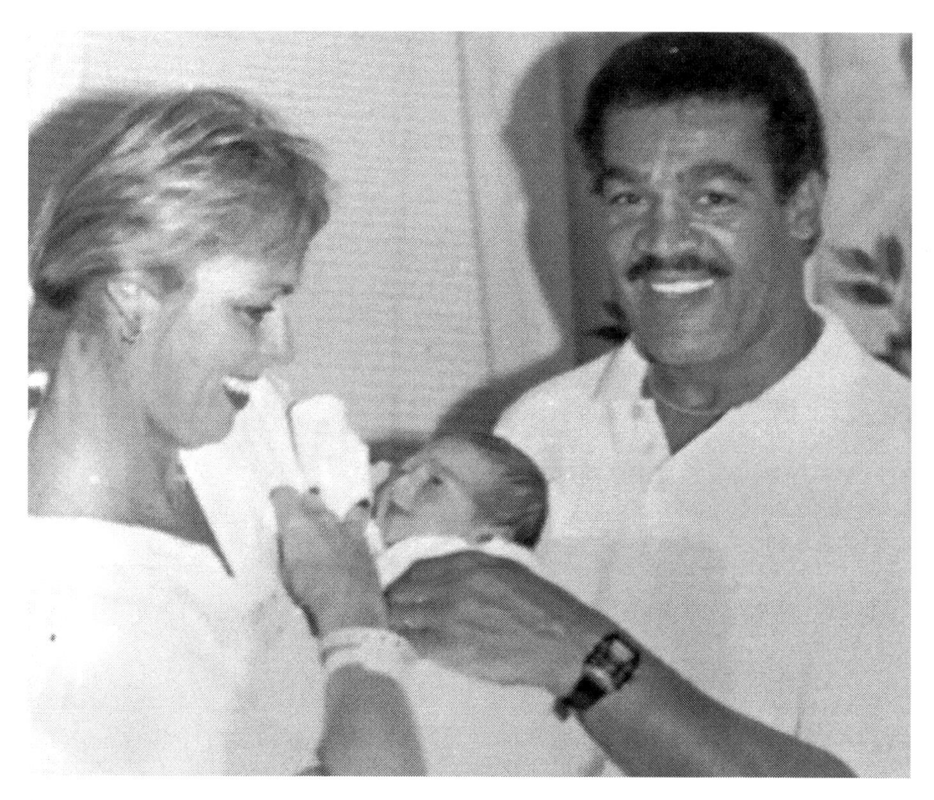

On Sept. 5, 1987, Lee and Timmy became the parents of their only child, Sean Timothy Brown. The child's birth led to Lee's parents finally accepting Timmy as part of their family.
COURTESY LEE HARTLEY

Lee, Sean, and Timmy at baby's first Christmas in 1987, with Hollie Vest (right). Timmy had met Vest in the early 1970s when he pulled up next to her at a gas station. They remained close friends for life. Vest became known for performing in the style of Tina Turner. COURTESY HOLLIE VEST

Sean Brown became a musician and then an actor in Southern California. He and his partner, Jennifer Van Camp, had two children, Ella and Leo. Lee joined them for this photo around the 2019 holiday season. COURTESY LEE HARTLEY

As Indiana officials pondered the future of the Soldiers' and Sailors' Children's Home, Timmy attended a 2009 rally at the state Capitol aimed at keeping it open, and signed a football for a raffle. It was won by Tom Bennett, a Morton Memorial 1960 graduate. The state voted to shut the Home anyway. TIMMY BROWN PHOTO COLLECTION

Tommy McDonald was one of Timmy's biggest fans from their short time together on the Eagles. In 2007, the team invited fans to vote on an all-time all-star team, and Timmy and Tommy were both elected to it. Tommy was accompanied to the game marking the event by his wife, Patricia. TIMMY BROWN PHOTO COLLECTION

Timmy holds Sean while getting a plaque from the Eagles in November 1990. To his left were Gene Kilroy and Ernestine Grice, at whose home he lived for many years. To his right was Tommy Mc-Donald. TIMMY BROWN PHOTO COLLECTION

Timmy on his last visit to Ball State University, in 2010, in front of Shafer Tower, which was built many years after he left. No matter where his life took him, he remained loyal to the school. By this time, his mental disabilities were becoming more prominent, yet until the end he always could turn on his public charm. CATHERINE TSAI / BALL STATE DAILY NEWS

HOLLYWOOD

CHAPTER SEVEN

A Star Rises, and Then Falls

H. Richard Hornberger Jr. was an Army surgeon during the Korean War. In 1956, he began working on a novel based on his experiences. He eventually called it "MASH: A Novel About Three Army Doctors," with the abbreviation standing for "Mobile Army Surgical Hospital." (The book did not use the now-iconic asterisks.) The novel, published under the name of Richard Hooker, and two less-popular sequels, "M*A*S*H Goes to Maine" and "M*A*S*H Mania," were based in part on Hornberger's experiences as a captain in the Army Medical Corps. In a foreword, Hornberger, who after leaving the service lived his entire life in Maine, wrote that the characters in the book were composites of people he knew or had heard about, and that he based the main character, Capt. Benjamin Franklin "Hawkeye" Pierce, on himself. Hornberger tried to get his book published for several years until William Morrow accepted it in 1968. It is unlikely that this New England doctor could have envisioned the entertainment empire that his book would launch. "M*A*S*H," the film adaptation of the first novel, was one of the most highly regarded movies of the 1970s and led to one of the most beloved television series ever.

The book introduces many of the characters who would appear in the film and the television series, including "Trapper John" McIntyre,

Col. Henry Blake, and Walter "Radar" O'Reilly. Among them is Oliver Wendell "Spearchucker" Jones, an African American neurosurgeon. Both the book and the movie feature a football game between units. Hawkeye works to add Spearchucker, his former roommate, to his team. Spearchucker by then had been assigned to the 72nd Evacuation Hospital in Taegu.

In the book, Spearchucker Jones is described as a fullback who was scouted and signed, ironically as it turns out, by the Philadelphia Eagles. When Jones arrives at the MASH camp, Trapper John asks, "Where'd you get that Spearchucker handle?" He answers, "I used to throw the javelin. Somebody started calling me that, and the sportswriters thought it was good and it stuck." Despite that explanation, "Spearchucker" was then, and remains, a racially charged term used to describe African Americans. The chapter that features Spearchucker can at best be called awkward, and reflective of 1950s stereotypes and prejudice against Blacks. An attempt is made to touch on the topic of race, but Hawkeye quickly brings it to a halt, saying, "The hell with this. Let's talk about something else."

Shortly after the book was published, the screenwriter Ring Lardner Jr. read it and thought it would make a wonderful movie. He also was hopeful that it might provide the comeback he needed. Lardner, whose father was a famous baseball writer, had been a successful screenwriter, winning an Academy Award for best original screenplay with Michael Kanin in 1942 for the Katharine Hepburn-Spencer Tracy comedy "Woman of the Year." But in 1947, Lardner testified before the House Un-American Activities Committee, created in 1938 to investigate suspected communists. Rep. J. Parnell Thomas of New Jersey grilled Lardner over his alleged ties to the Communist Party. The congressman, frustrated by Lardner's repeated refusals to answer the committee's longtime basic question, said, "It's a very simple question. Anybody would be proud to answer it – any real American would be proud to answer the question, 'Are you or have you ever been a member of the Communist

Party?'" A defiant Lardner answered, "I could answer the question exactly the way you want, but if I did, I would hate myself in the morning." Lardner, who was one of the writers later dubbed the "Hollywood Ten" for their actions before the committee, was found guilty of contempt of Congress and was blacklisted for years, forced to submit his work under pseudonyms.

By the late 1960s, the effects of the communist witch hunt had started to subside. Lardner saw his opportunity and wrote a screenplay about the MASH doctors in Korea. His instincts were correct, as he won the Academy Award for best adapted screenplay for "M*A*S*H." But even Lardner could not foresee what "M*A*S*H" would become, once saying, "'M*A*S*H' has no future as a television show."

Robert Altman, the movie's director, was, at the time of his death in 2000 at the age of 81, one of the most celebrated and critically acclaimed directors of the 20th century, with a filmography including "McCabe and Mrs. Miller," "California Split," "Gosford Park," "Short Cuts," "The Player," and, most notably, "Nashville." But in 1969 he was a struggling 45-year-old television director still looking for his first critically acclaimed or commercially successful feature. "M*A*S*H," made for 20th Century Fox, succeeded on both counts. As is often the case with movies, timing was key. America was entangled in the Vietnam War, with much of the country questioning the involvement in Southeast Asia. Although the setting for "M*A*S*H" was the Korean War, many of the themes resonated with Vietnam. And so, a movie made for $3.5 million with minimal expectations took in $81.6 million at the box office and won the Palme d'Or at Cannes, in addition to five Oscar nominations. Lardner repeatedly clashed with Altman, before, during, and after production over the director's penchant to have his actors improvise, but Lardner ended up being the only one to carry home an Oscar. Altman was outraged, as often happened, and was never shy thereafter to criticize Lardner's role in writing the screenplay.

As "M*A*S*H" began filming, Timmy got a call from Altman. It is likely that Altman was looking for real football players to bring added credibility to the football sequences that dominate the last quarter of the film. Altman's casting director had selected NFL great Fred Williamson to play Spearchucker Jones. According to Timmy, Altman had followed his career in the NFL and learned of his interest in acting only after Williamson had been cast, so he created a role for him – Cpl. Judson. But the part was a cameo with no dialogue. Thus the ending of the film seems inexplicable. In an epilogue, the P.A. announcer at the MASH unit announces the primary characters and actors, beginning with Donald Sutherland as Hawkeye and Elliott Gould as Trapper John. The film's other stars, Sally Kellerman (Maj. Margaret "Hot Lips" Houlihan), Robert Duvall (Cpl. Frank Burns), and Gary Burghoff (Radar), are also mentioned. The last to be included is "Tim Brown as Cpl. Judson." Why Altman featured Timmy while characters with much larger parts, including Williamson, were left out was never addressed.

Timmy would benefit from the brief exposure Altman gave him, whatever its reason. But in the early 1970s his "M*A*S*H" experience mainly led to a disappointing collection of small roles and guest appearances, on largely forgotten shows such as "Cade's County" and "O'Hara, U.S. Treasury." A 1972 role on "Mission: Impossible" epitomized how Hollywood seemed to view Timmy. The seventh-season episode is called "Cocaine" and guest stars William Shatner as the primary villain. Timmy plays one of his hired guns, Barret. The character's dialogue is clichéd and does nothing to stretch Timmy as an actor. Some producers hired him more for his celebrity on the gridiron than his acting. Timmy's appearance on a 1970 episode of "The Mary Tyler Moore Show" was a cameo as himself, and he is on screen only long enough to shake the hand of Lou Grant, played by Edward Asner. Timmy had wanted to be in the series about a Minneapolis TV newsroom and its staff and had tried out for the role of the sportscaster, but the role went to John Amos, who later gained more fame in the CBS series "Good Times."

(There would always be links between Timmy's gridiron career and

Hollywood. In both versions of "The Longest Yard," in 1977 and 2005, Timmy said, Burt Reynolds wore a jersey with his number, 22, and told him it was a tribute to his career. In September 2003, for the opening of the Eagles' new home, Lincoln Financial Field – with a "Monday Night Football" game that the Eagles lost by 17-0 – the team wanted Rocky Balboa to be part of the pre-game events. Sylvester Stallone came out wearing a No. 22 jersey, which the Philadelphia Daily News reported that he had picked to honor Timmy.)

Timmy's best roles during this era were in three episodes of the NBC police series "Adam-12," playing a different character each time. The two episodes available online ("Vengeance" and "The Militants") show Timmy's potential as an actor. He is particularly good in "The Militants," transcending now-dated and clunky dialogue such as "Little Willie James was murdered by the pig power structure."

According to Timmy, some of his frustration in obtaining roles came from his light skin color. "It was hard fitting their [casting directors and producers'] idea of what Black was supposed to be," he said years later. "To go in for a part that is supposed to be a Harvard lawyer, and you give them a reading, and they say, 'No, no, no.' They wanted more 'Black.' Well, what is 'more Black'? They didn't know how to cast Black. A lot of places didn't know how to cast Blacks at all." Once, he said, an agent told him, "'You're not going to get any great roles unless you get out and get darker.' I would go to the beach and get as dark as I could." Another indicated, "You're going to be hard to get work for because you're a good-looking Black man — light-skinned." Timmy answered him by joking, "I can get dark. Then I can be Dark Gable." Rick Whitfield, who maintained his close friendship with Timmy during this time, said Timmy competed for the role of Louis McKay in "Lady Sings the Blues," in which Diana Ross played Billie Holiday. In the end, the part went to Billy Dee Williams. Timmy kept running short on luck.

And then, "M*A*S*H" came back into the picture.

William Self, president of 20th Century Fox, may have been the first person to think that "M*A*S*H" had the potential to be a successful TV series. It was pitched to two networks, and CBS beat out ABC by committing to a pilot before seeing a script, a rarity in those days. Self first brought on board Gene Reynolds, a hot young producer, and the two flew to London to recruit Larry Gelbart, who among other successes had been one of the key writers on Sid Caesar's early television landmark, "Your Show of Shows." CBS was on a roll in the early 1970s. Having been known for years as the "country corn" network, with commercially popular but critically panned hits like "The Beverly Hillbillies," "Green Acres," and "Petticoat Junction," CBS changed course in the 1970s with a series of culturally relevant and superbly scripted and acted sitcoms.

The change started with "Mary Tyler Moore" in 1970. In 1971, CBS brought out "All in the Family," which broke more barriers than any show before it (or possibly since) and shattered ratings records while doing so. "All in the Family" proved that sensitive and controversial issues and commercial success were not mutually exclusive. Without "All in the Family," "M*A*S*H" the series might not have happened. Here was a sitcom that lived in a world of war, death, blood, and tragedy – but still, some scenes were accompanied by the standard laugh track. (It was not used during scenes in the operating room and disappeared altogether after a few seasons.) The continuing quagmire of Vietnam also played a role. Gelbart and Gene Reynolds were clear in stating that the series was really about Vietnam. In Suzy Kalter's "The Complete Book of M*A*S*H," Gelbart says, "I was not part of the Vietnam antiwar movement in the United States because I lived in England, so 'M*A*S*H' was the contribution I knew I would have made if I had been able." Reynolds was even more direct: "There was no question about it. We were literally in Korea but figuratively in Vietnam."

William Hornberger, son of Richard (who died in 1997 at age 73), indicated that his father "liked the movie because he thought it followed his original intent very closely, but my father was a political conservative, and he did not like the liberal tendencies that Alan Alda portrayed Hawkeye Pierce as having."

"M*A*S*H" debuted on CBS on Sept. 17, 1972, and was not an instant success. In the 1972-73 season, the series ended up 46th out of 84 shows. Critically, it fared no better, with Time labeling it one of the most disappointing new series of the season. In later years, as broadcasting and cable became more competitive, CBS likely would have canceled the series quickly, perhaps after 13 episodes and certainly after one season. But the CBS of 1973 chose patience, and it paid off. "M*A*S*H" ended 11 seasons and 256 episodes later, with the episode "Goodbye, Farewell and Amen" on Feb. 28, 1983, being the third-most-watched program in television history – and eight of the 10-most-watched programs are Super Bowl telecasts.

Over those 11 years, "M*A*S*H" survived changes in casting and emphasis through superb writing and outstanding acting, as well as its nature as an ensemble show, with episodes centering on different characters instead of just one star. Most of the characters in the film were initially featured in the series. Alda was brilliant as Hawkeye, but so were Wayne Rogers as Trapper John and Loretta Swit as Houlihan. Larry Linville shaped a minor character from the film, Frank Burns, into a villain audiences loved to hate. McLean Stevenson was wonderful as Col. Henry Blake. But only one actor from the film carried over into the same role – Gary Burghoff, whose Radar O'Reilly became one of the series' most beloved characters. Like Timmy, Burghoff was an alumnus of the HB Studio in New York, although there is no record of whether they ever worked together as students in the acting school.

One additional carryover character from the film was Spearchucker Jones, and for this role the producers turned to Timmy – making him the only actor other than Burghoff to appear in both the movie and multiple episodes of the series. In the pilot and the next five episodes, Spearchucker bunks with Hawkeye, Trapper John, and Frank Burns in the famous "Swamp" tent. According to Whitfield, when Timmy went in to read for the part, he thought that the casting director wasn't paying attention to him. He kept reading but got angry, and when she seemed to have lost attention in what he was saying, he slammed his hands on the table as hard as he could, then said his line. He thought that got her attention – and got him the part.

In Kalter's book, Gelbart says the writers and producers were "really feeling our way" in that first season. (He goes on to indicate that he shuddered years later when watching some of the episodes from the first year, especially in their treatment of women.) It is clear from watching these six episodes that the writing staff did not know what to do with Spearchucker Jones. Timmy's best episode is "The Moose," a GI slang for Korean women who would serve as girlfriends or even slaves. Hawkeye is outraged when he learns that a sergeant in camp has a 17-year-old "Moose." He schemes to buy the girl with the intent of setting her free. Several scenes show that Spearchucker could have served as a straight man for Hawkeye throughout the series. But that was not to be. There are many reasons given for Timmy's being let go by the series. He said the reason was that the show's staff discovered that there were no Blacks serving as Army doctors during the Korean War. He recalled that Patrick Adiarte, the actor who played Ho-Jon, the house boy, was let go because the producers also found out that house boys did not actually appear with MASH units.

Another reason was the breakout performance of Jamie Farr as Cpl. Max Klinger, who tries continually to get out of the Army by wearing women's clothes. His character was meant to be in only a few episodes, but was such a hit that he stayed with the series for all 11 seasons. In a Dec, 15, 2011, interview with the Archive of American Television, Farr said, "At that time, they had so many characters in that show. It was a half-hour show, and as we know, it's not a full 30 minutes, because you have commercials and you have titles for the show and the credits, etc. So they had Ugly John, they had Ho-Jon the house boy, they had Spearchucker, they had Lt. Dishy, they had Ginger the nurse, they had a guy from Oklahoma.... They had so many characters beside the leads that they had ... so they were looking for a shakedown. Too many characters crossed over – they were too similar. So they were looking for individuals."

Producer Reynolds told a different story in an interview on Aug. 22, 2000, available on the Archive of American Television website. His recollection was, "Tim Brown did a very strange thing. He could have stayed with that show, and he probably would have stayed with it for 11 years. But he came to me and said, 'Look, I have a chance to be in a feature.' So I said, 'Are you sure? You've got a pretty nice part here. You're one of the guys in the Swamp.' He said, 'No, my agent says I got a chance to star in a feature and I should do it.' Well, nobody ever heard of the feature, and I don't think anybody ever heard of Tim Brown again as an actor. It was not a wise decision."

In an article written by Sylvia Stipe for Ladies' Home Journal in December 1972, Timmy told a story similar to Reynolds'. Stipe wrote that "Brown said he left the series halfway through the season because, even though he was one of the three principals, he found himself standing around but with no lines in page after page of the script." In the same article, Timmy was quoted as saying, "It probably was one of the biggest mistakes I've made. The show will probably run for years as a smash hit, but I'm not sorry I left."

Kalter's book quotes Gelbart as referring to historical accuracy: "It was devised as a show with two more or less equal stars, with another surgeon, a black surgeon — Spearchucker — whom we lost early on when we found out that the research didn't bear us up. There were a lot of black soldiers but no black surgeons."

Whatever the reason, Timmy missed a golden opportunity to establish himself in one of the most popular shows in the history of television, and one that made a fortune for most of its stars. The film that Timmy made right after he left "M*A*S*H" was called "Sweet Sugar." "Too bad that was a lousy film," Timmy said in 1973.

"Sweet Sugar" (1972) stars the little-known Phyllis Davis as Sugar. The plot is about a group of beautiful women who are kidnapped to work on a plantation by its evil owner, but the plot is merely an excuse to show skin. The poster has the tagline, "Sugar gets what she wants ... when she wants it," and the phrase "Her machete isn't her only weapon" appears next to Sugar's well-endowed figure. Underneath Sugar's picture, the poster reads, "They're women ... they're warm ... they're wildcats." Roger Ebert gave the film one star out of four and wrote, "Now folks, there's a movie about those sexy victims of Caribbean slavery, the beautiful sugar-cane harvesters of Costa Rica. Unlike, say, your average sugarcane field hands, these are girls with an average age of 22. Double that and you've got their chest measurements. They wear Levi's hot pants and overflowing halters and, frankly, they look sort of ridiculous using machetes." Ebert goes on to joke about Sugar, "How she manages to look so great out there in the cane fields is beyond me." Timmy plays Rick, a guard on the plantation. Ebert wrote that Rick "looks like a cover boy for a weightlifting magazine. He's kind of dumb. One of the girls steals his pistol from its holster while kissing him. He doesn't notice. Later, another girl steals another pistol from the same holster. He still doesn't catch on."

In the early 1970s, a new genre of film had begun to emerge, known as Blaxploitation. Frustrated with the fact that Hollywood films were not portraying African Americans with any sense of reality, a number of filmmakers decided to take it upon themselves to present an authentic view. According to Novotny Lawrence in his 2008 book "Blaxploitation Films of the 1970s," Blaxploitation films were produced by the hundreds during the years 1970 to 1975. These films, highly controversial at the time, relied upon graphic sexual content and violence. A leading figure among African American filmmakers was Melvin Van Peebles; one could argue that he singlehandedly originated Blaxploitation. In his commentary on the history of the portrayal of Blacks in movies with Ebony magazine in 2005, Van Peebles stated that Black men originally were portrayed as "shuffling, quaking buffoons" and Black women as "mammies, huffing and puffing up on the silver screen." After World War II, Hollywood tried to depict the "New Negro" with more dignity, he noted, but while it was "slightly more sophisticated," the portrayals were entrenched in the "same ole racism." Van Peebles said most of these films contained "a moral lesson about justice and tolerance, always with a central sympathetic White character – a doctor, a teacher, or something like that, a liberal update of the function of the kindly slave owner."

In his view, while Sidney Poitier broke through barriers in his roles and Oscar nominations, the actor's roles did not relate to the Black community: "Sidney was a wonderful actor, and we were proud, but nobody could really relate, because the characters he was given to play were surreal, more from heaven than the 'hood." In 1971, Van Peebles released the groundbreaking "Sweet Sweetback's Baadasssss Song." He had made it largely by himself, writing, directing, editing, and – perhaps most important – producing. "Sweetback" opens with a title card that reads, "This film is dedicated to all the Brothers and Sisters who have had enough of the Man." The film revolves around a pimp (Sweetback, played by Van Peebles' son Mario) who sees racist Oakland cops beating up a Black man. Sweetback kills the cops and is forced to go on the run. The soundtrack was provided by a then-little-known funk band called Earth, Wind and Fire, who were elected to the Rock and Roll Hall of Fame in 2000 after a string of hits. The film was a smash in the African American community, although it is likely that few whites saw it. Made for $500,000, it grossed $10 million. (In 2003, Mario Van Peebles wrote, directed, and starred in the underappreciated "Baadasssss," a fictionalized version of the making of "Sweetback.")

The success of "Sweetback" set off the explosion of Blaxploitation. But the films' popularity did not bring about exactly the type of change that Melvin Van Peebles had hoped for. He said, "I also wanted to prove to Black folks that we could do it by ourselves, without Massa's grants, blessings or anything else. When the movie turned out to be a box-office success, I thought it would only be a matter of minutes before an army of homeys would come storming up the hill to help tear down the walls of Hollywood. I waited for reinforcements to arrive. Weeks, months, years rolled by.... The majority of Black filmmakers were being denied the big prize ... but Hollywood, for all practical purposes, remained a lily-white fortress." He said it was not until the rise of filmmakers like Spike Lee and John Singleton in the late 1980s that Hollywood started to see the full commercial value of films based in the reality of African American life.

Blaxploitation also came along at the same time as Sexploitation, films that featured soft-core nudity, were generally low-budget and independently produced, and had a thin plot that often existed only to highlight provocative and titillating violence and sex.

Both Blaxploitation and Sexploitation were popular in what were known as grind houses. David Church, in his article "From Exhibition to Genre: The Case of Grind-house Films," indicates that grind houses were "independently operated theatres located in downtown or inner-city areas, showing double and triple features of exploitation films at all hours for low admission prices." These films have since attracted a cult following and heavily influenced the work of directors including Quentin Tarantino and Robert Rodriguez. Many of Tarantino's films, including "Jackie Brown" (1997), the two parts of "Kill Bill" (2003-04), and his seminal film, "Pulp Fiction" (1994), have their roots in this genre. In 2007, Tarantino and Rodriguez teamed up to make "Grindhouse," released to look like a double feature of "Planet Terror" (Rodriguez) and "Death Proof" (Tarantino).

In the 1970s, the challenge for African American actors to find mainstream roles in popular Hollywood films was daunting. As a result, Timmy's career began to gravitate toward Blaxploitation and Sexploitation films, most of which are not readily available for viewing even in the internet age. While these low-budget movies generally included minimal dialogue and were action-heavy, they let Timmy carry prominent roles. "I was the star, but acting-wise, I didn't care for much of any of them," Timmy said.

Along with "Sweet Sugar," Timmy made "A Place Called Today," "Girls Are for Loving," "Bonnie's Kids," and "Black Gunn" in 1972. All were Blaxploitation and/or Sexploitation films. Timmy pointed out a major difference between these films and other Hollywood productions when he recalled, "In a big film, they would do 15, 20 takes if necessary. That's how they get to be so good. They can splice together what they want of them. Blaxploitation actually meant 'low budget.' Basically, they don't do 10, 15 takes like in the big films."

"FEAR IS POWER! You want your city — FIGHT FOR IT!" screams the tagline for "A Place Called Today," which clearly was influenced by the enormous popularity of Clint Eastwood's "Dirty Harry" – the poster shows a man's hand holding a gigantic gun. In an Oct. 3, 1972, article in the Philadelphia Tribune, a newspaper for the Black community, Len Lear wrote, "The last film Brown appeared in was a horrendous Blaxploitation work entitled 'A Place Called Today.' When asked about it, Brown displayed a disarming brand of honesty not very common among Hollywood actors. 'It was pure shit but I needed the money. After all, you have to start somewhere, and it had been a long time between jobs. It did lead to several other movie roles, although I would never take a part in a film like that now.'" In another article around the same time, Timmy stated, "I thought the script was better than the film."

Timmy spent five weeks filming "Girls Are for Loving" in the U.S. Virgin Islands. The listing on Amazon.com indicates that it is the "third film in the 'Ginger Trilogy.'" Ginger is played by Cheri Caffaro, one of the more popular Blaxploitation actresses, and is described as the "female James Bond." On the poster for this film, the tagline reads, "'Girls Are for Loving' … and Ginger's never going to let you forget it!" Above a picture of Ginger wearing a string of bullets to cover her breasts are the words "Ginger's onto something big." Timmy did enjoy the location shooting for this film: "The Virgin Islands has everything, beautiful scenery, great people, everything! The cooperation was superb while we were on location. Everyone in the crew agrees that the cooperation was the best they've ever had on location." But he said he was tricked into doing the film by not being made aware in advance of all it contained. "They did a lot of scenes that weren't in the script. When it came out, I said, damn, that wasn't in there – two women making love. It wasn't X-rated, but it was close. I don't know if it did [career] damage or not … but I didn't like it," he said many years later.

The poster for "Bonnie's Kids" tells a similar tale – well-endowed women showing their breasts, legs, and weaponry with a reference to a successful mainstream movie, in this case "Bonnie and Clyde." One sentence from the review tells you all you need to know about the film: "So, we've already got bare teenage boobs, voyeurism, phone sex, attempted rape, implied child molestation, pseudo-incest, and bloody murder of a (sort of) family member – before the opening credits even roll!"

"Black Gunn" may have been the best of the bunch – and what's more, it reunited T. Brown with J. Brown. Jim Brown appears shirtless on the poster (with several shapely women in the background) with the tagline, "Jim Brown is Gunn and Gunning 'em Down!" The cast includes Martin Landau, a well-known character actor who had recently starred in "Mission: Impossible" on TV (Landau won an Oscar for best supporting actor for playing Bela Lugosi in the 1994 film "Ed Wood"). And it has Vida Blue, the Oakland A's pitcher who had been the 1971 Most Valuable Player and Cy Young winner in the American League, in what may have been his only film role.

In a 1973 review in the Los Angeles Times, critic Kevin Thomas said the film is a "routine black action picture that's long on violence and short on subtlety." He said it "has strength at its core, thanks largely to Jim Brown's imposing presence and dignity, but lapses into parody of the entire brutal genre around the edges," and added that "sensation wins out over substance every time." But he also noted that "amid an enormous supporting cast, Timothy Brown is a standout as Gunn's right-hand man."

Timmy visited Philadelphia in 1972 to promote "Bonnie's Kids." To a Daily News columnist, he said he was in better shape than when he was playing football, and added that it was frustrating to compete for a football part in a movie and be told, echoing Lombardi, that "they didn't feel I looked like a football player. You take Joe Namath. He doesn't look like one either. What does a football player 'look' like? You've got to be a Deacon Jones in L.A." Jones, who had played for the Los Angeles Rams and who also pursued an acting and singing career, was 6-foot-5 and 275 pounds. An interviewer for the Philadelphia Tribune compared him favorably to, of course, Jim Brown, "who could never act his way out of a paper bag." He noted that Timmy "did not step right off the grid-iron into a movie studio with no preparation or talent," citing his acting lessons and experience in dinner theater as evidence. Timmy had kept working to refine his craft after leaving football, entering the Estelle Harman Actors Workshop in Los Angeles. Harman was a legendary acting instructor at UCLA who was recruited by Universal Studios in the 1950s to instruct its cadre of stars under the old studio system. She soon started her own school, whose alumni rival those of HB, including Carol Burnett, Tony Curtis, Rock Hudson, and Lee Majors.

Another famous alumna is Sharon Gless, who played Sgt. Christine Cagney in the CBS series "Cagney and Lacey" from 1982 through 1988, a role for which she won two Emmy Awards. Timmy met Gless at the Harman school in the mid-'70s. "I went back to acting class and Sharon was there," he said. "I'm getting up to do a scene — an improvisational thing — and she screamed out, 'Oh, that's the guy that got me my first job.'" According to Timmy, that job was "Bonnie's Kids." The director, Arthur Marks, was looking at some actresses for the small role of a waitress. Timmy suggested Gless, although he had never met her or seen her act; she had been serving lunch on the set. At the Harman workshop, Gless gave Timmy a hug, to which he deadpanned, "You're interrupting the scene!" "Everybody laughed," he said. "It was kind of nice. Kind of fun."

At Harman, Timmy took copious handwritten notes that he kept on index cards. The notes include advice on improvisation, cold reading, monologues, psychophysical action, emotions, loosening-up activities, sensitivity exercises, positive affirmations, role playing, physical presence, temperament, and other acting strategies. An example is a card labeled "Elements of Action: Subtext." The note read, "An actor must complete his character's biography in his mind from beginning to end, because knowing how the character grew up, what influenced his behavior, and what he expects his future to be will give more substance to the present life of the character and will give the actor a perspective and a feeling of movement in the role."

Many of Timmy's notes include advice from some of Hollywood's most notable stars, including Katharine Hepburn ("A piece of fiction doesn't exist until you make it exist"), Robert Redford ("Sacrifice the role to the plot"), and Jack Lemmon ("The one thing about acting is to be unafraid"). It is unknown whether the quotes on these notecards came from those actors serving as guest speakers or were taken from a textbook, but Timmy was soaking up the information he was getting in these classes.

As for the films he was making, Timmy knew they were not going to garner attention during awards season. "Black films are hot right now, but after a while they won't be," he said in 1972, "so a whole lot of people are trying to capitalize on them while they still can. They're doing the same thing whites did for so long. After all, turnabout is fair play." He also knew that movie stardom was fleeting: "In this business, you never tell from one day to the next. By next year at this time, I may be digging ditches or pumping gas," he said around the same time.

During this time, he and Ernie the Head reconnected in Los Angeles. Ernie Butler had been teaching at the Munich American School in the Department of Defense Dependents Schools (DoDDS) system. In 1971, he spent a summer in Africa studying with an anthropology professor, and in 1972 became director of the minority studies program for DoDDS-Europe secondary schools. As part of the job, it was expected that he would complete a master's degree. He attended the University of Southern California and received his master's in 1973. Since he needed to be back in the States in the summers of 1972 and 1973, he traveled on a "See America" airline ticket that allowed several stops. Flying from Europe, he went to Cincinnati, Indianapolis, and Detroit, then Los Angeles. There, he stayed in a place of his own: "I couldn't stay with Tim because he had an old scraggy dog – a Scottish West Highland white terrier named Tonnie – and I had asthma."

During the summers, he recalled, "as I was a student and had to attend classes and write papers, I couldn't hang out full time like back in the Philly days." What fascinated him was the amount of time that Timmy and Jim Brown spent competing with one another. He knew they were both former top NFL players, but he had a problem with how seriously they took their competition. According to Ernie, they would get together every day to compete. Chess. Swimming. One-on-one basketball. Timmy had learned the basics of chess at Ball State and loved to play. He recalled that at one point Jim was ahead by 30 games to 10, then 56 to 40, and finally 96 to 85. That's when they quit the chess matches, with Timmy admitting that Jim was the better of them. Jim bought Timmy a bottle of rum to celebrate. At other times, they would invent a new game, like throwing a bag closest to a chair, and put a little money on it. Whoever would win would brag about the fact that he had beat the other at throwing a bag closest to a chair. "We were all old," Ernie said. "These guys' knees were gone. They competed at a level of intensity that was almost silly. Tim was always trying to prove himself."

Ernie remembered playing Jim once in a one-on-one tournament where he was winning. Jim called a timeout and changed into a Superman T-shirt, apparently trying to psych him out. Several celebrities would participate in these contests, he said, "including Elliott Gould, Marvin Gaye and the likes. We had a lot of fun."

When Ernie would come back to America from Europe, he sometimes would wear a style that hadn't yet made it to the United States. Returning to L.A. for his last summer at USC, he dressed in an Italian style, wearing platform shoes and a little bit of a bell on his pants. In terms of height, Jim Brown was the tallest, then Ernie, then Timmy. When they went to a disco one night, however, Ernie was the tallest. Jim wondered, "How did this brother get taller than me?" Eying Ernie up and down, he spied the shoes but didn't say anything. About two weeks later they went to a disco again, and things were back to normal: Jim was tallest, then Ernie, then Timmy. Ernie noticed that Jim was wearing platform shoes. Jim, realizing that Ernie was looking, said: "Got to put the shit in the proper perspective."

But that was just life with Jim Brown. During the 1970s, Timmy, Jim and Fred Williamson were a regular nightclub posse. In his book, "Out of Bounds," written with Steve Dehlson, Jim Brown made it clear that he considered himself the alpha male: "I never competed with my friends for women. When I used to partner with Fred Williamson, we'd spend a lot of time with Timmy Brown.... Timmy was amazingly handsome, could get any woman in town.... When Timmy, Freddy and I rolled into a club, we made a serious impact. We all had good-looking bodies, wore our clothes tight. We'd wear that double-knit shit. Clinging. No underwear. Muscles bulging. Attitude. But in any club, Freddy and Timmy always owned the first five minutes. They were the First Line Lovers, got the 10s, everyone else fell in behind them. I was a 10-man too, but I'd wait for Timmy and Freddy, only then would I take my show. Jim Brown, Team Player." Brown noted that when the group went to the Candy Store, a club on the Sunset Strip, the Rat Pack would be there, as well as Clint Eastwood and Tony Curtis, with each claiming part of the club (and the women in it) as his territory.

Brown's book was published in 1989, clearly a now-bygone era, as it contains this passage: "I can't speak for track men or golfers, but women love those football players. Guys who play football have that manly, physical image – the gladiator – and women go crazy for it. Talk all you want about brain power, but the intellectual gets the secondary women. It's the physical giant who gets the premium women."

Timmy would get angry with Ernie when it looked like he and Jim were teaming up on him. Ernie would say, "You know you talk a little smack." If he could get a basketball rebound on Timmy, Ernie would shout, "It's a big man's game! It's a big man's game!" Then Jim would do the same thing after blocking one of Timmy's shots. "Oh, man, you make me sick," Timmy would say. "You guys ain't that big!"

"He had that little kid thing," Ernie remembered fondly. "That's one of the things that brought you to him. He had the openness to let it show."

One day in the summer of 1973, just before he left L.A. to return to Germany, Ernie played hard in a game of basketball during a smog alert, which he recalled as having been unwise. He was wheezing, his epinephrine pills didn't seem to work, and he wondered whether he should go to a hospital. He had a flight scheduled from L.A. to San Francisco, then to Chicago and Indianapolis. Timmy drove him to the airport. The air-conditioning at the airport and on the plane, and the pills, worked well enough that by the time he landed in San Francisco, he was feeling much better. On the flight from L.A. he had met a passenger who had just come from Hawaii, who told him that he that he could leave his bags some place and get to downtown San Francisco in 10 minutes by taking the Bay Area Rapid Transit train. The passenger encouraged him to see some of the city. "By the time I got there, the medicine had kicked in and I was feeling high from the epinephrine. By the time I got to town, my lungs were clear, and I fell in love with S.F." That trip was the last time that he would visit with Timmy in person. By 1975, he said, he believed that the DoDDS minority program was on solid ground and realized that he liked working with youngsters more than working with adults, so he returned to his Munich teaching position.

Football also maintained a hold on Timmy during this time, as not all of his media work was in scripted film and television. On July 25, 1973, he was signed to a contract with the NFL to serve as a CBS color commentator on a number of game broadcasts during the regular season. An unofficial listing shows Timmy working nine of the 14 regular-season games, including Chicago at Denver, Los Angeles Rams at Houston, Philadelphia at Minnesota, Chicago at Green Bay, Philadelphia at San Francisco, Chicago at Detroit, New Orleans at Rams, and both Philadelphia-New York Giants matchups. Timmy was paired with play-by-play announcers Jack Drees, Dan Kelly, and Jack Whitaker during these games. No recordings of these broadcasts apparently survive.

In the meantime, "Monday Night Football," the concept that Timmy had passed on when approached by Frank Gifford and Howard Cosell in 1969, had become a runaway hit. Keith Jackson was the play-by-play announcer when "MNF" premiered on Sept. 21, 1970, with Don Meredith as the color commentator and Cosell as, well, Cosell. Gifford replaced Jackson in the second season. For the 1973 season, Meredith left to pursue an acting career that failed to materialize. In his stead, ABC first turned to Fred Williamson, the original Spearchucker Jones from the "M*A*S*H" movie. Williamson didn't work out, and Alex Karras replaced him until Meredith's return in 1977.

In 1973, during his CBS analyst stint, Timmy looked back on his time balancing acting and playing. He told Inquirer columnist Judy Bachrach said that "in football, at least, you know exactly what you're doing. In acting you just never know how you've done.... I could go on a talk show tonight and people wouldn't know who I was. Oh, after a while, they might say, 'That's Timmy Brown. He once was dynamite.'" He had earlier noted that "football isn't going to do a damn thing for me when I'm through" and said Jim Brown "doesn't have those problems because he was always tops in football." He said he had been "the top bachelor in Philadelphia. I guess I was spoiled rotten in football, but when I ended that part of my career, I said to myself, 'OK. Now it is time to start my new life. Now give me my lines.'... You walk into a lineup and five people are looking at you like you're a robot or something. And then they say, 'Well, you're not quite our type.' And then all of a sudden, it's like I was ... a little boy again in that children's home having to prove myself again to the outside world.... Now, when I don't get picked out of an actors lineup, I just tell them to go fuck themselves." In 2010, Timmy still felt the same way: "With the Eagles I knew where I was. I didn't know to make a move out there, not knowing how Hollywood was."

Even so, after a year with CBS, Timmy said, he did not seek further work as a football commentator because of his desire to return to acting.

During 1973, Timmy met two women who would be significant in his life. One, Constance Kessner, he said he planned to marry. In the Black Sports interview, he described Connie Kessner as his fiancee: "She's a 1969 graduate of Colorado University. She'd come to Los Angeles about a teaching job, and I met her. I thought she was too skinny at first. But, you know, it's always ironic. I always liked girls with a lot of meat on them. All of a sudden, I'm going to marry a skinny girl. I guess that's the way it works, though." He went on to say, "You never end up with what you always think you were going to get. I always heard that when I was younger, but I never believed it. I said, well, they can talk that trash if they want to. I know I'm going to end me up with some girl with some meat on her. And here I am with my bone." In a June 1973 Inquirer article, writer Judy Bacharach confirmed the wedding plans. Timmy shared that "Connie wants to get married. It's sort of arranged. A June wedding at Jim Brown's house. But I don't know...." Bacharach pressed, asking if he was faithful to Kessner, to which he replied: "Let's put it this way. I don't embarrass her, and she don't ask. But I've changed a lot over the years since the Eagles." Timmy told Bacharach that he didn't trust women, which he said Kessner attributed to an experience with a former girlfriend. Timmy recalled, "One day she just drops in. She was engaged to some old fat dude in Miami, and he was showering her with jewels and stuff. And I started playing some old college records, like Fats

Domino. I played the flip side of 'Shop Around,' too. And then I played 'Bad Girl,' and that's a really dynamite song. You know how it goes?" He began to sing for the interviewer, "She's not a ba-a-ad girl just because ... 'cause ... she made me see ... she cheated on me...." He continued, "I put that on and she didn't like it one bit. She must have known it was her. Well, we rapped about four hours and then she wanted to dance and kiss .... But I said no. I put a value on strength. I told her to marry the rich dude. She was a queen in college. A real queen. But not very intelligent." As the woman had a Florida connection as well as one with Ball State, Timmy may have been referring to a visit from Sandy Collins.

Ernie Butler described Kessner "as a lovely lady" and said she and Timmy were living together in the summer of 1973. But little else is known about their relationship, and they never married. The other woman was Hollie Vest. They met in 1973 at a gas station on Santa Monica Boulevard just east of La Brea Avenue in Hollywood, when he was 36 and she was 21. She had just moved from the suburb of Inglewood and was the manager of a women's clothing shop in Culver City called M. Cole's. She also was singing nonprofessionally. Having just broken off an engagement with a man with whom she attended high school, she was sitting in her car, heartbroken and crying, while getting gas, and "this handsome guy pulled up next to me in a small white sports-model Mercedes." Timmy smiled at her through the window, and that made her cry even more. Her window was up, so he couldn't say anything to her. He made a sad little face and mouthed the words, "Your place or mine?"

Without any hesitation, she pointed to him and said, "Yours." He smiled and motioned for her to follow him. "For some strange reason, I completely trusted him," she recalled. "It was not something I would ever do normally. But with him, I felt totally safe." As it turned out, Timmy's place at 927 N. San Vicente Blvd., Apartment 2C, was around the corner from her new apartment. "He introduced himself and had this big, beautiful, sincere smile, and showed me where to park. He seemed like he was the happiest person on the planet, without a care in the world," she said.

They walked upstairs to his apartment, and he had her sit in the TV room. He asked if she was hungry and offered her something to drink. She was still crying and distraught. He got a couple of TV trays and brought in some fried chicken wings with honey, beer bread, and water. While she had eaten fried chicken wings before, she said in 2022, had never had them with honey and beer bread, and found them "delicious."

He asked what kind of movies she liked to watch, to which she responded: "Pretty much everything. I love to watch movies." She could not recall what they watched that day, but she remembered Timmy singing, joking, and doing his best to make her smile and have fun. They talked about everything. Timmy, she said, was the perfect gentleman and never put his hands on her. By the time she left him that day, she had gotten over her sadness. "Tim loved to bring joy to others," Vest said. "Following Tim home that day turned out to be one of the best decisions I ever made." Their friendship would last until his death.

After Timmy's brief stint in broadcasting ended, one of the better films that he made during the early 1970s was released. In "Dynamite Brothers" (1974), Timmy plays Stud Brown, who partners with Larry Chin (played by Alan Tang) to break up a drug ring in Los Angeles' Watts section. The film mixes Blaxploitation with the new kung fu craze that had begun with Bruce Lee's "Enter the Dragon." It also had, as a crooked cop, Aldo Ray, who had achieved some fame as a character actor in the 1950s. Typical of Timmy's films of the period, the plot is simple and mainly serves as a platform to create action scenes. Timmy did his own stunts in the film, but for a man with a history of knee problems from football, it was at a price. "I never had any stunt man. I didn't need them," he said later in life. "The bad thing about it, though, was my knee.... I faked running so many times doing takes that my knee would be killing me when I got home. But I had to fake it, they couldn't tell, I was taking the pain. I was running down this hall to get this guy, and I dive and roll over and come up with my gun, and we did about six takes on that for their angle, camera or whatever. I had it down the first one, but that killed me running up and down that hall. The dive and the roll-over and come up with the gun wasn't a problem, but running … and it just got worse and worse. In fact, when I did that movie, this leg was bowed out to here, and I was always trying to hide my legs. And they would say, 'Are you limping?' I said, 'No, I'm fine.' I knew I had to get back into the act. But I mean, that was killing me." Timmy remembered Jim Brown telling him, "If your knee had not been messed up, you would have been getting a lot more work in the action-type stuff." Although these films were not critically successful and appealed only to a cult audience, they were giving Timmy experience. But he needed a meaty role that would open doors for critical and commercial success – a role that would show that he could not only act, but could sing as well. That role came his way in 1974, and Timmy packed his bags for Tennessee.

After the commercial and critical success of "M*A*S*H," Altman had directed a series of well-regarded films that struggled to find an audience, including "The Long Goodbye" (1973), "Thieves Like Us" (1974), and "California Split" (1974), as well as "McCabe and Mrs. Miller" (1971) with Warren Beatty and Julie Christie. In the early 1970s, United Artists sent Altman a screenplay about a country music artist. Altman rejected the script, but the idea of putting on film the world of country and western music appealed to him. He asked screenwriter Joan Tewkesbury to determine whether a story suitable for filming could be made. Tewkesbury made several trips to Nashville. Her first visit was uninspiring, but afterward she kept a diary of her visits, much of which ended up in the film.

Altman's "Nashville" follows the lives of 24 characters over five days during the height of a political campaign. Its stars, in many cases playing roles based on or inspired by actual country artists, include Ronee Blakley as Barbara Jean, Lily Tomlin as Linnea Reese, Karen Black as Connie White, Keith Carradine as Tom Frank, Barbara Harris as Albuquerque, Geraldine Chaplin as Opal, Shelley Duvall as L.A. Joan, Scott Glenn as Pfc. Glenn Kelly, Henry Gibson as Haven Hamilton, Ned Beatty as Delbert Reese, Keenan Wynn as Mr. Green, Gwen Welles as Sueleen Gay, Allen Nicholls as Bill, David Peel as Bud Hamilton, Michael Murphy as John Triplett, and, in the best performance of his career, Timothy Brown as Tommy Brown.

Reviews of the film were euphoric. Roger Ebert called it the best American film since 1968's "Bonnie and Clyde," writing, "Sure, it's only a movie. But after I saw it I felt more alive, I felt I understood more about people, I felt somehow wiser. It's that good a movie." Ebert was no less enthusiastic in 2000 when he added the film to his "Great Movie Series," calling it a "tender poem to the wounded and the sad." He added that Altman was "almost alone among white American directors [in that] he never forgets that a lot of black people live and work in town."

In his 1975 review in the New York Times, Vincent Canby wrote, "I have no idea how to credit the superlative performances in the film except alphabetically," thus mentioning Timmy second to Karen Black. Timmy even received a telegram from Barry Diller, then the president of Paramount Pictures, saying, "Your admirable contribution to the excellence of 'Nashville' has already been noted by the critics. Please accept my personal congratulations and best wishes." This was high praise from one of the top moguls in Hollywood.

And movie critic Lou Gaul, writing in the Burlington County Times in New Jersey, noted that Timmy's cinematic career [had] seemed doomed when director Robert Altman heard Brown sing and offered him a role as a Black county singer in 'Nashville.'" "Nashville" was also celebrated when the nominations were announced for the 1976 Academy Awards. It was nominated for best picture ("One Flew Over the Cuckoo's Nest" won). Blakley and Tomlin were nominated for best supporting actress (Lee Grant took home the statue for "Shampoo"). Altman was nominated for best director (Milos Forman won for "Cuckoo's Nest"). The lone "Nashville" winner was Keith Carradine, who wrote and performed "I'm Easy," the winner for best original song. (In the summer of 1976, "I'm Easy" – not to be confused with Lionel Richie's "Easy" from the following year – became a surprise hit, rising to No. 17 on Billboard's Hot 100. The soundtrack peaked at No. 80 on the album chart.) Much to Altman's disappointment, the movie did not garner a nomination for best score. In addition, the academy overlooked Tewkesbury's screenplay, perhaps because of the perception that in classic Altman fashion, much of the dialogue had been improvised.

While Hollywood liked the film and critics loved it, those in the real Nashville's music business were not among its fans. They saw it as a slam of their world, if they saw it at all. Referring to the central scene at the end, when Barbara Jean is assassinated, the record producer and songwriter Billy Sherrill, famous for his work with George Jones and others, stated, "I'll tell you what I liked best about the film. When they shot that miserable excuse for a country singer." Loretta Lynn was more diplomatic in explaining why she boycotted the premiere, saying, "I'd rather see 'Bambi.'" In the end, "Nashville" never found a mass audience, grossing only $9.9 million. Altman's unconventional narrative, overlapping dialogue, and interlocking stories were taxing to follow, and unusual in movies of that time. But the film did find its audience among a generation of filmmakers, many of whom, such as Paul Thomas Anderson and Alan Rudolph, worked with Altman and drew inspiration from him. Its effect on film vocabulary can also be seen in films such as "Crash," the 2004 best-picture Oscar winner.

Around the time "Nashville" was being cast, Timmy had been relegated to one-off guest-starring roles in network series and appearances in Blaxploitation films. In an interview around this time, he lamented, "Parts are hard to get. Sometimes they'd tell me I wasn't black enough and talked too white. So I used to lay in the sun to get three shades darker. And I didn't want to take parts because of football, I wanted to do it on my own ability. Maybe I made a mistake. Maybe I should have taken the parts. At least they would have seen what I can do."

In a Newsweek article written by Charles Michener in 1975, Altman said "casting is 90 percent of the creation." Even so, he apparently did not feel that compensation and casting were linked. Michener wrote that Altman had offered his principal "Nashville" actors "rock-bottom fees of $750-$1,000 a week for eight weeks of shooting."

But even for relatively low pay, "Nashville" offered Timmy a golden opportunity. Timmy said his involvement in "Nashville" could be traced back to "M*A*S*H." "Bob Altman heard me sing at a party to celebrate the completion of his film 'M*A*S*H.' That was back in 1970, and Bob and his wife, Katherine, told me they were thinking of making a country-western type of film and might want me for the part. I thought they would forget, but I discovered that Bob has the ability to keep a performer in his mind. I was right for this part because he had a Charley Pride character in mind. Because of my upbringing, I don't have a Black-sounding voice."

Timmy was a natural fit to play a character based on Charley Pride. Born in Sledge, Miss., in 1938, Pride became the first African American performer to find success in the lily-white world of country and western music. Pride also had tried to make it in pro sports, although with significantly less success than Timmy. Before finding stardom as an entertainer, Pride wanted to play in the major leagues, but was never able to rise above the lowest reaches of the minors. The closest Pride came to making it in professional baseball was 1960, when he recorded seven innings and a 3.86 ERA as a right-handed pitcher for the Missoula Timberjacks, a Class C affiliate of the Cincinnati Reds in Montana.

After realizing he was not going to make it in baseball, Pride focused on Nashville, with staggering results. Pride faced tremendous racism – one record company tried to hide his race by releasing his initial recordings without showing his photo, for fear that radio stations would boycott his music. The company's apprehension was based in reality, because some disc jockeys did reject Pride's records once they knew his race. Even so, Pride rose to become one of the most successful country artists of his era. He had 36 No. 1 hits on the country charts and sold 25 million albums. His first top 10 single, "Just Between You and Me," was released in 1966, and his last charting song, "Amy's Eyes," was in 1989. He may be best known for the crossover hit "Kiss an Angel Good Morning," which reached No. 22 on Billboard's Hot 100 in January 1972. In 1971, Pride was awarded the Entertainer of the Year honor by the Country Music Association. He was inducted into the Country Music Hall of Fame in 2000, securing his place as the most successful African American in the history of country music to that time. In 1967, he became one of the first African Americans to play in the Grand Ole Opry at the historic Ryman Auditorium. And he realized his baseball dream as well, in 2010 becoming a part-owner of the Texas Rangers.

Timmy's previous work had helped him with the role, but he still researched the part. "I had tapes of about five different country singers that I just wanted to get. I was pretty good, because at the children's home and at Ball State, we had a lot of country music," he said. "I listened to them for at least two weeks while I was driving or when I was home, getting their sound down." The artists he listened to included Conway Twitty, Merle Haggard, and Jones. But, he said, "I wasn't imitating anybody. I just went with my sound." In film critic Jan Stuart's 2004 book "The Nashville Chronicles: The Making of Robert Altman's Masterpiece," Timmy says, "I wanted to have my own identity with it and show them that, hey, I could do any kind of movement. My comfort zone is with my body. Of course it had to be controlled with that audience, so that they didn't perceive it as rock and roll or blues. You had to keep it straight."

Timmy's performance on the Opry stage in the movie impressed country legend Roy Acuff, who reportedly pulled him aside and said, "Son, you want to make a whole lot of money? You should go into country music. What you did out there is just what they wanted Charley Pride to do."

But Timmy was unhappy with the fact that he was the only actor in "Nashville" who was not asked to write his own songs. Altman said that was because Timmy was hired too late in the process to allow him to write a song. The song that Timmy sings in the film and is on the accompanying soundtrack is "Bluebird," written by Blakley. Blakley contributed six songs to the film, including "My Idaho Home," "Dues," and "Tapedeck in His Tractor," which she performed as well.

Timmy also performed a second song written by Richard Baskin and Altman, called "The Day I Looked Jesus in the Eye," but the performance was dropped from the film, and the song has never been released by any performer. Timmy thought that some of his best work ended up on the cutting room floor, most notably some key scenes in the opening traffic-jam sequence. Timmy recalled attending a private screening of "Nashville" with "M*A*S*H" costars Duvall and Gould. At the conclusion, one of the two turned to Timmy and said, "Christ, what did you do to Bob?" This led Timmy to ask Altman what had happened. Timmy recalled Altman as saying, "Well, now you know who makes you or breaks you in this business." (Even with the cuts, the film ran for two hours and 39 minutes.)

Timmy believed Altman worked to blacklist him from roles in Hollywood after "Nashville." The reason, he believed, is that he beat Altman in a game of chess. According to Timmy, several film colleagues supported his theory. He said one told him, "You shouldn't have beat him, man," to which he responded, "What do you mean I shouldn't have beat him – he wasn't that good." The colleague responded, "Yeah, but he's the director."

Timmy did not turn totally hostile to Altman; in Stuart's book, he said, "I always felt like a son. He had a kid who was half-Black who reminded me of me, and he and his wife were always very nice. I don't want to sound bitter." Could a game of chess really have ended Timmy's path to stardom? It seems fantastic, and Altman, who died in 2006, never addressed the matter publicly. Perhaps something in Timmy's performance displeased Altman, but he never told Timmy. By Timmy's own admission, his performance at the Opry strayed from how Pride did his work. Pride normally stood stationary at the microphone when singing, whereas Timmy used his athleticism to move around. Whatever the reason, Altman was done with Timmy, and an acting career that could have received a major push was essentially over.

Timmy was not the only actor in the film to be snubbed afterward by Altman. According to Stuart, a number of actors felt the director's wrath, including Blakley. After "Nashville," Blakley felt that other casting directors saw her only as Barbara Jean, her character, so an ad for her second solo album, "Welcome" (1975), read, "Hello Ronee, goodbye Barbara Jean." Blakley was quoted by Stuart as saying of Altman, "He didn't approve of the ad that came out. That made Bob furious. I think he thought, I took her and gave her everything that she has, and now she says goodbye to it? Alan Rudolph (assistant director on "Nashville") had cast me in "Welcome to L.A.," and I was replaced with Geraldine Chaplin. That was heartbreaking for me. I screamed and cried." Both Rudolph and Altman denied that Blakley was ever cast in "Welcome to L.A.," a 1976 release directed by Rudolph.

And Timmy wasn't the only actor in the film with substantial work left on the cutting room floor. According to Stuart, ABC was interested in assembling a 10-hour miniseries (this was the era of miniseries such as "Rich Man, Poor Man" and "Roots") from the unused footage from "Nashville," but dropped the idea when the film underperformed at the box office and at the Oscars. The footage disappeared, so even the Criterion Collection's DVD release of "Nashville" in 2013 could not offer as an extra the work that Timmy was so proud of.

In 1975, Timmy's career was floundering. His father, John Brown Sr., had died on January 14 in Indianapolis, where he had worked as a custodian. But Timmy continued to draw strength from his friendship with Hollie Vest, whose forays into entertainment were getting more notice. She first teamed up with Rozlyn Keel and Tracy Harris as Mello, Chill & Shock. They released a single on the Shock Records label in

1976, "Feel the Music" with a B-side of "It's All Over." Shock Records was associated with Janus Records. In 1977 she quit her job at the clothing store to pursue an entertainment career full-time. Starting in 1978 she would front a series of bands, starting with Hotline. In late 1979, Vest had emergency surgery, after which Timmy would check on her. Once she was able, she said, they went to shoot baskets to help her regain her strength.

In 1978, perhaps as a result of the problems his knee had given him in acting roles, Timmy decided to act on the way football had damaged his body, continuing to cause him pain. He planned to sue the Eagles and the Colts. An April 5 letter, sent to Timmy by Santa Ana attorney Paul Leiter, referred to "Timmie Brown vs. Philadelphia Eagles and Baltimore Colts." In the letter, Leiter said, "We have reviewed your file and have reached the opinion that it would be to your advantage to have a medical consultation with a doctor of your choice, not in the employ of the insurance company." Leiter said the cost would probably be ordered to be paid by the teams' insurance company once the case was concluded. He indicated that an appointment had been scheduled with Dr. David S. Archer in Santa Ana.

In a May 26 letter sent to the attorney from an orthopedic surgery office in Inglewood, Dr. Anthony F. Daly Jr. wrote that he had been seeing Timmy for knee difficulty since 1970. Daly wrote: "His history is that he played professional football, always had difficulty with his knees while playing and mainly the pain was in the left knee over the medial aspect. As a result of football injuries, in December of 1969, by Dr. Leventhal, who was the team physician for the Rams, he had a medial meniscectomy carried out. He had intermittent difficulty following that, including periodic aspirations and injections with cortisone and tenderness over the scar. During the past eight years, he has continued intermittent difficulty with the knee, at one time requiring removal of a neuroma over the incision. In addition, he had a loose body on the right knee, which was removed at one time. He has continued to have occasional intermittent difficulty with both knees. He has been able to be active; however, I believe that eventually on the left knee he will need a joint replacement because of degenerative changes within the cartilage, as a result of his football injury."

In a Sept. 29 letter, Tustin attorney George Hill advised Timmy that a deposition had been scheduled for Oct. 23 at 2 p.m. in the Santa Ana law office of Mouser, Channels & Roberts, and that he would be there as his counsel. He asked Timmy to call him to talk about his testimony.

But the outcome of Timmy's suit is not clear, as no further paper trail existed in Timmy's records. At the request of the authors of this book, a legal analyst who had access to a university's legal research databases looked for results under the names Timmie, Timothy, and Timmy Brown against the Philadelphia Eagles and found no legal decisions. He said the case could have been settled out of court, if indeed the litigation was ever filed, and he was unable to determine if Timmy was deposed. He concluded that "since it appears his leg was badly injured even before he played pro ball, I doubt he had a viable suit in the first place."

Like Timmy, Altman went into a career slump after "Nashville." In the mid-1980s, there was talk of reviving his career with a sequel. Robert Harders – a screenwriter who had worked with Altman in the early 1980s – completed the first draft of a screenplay for one. Although Tewkesbury was nominated for an Oscar for "Nashville," she was not asked to work on the new screenplay, as she had also fallen out with Altman. The working title was "Nashville 12." In the screenplay, Tommy Brown has two prominent storylines. The first finds Tommy's son being hit by a car driven by Wade, a Black character who in "Nashville" accuses Tommy of cozying up to white people. Tommy's son eventually dies. The second – also involving race – has Haven Hamilton wanting Tommy to sing a song called "Black Sheep" on his show. Tommy refuses before being coerced into performing it. No one knows how many of the "Nashville" actors Altman would have brought back, but "Nashville

12" was dead by 1987, as was Timmy's acting career. Altman would continue to have ups and downs, with every strong film such as "The Player" being matched by a commercial failure such as "Kansas City." But the successes of "Cookie's Fortune" in 1999 and "Gosford Park" in 2001 put him on solid ground again. He was awarded an honorary Oscar in 2006; before the end of that year, he would be dead from leukemia at age 81.

After "Nashville," Timmy had one more noteworthy appearance, starring as Dawson with, of course, Jim Brown in "Pacific Inferno." Jim Brown's Clyde Preston leads a team of Navy POWs ordered to retrieve $16 million worth of silver from the bottom of Manila Bay, where it had been dumped by Gen. Douglas MacArthur before Japan took control of the Philippines in 1942. The film was shot on location for about six weeks. A highlight was when Philippine President Ferdinand Marcos and his wife, Imelda, hosted them for dinner at the Malacañang Palace, where, Timmy recalled, "they treated us like kings." The palace was where Imelda Marcos kept her famous collection of thousands of shoes, discovered after her husband was overthrown.

After that, the closest Timmy said he got to a regular role was when he was a finalist to play T.C. in Tom Selleck's popular CBS series of the 1980s, "Magnum, P.I." Otherwise, aside from a starring role in another low-budget movie, "Code Name: Zebra," Timmy was limited to guest shots on series such as "Remington Steele," "Gimme a Break," "T.J. Hooker," "Benson," and "The Colbys." In some of these shows, Timmy might only have a few lines. Timmy's last screen credit was as "Roof Man Billy" in a 2000 film called "Frequency," starring Dennis Quaid, but it was barely a role. An "Employment of Day Player" contract found among Timmy's possessions typifies the work that he was offered after "Nashville." It called for Timmy to receive "1 day guar." at the daily rate of $500 with employment starting on July 20, 1977, for the part of a "Cop." The contract is signed by both Timmy and Burt Reynolds on behalf of "Lawrence Gordon/Burt Reynolds Productions" and was for the movie "The End," a black comedy starring Reynolds, Sally Field, Dom DeLuise, Joanne Woodward, and others. Tim's role was so small that he is not listed in any casting summary on the internet.

So Timmy recognized by the 1980s that once again, it was time to move on. Over the years, the connections he made in the industry had led him to become a participant in civic activities in Los Angeles. In some cases, he used his athletic skills to help raise money, and in one event for the Youth Foundation of Pasadena in March 1976, he played in a celebrity basketball game as the captain of an all-star team to challenge the Jackson Five all-stars. Based on letters retained throughout the years, Timmy stayed busy with celebrity golf tournaments, speaking engagements, and other functions to help raise funds for causes including Athletes Against AIDS, the Jerry Lewis Telethon, the Cystic Fibrosis Foundation, Love One Another Missions International, the Leukemia Society of America, the Sickle Cell Disease Association of America, and the Greater East Los Angeles Special Olympics. Among Timmy's charitable efforts was work for the Probation Department of Los Angeles County. And that foreshadowed the final chapter of his professional life.

LOS ANGELES

CHAPTER EIGHT

Friends and Family

As Timmy's acting career began to wind down, he maintained many of his friendships and developed new ones. Over the years, Hollie Vest – Timmy often called her just by her last name, as he did with many people he knew – had met a few of his friends, but with a couple of exceptions, she said, she had never gotten to know them well. She hosted several jam sessions at her parents' empty bar on Prairie Avenue in Inglewood, next to their house on 106th Street, until they sold the property. At these, Timmy and others would party for four to six hours, starting early on a Sunday afternoon.

She also went to parties he gave at his apartment, most often, she recalled, for a small group of his friends from the Estelle Harman Actors Workshop. Timmy had the unusual talent of breaking out into the lyrics of a song based on a word that someone had used in a conversation, to the delight of those around. At his parties, people would hang out and sing along, karaoke-style, with Timmy's collection of 45 rpm singles. In 1980, Vest formed a band called the Main Event. One night, the band was performing at a club in Burbank when, about 45 minutes before closing, someone sent a glass of Grand Marnier to her on stage. She drank it and began to feel like she had been drugged. Unable to drive, she called Timmy, who came and took her home. "Timmy was there when I needed him," she said. "We always tried to be there for one another."

Around 1980, Timmy became friends with Jeff Gerrard, another student at the Harman workshop. Gerrard was both acting and working as a session director at a casting agency. He lived with Desirée Boschetti, an actress, about a mile and a half away in a 250-square-foot studio apartment. They quickly became part of Timmy's social universe. Gerrard said he enjoyed going to Timmy's apartment in part because it was so large for a one-bedroom unit. Timmy's white Mercedes-Benz also caught his attention. "Timmy was in love with it," he said. "I have a feeling he loved it so much because it showed what he got out of football. It was stolen twice," a fact Vest also was aware of. The first time, it was found and returned. The second time, Timmy had stopped to make a quick phone call and left the car running. He saw the robbers take it, but it was never found. Gerrard said, "He was heartbroken."

Gerrard, Boschetti, and Timmy hung out together on weekends for about three years. They went to the beach, played games, watched sports, and roller skated in Venice. "When we didn't have any money, Timmy would have us over and cook pasta," Gerrard said. "We also had beer bread and drank piña coladas."

One night, while Gerrard was in Boston to act in a play, Boschetti and Timmy had dinner in Beverly Hills. Timmy asked her if she would like to go roller skating, and she said she would. The next day, they and their friend Ari Itzak Barak skated up and down a parking structure in West Hollywood. They enjoyed the thrill all the more because skating was prohibited in the structure. Barak also would go to the beach with them. He appeared in TV shows including "Dynasty" and "Hardcastle and McCormick," and in the movies "Basic Training" and "Scorpion."

Gerrard said Timmy introduced him and Boschetti to Vest, who at the time was wearing Bo Derek-style braids as she continued her singing career. "She had a great set of pipes on her. We'd go to local clubs with him to see her," Gerrard recalled. He also saw her at some of Timmy's parties. "He loved music," he said. "We'd be getting ready [at his home], and Minnie Riperton would come on. He'd get the groove on." Riperton was a soul singer who had a No. 1 single on Billboard's Hot 100 in April 1975 called "Lovin' You." She co-wrote the song, and the record was co-produced by Stevie Wonder. She also sang background on songs by Bo Diddley, Chuck Berry, and others. She died from breast cancer in 1979. Her daughter is Maya Rudolph, the comedic actress who was a member of the "Saturday Night Live" cast and has been in movies including "Bridesmaids."

In 1983, Gerrard opened Jeff Gerrard Casting in Sherman Oaks. He recalled that Timmy probably acted in two of the commercials he cast. "One ... was a beer commercial. He was a football player trying to get the other players fired up. It was MOS [without sound] with the music building up." Gerrard couldn't remember the other one but said, "I got one more shot at hiring him, but he had started working as a probation officer and his hours were very restrictive to the acting business. He was unavailable.

"He was such a great-looking guy, with a great smile and charm that would win everyone over," he said. Once, he complimented that smile, saying, "Timmy, you've got the pearliest white teeth." Timmy responded, "You could have teeth like these too, if you paid the right price," explaining that because of the damage done to his mouth by football, particularly the revenge attack by Dallas, every few years he had to have his gums cut and false teeth replaced.

"He was a great, friendly, warm-hearted, happy-go-lucky, nice guy," Gerrard recalled. "When he would laugh, it was the funniest thing – a really good laugh. I can hear it right now. I would bullshit with him. Oh my God, the stories he could tell. He had so many, and so much history. He was a great storyteller. We were really good friends."

Over the years, Boschetti built a successful acting career in a number of TV series, including "General Hospital" and two seasons of the

TBS comedy "Rocky Road," as well as the NBC miniseries "The Gangster Chronicles" and the nuclear-holocaust TV movie "The Day After". She and Gerrard married in 1985. Over time, they drifted apart from Timmy. "As lives change, families grow, they get busy and lose touch. That's what happened," said Gerrard.

Also among the friends Timmy had made over the years was Gene Kilroy. After leaving the Eagles, he had become business manager for Muhammad Ali, whom he had first met at the 1960 Rome Olympics. Kilroy was with Ali for fights including the "Rumble in the Jungle" against George Foreman. Among other duties, he organized Ali's training camps and took care of his taxes. In 1978, he began working at the Dunes in Las Vegas; he would later work at Steve Wynn's Mirage, the Luxor, and the MGM casino-hotels. At each hotel, he said, he "reported to the president and oversaw gaming, advertising, promotions, and special events." Timmy would visit Kilroy in Las Vegas two or three times a year, staying free at the hotel Kilroy then was working for.

And Timmy maintained his friendship with Rick Whitfield. In the early 1970s, Whitfield sang with a band called the Great Crowd. It had 15 members, including a horn section and four female singers. The group got its name from Revelation 7:9-10, which in the Darby Bible of 1890 is phrased: "After these things I saw, and lo, a great crowd, which no one could number, out of every nation and tribes and peoples and tongues, standing before the throne, and before the Lamb, clothed with white robes, and palm branches in their hands. And they cry with a loud voice, saying, 'Salvation to our God who sits upon the throne, and to the Lamb.'" Phil "Fang" Volk, who had been the bassist with Paul Revere and the Raiders, a band that had a successful 1960s run of singles including "Hungry" and "Kicks," was a leader of the Great Crowd. Through the band, Whitfield met Johnny Mathis, Timmy's former fellow Mercury recording artist, because Mathis' brother Michael was a band member and his roommate. He also met Johnny's younger brother Ralph, whose wife, Irene, was Volk's sister. Whitfield didn't perform publicly with the band, but recorded songs with it for Lute Records at the Gold Star Recording Studio in Hollywood.

Whitfield also recalled playing backup in 1978 for the Trinidadian soul singer and percussionist Vin Cardinal in Las Vegas and at Playboy Clubs across the nation. Cardinal had moved to the United States in the early 1970s after becoming a sensation in Scandinavia and Europe. His band Vin Cardinal and the Queens recorded the hits "I Need Your Lovin'" and "I'm Gonna Cry." But he never gained the level of popularity in the U.S. that he had abroad.

In 1979, Whitfield formed a band with Greg Watson and Jan Harrington. They toured Japan for six months and Canada for four. When he wasn't touring, he said, he was in touch with Timmy regularly.

After touring with Watson and Harrington, Whitfield formed the Rick Whitfield Band, with which he continued to perform into the 2020s. In the 1980s, they were playing at Reflections, a club in Glendale. Timmy came one night to see him play. In addition to Timmy, there was Whitfield's friend Bradley Lockerman, who appeared later with Whitfield and Timmy in a CBS daytime series, "Capitol"; Australian model David Thorenson; and actor Steven Mendel. Whitfield recalled that "girls were calling their friends and freaking out, saying, 'What the fuck? You got to see these guys. Super handsome.' It would be like having Brad Pitt and Harrison Ford when they were young in the same room. Really funny.

"After I finished performing [one night], Timmy and I went to a little place nearby," Whitfield recalled. "Someone there made a racial slur. Timmy got so mad, we had to go outside. He was ready to fight. I was afraid he was going to kill somebody, because he didn't take that shit."

Whitfield said Timmy was instrumental in getting him into modeling: "We were with Joan Mangum Agency Inc. and Mary Webb Davis." Whitfield's image appeared on numerous billboards, advertising Kool and Benson & Hedges cigarettes; Grand Marnier, the French liqueur; and a clothing line, for which he wore a hard hat in a riff on the

Village People. He recalled seeing that ad on a billboard as he drove on Sunset Boulevard. From his mid-20s into his 30s, modeling was part of how he made his living; in three of those years, he said, it was the only work he did.

Timmy "told me stuff about women," he added, such as that "it was always easier to get along with women who weren't beautiful and celebrities. He was such a handsome guy. He liked women and was slick with them. But I never saw him run around with a lot of girls. If he was a playboy, he wasn't obvious about it."

He also liked Timmy's sense of humor. "When we went to movies," he said, "he would buy chocolates and hand them to me one at a time." Timmy would butcher movie titles to get a laugh, calling "The Color Purple" "The Colored People" or "Poltergeist" "Polly Geesed." He made up names for people, likening them to animals, and would come up with one instantly upon looking at someone. This first occurred with Whitfield on the set of "Capitol." The daytime series was about the political feuding and personal conflicts between the wealthy Clegg family and the middle-class McCandlesses. It starred Rory Calhoun as Judge Judson Tyler, Constance Towers as Clarissa McCandless, and Deborah Farentino as Sloane Denning Clegg Mamoud. One of the biggest stars to appear on the soap was Carolyn Jones, who played Myrna Clegg for 786 episodes. Jones had starred as Morticia Addams on ABC's 1960s sitcom "The Addams Family." Country singer Tammy Wynette appeared as Darlene Stankowski, a hairdresser turned singer. Whitfield played the role of a dock worker, and during the 1985 season, Timmy portrayed a nice-guy lawyer called Marshall Devane.

One day Whitfield pointed out a wardrobe girl who was drinking water. She had a protruding lower lip, so Timmy instantly tagged her "Camel." He called Whitfield "Mongoose" because of his green eyes. Off the set, he referred to football players-turned-actors Marcus Allen as "E.T."; Fred Williamson as "the Horse"; and, of course, Jim Brown as "the Bear." He also had a name for O.J. Simpson that Whitfield said he could not recall. They often goofed around with nicknames for themselves, with Whitfield calling Timmy "the Badger" and Timmy referring to himself as "the Deer," thinking of himself as the better-looking one.

"Timmy wasn't as interested in the whole Hollywood scene as the other guys were," Whitfield said years later. "He liked those guys, but he didn't hang with them that much. He cared about his friends. He preferred hosting parties at his house and inviting regular people."

By the mid-1980s, Timmy's life looked to have settled into a routine – fun with friends like Whitfield, Vest, and Gerrard; the occasional television role or commercial; basketball games; and from time to time a charity tournament or appearance. Although he knew many women, he was not romantically involved. But Timmy had long been enamored of the actress and singer Doris Day, seeing her as a wholesome, All-American girl next door – the kind of woman he imagined would be his wife someday. Now, he was to meet a woman who would upend his routine and fulfill that dream.

Debra Lee Hartley was born on Jan. 2, 1955, in Norfolk, Va., to Bishop Melvin Leo Hartley, known as "M.L.," and Vera Elizabeth Hartley. She was the fifth of six children. She had two sisters, Glenda, six years older, and Judy, four years older, and three brothers – Kevin, a year younger; Roger, two years older; and Ronald, 10 years older. M.L. Hartley was responsible for selecting pastors for 126 congregations of the Church of God of Prophecy and, according to his daughter, held revivals seven nights a week during 20 weeks of the year.

The Hartley family accompanied M.L. to revivals, and his wife and children performed at them as a gospel-music group. When she was 3, Lee – she would start going by her middle name at age 19 – began singing with them. Eventually, they branched out to festivals and other venues. A recording company wanted to sign them, she said, but M.L. said, "Definitely not!" In the group, Judy sang, Ronald played guitar, and Roger played guitar and banjo. Their mother, who went by Elizabeth, and Glenda also sang. Kevin never performed with the group, Lee said, although he had a beautiful voice. Lee recalled standing on a metal milk-bottle carrier and singing "Sorry You Can't Go With Me," a song about a father going to Hell. As she sang, she said, she imagined not being with her father in Heaven, and cried.

At 10, she became the lead singer – standing on stage between Judy and Glenda, their arms around one another in a manner similar to the Lennon Sisters, whom they idolized. The four Lennon Sisters, tagged as "America's Sweethearts of Song," appeared on "The Lawrence Welk Show" from 1955 to 1968 (two of the sisters were still performing in 2022). While the Hartleys could watch them on television, the girls were never allowed to sing any of the Lennon Sisters' songs, because they were not religious in nature. Like the Lennons, they did wear dresses to perform, but makeup and jewelry were forbidden. In terms of music that they actually could sing, the most influential and popular gospel group that the Hartley girls followed was the Rambos. Buck and Dottie Rambo began performing in the 1950s as the Gospel Echoes and changed their name to the Singing Rambos when their 13-year-old daughter, Reba, joined them. In 1968, Dottie Rambo's album "It's the Soul of Me" won the first Grammy ever given for Best Soul Gospel Performance. Billboard recognized Dottie Rambo as "Trendsetter of the Year" because she sang with an all-Black choir. Songs she wrote were recorded by artists including Elvis Presley, Johnny Cash, Whitney Houston, and the Oak Ridge Boys.

Until she was 18, Lee performed with the singing Hartleys as the family moved from Virginia to Maryland, West Virginia, and Missouri. Lee had become the lead singer without taking singing lessons. She wanted to take lessons in junior high, but a teacher said, "No, she sings naturally, and I don't want to ruin that." She came to regret that decision, imagining how much she could have learned. She expanded her interest in music while in seventh grade in Milton, W.Va., when she started playing saxophone. She was recognized for her skill by being selected first chair.

The family moved to Van Buren, Mo., in 1970, and she graduated from Van Buren Senior High School in 1973. She had stopped playing the saxophone while in 10th grade there, as there was no band, but she sang in the school choir. A popular student, she was selected Homecoming queen in her junior year. In her senior year, she looked forward to attending prom. However, M.L. told her she could not go. She sneaked out and went anyway; he went to the prom, got her, and brought her home. A highlight of that year was her recognition as Miss Teen Van Buren and, as a representative of the city, going to St. Louis to compete for Miss Teen Missouri. She recalled that even though she wore no jewelry or makeup, she finished 10th. When the competition was over, she said, others among the top 10 were talking about how the winner had been smoking pot. Lee didn't know what pot was.

In Van Buren, Lee started a Sunday service for children in the basement of the church where her father preached. She appointed children to different responsibilities – someone to lead the singing, someone to read scripture, someone to share a message, for example. In addition to instilling responsibility and engaging children in religious study and celebration, Lee's Children's Church let the older parishioners hold a service without being interrupted by the children. "On occasion," she reflected, "the children would become so spirit-filled – like the power of the Lord just came down on us – that they shouted so loudly that the adults would stop to listen." She said she wanted the children to "feel like they had their own church."

After her high school graduation, Lee, Kevin, and their parents moved to Batesburg, S.C., about 60 miles from Charleston, where they lived in a large campground with a church, a parsonage, a swimming pool, and facilities for hosting a three-month summer camp. Judy and Glenda, who were both married, stayed in Missouri, so the move spelled the end of the gospel singing group, although they would continue to sing together at family gatherings and occasionally at church. M.L. then helped establish a statewide Children's Church organization, and Lee developed a newsletter. When her father traveled to churches, she would often accompany him in an effort to build the network of Children's Churches.

In the fall of 1974, she arrived at the University of South Carolina in Columbia, about 35 miles east of Batesburg. She was the first member of the family to leave home without being married and also the first to attend college. (Later, Judy and Kevin would graduate and become teachers, and Roger would attend for a couple of years before working for a number of businesses.) Not understanding what to expect on a campus, Lee failed to attend orientation. Later, when she met with an adviser, she got a course schedule for beginning a program in early childhood development and was told there was only one dormitory room still available. To her surprise, it was in the middle of campus, in a building known as Capstone House that she said was meant for seniors. It was a highly prized residence, capped by a revolving restaurant. She continued work on the Children's Church newsletter in her first year. However, she didn't have much time to devote to it, because she needed to earn money to pay for college. For a time, she sold Kirby vacuum cleaners door to door. She also worked the graveyard shift at a Denny's restaurant in Columbia.

In addition to coursework during her freshman year, she sang in the choir. Along with two roommates, she went to Florida during spring break of her second year and enjoyed the experience so much, she thought she might want to move there. At the end of the spring term in 1975, she left college with a two-year certificate that enabled her to work in early childhood education. But during her student teaching, she had realized that while she loved working with children, she didn't enjoy the hours or pay that would come with it.

She went home for a couple of weeks, then followed through on her desire to live in Florida. She drove an old car she owned to Miami, where she worked in a Greek restaurant and rented a room from a Lebanese woman who also housed another girl. After working there for some time, she flew to England and Ireland and visited Roger, who was studying the development of big-box stores there.

On her flight back to Miami, Lee sat in front of a mother with two children. She noticed that the mother was struggling to take care of them and offered to help. The mother appreciated Lee's help and offered to pay her, but she declined, saying she had enjoyed being with the children. The mother then asked Lee what she was doing for work. Lee said she was returning to Miami to see if she could get a job with Carnival Cruise Lines. The woman handed her a card and told her to present it at the Carnival office. Her husband happened to be a Carnival vice president. Because of the connection, Lee, to her surprise, landed a job immediately.

Lee traveled the Caribbean by cruise ship for 1½ years, doing a variety of jobs on board but never singing. She wasn't aware of the opportunity to work as a singer on a cruise ship when she applied. Early on, however, she was able to watch a nightclub act. Standing in the shadows, she was spellbound by the spotlight shining on a big-eyed, beautiful singer – her first name was Shirley, but Lee could not remember her last name. "It was beautiful," she remembered. She met Shirley and her boyfriend and pianist, Randy, a lanky man with long hair and a beard. He began working to expand her repertoire from gospel music to include jazz standards. Sometimes they met on stage after one of Shirley's performances or in his room, where he had a piano.

Her work on the cruise ship ended abruptly when she missed boarding time one day. She caught up with the ship at one of the stops, but on the day before its final docking, she was informed that she was being terminated. Randy encouraged her to go to the campus of the University of Miami, where there was a music school, and look on the posting boards for audition opportunities. He assured her that there were always auditions for singers. Within a day, she had landed a job with three males in an R&B band.

She drove her car from her parents' house – they had moved again, to North Carolina – to the Florida Keys. It barely made it, she said, as it was out of oil and the tires were nearly bald. One of the band members' parents owned a home in the Keys, close to a resort where they played for three months in the summer. In 2022, she didn't recall the name of the band or the members, but remembered that they were "just a bunch of college kids." She lived in a "casita" near the home, where the males stayed and the band rehearsed. She remembered being influenced by the work of Carole King and Phoebe Snow as a result of playing with the band. At the end of the summer, she nursed the car back to her parents' house. "I didn't have a bedroom or anything anymore," Lee said. "I was considered on my own. My dad disowned me for singing jazz. He was angry at me."

Now in her early 20s, she spent several weeks at her parents' house, thinking about what she might do next. In the fall, she received a call from a male friend in New York, who asked her to come visit for a couple of weeks. Her car had broken down, so she took a train. At the time, she had $100 and a few clothes, which she packed into a small suitcase. She wore a white suit and had a little fur wrapped around her neck when she arrived at the train station in Manhattan. She said she felt out of place, as everyone seemed to be wearing black. Her friend, who met her at the station, told her that her outfit wasn't the way New Yorkers dressed.

In New York, she said, she found a place to live with an ailing supermodel and her teenage daughter. She became their vegetarian cook and was responsible for cleaning up afterward. Every night she could, after cleaning up, she walked across the street to the Village Vanguard, the legendary jazz club on Seventh Avenue South in Greenwich Village. She sat at the bar to avoid the cover charge, but didn't order a drink. At the club, she heard performers such as the pianists and composers Horace Silver and Junior Mance, and the saxophonist Benny Carter. After one performance, the bass player for Silver approached her. Having noticed the white blonde in a white suit, he said, "You look like a sore thumb." She knew she had been naive about dress when coming to New York, but she hadn't yet earned the money to add to her collection of clothes. For a time, she knew she would have to endure some embarrassment and discomfort. She was also naive about safety in the city, she soon realized. After talking for a while one night, about 1 a.m. she told Mance that she was going to walk back to her apartment. Mance responded forcefully, "You can't walk over to your place at 1 a.m." He escorted her to her apartment and left.

While her friend had imagined that she would have a short stay in New York, Lee ended up living there for about a year. She met numerous jazz musicians and learned a variety of songs, building her interest and knowledge of jazz. She also took voice lessons from Claude Garvey, musical director for the comedian Nipsey Russell. Garvey helped her with speech and diction. But she found living in New York to be very expensive, and when an opportunity arose, she left.

It came when Randy, who had performed on the Carnival ships, got in touch with her. He said he had a gig with a band led by a singer named David Blaylock, and asked if she could join the group. She took a train in the winter snow to Mount Clemens, Mich., just north of Detroit. Lee became the lead singer for the "dance sets," which did not include Blaylock and which encouraged audience members to dance. She then sang backup when Blaylock, wearing a velvet jacket and sideburns, did a Tom Jones-like act. Lee toured with the group from the Detroit area to Cleveland; Albuquerque, N.M.; Dallas; and Las Vegas.

On the way to Nevada from Texas, the bus broke down about an hour outside of Las Vegas. Lee and another singer in the group hitchhiked to the city in a semi-trailer truck. There, she was introduced to a couple who took her to see her first Vegas show, featuring Raquel Welch. The man told her that he could get her an audition with Marvin Gaye. Surprised but excited, she agreed. The couple gave her an airline ticket to Palm Springs and told her she could stay at their house. When she arrived at the airport, friends of the couple picked her up and took her to the house. Not long after that, one of the couple's friends received a call from the man, and relayed the following message: "You can't audition. [The man was] in trouble. Forget you know him. But you can stay in the house for a couple of weeks."

At the time, Lee recalled, she had $40. She spent $12 to rent a bicycle to look for a job and a place to live. She landed a position as a hostess at a restaurant around the corner from the house. She later remembered how kind the restaurant staff was, knowing that she was working as hard as possible to get out of a difficult situation. She knew that she could not call her father, as he had told her to "never call home for money or help." Then she met a contractor who owned three houses. He told her that if she would clean the houses, she could stay in one at no cost. He also drove her to work at the restaurant every day.

In Palm Springs, she went to a small jazz venue on Palm Canyon Drive, where she met Pat Rizzo, who had played saxophone and flute with War, Sly and the Family Stone, Tito Puente, and others. According to an article by Brian Blueskye in the April 16, 2021, Palm Springs Desert Sun, "One day, Rizzo got a call to play a gig at the Trinidad Hotel in Palm Springs. He showed up and only saw Sinatra in the audience. It turned out the Rancho Mirage resident was auditioning him for his big band. He got the gig, but didn't have to do swing music exclusively. He went back into the studios and became an in-demand session player." According to Lee, Rizzo also played at Sinatra's parties.

Rizzo was a celebrity in the community and was known as "Riz." He sang in the style of Tony Bennett. He hired Lee for a variety of jobs, focusing on funk, jazz, swing, and standards, with artists ranging from the band Rufus to Miles Davis. They performed several times at Los Angeles Lakers owner Jerry Buss' Ocotillo Lounge. When she performed with Rizzo, she said, it was "off the cuff." They never had a song list and never prepared. Rizzo would call her onstage and give her the name of a song, like "They Can't Take That Away From Me," and tell her the key in which to perform it. On occasion, she helped him book acts. Rizzo gave her tickets and backstage passes to take friends to see Kenny Rankin, Sly and the Family Stone, Willie Bobo, and others. "He always treated me fairly," she remembered.

Lee performed with other groups while in Palm Springs. "The thing with jazz in those days," she said, "was that people just showed up to play. I was one of those who always showed up. There were a lot of gigs around town. Sometimes I was hired. People knew that I had been on the road with David Blaylock, and had background and experience."

By the spring of 1983, Lee had moved to Westwood. In April, she was contacted by Associated Booking Corp. in New York to replace a singer who had dropped out of a commitment to perform at two Playboy Clubs in Japan. She flew from Los Angeles to Tokyo on May 20. From May 23 through July 3, she performed at the Tokyo Playboy Club, and from July 18 to Aug. 14 she was at the Osaka club. She left Osaka on Aug. 16 and returned to Los Angeles. While in Japan, for six days a week she was required to either perform three shows per night of 30 minutes each, or two shows per night of 45 minutes. Playboy provided a free place to stay, as well as lunch and dinner at the club with the exception of her days off. Since she spoke no Japanese, Playboy Bunnies helped her translate. She quickly learned how to get taxis, order food, and converse at a level where she could function effectively. She recalled, "Everyone invited me out and wanted to be seen with me."

The Japanese promoter regularly took her to see shows of noted musicians, such as Benny Carter, and made certain she had a front-row seat and access backstage. She said she spent time with the pianist and composer Joe Sample, noted as one of the founders of the Jazz Crusaders, who was performing with a band featuring Larry Graham Jr., who had been bassist and singer with the Family Stone.

Upon her return from Japan, she moved to her own "little place south of Pico in Beverly Hills, close to Saks Fifth Avenue." She took a job as a massage therapist at the Sports Connection at 8612 Santa Monica Blvd. in West Hollywood – less than two miles from her apartment. That was where, in October or November 1984, she met Timmy. He was now 46 and she was 29. She had a day off, so she decided to have a steam and sauna. Afterward she went to the desk to see if there was an opening for a massage, and met Helen, the owner, who said, "Oh, you should meet Tim." Before she knew it, Timmy was shaking her hand as Helen continued talking: "He's a pro football player. He knows all kinds of people. He probably has lots of fans who would want to use your service." Lee said she was thinking: "No, no, no, no, no, no! I'm not looking for a football 'player.'" The word "player" stuck in her mind. "I really didn't want to get in with that whole Hollywood scene," she recalled. Timmy didn't let go of her hand. She had no makeup on, and her hair was wet from the sauna. She was embarrassed and felt like she wanted to run out of there – to anywhere.

After that meeting, he started calling her. He called a few times to get an appointment for a massage. Every time, she told him that she was booked. Finally, he asked, "When can I take you to dinner?" Each time, she said she was working and couldn't go. According to Lee, this went on for about three months.

One night, Lee decided to go to a club to see some friends perform. She told Timmy, "We'll go over to the Valley." She drove to his place, and then he drove them to the club. "He was the worst driver," she recalled. "He drove like he was running a touchdown. He would dive in front of cars. Wouldn't use the blinkers." As he wheeled in and out of traffic, he said, perhaps thinking back to his football days: "Why would you use a blinker? You can't let them know where you're going, you know."

When we walked into the club, "you would have thought the ocean had parted," Lee remembered. "All the women wanted to know who he was, saying, 'Oh, my God, who is this guy?' He was so good-looking, polite, kind, and down-to-earth."

Timmy gave her all of his attention. Later, he told her that he "was smitten" and that it was "like seeing white on rice" – an idiom, popular in the 1980s, meaning that the color of rice and rice itself are so closely intertwined that they are inextricable. They had a wonderful time. They got back to his house, after which Lee felt "totally paranoid of him ever driving again." But she went home still very concerned about getting involved with a "player." For about a month, they went to clubs and were together at parties Timmy threw at his apartment. Then, during the holiday season of 1984-85, Timmy asked her to marry him. She accepted.

Timmy said later of his feelings for Lee, "I told her that she was my Doris Day, who I was in love with as a kid. I would go see her in the movies. She was the ideal woman." Timmy may have been enchanted by watching some of Day's movies from the 1950s and 1960s, when she was one of the biggest box office stars in Hollywood, including "Send Me No Flowers," "Please Don't Eat the Daisies," "That Touch of Mink," or her Academy Award-nominated performance in 1959's "Pillow Talk." Or he may have followed her singing career through Hit Parader and enjoyed songs like "Dream a Little Dream of Me," "Sentimental Journey," "Secret Love," or her signature, "Whatever Will Be, Will Be (Que sera, sera)." Day had started out as a Big Band singer, then went on to star in movies from 1948 to 1968 while still releasing records. She often co-starred with Rock Hudson in rom-coms. As attitudes toward sex changed in the 1960s, Day's film persona did not; she was referred to as "The World's Oldest Virgin," and turned down the role of Mrs. Robinson in "The Graduate" because she found the script morally offensive.

The idea that Timmy would get married came as a shock to most of his longtime friends, among them Hollie Vest. She had continued to perform with various bands she led, and starting in 1981, she was booked for every New Year's Eve at a Holiday Inn in the South Bay suburb of Torrance. In 1984, she was appearing with a group she had formed that year, Hollie Vest and the Blazers. That spring, Tina Turner had released the song "What's Love Got to Do With It," her only Billboard Hot 100 No. 1 single. This was Turner's second go-round with fame after breaking up with her abusive husband, Ike Turner, in 1976 (their relationship is chronicled in the Academy Award-winning film, "What's Love Got to Do With It," staring Oscar nominees Angela Bassett and Laurence Fishburne). As the Ike and Tina Turner Review, they had released hits such as "River Deep – Mountain High" and "Proud Mary" in the 1960s. In preparing for her annual show, Vest went to Hollywood Boulevard and bought a private dancer wig similar to Tina Turner's, and made her first Tina costume out of items in her own closet – a short skirt, five-inch heels, and a metal-mesh halter top. Typically, she sang "Auld Lang Syne" at midnight. But this year, she told her band to bring up "What's Love Got to Do With It," and surprised both the band and audience by performing as if she were Tina Turner. Her act was a hit, and eventually she added a full show on Friday and Saturday nights.

There was a little tension between Vest and Lee after Lee accepted Timmy's proposal. According to Lee, Vest had thought that Timmy would never ask anyone to marry him, and was wondering what was going on. "Hollie and Tim had a sister-and-brother relationship. At one time, it was a boyfriend-girlfriend relationship," Lee said she believed. "They were having fun enjoying life. She had boyfriends and he had girlfriends. I thought they were a little too friendly. She's on his lap at Christmas while I'm in the kitchen cooking." After a while, Vest understood what Lee was thinking and said, "Oh, no." She hugged Lee. "She was just so engaging – constantly calling Tim. She would end the call to Tim saying, 'Tell Lee hello.'" Lee recalled that another woman, named Carol, also was vying for Timmy's attention. "They always came over. He loved company. We were always having people around. I would be gone and come home, and there would be a whole house full of people."

When Timmy told Kilroy that he was engaged, his reaction was close to Vest's. Indeed, the proposal had come as a shock to Lee. Shortly after accepting it, she called her parents to seek their approval. M.L.'s first reaction was, "Isn't he Black? You know, I'm a Christian man, but I'm also a Southern man. I can't approve of this." Elizabeth insisted on time to think about it, but made no promise, saying: "We're going to pray about this." Her mother fasted for three days and prayed, then said to M.L.: "He's never been married. She's never been married. You have to bless this." But M.L. still kept his distance.

Once over his shock, Kilroy swung into action. On March 24, 1985, Timmy and Lee were married at the Dunes. Kilroy hosted the wedding and had told the couple he would take care of everything. That included getting a marriage license, which they had forgotten to do.

The officiant was a justice of the peace, another detail Kilroy had taken care of. Kilroy was Timmy's best man. Lee's three best friends – Karen, Michelle, and Sharon – were bridesmaids; they remain close friends. Michelle was matron of honor, and her husband walked Lee down the aisle; their children served as flower girl and ring bearer. Pianist Peter Clark played the wedding march and accompanied Lee when she sang Leon Russell's "A Song for You" to Timmy.

Lee's parents were not there. But from Timmy's family, Juanita, Buddy, Polly, and Trixie were. They, like Timmy, had relocated to the Pacific Coast. Buddy had been awarded a doctorate in educational administration by Northwestern University in 1979. He had worked as executive secretary of the Midwest Teacher Corps Network at the University of Minnesota, and since 1980 had been executive secretary of the California Commission on Teacher Preparation and Licensing. But over time, his star was dimmed by California educational politics, and under pressure, he would resign in July 1985.

According to Lee, "All of our friends from before we met were there. We had everyone there. It was just one big happy family." When Whitfield arrived in Las Vegas, he was wearing a tuxedo. Lee said, "You don't have to be dressed yet." He said, "No, this is all that I brought to wear." He had rented it in Los Angeles and had to return it there.

After the ceremony, most of the guests hung out, drank, or gambled into the morning. Timmy and Lee celebrated for another day, then drove back to his little apartment in L.A., which would be their home. After the wedding, according to Lee, they received a bill from the Dunes. Timmy said, "What's this?" He called Kilroy, who said he would take care of it.

The transition to married life wasn't easy for Timmy. "He was in shock," Lee said. "I didn't understand why he was in shock, but he had been raised in an orphanage – so institutionalized. He had never allowed a woman to spend the night, literally timing everything so they had to go home before it was dark. There were some big adjustments." At the Home, a bell rang when it was time to eat; in their apartment, Timmy had a row of bells for her to ring when she had cooked dinner. She said he could flip out over the milk carton spout being turned the wrong way, chiding, "Who put the milk in the wrong way?"

"It was a big deal," Lee recalled. "He had a temper." He had an assortment of spoons that did not match, but each had a purpose. One he called his "ice cream spoon," another his "oatmeal spoon," for example. Lee recalled that he wanted to sleep in total darkness and total silence. He wore earplugs and an eye mask, and had a routine before he went to bed.

"I was used to constant tactile energy, being from a big family and sleeping with my brothers and sisters in the back of a car traveling while my father was doing revivals," Lee said.

"But when he was sleeping, if I touched him, it would startle him. He had this whole thing about that.

"Tim was very clean, immaculate – all things were in a certain way, yet the house was a mess. He had lots of clutter," Lee discovered. She wanted to redecorate. Timmy had a brown wrap-around leather couch whose arms had been fixed with duct tape, because they were cracked and worn. "It was the ugliest thing I had ever seen," she said. Timmy said, "We can sell it." She said it would have to be reupholstered first. "We argued for months about this," Lee recalled. "Eventually we had to pay someone to take it to a dumpster, which was very expensive to do." She wanted to get new curtains, so she bought fabric and made them. "He was always comfortable with things as they were," she said. "Not interested in making quick changes."

Lee said she and Timmy were still a "young couple" in terms of time together, though not in age. And now that she was his wife, Timmy told Lee that Vest and Carol didn't mean to him what she did. Still, she wasn't pleased when they would continue to sit on his lap or vie for his attention after they were married. He said it was all in fun. So she asked him, "Would it be OK if I sat on Jim's lap or Rick's lap," referring to Jim Brown and Rick Whitfield. Timmy said, "No, it wouldn't." She responded, "Now you get my point. Don't disrespect me." Then she let Tim take care of it.

About six months after they were married, she and Timmy met the owner of a blue Mercedes to look at the car. At first glance, Lee exclaimed, "That's the most beautiful car!" Seeing her reaction, Timmy bought it for about $2,500. She was surprised that he bought it, as "they really didn't have the money for it," Lee recalled. "It was in mint condition, but the mechanics were horrible." Over the ensuing months, it cost about $10,000 in repairs. They finally unloaded the car for about the same amount that Timmy had paid for it.

After getting married, Lee continued performing jazz at restaurants and clubs in the Los Angeles area, and recorded as a lead and background vocalist for various groups. "I was gone a lot," she said. "This gave some space to Timmy, who was used to having time to himself." She no longer worked at the Sports Connection, but continued to work as a health care professional. "I got all the top-notch clients," she said. "A lot of times, they'd be surprised that I was married to a pro football player. 'Like, why are you working?' they asked." She said Timmy, long a man about town, had found her different than other women he had dated. "It was ironic," she noted, "that a lot of the Hollywood women that he had dated were my clients."

Soon after their marriage, Timmy and Lee traveled to Philadelphia. She had no idea how huge a star he was there until they arrived. "As soon as we got off the plane, everyone noticed him and said, 'Oh, Tim Brown,' asking if they could carry his luggage and do things for him. The Eagles sent a car to pick us up. It was like a big parade, with everybody celebrating. We went to restaurants and Philly cheesesteak places – I had my first Philly cheesesteak sandwich there, which I loved – and when we walked in, the red carpet was rolled out and we were told, 'It's on us, whatever you want.'" They attended an Eagles game. Timmy took her to meet Al and Ernestine Grice and see the house on Pine Street where he had lived. During the visit, she came to understand how kind, generous, and supportive the Grices had been to Timmy.

Timmy and Lee also became couples friends with Bobby and Linda Bell. Timmy had met Bobby Bell through football. He was a Hall of Fame defensive back who played for the Kansas City Chiefs from 1963 through 1974. Just like Timmy, he had left college to play football without earning a degree – in his case, the University of Minnesota in 1963. Also, like Timmy, he eventually completed his degree, though much later in life; 52 years after leaving the university, Bell graduated on May 14, 2015.

Timmy was best man at the Bells' 1985 wedding. He also helped Bobby Bell promote his barbecue restaurant chain in the Kansas City area, which he had started in 1981. Bell had a jingle written and scored by Lee's brother, Roger, called, "I Smoke Ribs (Bobby Bell's Barbecue)." Bobby asked Timmy to sing it; he did, and was paid $500.

Bell's barbecue drew national attention in 1985, according to an article in the April 7, 1991, Kansas City Star. It said that when U.S. Rep. Thomas Coleman, from Kansas City, went back to the capital on Air Force Two, "Coleman's staff smuggled Bobby Bell's barbecue on board for Coleman's forthcoming birthday bash [scheduled for May 29]. Assessing it was for him, [then-Vice President George H.W.] Bush appropriated the tasty treat. He later paid for it with vice presidential goodies for the Coleman family."

The four first met for dinner in Las Vegas. Lee recalled how elegantly dressed they were. She described Linda, an airline stewardess, as "stylish and pristine," noting that she ironed everything. Lee was amazed at how much Linda could jam into a bag – cosmetics, underwear, shoes, everything she needed – and how heavy it was. "Bobby had a preppy look," she said. "He was the first guy I had seen who folded a sweater around his neck."

She and Linda spent time together shopping and going to the swimming pool. "The first time we met at the pool, we wore identical white bikinis," she said with a laugh. On another occasion, she and Timmy met the Bells for dinner at a hotel in Beverly Hills. On a couple of occasions, Lee and Linda stayed at Lee's parents' home in Gastonia, N.C., about 30 miles from Shelby, where Bobby grew up. The first time was in 1986, when both Lee and Linda were pregnant.

Bobby and Linda came to L.A. to join the Browns at the Jan. 25, 1987, Super Bowl XXI between the New York Giants and the Denver Broncos. A limo driver had been hired to take the four of them to the Rose Bowl. They never made it. The driver smelled of marijuana, didn't seem to know where to go, and admitted that he had received the call at the last minute to pick them up, Lee said. Then Bobby found out that the driver didn't have a pass needed to let him drive them close to their seats. As both women were pregnant and dressed up for the occasion, Bobby said, they didn't want to walk a long distance. They also wondered where they would be picked up after the game. Given all this, they decided to sell their tickets. Seeing several fans wanting to buy tickets, Bobby had the driver stop, spotted a buyer, and told him that he would accept cash only. The buyer handed him more than he expected. The driver stopped so they could buy food while heading back to Timmy and Lee's place. From there, they watched the Giants defeat the Broncos by 39-20.

Bobby also played golf with Timmy and other members of the National Football League Alumni Foundation. In a March 3, 1987, article in the Kansas City Star, writer Mike McKenzie noted that Bobby had just begun playing golf that year, at the age of 46. He noted that funds raised helped to support "players in the NFL before 1959 [who were] not eligible for the major-dollars retirement benefits that retired players from 1960 on" received.

McKenzie said Bobby "played in 18 tournaments, including four in the span of 11 harried days in Phoenix, Las Vegas, Los Angeles, and Reno." Timmy, because of other commitments, played in fewer. Both Bobby and Lee remembered that the Camelback Resort in Scottsdale, Ariz., was a favorite location. Whenever they went to a tournament, while Timmy and Bobby were playing golf, she and Linda swam in the pool, sunbathed, or shopped. At night, the four of them met for dinner. Typically, they added a day or two after the tournament to spend more time together.

Eventually, Bobby and Linda separated. Lee recalled that she and the Bells maintained their friendship for some time. After the Bells divorced, Lee lost track of Linda but has continued to talk with Bobby to this day.

Also becoming part of Lee's life as Timmy's wife was, of course, Jim Brown. Timmy and Lee got together with him about 45 times, she recalled. "Jim came over to the little apartment all the time," Lee said, and they went to his nearby home as well. Sometimes Lee's nephew Greg Powell and niece Dee Dee Powell went as well. The couple also went to parties at Jim's place, but Jim told her and Timmy, "I don't invite you to all the parties. I invite you to ones for the family – you've got your lady here." For about 2½ years, Lee would baby-sit Jim's daughter Kimberly, who was of pre-K and kindergarten age. She recalled, "Jim would have to run and do something and would say, 'Can you guys watch Kim?' I loved and was crazy about children, so I found it delightful." (Now known as Kimberly B. Brown, she had a role as the wife of boxer Sonny Liston in the 2020 Academy Award nominated film "One Night in Miami," directed by Regina King, in which Aldis Hodge played Jim Brown.) But taking care of Jim's daughter didn't mean he was really paying attention to Lee. At one point, she said to Timmy, "You know, I don't think Jim knows my name." Timmy responded, "Oh, my God. Yes he does. You're crazy!" She reiterated, "No, he doesn't know my name. When he introduces me, he always introduces me as 'Tim Brown's wife.'" Coincidentally, about 10 minutes later Jim called. Timmy immediately said, "Jim, I got a question for you. This is it. What is my wife's name?" There was dead silence. Then Jim said, "Oh, man, Tim. Just forgive me. I'm just not thinking right today. Tell me. And I'll never forget."

Another old friend of Timmy's, Dionne Warwick, invited them to a couple of events. One was to a Whitney Houston performance on Sunset Boulevard, close to where they lived. Lee was excited, but Timmy didn't want to go and shrugged it off, saying, "She's just some cousin of Dionne's." Lee has always regretted not going. Houston had 11 singles that reached No. 1 on Billboard's Hot 100, including seven consecutive No. 1 singles between 1985 and 1987, and her version of Dolly Parton's "I Will Always Love You," which spent 14 weeks at No. 1 in 1992. Houston's first two albums, "Whitney Houston" (1985) and "Whitney" (1987), each reached No. 11 and sold more than 20 million copies worldwide. By the time of her death in 2012, she had established herself as one of the most popular singers in pop/rock history. The other event was a Warwick birthday celebration at a hotel in Beverly Hills one December, which they did attend.

Timmy also continued his civic engagement efforts. One agency to benefit from his time was the Los Angeles County Probation Department. His association with it had begun in 1986, when he worked as a volunteer for Youth of America Week '86. In February 1987, he was selected as volunteer of the year by the department. A letter of congratulations from director R. Michael Lindsay stated, "This is indeed an honor, since we have volunteers at numerous camps, juvenile halls and area offices. Personally, I can't think of a better choice than you, since you have done so much for our young people through your work with the NFL alumni." The letter asked Timmy to appear at the Dorothy Chandler Pavilion in downtown Los Angeles on April 22, 1987, for a luncheon at which he would receive the award. The still-pregnant Lee sang Whitney Houston's 1986 No. 1 single, "The Greatest Love of All," which focused on the belief "that children are our future," during the ceremony.

A photo of the occasion shows Timmy, next to emcee Henry Winkler, holding a plaque. Winkler had become a 1970s icon and the epitome of cool as Fonzie on "Happy Days," with his motorcycle, leather jacket, thumbs-up gesture, and phrase "Aayyyy!" Winkler has enjoyed a career comeback in the HBO series "Barry" and won the Emmy for Outstanding Supporting Actor in a Comedy Series in 2018. Though Winkler suffered from dyslexia and major depression, unlike many other 1970s stars who rose to fame quickly and developed "big heads," he managed to stay well-grounded. He was said to have become even more polite and agreeable after his popularity soared from the series, which ran from 1974 to 1984.

On Sept. 5, 1987, Sean Timothy Brown was born at what was then Brotman Medical Center in Culver City. Lee was in labor for 18 hours, vomiting after eating chili dogs that Timmy had made. Sean weighed 8 pounds, 11 ounces when born at 2:52 a.m. Lee was served a lobster dinner afterward. Timmy described the birth of a son as his greatest accomplishment. "We had been trying," he said, "but had a failure on the first one," when Lee miscarried. "I had given up." Lee said Timmy was a "hands-on father who changed diapers, burped him, fed him – did everything." As he got older, Sean followed Timmy around, showing a "sweet and beautiful bond."

Lee's father, M.L. Hartley, the self-described "Southern man," had been reluctant to let the couple into his life. For two years, he refused to meet Timmy. The birth of Sean and the cute photos of him that Lee sent to her parents caused a change of heart. His wife, Elizabeth, chided M.L., "You have to let them come home for things – Christmas or Thanksgiving or something. You have to. Never let your wife be this mad at you." M.L. relented, and Timmy and Lee were told, "You guys have to come home."

Timmy was somewhat reluctant to go to South Carolina to visit the family. "He was afraid. He'd never been to the South. He had this fear of going back to meet my dad and he couldn't sleep." She finally asked: "Why are you up all night?" He said, "Because I keep seeing myself getting lynched."

He overcame the fear. Lee fondly recalled that "when my dad met Tim, what he saw was an elegant, beautiful man, and so well-spoken, and he fell in love with him. I mean, he literally fell in love with him. He knew he was wrong and learned a lesson. It was a beautiful healing for the family and church people."

M.L. and Timmy played checkers and dominoes for hours while singing Elvis songs. He asked Timmy about Ross and Warwick and football, living vicariously through the stories. He was so taken by Timmy that he took him to all the churches he oversaw – Black and white – to "show him off," according to Lee. As a result of the visits, Lee said, M.L. became known as a "civil rights equalizer."

One evening at dinner, Lee's oldest brother called. Everyone at the dinner table heard the conversation. Her father said, "No, Ronald, you have to come home. We were wrong. We were so wrong. You know, you know, you just can't, you can't, you can't judge a book by its cover. You got to come home, you got to meet him." Lee recalled, "And sure enough, when my brother met Tim, he fell in love. My whole family really loved him. We went to visit them at Christmas and one other time." While Elizabeth flew to L.A. on a couple of occasions to visit Timmy, Lee, and Sean, M.L., who was afraid of flying, never did.

When Sean was a little older, he and Timmy played at being Batman and Robin. When Sean went to sleep at night, he said later, he believed that he and Timmy went on excursions across the city to save people. He once said, "Mom, I really believed I was Robin." He never wanted to take his Robin pajamas off, because he knew he would have to get dressed in them while he was sleeping. Lee said this brought joy to both Sean and Timmy. "I'm glad that Tim was able to experience part of what he missed in his childhood through Sean," she said. "Sean was crawling all over him and riding on his shoulders."

After Sean's birth, Timmy rarely got even minor roles in television and commercials. "I haven't given up," he told Philadelphia Daily News writer Ray Didinger in a Sept. 27, 1990, article, "but I'm trying to be realistic." He continued his civic volunteer work, including with the county Probation Department. Lee said Timmy "kept going out and they kept calling him.... He was a very generous person with his time, and he just loved people and people really loved him." Based on the positive feedback to his volunteer work, he was encouraged to apply for a counseling position with the department.

At first he didn't think the overtures were serious, and declined in a self-effacing way. Because of this and his notoriety, according to Lee, those at the department who wanted to hire him didn't think he would accept a job there. Eventually, Timmy contacted the department to ask about a staff position. In his application, he referred to his work in Orange County for the Goals for Life program, in which former football players counseled L.A.-area youths identified by their teachers as at risk of getting caught up in gangs or other things that might jeopardize their future. He also mentioned his counseling work, his childhood experiences at the Home, and his professional sports career. He prominently mentioned the 1987 Volunteer of the Year Award on his resume. He was accepted, completed counselor training, and attended the Juvenile Counselor Core Graduation Ceremony on April 20, 1990, where he received a certificate and a badge. To Timmy's copy of the program were attached two Graduation Roster pages – one dated March 28 and the other Feb. 14, with his name appearing on the latter with assignment to Camp Kilpatrick, on Encinal Canyon Road in Malibu. Of the 40 graduates, he was the only one assigned to Kilpatrick. Lee remembered that "he was very happy to get the job there."

Didinger noted that Timmy had visited several youth centers on behalf of NFL alumni, so "had a few contacts in the system" when looking for employment. He said Timmy took the job because the family needed another source of income. Timmy told him, "I still read scripts and keep my eyes open, but I'm becoming more and more involved with my family and my work at the camp. After all those years of just thinking about me, me, me, it's kinda nice to think about other people for a change." Later in life, Timmy said that in addition to needing the money, he wanted to have a normal job with predictable hours, so he could not only be available for Sean but could model what he believed a responsible father should do. Trying out for ads and small roles wasn't the model he desired.

Camp Kilpatrick was about a 45-minute drive from his home. Each Thursday and Friday, and a half-day on Saturday, he served as a live-in counselor to boys 14 to 18 years old who had been placed there as wards of the court. His job had elements of what he remembered from the Home. He made certain that the boys got up at 5:30 a.m. and made their beds. He had them line up, shower, dress, and go to breakfast. He was responsible for getting them to lunch, dinner, and, at lights-out time, bed. He was required to meet one-on-one with each of them in a counseling session for 30 minutes once a week, hold a group session at least every other shift, and keep detailed records on their progress. He was expected to know how many were under his supervision and where they were at all times. He had to inspect all incoming and outgoing mail. He had to watch for any signs of gang association or activity, looking for gang-related colors, styles of dress, accessories, nicknames, words or phrases, and mannerisms.

As a reward for good behavior, Timmy often showed movies. When the movie was over, he would ask them questions about it. For correct answers, in the classic Timmy style, he doled out pieces of candy from a bag that he brought. In Didinger's article, Timmy characterized the youths in the probation program as "one step away from hard time. Our camp is like the last chance. We have to reach these kids, because if they leave us and return to their old ways, the next offense means the slam.

"Most of our kids come out of the gang environment. There's a lot of drugs, a lot of violence, total disregard for the law. Drug dealers use these kids. They say, 'Look at all the money you'll make if you work for me.' Show a teenager enough money and he won't care about the risk of getting caught.

"What we have to do is convince them there is another way to make it," he told Didinger. "We have to show them that where they're headed is all wrong. The first step in doing that is to show them that we [the staff] care and we want to help. That's the hardest part, breaking down that wall and getting their trust."

In an interview, Timmy recalled that at first, he wasn't respected because he was seen as too lenient: "I tried to be myself. I thought I had to treat these kids right. I wanted them to see another side." One incident he recalled illustrated his demeanor. One of the youths, named Contreras, was acting up after lights out. Timmy admonished him to lie down in his bed and be quiet. Contreras responded defiantly, "Ain't gonna do it!" To which Timmy warned, "You don't want me to come over." "Fuck you! Fuck you!" the boy yelled. Timmy said he laughed and again told Contreras to "get flat and be quiet." Then, more seriously, he said, "I'm giving you a shot here. If you fight, you will be in lockdown for two weeks." He repeated, more forcefully, "You really want me to come over?" Contreras apparently continued his defiance, because a short time thereafter, Timmy put him in a headlock and walked him to the door. He told him that two or three other staffers were coming. Shortly afterward, the staffers arrived, and one asked Timmy if he wanted Contreras taken to lockdown. He said, "No. He's OK." Looking at Contreras, he said, "Go back to your bed, Contreras." "Yes, sir," the boy responded, and lay down on his bed. Timmy concluded, "I had to get respect. Once I did, things were pretty good."

Not all of the probation officers treated their wards in the way that Timmy did. A few who had been on the job longer and had bad experiences, such as being attacked in the cafeteria, acted nervous. According to Timmy, some of the staff "beat them up, talked about their mothers in [disparaging and vulgar] ways, enticed them to fight, and showed no respect."

What Timmy observed "did not sit right with him." He determined he couldn't allow his charges to be abused physically, verbally, or emotionally, and would have to report it if it occurred: "I'm going to make some enemies on this, but I'm going to do it because it's not right for them to do this to these kids."

The advocacy, compassion, and care that Timmy felt and showed toward the youths were captured by Didinger in his article: "The camp recently had an open house with a cake sale and a magic show for families and other visitors. Brown noticed that five kids from his dorm were left out. None of their relatives came to visit, so they were off by themselves. Brown rounded them up, treated them to lunch, rented a movie, then played basketball with them the rest of the day. Said Brown, 'I had been in their position, and I know how it hurts. I just wanted them to enjoy the day, the same as everyone else.'"

Later in life, Timmy recalled building trust, respect, and positive interactions with the youths. He remembered that on occasion later in life, when he was in downtown L.A., some of them would see him and shout, "Mr. Brown! Mr. Brown!" They would tell him how they'd turned their life around after being released, thanks to his help and guidance, and that he was their favorite teacher.

Sean reflected these sentiments in a March 22, 2022, Inquirer article, in which he was quoted as saying, "Everybody loved him at the camp, the kids and staff alike. The kids especially. He was a lot of fun for them, even though they were in a place that wasn't necessarily going to be fun for them. He treated them with a lot of respect and showed them a lot of love, even though these kids didn't really get a lot of that in their lives."

Timmy also continued his volunteer work with the department. In 1990, a letter shows, he was chairman of Youth of America Week, enlisting other former NFL players to "join alumni across the country [from Sept. 10 to 14] in focusing our time and efforts on worthwhile projects with area young people." Other volunteer work with the department included a speech on May 12, 1990, at the Parent of the Year Awards Breakfast; a talk with students on Feb. 26, 1991, at Westminster High

School during lunch hour, about a program to help migrant students stay in school; and participation on May 30, 1991, in a Career Day at Mount Vernon Junior High School in Los Angeles.

Youth Development teacher Dennis DelValle from Waite Middle School in the Norwalk-LaMirada Unified School District praised Timmy's work with youths, saying: "Tim Brown is doing more than just teaching student goal-setting techniques. He is, through a caring relationship, assisting the students to internalize that they have worth and value: one of the most important truths in life. Every week kids come to me begging to be in Tim Brown's group."

According to Lee, Timmy had been asked to talk to kids and give them a boost – sharing his life and what he had accomplished. He would encourage them, saying, "Look at what I did. If I can do this, you can do it, too. Believe in your dream!" He also spoke to youths whose dreams had been dashed by bad decisions.

Jim Herron Zamora reported in a Los Angeles Times article on Sept. 17, 1992, on Timmy's remarks to "40 inmates in a high-security cellblock [at Sylmar Juvenile Hall] for boys charged with or convicted of murder." Timmy told them, "You guys turn 13, start growing face hair, and you don't want to hear anyone talk to you like a kid. Trouble is some of you will never grow up. You'll keep making the same mistakes.... You'll end up dead in the street." Also speaking at the event was Reggie Berry, who was a kickoff and punt returner for the San Diego Chargers in 1972-74 and who had founded Goals for Life in 1989.

"'I wish somebody had told us about this earlier," said one boy with gang tattoos on his neck, according to the Times article. "Maybe I wouldn't be here." Another boy, whose "scarred, weathered face made him appear far older than 17, agreed. 'I'm facing murder as an adult. I don't have a life.'"

Timmy was on occasion able to supplement his income from his weekend Probation Department work. When he could, he worked for Goals for Life. A Jan. 29, 1996, article by L.A. Times reporter Jeff Leeds noted that "school districts contract with the program," run by Berry "from a hospital office in Norwalk, to send athletes to campuses several times a week for 24 weeks. Under each $5,000 contract, the players meet with teachers, look over students' report cards and attendance records, and chat privately with small groups of students." Field trips and other activities were also available.

Timmy and Lee found plenty of time to attend NFL and Probation Department-related activities, as well as travel and visit with family and friends, and continued to host house parties at their place. One tradition at these parties, as it had been for Timmy since his college days, was beer bread. "He was always making beer bread, which was legendary," Lee said. "He always picked it for every single party. It had 20 steps to it. It was a whole drawn-out thing. He would take the batter and had to dry it out. It had to do this [and that], and it had to be right. I didn't even know how he made it. He never shared it with anyone. I don't even know where he got the recipe, but it was crunchy on the outside. And it had so much flavor on the inside, with tiny pieces of onion and butter. It was unbelievable."

Lee recalled going to an NFL-sponsored event in Mexico that was organized by Arthur Ashe, the Black tennis player who won three Grand Slam singles titles. She remembered spending time on the beach and playing tennis. Lyle Waggoner, who played the straight man on "The Carol Burnett Show" for seven years, and one of her favorite singers, the jazz vocalist Nancy Wilson, were there. So too was a "who's who" of boxers, all of whom had come from Las Vegas. During Wilson's performance, Lee asked her if she could sing "Midnight Sun." Wilson said it was not in the set, but then sang the entire song to her. Sean, who was 4 at the time, enjoyed interacting with the boxers while riding on the bus. They showed him different moves and how to throw punches. At the end of the trip, Lee recalled, it was raining as they began to depart. "One of the boxers was held back and wasn't able to leave until he paid Mexican authorities," she said. She was told that the practice was not uncommon at the time, which caught her by surprise.

Lee remembered attending other NFL events in Los Angeles on occasion, including one where she saw O.J. Simpson and his wife, Nicole, whom he later would be accused of killing. She also met Wilt Chamberlain at an L.A. gathering. Timmy and Chamberlain had roomed together at a celebrity event in Philadelphia once, and knew one another while Timmy was playing for the Eagles. "Everybody was trying to see Wilt while we were there, and Wilt was trying to find Timmy. Wilt adored him," she said. After they connected, at one point Chamberlain said, "Come on, let's get in the elevator. I've got to go up to the other floor." Timmy and Lee accompanied him. When they got on the elevator, Lee noticed that Chamberlain had to bend over to ride in it. "He was not only tall, he was massive. He made Timmy look like a little shrimp." When they got on the elevator, Timmy and Wilt hugged.

"I was looking at his feet, that looked like boards, and asked him if I could ask him a question. He anticipated that I would ask him about the size of his feet, but I didn't. I asked, 'How do you drive a car?'"

"That's a good question," she said he responded. "I had to make changes in my Rolls Royce, taking out the front seat, and moving and customizing the door to get in. I thought you were going to ask me what size shoes I wear."

She instantly said, "Size 26."

He laughed and said, "That's right."

On March 16, 1990, Gene Kilroy celebrated his 49th birthday at the New York-New York Hotel & Casino in Las Vegas. Timmy attended, along with other celebrities, including several heavyweight champions. One of them was Mike Tyson. Tyson would post a 50-6 career record with 44 knockouts. But at the party, "Iron Mike" was still sulking from one of the biggest upsets in boxing history, when James "Buster" Douglas had beaten him in the 10th round on a technical knockout on Feb.11.

Heavyweight championship boxing at that time was a tightly knit world, as shown by three other guests, Larry Holmes and the Spinks brothers, Michael and Leon. Holmes knew Kilroy because he had been a sparring partner for Muhammad Ali. In a much-publicized match between friends, on Oct. 2, 1980, Holmes defeated Ali when the fight was stopped in the 10th round on a TKO. Ali, at 38, was trying to make a comeback but lost every round, according to the judges, in what was widely described as a "fearful, horrible beating."

Holmes defeated Leon Spinks by a TKO in June 1981, but lost two consecutive matches to Michael Spinks, the first on Sept. 21, 1985, and the second on April 19, 1986. After losing his rematch, Holmes retired temporarily. He returned to the ring on Jan. 22, 1988, to fight Tyson. The fight was stopped in the fourth round after Tyson knocked out Holmes. (To complete the circle, Leon Spinks had fought Ali on two occasions, and Michael Spinks' last fight ended after 91 seconds in the ring with Tyson.)

Another guest, the actor Burt Young, had also boxed. While in the Marine Corps, he won 32 of 34 matches, and he went on to win all 14 of his professional bouts. However, he was best known through a different boxing connection, playing the role of Paulie Pennino, best friend and brother-in-law of the Italian Stallion, in the "Rocky" film series. The artist LeRoy Neiman, famous for his flashy expressionist works, also was there. Neiman's work concentrated on athletes and sporting events, musicians and other well-known figures, famous places, and animals. According to a New-York Historical Society announcement of a Dec. 11, 2016, to March 26, 2017, exhibit, "Muhammad Ali, LeRoy Neiman, and the Art of Boxing," "In the early 1960s, Ali found friendship with … Neiman, with whom he shared an affinity for boxing, the limelight, and breaking with convention. Neiman even taught and encouraged Ali to draw." The exhibit contained some works by Ali and several by Neiman focused on Ali's most memorable fights, such as the "Thrilla in Manila" and the "Fight of the Century" against Joe Frazier.

In November 1990, Timmy was named to the Eagles Honor Roll (later renamed the Eagles Hall of Fame). Timmy and Sean left Los Angeles on Saturday, Nov. 24, for Philadelphia to attend the fifth Honor Roll ceremony. The Honor Roll had been started in 1987, and this was the first year in which only one former player was selected. The ceremony came at halftime of the Sunday game between the Eagles and the New York Giants. Timmy, holding Sean, stood at midfield with Ernestine Grice, Tommy McDonald, and Gene Kilroy. Bill Campbell, who had been the "Voice of the Eagles" during the time that Timmy played and who was then hosting a radio show on sports talk WIP-AM, led the ceremony. In the Nov. 26, 1990, issue of the Philadelphia Daily News, reporter Didinger captured Timmy's sentiments about Grice, who with her husband had taken Timmy into their home: "She gave me a place to live, she treated me like one of her own. You don't forget that sort of kindness. Coming back here this weekend allowed me to visit with her and a lot of old friends."

Campbell pointed to the Phanavision jumbo screen and asked the crowd to watch "some of the great videos of Timmy Brown, actor, singer, player," that were being shown. He said that "few created more excitement ... when he had his hands on the ball, to hear 60,000 fans come alive as one, and usually the result brought thunderous fury."

He continued, "Let me jog your memory," highlighting Timmy's 105-yard kickoff return in the opening game in 1961 against the Cleveland Browns, at that time the longest return in Eagles history; having twice as many yards on kickoff returns than any other Eagles player; his record of 341 total all-purpose yards in a game against the St. Louis Cardinals in 1962, and his 90-yard return of a missed field goal for a touchdown that same year; returns of two kickoffs for touchdowns in 1966 against the Dallas Cowboys, one for 93 yards and the other for 90; and his selection to the Pro Bowl in 1962, 1963, and 1965. Ending his introduction, he reminded the crowd that Timmy had been a 27th-round draft pick by the Green Bay Packers and called him the "bolt of lightning from Ball State." The crowd roared in a standing ovation.

Timmy had looked at the Phanavision, and Didinger reported that "he saw ... old 22 slashing through the open field. He smiled at how easy it looked, the balletic moves, the fluid, breakaway speed." He later told Didinger, "It was nice to see I had two good legs at one time. I can't move like that anymore, not with my knee the way it is. That was why I had Sean run onto the field with me. I was hoping he would take people's eyes off my limp.... The doctors want to replace my knee [with an artificial joint], but I haven't done it because I don't want to be completely inactive" during recuperation. "It's bone on bone," he said, which Didinger translated as "meaning that the years of continuous NFL pounding have worn away the cartilage in his left knee." Timmy said, "That's the price you pay for getting older, I guess."

Timmy was dressed impeccably, in a black suit, white dress shirt, and red tie. He held Sean, who was warmed by a black flight jacket with colorful decals and a furry collar, in his left arm. Without notes, Timmy spoke briefly, saying this was a great day for him and his son. He expressed appreciation to key Eagles officials of that time – owner Norman Braman, general manager and president Harry Gamble, and Jim Gallagher, who had served in roles ranging from personnel director to public relations. He especially thanked Gallagher "for having me back ... to look at the fans one more time." To the fans, he said, "I feel very special with you because you got me in this game. Some of you were here when I played. I hope you are out there today to help cheer this moment." The crowd erupted. He thanked them and continued, "It's an honor for me to join my old teammates Tommy McDonald, Pete Retzlaff, Tom Brookshier, and fellows I didn't play with, Harold Carmichael and Wilbert Montgomery." Then he concluded: "It's an honor for me, and I hope the Eagles can take the Giants today," to which the crowd again cheered. The Eagles won by 31-13.

Throughout his father's remarks, Sean was quiet and attentive. But when Timmy had finished, Sean saw a person dressed as an eagle and began wriggling in his arms, pointing and screaming, "Bird! Bird! Bird!" Years later, Sean reflected on how much he appreciated being included in the honor: "He could have done it alone. He always involved me.

Never made me feel that I was distracting or making his plans more difficult. He wasn't even fazed by my reaction to the mascot."

However, Lee had not accompanied Timmy and Sean to Philadelphia. Their relationship had deteriorated, and Lee had become very restless. With his work schedule and daily routine, she recalled, she felt like she didn't have any contact with Timmy. It was like she was his mother. She said, "He wanted me to come home and make his dinner and feed the cat. He worked out at the same time every day. He went down to the game center and would set the high score on a Pac-Man game every single day. It was like clockwork. And then he would want to go down again later that night to see if the high score was still there. He still had that competitive thing in his body that he just wanted to beat something every day.

"The breaking point was when he asked me to sleep in the other bedroom. There was a total lack of energy between us. With his job, my work, taking care of Sean, and Timmy's expectations, we spent less and less time together, and grew further and further apart. It was very personal. We went to therapy. But it was not successful." It led to their separation in January 1991. In retrospect, she regretted it. "I wish that I could have been more understanding," she said. "I didn't understand the pain he had from being reared in an orphanage. I didn't understand how institutionalized he was, and that he may have been experiencing [symptoms of] Alzheimer's at this point, because he did everything in a routine.

"We really loved each other," she said. "I had a vision of what a marriage was. He thought being in the same house was a marriage. He didn't have any example. I wanted something more." Timmy remained in the San Vicente Boulevard apartment, and Lee and Sean moved to an apartment at 4913 Cahuenga Blvd. in North Hollywood.

Timmy now was working for the Probation Department during the week, from an office in North Hollywood. As an adult probation officer, he held weekly or monthly meetings with adults who had served time. He gave them drug tests and made sure they were staying on track.

He was off on weekends, when Lee worked, so he was the parent on duty then. He would either take Sean to school on Monday morning or back to Lee's on Sunday night. Sean's school was just across the street from their new apartment, so Lee typically walked him there and home every day. A housekeeper spent time at Lee's during the week and at Tim's during the weekend. Lee remembered that she watched cartoons with Sean and taught them how to cook Mexican food.

One day while Sean was in preschool, Lee recalled, she went to the supermarket, and when she came back the house was full of kids. She asked the housekeeper what was happening, as she was cursing in Spanish and carrying on. Not getting an answer, she asked Sean, "What's going on?" Sean said, "Oh, Mommy, I call my friends and I tell them we have a pauty." Surprised, Lee asked, "How do you know their phone numbers?" Sean responded, "I memorized them." He had memorized the phone numbers of 12 children in his preschool class and had invited them to his place.

Lee called the other mothers and asked what had happened. They repeated the same story: "Your son called and said you guys were having a party today. I just figured you just ran to the store to get some food for everybody." Lee thought, "My child created this whole thing. It was funny. We laughed about it later." At an early age, it seemed, Sean had inherited his father's love of throwing parties at his home.

Sean could draw attention as a party guest as well. When he was 4, he said in an online post in 2019, "I went to a little girl's birthday party and before we could all have cake, I decided to smash the Little Mermaid cake to pieces, thus ruining the party and crushing the little girl's heart." The girl, who was one day younger than Sean, was Jane Carrey, daughter of the actor Jim Carrey. In 2019, Sean met Jim Carrey, "and he immediately had to have a picture with me to send to his daughter."

During his separation from Lee, Timmy continued his volunteer work. In April 1991, he joined a rally with other celebrities to raise money for environmental and children's agencies for the Permanent Charities Committee in Los Angeles. He was invited by Clint Eastwood, the 1991 chairman, to participate in Earthwalk 1991. And he also picked up some money on the side working with Goals for Youth, a program specifically for migrant youths developed in connection with the NFL Players Association. From Sept. 30 to Dec. 31, 1991, he worked with the program for the Fresno County Office of Education and was paid $5,400, according to a contract. Shortly afterward, he worked for 12 weeks at Sierra Intermediate School in the Santa Ana Unified School District, and in the spring of 1992, he again worked in the program, this time at Westminster High School in the Huntington Beach Unified School District.

During this period of separation, Grayce Butler Shadd came to visit Timmy over the Christmas holidays. Timmy had invited her during a phone conversation. She was divorced and living in Cincinnati. Timmy, she said later, had told her that he and Lee were divorced. When she got to California, she found to her surprise that they were not.

Grayce gave him a composite of photos that her son Dirk had taken. They were high-quality headshots as well as photos of her in aerobics and tennis. At the time Dirk took them, he was working as a photographer with the Long Beach Press-Telegram, having arrived there after one year with the Philadelphia Inquirer. In addition, she brought a cassette of music they had listened to while in college. She was very proud of it, but he didn't listen to it while she was there. (She said she later asked him about the cassette and he said, "It was so faint, I could hardly hear it." "He wasn't impressed," Grayce recalled, disappointed given what it had meant to her.)

Timmy was recovering from knee surgery. They went to a park, where she watched over Sean while Timmy was "shooting hoops with the guys." "I thought it was funny," she said, "that he wanted me to watch him play basketball, the same way he had wanted me to watch him play ping-pong at Ball State." She said she wondered to herself, "What's this all about, Grayce? You're watching this guy, so happy and so proud, and he had to show."

They also went to see his mother, Juanita. And then they went to the Beverly Center, an eight-story shopping mall at the edge of Beverly Hills and West Hollywood. Grayce remembered being excited because she liked to shop. Once inside the mall, Timmy and Sean walked directly into a game room, where he and Sean played a couple of games. Then Timmy told her, "Now you take Sean away for at least an hour."

"I was a Montessori teacher at the time with a master's degree," she recalled, saying she thought, "OK, Grayce, remember how you feel. Remember the feeling you have now. This is Tim. Now think about it. Would you want to leave everything you've got and come here to a person who every morning at breakfast would pour himself a big bowl of cereal and read his newspaper, and no one could talk to him for an hour while he was reading?"

With money to spend, passing shops she wanted to visit, she took Sean to a play area. Then she bought him some pizza at the food court. They returned to meet Timmy after an hour. He asked, "What did you all do?" Sean said, "Grayce bought me some pizza." Timmy said, "What? Why would you feed him pizza? You know he's got a cold. That cheese is going to clog him up."

Grayce said, "I looked at him and thought, 'Remember this feeling, Grayce. Remember this feeling. Do you want to have this feeling for the rest of your life?' No. So that was the last time I saw him."

A few months after that visit, she returned to California. She had called Timmy and told him she was going to visit Dirk. He said, "Oh, you've got to come and visit me. Sean wants to see you, too." She thought, "Yeah, I could. I am coming to visit *my* child. My child and I are not going to see him and his son, especially when I remember that cheese was going to clog him up."

They continued to talk by phone on occasion. During one of their conversations, they talked of getting together during the summer. At the time, according to Grayce, she had met a man and decided not to visit. A few months later, Timmy returned the composite photos to her with a note saying: "Lee and I are going to try it again." She concluded that during her earlier visit, Lee had sent Sean to be with Timmy for a few days, to make sure that she and Timmy weren't able to be by themselves. She was relieved that she had decided not to visit him in the summer.

Timmy and Lee started doing things together again, such as attending Dionne Warwick's birthday party on Dec. 12, 1992. "I had invited all my football friends," she said in 2022. Timmy, of course, had first interested her in the game back in the 1960s. "I am an avid, diehard fan of the Raiders.... He used to tease me about that.... He said, 'What about the Eagles?' And I said, 'What *about* the Eagles?'"

Timmy and Lee got back together in January 1993, moving to 5534 Saloma Ave. in Sherman Oaks. The property had a small lap pool and two tennis courts. They lived in a house with two master suites. After a week of living in one suite with him, she moved into the other. He was very upset that while they were separated, she had dated a musician who played piano for Natalie Cole and Sarah Vaughan. "That one didn't sit well with Tim," she said. "He was never able to get over it. We went to therapy. He had felt rejected his whole life. The lack of having a mother was traumatizing."

On Nov. 7, 1993, Timmy and Lee separated again, with Sean and her moving to a two-story, two-bedroom, two-bathroom apartment very close by. Timmy stayed on Saloma Avenue through the end of the lease in January, then moved into an apartment at 6212 Fulton Ave. in Van Nuys.

In a Marital Settlement Agreement dated Dec. 21, "irreconcilable differences" were cited to have "led to the irremediable breakdown of the marriage." Timmy and Lee agreed that "no further waiting period, marriage counseling, or conciliation efforts would save the marriage." Each was responsible for individual attorney and court-related costs. "Joint legal and physical custody [of Sean], subject to rights of reasonable visitation," was provided. Timmy was required to pay Lee $500 per month child support – $250 on the first of the month and $250 on the 15th. He was required to maintain Sean on "his employer's medical and dental insurance plan" and was to "be consulted before any medical or dental expenses [were] incurred other than for normal periodic examinations and treatment or in cases of emergency." Child support was to be continued to age 18. Timmy could claim Sean as a dependent on his federal and state taxes as long as he was not delinquent in paying child support "in excess of 15 days in any one instance nor a 45-day cumulative period."

In the settlement, Lee retained her 1987 Chrysler LeBaron; any and all retirement benefits accruing to her; one-half of the community furniture/furnishings in the apartment at 927 N. San Vicente; and a time-share condo at the Palm Springs Tennis Club that they had bought in 1987. Timmy retained his 1977 Volvo 264 GL, his pension and retirement benefits, and the other half of the furniture. Lee claimed that Timmy didn't sign the divorce papers for some time, but said he did follow the decree's terms.

Their divorce was granted on Jan. 4, 1994. Lee's family had been upset when she had separated from Timmy and was no less disappointed by the divorce. M.L., Elizabeth, and the family loved Timmy, and Timmy loved the family. Elizabeth and Timmy continued to communicate, writing inspirational letters to one another, and exchanging birthday and Christmas greetings.

PALM SPRINGS

CHAPTER NINE

Reeling in the Years

After Christmas 1993, Sean wanted to go to Palm Springs to stay in the timeshare at the Palm Springs Tennis Club. Lee, Sean, and a friend left a couple of weeks before a 6.7 magnitude earthquake hit west of the San Fernando Valley at 4:31 a.m. on Jan. 17, 1994. A Jan. 16, 2020, story on a City of Los Angeles webpage, "Remembering the Northridge Earthquake," described its impact: "By the time the sun began to rise, the impact of the Northridge Earthquake was incalculable. Portions of the Santa Monica Freeway were damaged, cars were discovered among rubble from the collapse of Interstate 5, a total of 466 fires occurred that Monday (some from the eruption of natural gas mains and valves), and structural damage ranging from apartment buildings to historic structures like the Los Angeles Memorial Coliseum were beyond apparent. The quake killed more than 60, injured more than 9,000, and caused damage amounting to over $20 billion."

Timmy, who was staying at the apartment on Fulton Avenue, described the quake as "the Devil had the walls and was shaking them." Lee recalled thinking that if they had been in their apartment, they would have been killed. It took four months to clean up the apartment and get their stuff out. Then she and Sean left Los Angeles for Palm Springs.

Also leaving L.A. after the quake was Hollie Vest. She was beginning to achieve greater success as a Tina Turner tribute artist. In the late 1980s, Vest had been performing at the Industry Hills Sheraton Resort with her then-current band, the Blazers. One evening after her midnight Tina Turner tribute show, she was invited by Frank Gorshin, the impressionist and actor who played the Riddler in the "Batman" series that aired on ABC in the mid-60s, to join him at his table.

Gorshin told her he enjoyed her performance. Vest thanked him and asked, "Can I ask you a personal-professional question?" He said, "Yes, of course." She asked, "Do you ever resent making a living doing impressions of other celebrities' voices?" He responded, "Oh, so you're at that stage. Let me ask you a question. Who is your favorite singer?"

Vest said, "Tina, of course, and many others. Too many to name." Gorshin said, "Exactly. And how many of them can do a show like yours?"

He told her that not every performer has the ability to do impressions and impersonations, that it was a unique talent to be appreciated. He suggested she read, watch, and learn everything she could about Tina Turner. "It's important to fall in love with your character and make the character your friend," he said. "Re-create the illusion of the character as respectfully and believably as possible, but have fun."

Until this, Vest said in 2022, she had not had much respect for or understanding of the art of impersonators. She wanted to be known as a song stylist and original artist and songwriter. Gorshin encouraged her to recognize a talent that others did not have. In time, she found it ironic that she preferred performing as a celebrity character rather than as herself. She said he helped her to perfect her act, and make peace with getting more applause as Tina than as herself.

After the Northridge quake, Vest said she believed there was nothing left for her in Los Angeles, so she moved to Las Vegas. She dissolved her band, the Wiseguys, so she could travel doing her Turner tribute. She performed in South Africa for 19 months in 1996 and 1997. While performing at the Sun City Resort Theatre, she was able to watch the real Turner during six weeks of dress rehearsals for her "Wildest Dreams" tour. She hung out with Kenny Moore, Turner's musical director and keyboard player since 1977, and would sit at the front of the stage so she could watch Turner closely.

At one rehearsal, Moore yelled, "Hey, Tina, there's Hollie. She's the one who impersonates you." Turner pointed to Vest and said, "If you're going to do it, do it from the heart," then blew her a kiss and launched into the song "Thief of Hearts." (Moore died the following year at age 45 while with the tour in Australia.)

After Vest returned from South Africa, she spent three days caring for Timmy after his cataract surgery. "I had purchased a large-screen television for my mother and me, and I also got one for him. I told him, 'We are going to watch movies in style, buddy.'"

After leaving Los Angeles, Lee and Sean first moved to a residence at the Bermuda Hills Country Club in Bermuda Dunes, 19 miles east of Palm Springs, living for about a year with a friend who had two children and needed some help. Sean attended first grade there at James Monroe Elementary School.

They next moved to Desert Flower Apartments at 2500 E. Palm Canyon Dr. in Palm Springs, where Sean attended second and third grade at Cahuilla Elementary School. On a Valentine's Day when he was 8 or 9, he asked Lee to get flowers for him to take to a teacher. They went to a Ralph's supermarket. There, she met Steven Ader, who had been involved as a producer or writer with the films "I Spit on Your Grave" (1978) and "Zombie" (1979), and had developed the story for the 1990 Chad Lowe movie "Nobody's Perfect." He had also played basketball in Italy. They soon began dating.

From 1994 to 2001, Timmy and Lee coordinated custody schedules for Sean on weekends, holidays, and summers. Sometimes Lee worked in L.A. and dropped Sean off to stay with Timmy. Sometimes, Timmy would drive to Palm Springs and stay at the timeshare that he and Lee had purchased and she now owned, or on rare occasions at a hotel. Often, they met between L.A. and Palm Springs, at a Popeye's chicken restaurant in Riverside, to exchange Sean. This continued even after Timmy retired from the Probation Department in May 2000.

After the Desert Flower apartment, Lee and Sean moved into a two-bedroom condo at Shadow Mountain, on Golf Club Drive. They moved there as he entered the fourth grade, according to Sean, because he had been selected to participate in a program for gifted students available at Cielo Vista Elementary, the California Gifted and Talented Education (G.A.T.E.) program. He recalled "doing really well in the patterns section of mathematics." He remembered an assignment in the fourth grade when students were asked to pick a book about a famous American and write a short biography from it. While others chose figures from history, such as George Washington or Martin Luther King Jr., he went straight to books beginning with "B," since his last name began with that letter. He found a book about a great athlete, activist, and advocate. It was, of course, Jim Brown. He shared his choice with Timmy, who arranged a trip to Jim's home in the Hollywood Hills. Sean recalled the spectacular view of downtown Los Angeles from Jim's pool, and treasured the opportunity to ask Jim personal questions. "The visit set a tone about how I felt about celebrities," he said. "They are just people who excel in their field and have strengths and flaws like any of us. As a result of that experience, I was never intimidated by a celebrity."

A couple of years later, Sean recalled, he and Timmy stopped at a Taco Bell and ran into Muhammad Ali. Sean was aware of Ali's famous proclamation, "I'm the greatest!" To his surprise, the Champ put a twist on it, saying, "Yo daddy's the greatest!" Another time, Sean met Gerrard and Boschetti, who ran into him and Timmy at a mall where they were buying sneakers.

In the G.A.T.E. program, Sean didn't feel like he was special and thought of himself as just another student. However, his skill in basketball set him apart. In fourth grade, he began playing on travel teams. He enjoyed watching NBA and college playoff games with his father, saying "two of our favorite NBA players were Michael Jordan and Charles Barkley."

Over the years, his mother and Ader had become a couple. Ader had a second-floor duplex in Westwood that his best friend also used when he visited Los Angeles. Sean said, "Steve was staying a lot more with his mom in Palm Springs because she was getting older and needed more help." Lee also spent time with Ader in the duplex, when she worked with clients in Los Angeles. When she was there, they would drop off Sean with Timmy.

In 1998, Ader sold the duplex to his friend. That same year, when Sean was 11 and in the fifth grade, Lee and Ader married. With their family now including their baby daughter, Alexandra, they moved into a three-bedroom, 2,700-square-foot condo on Bogert Trail in the Andreas Hills neighborhood. Sean had his own bedroom and bathroom downstairs, close to the entrance, so he could come and go as he wanted. "He was sneaking out all the time and I couldn't hear him," Lee recalled. "He was getting into a lot of trouble that I didn't know about."

Sean attended grades six, seven, and eight at Raymond Cree Middle School. He said, "I continued to play basketball and won awards for most points scored (40 in one game) and most assists. I was playing center because I was the tallest on the team, though I was not quite six feet tall. I also was considered the best shooter, passer, and ball handler." He still spent weekends in Los Angeles with Timmy, where "the neighborhood basketball competition was much stiffer than in Palm Springs."

In 1998, as summer approached, Sean was ready to live with Timmy in Los Angeles. In Palm Springs, he grew restless and frustrated. It was hot and he was bored, wondering, "Why can't I go to L.A. to be with my friends?" Looking for something to do, he discovered a dusty guitar with just three strings that his mother had bought him years earlier. Over the next two years, he practiced on it often.

After returning to Palm Springs at the end of the summer of 2000, he got a new guitar for his birthday, and soon began playing in bands. The first one, made up of friends, was called Philosophy 2. "It was a terrible band," he said. But as the year went by, he started "doing music – writing songs." He began to see a future in songwriting and thought, "If I start making it now, I will be good at it by the time I am 23 or 24." He stayed in Palm Springs a few extra weekends the next summer to play in bands, and as a result, Timmy began to think that Sean wanted to stay there for good. But Sean hungered for L.A. "I wanted out so bad, I would have gone to school anyplace in L.A.," he said.

Going into the summer of 2001, Sean thought he would be living mainly with Timmy in the fall so he could focus on sports. He had his heart set on it. He recalled that his father had imagined that he would attend Mater Dei High School, a private preparatory school in Santa Ana that was an athletics powerhouse. However, Timmy had decided that Sean wanted to stay in Palm Springs, to continue writing songs and playing in bands. And now that he had retired, he had no special reason to stay in Los Angeles. So he informed Sean that he was going to move from L.A. to Palm Springs by fall. Sean had no warning that Timmy was thinking about this, or input into his decision. "Tim never pressured me into sports, but if I had moved to L.A., he would have pushed sports," he said. "So, it was a blessing to stay in Palm Springs, where he encouraged me to consider music and acting. He was incredibly supportive."

Timmy rented a two-bedroom condo at 505 S. Farrell Dr., at the Mesquite Golf and Country Club in Palm Springs, from Nov. 1, 2001, to May 1, 2002. He had not seen the unit and had relied on Lee to find a place. Lee told Ader that Timmy had never owned a residence and she would like to help him. Ader liked Timmy, so he agreed. She co-signed the lease "For Timothy Brown (Lessor) by Debra Lee Hartley (Lessor)." A down payment of $3,000, including a $500 security deposit, and first-and-last-month installments of $1,250 were made. For the remaining months, $1,250 was required on the first of the month. At the end of the lease, Timmy bought the place. Sean moved in with him and completed grades nine through 12 at Palm Springs High School.

When Sean moved in with Timmy, it wasn't a situation where Lee, Ader, and Alexandra "were here" and he was "over there," Lee said. "We took a trip or two a year. If we were going someplace, Sean would always be invited." On one occasion, for example, Ader, his two older daughters, Alexandra, Sean, and Lee flew to New York City. "We stayed in this tiny apartment in Times Square," she said. "It was so small we could barely open the refrigerator."

After Timmy moved to Palm Springs, it became harder for him to keep up some of his longtime friendships. Starting in 2000, Rick Whitfield had been playing with his band at the Crustacean in Beverly Hills, and he continued to perform elsewhere with other bands and by himself. He lost touch with Timmy after the move. Gerrard called Timmy once after he moved to Palm Springs. Gerrard's mother-in-law had moved from Connecticut to Palm Desert, less than 15 miles away, and he thought about going to see Timmy, but never did. "If I had," he imagined, "we would have been bullshitting for three hours." They never met again.

Vest continued to see Timmy as her work allowed. She worked on cruise ships and in Canada and Australia, as well as at casino hotels in the South. In 2000, she performed as both Tina Turner and Carmen Miranda in Barbados at the Variety International Children's Charity event, hosted by Monte Hall and honoring Harry Belafonte with the humanitarian award. At other events, she was performing as Ethel Merman and Peggy Lee. That same year, she opened for Chubby Checker at the National Apartment Association convention. A year later, Timmy, Sean, and Vest went to see Checker perform in Las Vegas. Checker pulled Timmy on stage, where they laughed and told stories. Timmy then moved to introduce Vest to Checker, but Checker seemed to not see her. "Oh, you don't know, do you," Timmy said. Finally, Checker said, "I thought you were a Black woman." He had not realized that the woman who sang as Tina Turner wasn't Black.

Sean said in 2022 that "we would usually see Chubby in Long Beach or L.A. a lot of those years, and then he started playing at casinos in Palm Springs. When he did, we saw him there and he came by the house a few times. My friends don't know who he is. They have a cartoon caricature image of him. The 'Twist' guy. No, Chubby. He's a person. He's a dude. I've heard him talk about some very personal things with my dad."

Ader's sister and her husband had been living in Woodland Hills, but had moved to the Mariner's Point community in Carlsbad, just north of San Diego, and wanted Ader to move there so they could be "one big happy family," Lee recalled. She said Ader's mother, who had a large house in the Hancock Park section of Los Angeles as well as her place in Palm Springs, had moved there as well. So Ader told her, "We're moving there." Their home was built on a hill with a slight ocean view, in a planned neighborhood with a park, a school, a church, and a Costco store. "It had everything," Lee said. "It was an ideal place to rear a child. Alexandra was 6 and Sean 16." But Lee had conflicting feelings. Alex was starting pre-school in Carlsbad, while Sean's high school was in Palm Springs. She felt that she needed to be available to her children in both communities.

Timmy, having just moved to Palm Springs, also had thought Lee and Ader were staying in the desert. "I had a little bit of a meltdown and reaction to moving away, because Tim had just moved there and that he would be mad," Lee recalled. "And he was. Serious. Very mad. Not at Sean, but at Steven and me."

Ader sold the Andreas Hills place, but in addition to the home in Carlsbad, he bought a condo at the Desert Princess Country Club in Cathedral City. This let Lee return to the Palm Springs area on a regular basis to spend time with Sean. "I was there every week," Lee said. "I know it's different if you are not living at a place. I saw him play football and later perform in high school plays, and, for a short time, dance. I still saw Sean a lot, but Timmy never acknowledged it, because he had so much anger toward me at that point."

In 2001, during his freshman year of high school, Sean played defensive tackle in football. "I understood the sport and played well enough to be moved to the varsity team when it started competing in the playoffs," he said. He knew he could make varsity in his sophomore year. He understood that he could play a number of positions, but he wanted to play quarterback. But one of the assistant coaches had a son who was tabbed to play the position. That didn't diminish his interest in playing. But an incident during the second week of practice camp did.

Sean said a coach who knew that he had taken classes in theater and enjoyed acting confronted him, saying: "So, are you going to commit to this queer theater or play some football?"

Sean responded, "My theater teacher would never give me an ultimatum like that."

The coach said, "What do you mean?"

Sean answered, "I know 'ultimatum' is a big word for you, but my theater teacher would never put me in this position."

The coach countered, "So, you think you are a smart ass."

Sean started to walk away. "Where are you going, Brown?"

"Not here," he responded simply. Unlike his father, who had walked off the football field at Ball State his junior year but returned to play, Sean never did go back.

"We were devastated and shocked," Lee said. "It was like a slap in the face."

A week later, Sean auditioned for a school play and was selected. He considered the high school drama teacher, Rosemary Mallett, an inspiration who led him to pursue a theater career later. One of the classes Sean took was in dance. On the first day, he walked into the room and saw a girl lying on her back, stretching spread-eagle. He thought, "This is definitely where I'm supposed to be, not in the heat of Palm Springs playing football and sweating my butt off."

Sean continued to play basketball into his junior year, on what he thought was a "terrible team," and became more frustrated over time.

Not quite 6 feet tall, he went up against players 6-7 and 6-8. Reflecting on the experience, he laughed at the coach's giving him a hard time for not being able to rebound. Convinced that nothing was going to change, he stopped participating with the team.

In 2003, Alex turned 6, and Lee and Ader got a dog, named Muffin. They also bought a house in Carolina Beach, N.C. It was a five-bedroom, five-bathroom vacation home with an elevator, two huge wraparound porches, and a private walkway to the beach. Ader had wanted a home with a panoramic ocean view but couldn't afford one in Carlsbad. Upon seeing the Carolina home under construction, he said, "This is my dream house." Lee said, "We were going to rent it, but we bought it. My family was down there all the time, since they [now] lived in North Carolina. I got to spend a lot of time with my mom and all her brothers and sisters and their families, and all my brothers and sisters and their families. It was such a wonderful, wonderful experience. Tim never came, but Sean did." They kept the beach house for about four years.

Over time, Sean not only stopped participating in school sports, but in school overall. According to Lee, he "stopped going." When he graduated at age 17 in May 2005 from Palm Springs High, she said, "he graduated with the most absentees that they ever had in their school history. He wouldn't do any of the homework. The teachers would test him and he would pass all the tests with A's. So then his grade would be C. He had a rebellious attitude. He said it was because he was bored."

The year 2005 was also when Timmy met Mary Lee Henderson, who would prominently figure in his life for the next 10 years. They met early in the year at the Mesquite Country Club. Timmy said he had seen her a few times on the practice putting green, always by herself. He felt she was lonely, so approached her and began talking. In short order, he arranged a time to give her putting tips.

Henderson, who at age 73 was about five years older than Timmy, was a former travel agent from Chicago. She had graduated in 1950 from New Trier High School in Winnetka, Ill., and in 1954 from De-

Pauw University in Greencastle, Ind. She had lived in Orange County for some time, and had moved into a condo in the same complex, one that was within a three-minute walk of his.

When Timmy began spending time with Henderson, it perplexed a couple of his friends. She was older and soft-spoken, and while attractive, she was not the strikingly beautiful, outgoing celebrity type to whom he was historically drawn. One friend recalled a time when Timmy had been serious with a girl whom she thought he might marry, but broke it off. She remembered his explaining that the girl didn't need him, that there wasn't anything he could do to improve her. Another friend thought that Timmy was seeking a mother figure – someone who would support him, take care of things, and look after him.

Timmy was aware of his friends' feelings. In 2010, he said, "I have people look at me crazy, or funny, those that know me, and say, 'What are you doing with Mary Lee?' And I said, 'She's a great lady, she's a great person. I have more fun. I laugh with her more than I do with Diana Ross or all these other people who are always looking to see if they can get something better or prettier." His relationship with Lee had clearly left a scar: "Most people are not with the person long enough to find out about the person.... They fall in love, get married after six months, like I did the first time. And it's OK. She was everything I thought she was. But her ambitions, I wasn't helping. I wasn't pushing her ambitions through my acting and stuff."

Timmy and Henderson went for a time to the nearby Desert Chapel Christian Church. Timmy introduced her to sports, and they often watched NFL and NBA games. They were regular movie-goers and always looked forward to watching Oscar-nominated movies at home in December and January. Timmy received the "for your consideration" DVDs because he was a voting member of the Academy of Motion Picture Arts and Sciences.

Also that year, Timmy attended a reunion in Indiana – the 50th anniversary of the Morton Memorial Class of 1955. Earl Lambert, who had been his classmate and friend there, said that since they had graduated, he hadn't kept in touch with Timmy or anyone else from the class until this event. "We got to spend some private time together," he recounted. "Tim needed a ride to a party we were having in Greenfield, so I drove and took him to it." Timmy talked to Lambert about his movie and television career, telling him that he had had many disappointments. One, Lambert recalled, was that he was turned down for acting roles because his skin color was too light. Timmy told how much he enjoyed working with young people as a probation officer and said he hadn't been happy with his life until he got that job. He never mentioned football or his life at the Home.

After his 2005 high school graduation, Sean lived on his own for a year, doing what he considered his "first real job." He started working that summer. He used a large screen-printing machine to produce merchandise that he sold for bands with which he toured. Sean said that in addition to creating the merchandise, his work for the company sponsoring the tours involved inventorying stock and restocking, reporting all sales, and turning over the cash at the end of the night. From $3,000 to $4,000 was generated each night. He also drove a 12-passenger van with a trailer hooked to it. He reported to a man who worked for the merchandise company and was the tour manager. The first tour took him across the United States with Mêlée, a band recording for the independent Subcity Records label. They opened for Lucky Boys Confusion and Daphne Loves Derby. Sean, the manager, and the four members of Mêlée rode together in the van. The second tour, from late November to mid-January 2006, was larger, because Mêlée now had a Warner Bros. contract. The same group rode together in the van. The other bands on tour included the Spill Canvas, Dropping Daylight, and Copeland. Although Mêlée never charted in America, it did have some success in Europe in 2007.

Sean also continued playing in bands. Until he was 21, he played mostly with the same people who had been in Philosophy 2. Their next band was Here on Out, which he was with until he was 19. From ages 19 through 21, he played with the Kiss Electric – a wordplay on the sparks that fly from the first romantic kiss. He thought it had the most potential and accomplishments: "I pushed really hard. My heart and soul was in the band." It opened for other bands and did shows across California and Arizona, performing at venues that Sean had never thought he would play – the Viper Room and Whisky a Go Go in West Hollywood, and the Glass House in Pomona. A highlight was playing in residence at the Roxy Theater in West Hollywood for nearly two months. Because alcohol was served at many places they performed, Sean said, the band members for a while had to lie about their ages. "No one asked," he said, because "we had beards and looked old enough and sounded mature enough." The group progressed from heavy, dark music to melodic pop rock. When the Kiss Electric broke up, he continued working with one of the band members, then went solo for a couple of years, billing himself as SA!NT.

CHAPTER TEN

All We Will Remember

As Timmy moved toward his 70s, everything looked rosy on the surface. He had maintained his friendships with Vest and Kilroy, whom Sean called Aunt Hollie and Uncle Gene "because they were the closest thing to an uncle and aunt on my dad's side." Timmy would fly to Vegas two or three times a year to see Kilroy, according to Sean. "My dad could have called any time he wanted, but he wouldn't do that. Uncle Gene would call and say, 'Come out. There's a show you should see.'" Sean often would go along. Typically, they stayed for two nights and three days on a weekend as Kilroy's guests at a casino hotel where he was an executive. They could check in as early as they wanted and check out as late as they wanted. If it was a holiday, they might extend the stay. "We would see Aunt Hollie at her home and visit" when she wasn't performing elsewhere, Sean said.

Sean remembered that they would meet Kilroy, eat a meal with him, walk around, and talk every day they were there. When Timmy gambled, he would give Sean $20 to play video games. "My dad did special things. He took me to see one of my favorite groups, Boyz II Men. We saw Destiny's Child with Beyoncé Knowles before she went solo. I got to meet them backstage. I saw Tom Jones, the popular Welsh singer with hits like "It's Not Unusual" and "She's a Lady," who Timmy would link up with at least once a year. They couldn't stop laughing. It was like two hyenas. It was crazy. Almost embarrassing."

But Sean became aware of changes in his father's behavior in 2006, when Timmy was 69 and Sean was 19. Timmy was a celebrity at a couple of restaurants in Palm Springs where he often had breakfast – Rick's Restaurant & Bakery on North Palm Canyon Drive and Elmer's on East Palm Canyon Drive. Waiters, waitresses, and managers looked forward to his coming. As soon as he entered, someone would greet him respectfully as Mr. Brown. They would ask how he was doing and, knowing where he liked to sit, would escort him there. As Philadelphia Inquirer columnist Mike Sielski wrote on May 17, 2020, Timmy would often entertain with a story about his days in professional football or entertainment, which would prompt questions: *You played in Super Bowl III, Mr. Brown? You dated Diana Ross? Wow!* But as Sean told Sielski, over time, "Timmy's anecdotes were becoming circular and repetitive." People who were "captivated" by the stories didn't notice. "But Sean knew," the article said. He "had known for a while. At first, Sean kept his concerns to himself, because the stories were still wonderful, and his father still told them well."

According to Sielski, Sean thought to himself, "You're telling the Muhammad Ali and Jim Brown one again? OK. I'll listen. I've heard this a thousand times, but it's Muhammad Ali and Jim Brown, so I'll listen again." But over time, Sielski wrote, "the tales grew more tangled, and Sean thought back when he was a teenager, when his dad would get 'forgetful and weird and paranoid.'"

"It had been showing itself for some time," Sean recalled in a separate interview. "He didn't want to acknowledge it. My dad was never accusatory, rude, or short. But he was getting that way." For example, he thought that the housekeepers or Sean had stolen money. "I had very broke moments when I had little to no money," Sean said. "I would take [my own] coins to Coinstar to get 20 bucks to eat the next two days." He pleaded with Timmy, "If I was stealing money from you, I wouldn't have to do that. You'd give me anything I asked for. You'd give it to me in a heartbeat. Come on, Dad, you're accusing me of things that I would never do." He didn't understand where Timmy was coming from. Sean eventually asked him if he would consider having a doctor examine him. Timmy didn't want to hear it. "He wasn't happy. It wasn't the best of times. We were already arguing, and I brought it up."

As a result, their relationship was strained when, on April 5, Timmy went to Philadelphia to attend the induction of the 1960 Eagles championship team into the Philadelphia Sports Hall of Fame. A photo in the April 7, 2006, Philadelphia Daily News shows him smiling and talking with Eagles coach Andy Reid and his longtime friend Tommy McDonald at a cocktail reception on the evening of April 6. The individuals inducted into the Class of 2006 – the hall's third – were Herb Adderley, Packers defensive back from Philadelphia; Roy Campanella, Dodgers catcher, also from Philadelphia; Ray Didinger, longtime Daily News sportswriter; Bill Ellerbee, a high school basketball coach; Del Ennis, Phillies outfielder; Joe Fulks, a former Philadelphia Warriors player; Hal Greer, a member of the 76ers 1966 championship team; Gene Hart, announcer for the Flyers; Reggie Jackson, baseball's "Mr. October," from the suburb of Cheltenham; Willie Mosconi, a Philly native, considered the greatest pool player of all time; Jack Ramsay from Delaware County, who retired as the second-winningest coach in NBA history; Helen Sigel Wilson, a Philly native who won 350 golf titles; Al Simmons, outfielder for the Philadelphia Athletics; and Anne Townsend, a multi-sport player who had captained the University of Pennsylvania's women's basketball team. Then came the 1960 Eagles as a team and the Palestra, the storied home of Big 5 basketball, as a venue.

Not long after Timmy returned to Palm Springs, he and Sean got into an argument about taking the trash out. "He was so fixated over a little thing," Sean recalled. Timmy told Sean that in Philadelphia, he had had a few drinks with friends the night before returning, and had fallen and hurt his shoulder. "I knew how well he masked things," Sean said. "He had a very high pain tolerance, physically and emotionally. He would suffer in silence, all the while smiling and being very jovial. I wanted to make sure he was getting more accountable for himself. I told him again that his memory wasn't very good. That was the last straw." Timmy kicked him out.

For two weeks, Sean said, he lived with Lee, and for the rest of the summer, he lived at the Desert Princess condo. In August, he moved in with Ader and Lee in Carlsbad to attend the fall semester at Mira Costa College. "Part of what pushed me to Mira Costa was that I wasn't talking to my dad and I didn't really want to be in the desert," Sean confided. In addition, he said, "by having enrolled in August, before my 19th birthday, I was able to keep my health insurance coverage." He took courses in guitar, theater, music, programming, music theory, and philosophy. He didn't take any prerequisites and was told that without them he wouldn't get a certificate. "But I didn't care," he said. "I wasn't there for that, right then." It would be 10 months until Sean would again live with Timmy.

That spring, Dave Chapman, one of the Richmond neighborhood friends whom Timmy had played with before he went to the Home, got a call from a local writer who wanted to do a story about an athlete from that city who had found major success in a sport. Chapman's father had played for the Brooklyn Dodgers. As they talked, Chapman told the writer that he should consider writing about Timmy Brown. The writer asked if Chapman had his phone number, and Chapman told him to try the Ball State Alumni Office. Soon, the writer called back to give Chapman Timmy's contact information. Chapman had not seen Timmy since attending the San Francisco game in 1966.

In 1997, Chapman and his wife, Dorit, had bought a timeshare in Palm Desert. He realized that he had been vacationing for nine years within a half-hour's drive of Timmy's condo. He called Timmy to arrange a get-together. On June 6, the Chapmans and two friends met Timmy for dinner at the Kaiser Grill in Palm Springs. Chapman updated him on Richmond, and Timmy talked about his work with the Probation Department. Chapman and Timmy later played golf and met again for dinner.

"We went to see him every year" thereafter, Chapman said in 2022. "We played golf, went out to dinner – the Yard House, Kaiser Grille, Las Casuelas, Mario's, and Manhattan in the Desert, and enjoyed visiting." It wasn't until their second trip in the summer of 2007 that they met Mary Lee, but from then on, she was with Timmy when they got together.

As always, Timmy had held onto an old friend. More surprising is that he and Lee's second husband, Steve Ader, had also become buddies. They played golf and watched movies together. Lee, Timmy, and Ader would also get together, sometimes to celebrate holidays and birthdays, other times just to hang out. "It was just whatever worked out with anybody," Lee said. "It could be last-minute." She noted that "Tim and Steve actually got along really well. Tim accepted Steve, because I also had a child with Steven." But when Timmy began his relationship with Henderson, he told Lee that Henderson "wasn't comfortable with her around." Lee believed that Henderson "was a little bit intimidated" by her continued friendship with Timmy. She said she understood Henderson's feelings, so she cut back on dropping by his home and spent less time with him while they were together. Still, she called him on occasion, and routinely sent him a Christmas card and a birthday card. Lee said Timmy told her to just come by even if it made Henderson uncomfortable. She said she saw Henderson five or six times a year, when she dropped things off for Sean. On one occasion, Lee recalled, she had dinner with Timmy, Henderson, and Sean.

In the fall of 2006, Timmy returned to Ball State for a reunion of Cardinals basketball players from 1955 to 1959, held at the Alumni Center on Sept. 8 and 9. The event was the inspiration of two former players and friends, Wilbur Davis and Norman Jones, who had met up in Milwaukee in November 2005, shortly after Jones had published his memoir, "Growing Up in Indiana: The Culture and Hoosier Hysteria

Revisited." They worked with the Alumni Association to organize the reunion, which was attended by 47 alumni and family members, according to an article by Laura Ford in the November 2006 Ball State Alumnus magazine. Jim Hinga had coached the varsity for all four of those years, so most of the alumni attendees had played for him. Timmy, who had only played on the freshman team, had not played for Hinga, but still, he was prominently shown in two photos in the two-page Alumnus piece. The caption below one photo read, "Tim Brown, former Cardinal football standout and pro football running back, joins Wil Davis, Al Cook, Jim Harris, and Norm Jones." It was his fame in football that garnered him an invitation.

According to Ford, "the two days were filled with reminiscing, introducing families, and catching up on nearly five decades of life events." The guests visited the parts of campus where they had lived, studied, and played, and also saw the newer parts. Ford wrote, "Apart from physical improvements to campus, there were other, perhaps more personal changes the former players noticed. Racial tensions had been high the last time many of the players were together, the civil rights movement was on its way." Ford said one of the reasons for the reunion, according to Davis and Jones, was "to create a friendship and bond among them that didn't, and couldn't, exist during their years on court." Davis recalled, "There was warmth among the guys at the reunion [that didn't exist] when we were in school playing together. We had different life associations [then] and came to feel differently about things, as well as times changing. [This time] there was a special bond and, almost to the man, you could feel it."

The past reached out to Timmy in 2007 in another way when Eagles fans got to vote on an all-star team to mark the club's 75th anniversary. They selected Timmy as the greatest kick returner in Eagles history. His teammates on this Football Heaven team from their days playing together were his old friend McDonald as wide receiver and iron man Chuck Bednarik at center and middle linebacker. (In a nod to then-current stars, Donovan McNabb was named the top quarterback of all time and Andy Reid the top coach. McNabb then led the 2007 Eagles, coached by Reid, in walloping the Lions by 56-21.) Henderson called the trip a highlight of her life. She was in awe at how Timmy was treated by everyone. She was particularly impressed by how the Eagles organization handled all aspects of the trip, which she described as "first class." She enjoyed getting to meet players whom Timmy had talked to her about. She especially enjoyed visiting with McDonald, who in addition to his Eagles honors had been voted into the NFL Hall of Fame, and his wife.

After the 2006 fall semester, Sean left Mira Costa and Carlsbad, and returned to living with Timmy in Palm Springs. For the 2007 fall semester, he enrolled in the College of the Desert in Palm Desert, and took a course in choir and one in theater. While he had found the coursework at Mira Costa "really great," he found the new school "really low level, not my vibe at all. I decided to bail on that."

In Carlsbad, Lee had been working with a girlfriend who owned a science laboratory and production facility. Since her mid-20s, Lee had been interested in health food and healthy living, and enjoyed mixing and blending ingredients to make botanical wellness products. Her girlfriend suggested she develop a label for promoting it. She began exploring the idea while continuing to share her products with others.

In the late 2000s, Timmy became involved with the BookPALS in the Coachella Valley program. BookPALS was developed in Los Angeles by the Screen Actors Guild Foundation (later the SAG-AFTRA Foundation), with PALS standing for "Performing Artists for Literacy in Schools." It was established in 1993 by Barbara Bain, who had been among the stars of "Mission: Impossible" and was the wife of another "M:I" star, Martin Landau. The program in Palm Springs began in 2007; during the Great Recession, local funding switched to Palm Springs Women in Film and Television. BookPALS sent more than 70 volunteers into Palm Springs area schools weekly to read aloud to elementary-school children, and arranged events with stars such as Cheech Marin and Mary Hart at museums and the YMCA. Timmy was assigned to read at Cathedral City Elementary School. Decades after getting his degree from Ball State, he was finally in front of a classroom. He continued volunteering for many years.

In 2008, Timmy again returned to Indiana. On Saturday, Nov. 22, he flew from Palm Springs to Indianapolis, and was taken to the L.A. Pittenger Student Center at Ball State, where he stayed in a suite. He toured areas of campus he remembered, and went to Richmond to see his childhood home and haunts. Also, he briefly visited the Home, and met with Bonnie Brewer, the widow of his basketball coach in the mid-1950s, Bill Brewer, who had died the previous year. He also talked with other staff members. The future of the Home was being threatened by changes in state government priorities, and Timmy added his voice to those wanting to keep it open. But given the short time of his scheduled visit, his was a whirlwind tour.

On Monday, Nov. 24, he made a presentation at 7 p.m. in Teachers College Room 102 to an audience of around 100 faculty, students, community members, and fans on the topic "Race, Sports, and Society." He mesmerized the audience with his quips and stories of his experiences in football. He said that when he started playing, there was an unwritten quota on the number of Black players that a team could carry, and gave examples. He shared an elaborated version of his contentious interaction with Lombardi, saying the Green Bay coach had described him as "cocky," to which he responded, "Where I come from, we call it confidence." He said he never worried about getting hit, because "God was on my shoulder, telling me, 'Get the ball and run, and I will protect you.'" After speaking, he responded to questions from the audience, and then stayed to talk with individuals and sign autographs.

The next night, before the start of the game between Ball State and Western Michigan, Timmy was driven in a cart to the center of the field for the coin toss. He enjoyed the game from the President's Suite, visiting with university president Jo Ann Gora and other administrators, donors, and alumni. There were 23,861 fans in attendance, which remains the largest crowd ever for a Ball State home game. Going into the game, Ball State was 11-0, its first undefeated season in 60 years. The Cardinals defeated Western Michigan by 45-22 to clinch a spot in the Mid-American Conference (MAC) championship game. It was a great season for the Cardinals, who had been ranked as high as No. 12 in the nation by the Associated Press, and had beaten the Big 10 Indiana Hoosiers by 42-20 on Sept. 20. Their final AP ranking dropped to No. 23 after losses in their last two games.

Late in the afternoon before the game, Timmy visited Worthen Arena, home to the school's basketball teams and other squads, to see a plaque recognizing him and other athletes from all sports on an honor wall. He was shown another plaque recognizing him when he toured the football facilities next to the stadium.

While in Muncie, Timmy dined and talked with faculty and community members, and participated in interviews for this biography. On Nov. 26, he returned to Palm Springs.

The year 2008 also saw the start of a brief effort to get Timmy named to the Pro Football Hall of Fame, which, according to him, Pete Rozelle had said he would never enter. The move was led by Norman Jones, who had helped organize the basketball reunion. Jones had graduated in 1959 and stayed in Muncie to earn a master's in 1963, followed by a doctorate from Mississippi in 1966. He became a writer of books on motivation and human development, and he didn't stop there. In addition to his memoir, he had been recognized as a prolific writer of Letters to the Editor by the Chicago Tribune.

In 2008, he wrote an article about Timmy for the Indiana Historical Society magazine, headlined "From an Indiana Orphanage to the NFL." On Nov. 10, he was watching a "Monday Night Football" game between the 49ers and the Cardinals. San Francisco's Allen Rossum returned an opening kickoff 104 yards for a touchdown. One of the announcers noted that it was the longest such run since Timmy's 105-yard dash for the Eagles in 1961. The next day, Jones wrote to the Hall of Fame Selection Committee to recommend Timmy; he wrote Timmy the same day to tell him. He enlisted in the effort Jim Tunney, the longtime NFL official who had been an admirer of Timmy's play and attitude. Tunney noted that it was too late for consideration in 2009, but that Jones should try again in September for the class of 2010. Timmy is still eligible for the Hall of Fame, since, unlike baseball's hall, there is no end date for consideration. Kilroy said later that if Timmy doesn't get into the Hall of Fame, they should tear it down and replace it with a 7-Eleven.

His Hoosier past reached out to Timmy again in June 2009, when he got together with childhood friends from Richmond Harold Jones and George Walker, as well as Chapman, for a golf outing at Mesquite Country Club. Chapman said they spent three days together and played golf two or three times. They enjoyed eating, drinking, joking, and laughing about old times. Henderson often joined them. Gil Jacobs and Joe Agro wrote about the outing in their book, "Harold Jones: The Singer's Drummer." Jones, they noted, had been on the Richmond High golf team. "Though he loved the game," they wrote, "he invested his time on the drums because he loved that even more."

As the book relates, "George Walker had been a representative for the Yonex [golf equipment company], so he knew how to play. Timmy Brown was a great athlete who had played pro football for the Philadelphia Eagles and he knew how to play. David Chapman, also a good athlete, was a college quarterback and he knew how to play. And there was Harold Jones, a world-class drummer, who probably could not play golf at the level of his compatriots. Or so they thought! Well, you guessed it; Harold and George teamed up to play the two athletes and were victorious.... Apparently, Harold had developed his game over the years and he is now as adept with golf sticks as he is with drumsticks!"

Jones recalled that they wore specially made hats for the occasion that read, "Old School." He said, "We were playing for the International World Championship of bragging rights. The five-minute rule for looking for your ball went out the window on the first hole. It was fun!" It was the last time that Jones and Timmy saw one another. Jones played drums for Tony Bennett, and about a year after the golf outing, Bennett was performing in Palm Springs. "I invited him and his guest to the show," Jones said, "and he didn't think he could make it." And he didn't. It was also the last time that Walker and Timmy saw one another.

The last trip that Sean made with Timmy to Las Vegas was the weekend of the NBA All-Star game, played on Feb. 14, 2010, at Cowboys Stadium in Arlington, Texas. Sean was going to perform as SAI!NT in a record store there. When Timmy found out, he said: "Oh, you're doing a show in Vegas. I'll call Gene and he will get us rooms. I'll go with you. I want to do the Vegas Strip." Sean, Timmy, and Henderson drove to Vegas for the weekend. Sean remembered, "A lot of friends went to the show, as well as Gene. It wasn't a big turnout." Henderson was introduced to Kilroy and Sean's friends.

During the visit, an incident upset Timmy so much he rode in the car back to Palm Springs without uttering a word. Reflecting on the experience, he said: "When I get mad, I don't get angry. I get quiet." This was the last Vegas trip that Sean took with Timmy. "By the time I was of age to gamble, he had already stopped doing that so much. Eventually, he didn't want to go," Sean said.

In 2010, Timmy and Sean went to Philadelphia for a Sept. 12 ceremony marking the 50th anniversary of the 1960 championship Eagles team. Sean felt he had to go to assist Timmy. They left a day or two before the regular-season opener against the Packers, at which the ceremony was to be held. To at least Sean's surprise, Henderson showed up as well. He recalled, "I wasn't aware of her plans and don't think Dad was either, but he may have been. He didn't look like it when we saw her. She paid for her airline ticket, room, and other things."

At halftime of the game, 22 members of the Eagles organization and representatives met on the field with Bill Campbell, who just as in

1990 was the master of ceremonies. Timmy stood next to McDonald, and they were the second and third players to be introduced. Others were Billy Ray Barnes, Pete Retzlaff, Chuck Weber, Bill Lapham, Maxie Baughan, Chuck Bednarik, Gerry Huth, John Wilcox, Eddie Khayat, Riley Gunnels, Jimmy McCusker, J.D. Smith, Dick Lucas, and Jerry Wilson. Tom Brookshier had died on Jan. 30 of that year, and was represented by his wife, Barbara. Also honored were Campbell; Jim Gallagher, a 46-year executive with the Eagles who had been a favorite of Timmy's; and Leo Carlin, the longest-serving ticket director in the NFL at that time.

Unable to attend were Sonny Jurgensen, Ted Dean, Jimmy Carr, John Wittenborn, Marion Campbell, and Gene Gossage. And in addition to Brookshier, 18 members of the team were deceased: coaches Charlie Gauer, Buck Shaw, Jerry Williams, and Nick Skorich, and players Howard Keys, Jessie Richardson, John Nocera, Norm Van Brocklin, Joe Robb, Bobby Walston, Gene Johnson, Don Owens, Bobby Freeman, Stan Campbell, Don Burroughs, Clarence Peaks, Bob Pellegrini, and Bobby Jackson. Unlike 1960, the Packers won this game, 27-20. For Sean, it brought back memories of a decade earlier, when Timmy held him in his arms on the field. A day or two after the ceremony, Sean, Timmy, and Henderson returned to Palm Springs.

On Friday, Oct. 8, 2010, Timmy again returned to Indiana, this time for a lengthier visit. As before, he stayed in a suite at the Ball State student center. On the afternoon of his arrival, he attended a practice session with the football team. Stan Parrish, the head coach, introduced him as the greatest football player in Ball State history, and also mentioned his famous kickoff-return game against Dallas and his three Pro Bowl selections. Timmy said how happy he was to be there, how much he had enjoyed playing football at Ball State, and how fortunate he had been in his NFL career. He wished the team success in the next day's game against Western Michigan. But from the President's Suite, he had to watch the Cardinals lose by 45-16 to the Broncos, ending the year with a 4-8 record.

During this visit to campus, he walked more extensively around areas he remembered as a student and reminisced – about the student center, where he sang Elvis songs and hung out with friends; the Elliott Hall grounds where he lived; the grassy area that was Ball Field, where he played football; Ball Gym, where he played basketball and dressed for football games; the Administration Building, where he visited with president Emens; and the buildings where he took courses, many of them renamed since he attended – the Practical Arts Building, the Fine Arts Building, the Burkhardt Building, and North Hall, the former library. He also went to Richmond and to the site of the Home, which had closed in May 2009 and become the National Guard's Hoosier Youth Challenge Academy. Timmy was saddened by the Home's closing; he had supported efforts to keep it open, including attending a rally with other supporters in Indianapolis on Jan. 26, 2009. This visit, he spent more time there than in 2008, walking the grounds and talking about his experiences there.

A significant amount of time during this visit was devoted to interviewing for this biography. As before, he found time to visit with university administrators and faculty, and community members and fans – all interested in his life and his stories. He returned to Palm Springs on Sunday, Oct. 17. He would never see Indiana again.

The Nov. 8 issue of the Ball State Daily News highlighted his visit with a front-page photo of him standing in front of Shaffer Tower beneath the headline, "The First and the BEST." Sports editor Teddy Cahill characterized Timmy's being the first Ball State player to be drafted to the NFL as "once so unthinkable … [that Brown] seriously considered not going to training camp." He then recounted Timmy's career in entertainment.

In 2011, at age 24, Sean played with his last band, Drop the World, which he considered his most successful group. "We aspired to be more than a local band," Sean recalled. But Drop the World ended up just being a regional band, playing largely in the Coachella Valley with a few performances in San Diego and Los Angeles. The first version was a five-piece hard-core band. The last version was a three-piece group – guitar, bass, and drums – that played together for about 10 months. The group focused on progressive rock, pop, and punk. "It was the most fun," he said. "A part of the fun was doing everything I had to do. I was the main songwriter, promoter, designer of flyers; printed shirts for us, handled insurance for the 12-by-17 travel trailer and the equipment and everything in it."

Drop the World had the "biggest crowds and most anticipation," according to Sean. "We were recording demos and getting good opportunities. But we weren't quite ready for the steps coming ahead to be successful. We didn't expect and prepare enough." The band was set to go on tour, but drug issues, infighting, and accusations caused an abrupt breakup after a little less than a year. The last scheduled appearance of the band was for the 111 Music Festival, an event promoted by a local arts organization in which bands were to hop on and off city buses on Highway 111 to play for riders one Saturday. Sean was the only member of the band who showed up, and played on the bus by himself.

When Drop the World fell apart, it left Sean feeling stranded. "Like a three-headed dragon, two disappeared and I was left by myself," he remembered. "It was like Icarus flying too close to the sun. Exploded. Imploded. It was a blurry ending. I was depressed. At age 24, I wondered what I would do next, but I knew that I wanted to do something different."

Since he was 18, he had been doing seasonal part-time work with the Palm Springs International Film Festival, which put on an annual event each January as well as a festival for short films each June. By age 22, he had been asked to do more than box office work. At one Short Fest, his boss asked him if he would be interested in box office management. By 23, Sean said, "I became a co-manager – one of the youngest ever and one of the first local hires in that position."

While in that role, he met Jennifer Van Camp, who was working in the development department as coordinator of sponsorships. She was born on June 28, 1978, to Michael and Mary Van Camp in Naples, Fla. She had two brothers – half-brother Rusty was 11 years older, and Christopher six. The family operated a kennel and boarding facility for dogs and horses, a business started and largely run by her mother. When she was 7, Rusty got a new car for his 18th birthday. He "wasn't supposed to drive it on the highway yet. My parents had gone to work. Christopher and I [had] missed the bus, so Rusty decided to drive us" to school. On the way, a semi-trailer truck crashed into their car. Rusty died in the crash.

The tragedy propelled the family into a downward spiral. The emotional and psychological toll, coupled with mounting financial challenges, resulted in the loss of the business. The family moved to Miami for a couple of years, and when she was 9, they moved to the Big Island of Hawaii.

The move was a major adjustment for the family. Jennifer recalled that Christopher, who attended a public school in Honoka'a, about 40 miles northwest of Hilo, had a hard time, as he was bullied in school and was constantly getting into fights. During their first year in Hawaii, Christopher moved back to Naples to live with their grandmother. But he continued to have challenges in school there, and ended up graduating from Riverside Military Academy, a boarding and college preparatory school for boys in Georgia.

She attended St. Francis School, an all-girls Catholic boarding school in Honolulu – an experience she described as "very difficult." She said, "I was unsupervised, sneaking out, and getting into a lot of trouble. The ramifications were damaging to my life." The family was falling apart; she called it "tumultuous times." There was verbal and emotional manipulation and abuse. "I didn't grow up in a very healthy, balanced home. My parents were dealing with things I couldn't understand at the time – stresses of life."

A few months into her 10th-grade year, her parents moved to Palm

Desert, leaving her at the Honolulu boarding school. She moved back in with them in June. Christopher, she recalled, never moved back in with them, although he would visit.

In 1996, she graduated from Palm Desert High School. For the next two years, she attended the College of the Desert. In 2001-02, she attended the Fashion Institute of Design and Merchandising in Los Angeles. Before the film festival, she worked in a variety of sales jobs, including alarm systems. Her favorite work was in interior design, which she loved and found remunerative. But the 2008 housing crash erased that job.

Despite being nine years apart in age, Sean and Jennifer built a friendship over time, then began dating and increasingly spent more time together. The first time she met Timmy, Jennifer said, "he liked me right away." He teased Sean: "She's too pretty for you. You don't know what you are doing. Why are you even with her?" To which Sean bantered, "OK, old man. Watch it. She's with me. Calm down over there."

Sean and Jennifer would hang out with Timmy, watching movies, sports, or television programs, or just talking about things. "We were over there a lot," she recalled. "He was very warm and welcoming. All smiles. Very polite. And funny. He was just so sweet."

On occasion, they would "double date" with Timmy and Henderson. When they did, they predictably went to Yard House, where Timmy and Henderson would split their usual: the large chicken nacho plate, often preceded by an onion ring tower. He would drink a couple of beers and she would have a couple of glasses of wine.

Around August 2011, Jennifer's lease was up, and she and Sean moved into what she described as a "unique, artsy, funky, cool little place off of Palm Canyon, close to restaurants and art galleries." A real estate firm occupied the lower level, an architect had the upper, and there were two apartments in the remaining space. While it was their home, Sean was still spending time at Timmy's condo, where he still had his room and kept clothes and other belongings.

The next year, the young couple moved into an apartment at Bermuda Palms, 650 E. Palm Canyon Dr. By this time, Sean had moved out of the condo. They lived there for the next four years. Early in their stay, they bought a pit bull puppy they named Layla. Sean's adult life was taking shape. But Timmy's was starting to fall apart.

Timmy and Henderson had begun taking an annual cruise to Mexico in 2009. For 2012, they went on Princess Cruises' Sapphire Princess, which could carry 2,670 passengers. Timmy and Henderson had enjoyed drinking, eating, swimming, reading, and relaxing while on their first cruises, but over the years, Timmy's increasing mobility issues led to their spending most of their time on the ship. In a March 3, 2012, note to a friend, Henderson said Timmy's "back pain continued [and] kept activities few." Coupled with her growing concern about Timmy's memory problems, this was their last cruise.

In 2011 and 2012, Rick Whitfield tried to reconnect with Timmy. About every six weeks, he performed with the Rick Whitfield Band at two casinos close to Timmy – the Morongo Casino Resort & Spa in Cabazon, and the Aqua Caliente Resort Casino & Spa in Rancho Mirage. He said he called Timmy several times and invited him to see him perform and visit, but Timmy never came.

Sometime in 2013, he was playing at the Crustacean in Beverly Hills and recognized someone in the audience. It was, of course, Jim Brown. Whitfield remembered that Timmy and Jim had been friends and had gone together to the Candy Store club. He thought that Marcus Allen and O.J. Simpson had been there with Timmy on occasion. Whitfield had never met Jim Brown, but after the performance he approached him to say that he and Timmy had been longtime friends. He said Jim asked, "You've been in touch with him all these years?" He said he had, to which Jim asked, "You have Tim's phone number?" Whitfield called Timmy, and Jim and Timmy talked on his cell phone for about 40 minutes. In gratitude, Jim gave Whitfield his phone number and said he could call him any time he wanted.

On Oct. 31, 2013, Henderson sent an Alzheimer's Association pamphlet, "Know the 10 Signs: Early Detection Matters," to a friend of Timmy's because of her increasing concern about his behavior. In particular, she had noticed six signs from among those listed in the pamphlet: (1), "Memory loss that disrupts daily life"; (2), "Challenges in planning or solving problems"; (3) "Difficulty completing familiar tasks at home, at work or at leisure"; (4), "Confusion with time or place;" (7), "Misplacing things and losing the ability to retrace steps"; and (8), "Decreased or poor judgment."

Based on this information and his own observations, the friend arranged for Timmy to see a neurologist on Nov. 14. Timmy was reluctant to go, but at the doctor's office was friendly and outgoing, trying to do whatever he could to show there was nothing wrong with him. If he didn't remember something, he made a joke about it. The results of the tests, however, were clear. He was experiencing symptoms of chronic traumatic encephalopathy (CTE) and the onset of Parkinson's disease.

While Timmy had been stubborn and in denial until then, when he got the results he called Sean and said, "You were right." This was unusual, because he typically would begin a phone conversation with "How are you?" Sean responded, "About what?" His father said, "Dementia and Parkinson's." According to Sielski in his 2020 column, the doctor told Timmy he probably had been suffering from the condition for 10 years. Shortly thereafter, Timmy called Vest and had a similar conversation. Vest had just retired from performing to care for her mother. Her last performance had been on June 6, 2013, at the New Orleans Superdome, at an event where she followed a speech by Saints (and Purdue) quarterback Drew Brees. She was now driving from her home in Vegas to her mother's home near San Diego regularly. She routinely stopped in Palm Springs to visit Timmy, if only for a few minutes. She had felt that he was getting forgetful, but learning of the results was devastating. They both cried on the phone.

This happened just a month after Mark Fainaru-Wada's and Steve

Fainaru's book, "League of Denial: The NFL, Concussions and the Battle for Truth," had been released. The authors chronicled the identification and impact of CTE on NFL players, beginning with what they considered "one of the most significant dates in the history of American sports" – Sept. 28, 2002, when forensic pathologist Bennet Omalu cut open the skull of Mike Webster, a former center for the Pittsburgh Steelers, who won four Superbowls with Webster as their center, who had died suddenly after experiencing years of cognitive impairment and mood disorders, including suicide attempts. "That decision – and its consequences, growing by the day – [was] the subject" of their book, they wrote. They went on to say, "There has never been anything like it in the history of sports: a public health crisis that emerged from the playing fields of our 21st century pastime. A small group of research scientists put football under a microscope – literally."

While increasing evidence showed a relationship between the pounding that pro football players endured and memory loss, psychological issues, physical deterioration, and untimely death, the NFL brought in researchers to wage a war of denial. "With each new study," the authors noted, "the NFL was mounting a scientific argument ... [amounting to]: Don't worry, be happy. Concussion rates in the NFL are extraordinarily low. The number of concussions is a meaningfulness predictor of future injuries; theoretically, one can have an infinite number of concussions and still be fine. There is no link between football and brain damage because football players don't get brain damage. To those on the other side of the argument, there was a kind of ham-fisted logic about this science of denial."

On April 26, 2005, a federal judge in Maryland ordered the NFL to pay an estimated $1.6 million, including interest and fees, to Webster's estate. The judgment was upheld on Dec. 13, 2006. This and other events led the NFL Players Association and the league's Management Council to develop the 88 Plan, to address the relationship between the game and dementia. The plan was named for John Mackey, Hall of Fame tight end for the Baltimore Colts and former president of the NFL Players Association, who died at 69 "from frontotemporal dementia, a disease he had battled for 10 years." A September 2007 copy of the 88 Plan provided details related to player eligibility for "reimbursement or payment of medical and custodial expenses" for dementia, approved definitions of dementia, how to apply, costs covered, amount of funds available for the duration of coverage, and other matters.

Timmy began to show signs of increasing memory loss as well as physical changes. On one occasion, Vest got a phone call from Timmy, who said he couldn't find his way home. He had gone to the Aqua Caliente Casino in downtown Palm Springs and was trying to get back to his condo, a little over two miles away. Vest quickly drove from Las Vegas, more than four hours away. When she arrived, she found him "lost, scared, and exhausted." Thereafter, she said, "his keys and driver's license were taken from him." Kilroy said that on two occasions when Timmy was visiting him at the MGM in Las Vegas, he got a call from security after midnight. Timmy had been found lost and wandering down hallways, looking for his room.

On March 9, 2014, Timmy and Henderson visited Checker before and after his performance at Sun City Palm Desert, a seniors community. They didn't talk much before the show because Checker had to get dressed and was negotiating a possible tour in Russia. Checker played to a full house and didn't disappoint his fans. The crowd twisted, shouted, and rocked with every move he made. He was 73, a few years younger than Timmy, but still in great shape. After the show, Timmy and Henderson reconnected with his old friend. Timmy and Checker reminisced and shared developments in their lives. One of the developments in Timmy's life was that he now had to use a cane because of Parkinson's, although he despised it.

Henderson began making Timmy a daily schedule and paying his bills. According to Sean, Timmy at one point had fallen a year and a half behind on his mortgage payments and nine months behind on his electric bill. Henderson took over these responsibilities, but Sean was unaware of them, saying, "She had masked a lot of things." He said later that he now believed he should have taken on more responsibility when he was 18, when he first started noticing his father having problems, but "was too young at the time.... I was never ungrateful for what she did for my dad – the time she spent with him and cared for him."

Henderson "would have been with him all the time, if she could have," Sean said. "While my dad wanted to maintain the idea that he had only been intimate with my mother, I knew that it wasn't true. But I understood that he didn't want to show any disrespect for my mother."

However, Sean said, he and Henderson "never got along. She acted like I was after his pension money. She could never say anything nice to me. I once said to her, 'I just said something nice to you, is there any reason you have to be mean to me all the time?'" Sean felt that she was jealous and possessive: "She had to try so hard to get my dad's attention, and forced her presence so often that he would have to tell her to leave.

"She didn't understand the relationship that I had with my dad," he continued. "It was so symbiotic and so easy to maintain. We didn't have to try to be best friends. We just were. My dad wanted to spend time with me. When I showed up at the condo, he wouldn't say, 'Oh, I'm busy right now, can you come back later?' Rather, he would say, 'Let's hang out and watch a game. Crack open a beer. Let's have a good time. Come over. Bring your friends. Anytime.'"

He added, "On occasion, we would laugh about a time from the past. Mary Lee would be suspicious that we were talking about her." On one occasion, Sean said, he noticed her reaction and said, "We were just laughing about something that had happened when I was an 11-year-old boy. Why would you know that? Nothing against you. My dad and I are allowed to have inside jokes."

Sean said, "Mary Lee thought I was imposing. She didn't think I was coming to check on him, but to make sure that I was getting my inheritance. On the contrary, I wanted to make sure my dad was good, getting his newspaper, keeping him entertained, doing his crossword puzzles, watching some Laker games, keeping his mind as sharp as possible. I wanted to make sure he had the best quality of life.

"I got over it once I understood it. It was Jennifer who pointed it out to me: 'Why is she so rude to you when you are coming to say hi to your dad and check on him?'" Jennifer thought Timmy and Sean's relationship was wonderful. "Timmy was so unique. I never met anyone like him," she said.

Henderson died at her condo on May 8, 2015. Jennifer recalled that Timmy was with her when she died. Henderson had been diagnosed months earlier with melanoma on her left cheek. "For a long time, she hid it from Timmy by using a concealer. Eventually she covered it with a patch." While she was under the care of a home nurse, Timmy would sit with her. Jennifer brought food by on one occasion and Timmy met her outside the condo to get it.

For about a month after Henderson's death, Timmy would occasionally say that he hadn't heard from her. Sean had to remind him that she had died, to which he would respond: "Oh, yeah, that's right, I remember now." Henderson's death was just part of Timmy's world getting smaller. His mother, Juanita, had died in Los Angeles on Feb. 26, 2010, at age 97; his sister Trixie died just a few months later, on May 8. Polly had passed on April 9, 1988, and Betts on April 5, 2007; like all of Timmy's childhood family except for his father, they had moved to California as well.

Shortly after Trixie's death, Timmy looked back on the breakup of his family when he was a child: "I was very, very hurt. More so, probably, than my other siblings. I don't know, mine are now all passing away, it's just me and my brother and young sister. And we weren't even close to the others. The one that died two weeks ago, we were close at one time, I don't know what happened.... I would call and she would say, 'Oh, we're going out. I'll call you, don't call.' She would never call, so I just quit calling." He said Buggs had gotten the same shutout. The scars Buddy had left starting at the Home had not healed, even though Timmy continued to look up to him: "My brother … is an intellectual guy, great athlete. But he kept that on his shoulder…. I saw him at my mom's bedside. I hadn't seen him for a while. He don't like me. He never did…. He was spoiled by my three older sisters." Buddy would die in Los Angeles on Nov. 27, 2014. His career had never recovered after he was forced out of his state commission job in 1985.

During the years that Timmy and Henderson were together, Lee had continued to develop her botanical wellness products. She spent more time working on them after 2011, when she and Ader divorced and she kept custody of Alex. She branded them as A Love Lee Heart, and licensed and promoted them privately. Much of her time was taken up by her passion for music. In 2011, "Whole Lotta Somethin'," her first CD, was released. Later, she performed with several big bands – once with Jimmy McConnell's, and another time with Paul McDonald and Les McCann's. For about 10 years, she sang on and off with Ted Herman. She also toured with McCann for eight years. McCann was a jazz pianist who had become prominent in the 1960s with the album "Swiss Movement" and its single "Compared to What." His subsequent work put more emphasis on his vocals. Lee called him a mentor, friend, and buddy whom she had met before Timmy. McCann came to know Timmy, playing basketball with him when he visited Lee. "I didn't sing with him," she said, "we were just friends for 30 years." Then, one day, McCann asked her why she hadn't asked to sing with him. Lee said, "You hate singers." McCann responded, playfully, "Yes, I do. Let's sing together." They performed at venues including the Lyric Theater and Cultural Arts Center in Lexington, Ky., McCann's hometown and home of the Les McCann School for the Arts, on May 9, 2015, and Jimmy Mak's jazz club in Portland, Ore., on Sept. 23, 2015, where they celebrated McCann's 80th birthday.

While Lee and Ader had divorced, they were still getting together with Timmy and Sean. "Steve and Tim didn't play golf as much as they grew older," Lee recalled. "But they still watched movies together. Both of them would still come over. There was never a separation of our families. Steve was on board with all of us being a family. Tim didn't seem to be uncomfortable with it. Steve and Tim didn't talk about me. I would always ask them if they did. They laughed and said, 'No, we're way beyond talking about you.'"

A few weeks after Henderson's death, Sean and Jennifer moved from their apartment into Timmy's condo so they could take care of him. Sean had worked with a friend on renovations so that the condo would better accommodate them as well as their first child – Ella, born on July 11, 2015 – and their dog Layla as well as Timmy.

On the morning of Oct. 14, 2015, Timmy and one of the authors of this book were at Elmer's to review a chapter draft. The author's wife, who had become friends with Timmy and assisted in some of the research, also was there. Their typical approach for reviewing material was for the author and Timmy to take turns reading what had been written. Timmy relished reading drafts. If he saw inaccuracies in what had been written or thought of information that should be added, he shared it.

On this occasion, Timmy listened to the description of Muncie and the establishment of Ball State Teachers College, and his arrival there. Suddenly he said, in a strong yet matter-of-fact tone, "I didn't go to Ball State. I went to Butler. My brother went to Ball State." Knowing that Timmy liked jokes, the author responded: "Come on, Timmy, you're playing with me, aren't you," and chuckled. The expression on Timmy's face didn't change, and he repeated what he had said. The author, now perplexed, asked: "Are you serious?" Timmy again said, "I didn't go to Ball State." The author and his wife glanced at one another, and redirected the conversation to what they planned to do in Palm Springs. It was the last time the author and Timmy met to solely discuss the details in the book.

Just a few weeks later, on Nov. 11, Timmy, Sean, and Jennifer flew from Palm Springs to Philadelphia for Timmy's induction as an individual into the Philadelphia Sports Hall of Fame the following day. (The previous induction was for the 1960 team as a whole.) They shared a room with two double beds at the Sheraton Society Hill. Sean didn't believe that Timmy should go to Philadelphia alone or have his own room. He had noticed that the confidence Timmy had always exhibited had been diminishing. Timmy was often apprehensive and confused. Sean had been invited to other events involving Timmy over the years, but this was the first one that he felt he had to attend, because he was afraid that Timmy might not be able to get through it on his own. He also figured this would be the last time that his father would be able to make such a trip.

Sean had just started working at Trina Turk, a store noted for high-end attire. "I bought some nice clothes for us," he recalled. "I picked out clothes that would make him feel and look good for the ceremony. We were the best dressed."

On the plane to Philadelphia, Sean and Jennifer sat together in one row and Timmy sat in the row behind them. Every few minutes, Timmy asked, "Where are we going?" Each time, Sean said, he responded, "We're going to Philadelphia, where you are going to be given an award." In the past, when Timmy forgot something, he often made a joke of it, but not this time. Jennifer recalled thinking, "This is more serious than I even thought it was. This is something that he will never get over."

At the hotel, they settled in and slept late the next day. That afternoon, Timmy had been scheduled for an interview on a local radio station. As the three of them approached the spot in the lobby where tables and chairs had been set up for the interview, Jennifer recalled, "Timmy looked like a deer in headlights." Sean comforted him, saying, "I've got you, Dad. We're going to kill this interview." With Sean's help in carrying the conversation, the interview went smoothly. Following the interview, they mingled with fellow inductees, dignitaries, and others at a reception. At 7:30 p.m., the ceremony was opened by emcee Pat Williams, senior executive vice president of the Orlando Magic. A program provided a two-page background of each of the 14 inductees. Sean and Jennifer had written the one for Timmy, which appeared with three photos. Sean and Jennifer were among those acknowledged in the program for having "given their precious time and energy to make the Class of 2015 Induction Ceremony such a success."

The other inductees, some deceased, were: NFL quarterback Rich Gannon, a Philadelphia native; NBA player and college coach Walt Hazzard, now known as Mahdi Abdul-Rahman, also from the city; Rick MacLeish, who played 12 seasons for the Flyers; Garry Maddox, a Phillie for eight seasons; Roman Catholic High School basketball coach Billy Markward; Benny McLaughlin, a soccer player from the 1940s and 1950s and a native Philadelphian; Bob Montgomery, a lightweight boxer who began his career in the city; Lou Nolan, public address announcer for the Flyers; field hockey player and coach Karen Shelton, who attended college in the area; Sam Thompson, a 19th-century player for the Phillies; lacrosse player and college coach Cindy Timchal, who grew up in the suburbs; former Eagles coach Dick Vermeil; tennis player R. Norris Williams, whose family came from Philadelphia and who survived the sinking of the Titanic; and Dave Zinkoff, the legendary announcer at 76ers games.

Each living recipient had a brief time to make remarks. When Timmy learned that he would have to speak, he had a friend, who was visiting him in Palm Springs, write what he wanted to say, so he could have the words in front of him and could use them to rehearse. Before speaking, he wanted to make changes, and Jennifer rewrote portions of it. When he got to the lectern and began his remarks, he struggled. Jennifer recalled, "It was the first time I looked in his eyes and saw that he looked lost. He was nervous. Sean had to go to the podium to help him. It was hard to watch. I was choking back tears. This was highly unusual and reflected his anxiety and uncertainty. In the past, he would have killed the speech and would not have had written down any of the words."

They returned the next day to Palm Springs. Knowing that he

didn't have to do anything else and was going home, Timmy was relieved and relaxed. It was the last time that he participated in an event of public significance.

In April 2016, Sean began a new career as an actor. The play was "Bad Jews," written by Joshua Harmon and presented by the Desert Ensemble Theater Company (DETC) at the Pearl McManus Theater in Palm Springs. This was the first of a number of plays in which he was directed by his former high school theater teacher, Rosemary Mallett. Sean played one of three Jewish family members discussing who should get his deceased grandfather's pendant, saved from a Nazi concentration camp.

The following year, Lee also ventured into a new career. She told Alan Schultz, manager at KAJI, a jazz radio station in the Palm Springs area, that the station should have a female DJ. She had no training or experience. They talked for two hours about jazz, after which he said, "OK, you can do it." He put her in the booth, and showed her how to load CDs and operate the microphone. She introduced some records. Shultz asked her what days she wanted to work and advised her, "Just be natural. Just don't think about your voice. Your voice is fine, because you are a singer. Enunciate, be clear, and have fun." (In 2022, she was continuing to host a jazz show on Tuesdays and Thursdays at 11 a.m.)

As Lee and Sean opened new pathways, Timmy's physical decline was continuing. On Sept. 15, 2017, Sean posted a photo of himself as a child with Timmy and wrote, "As most of you know, I have been my father's caretaker for almost 4 years. My dad is my hero and it's been hard to see him struggle. I'm so fortunate to have had a father that taught me how to treat people, how to embrace the things I love, no matter what others think.... His mobility in the past week has taken a bad turn. And he is unable to leave our home now without a great deal of assistance.... I'm literally just learning how to take care of myself and my daughter. And I worry that I'm not doing enough for him. It has been the most difficult challenge of my young life."

Sean and Jennifer became parents for the second time when their son, Leo, was born on Feb. 22, 2018, by emergency C-section. Sean was there for the birth. Afterward, Lee, who had been babysitting Ella, came by with her so that she could see her parents and meet her new brother. After the visit, Lee drove to the condo to pick up some things for Ella and to check on Timmy. When she drove up to the entrance gate to the complex, to her surprise, she saw Timmy there and said, “”Hi, Tim. It’s Lee. Let’s go back.”

He asked, “Where are we going?”

“Just back home,” Lee said. She was able to coax him into the car and took him back to the condo. Lee called Sean to tell him that the friend whom they had asked to watch Timmy was not there, and that she would stay until he returned. Sean rushed home to check on Timmy and admonish the friend. According to Jennifer, this “was the beginning of the end of Tim’s living with us.”

Leo’s birth came while Sean was acting in another DETC play, “Election Day” by Josh Tobiessen. Sean played the boyfriend of an attorney who expects him to vote in a mayoral election.

As it turned out, the births of both of Sean’s children’s had coincidental numerical links to Timmy’s football career. He wore jersey No. 22; Ella was born at 10:22 p.m., 22:22 in military time; and Leo was born on 2/22. While one of Sean’s favorite photographs is of Timmy holding Ella for the first time, when Leo was born, there was a special bond. They looked at one another, thinking “I’m you and you’re me,” Sean recalled. There was “something very unspoken and cool about when they looked at one another. You could just see they had this link. We both had a link with my dad through shared names – Leo Thomas Brown and Sean Timothy Brown.”

Sean had been hoping for another daughter, saying, “I’m a girl dad and I love being a girl dad. I was hoping to have princess parties my entire life. I was told it was going to be a boy. I said, are you sure? Are your machines accurate? Oh, man, I’m going to have some dude punching me in the face when he’s 15 because he wants to take the car.”

Ella loved playing around Timmy and showing off any new moves she had. Both children seemed to understand that he had been an exceptional athlete. They called him Grandpa Ball, because they saw him holding a football in photographs. "The greatest joy of my life was to see my dad interact with my kids," Sean said. "To laugh at them. Watching him worry about them slipping. He was shocked at them running around. I told him, 'They're only going to get bigger and wilder, dude, if you recall.' It was funny to see him helicopter dad his grandkids. That's how I am. I guess I got that from him. He never expected to be a grandparent. That was probably my greatest gift, besides my time and energy to make sure he was comfortable."

Soon after Leo was born, Jennifer recalled, "Timmy started to decline rapidly. In addition to dealing with growing memory loss, we were having to change his diapers. Taking care of two children and Timmy, and Sean working, it was overwhelming. I couldn't physically or emotionally deal with things. It was one of the hardest times of my life."

The decision to move Timmy to another place was difficult. Sean felt guilty about the idea. "We couldn't take care of Timmy properly anymore," Jennifer said. "Our relationship was strained. It was absolutely the thing to do." Sean finally agreed.

"About a month and a half before we moved him into a facility," Sean recalled, "one night [Timmy] asked me to come into his room and sit on his bed. He was very clearly looking at me. It was the clearest moment that I had of my dad the whole time I was taking care of him. He was still there. At the time I was caught off guard."

He said Timmy asked him, "I'm sick a little bit and have trouble remembering things, right? You've been taking care of me ever since they told me that, right?"

Sean responded, "Well, yeah, Dad, of course I have." Then Timmy said, "I love you so much and want to thank you for that." Sean reflected later, "Very cool thing that I cherish. I think about it often. Really clear in thought. Speaking clearly. Sitting up straight in bed. I felt like I was in his room when I was a kid."

Sean had sole responsibility for selecting care facilities. In addition, Sean used the NFL's Plan 88 for financial support to offset the cost of facilities and medical care. "I wish I would have known about it sooner," he recalled. "There were about five years where we could have been benefiting from it. But I wasn't aware of it." He also used money obtained from the settlement of thousands of retired players' lawsuit against the NFL over medical conditions resulting from concussions. Of that money, he said, "People think it's millions of dollars. It was around $70,000."

He chose Atria Hacienda, an assisted living facility in Palm Desert. They took Timmy to visit. He was in a bad mood and very argumentative, as he knew what was happening. Sean and Jennifer told him that "this is going to be your new place. It's going to be really great."

Timmy moved there in May and seemed to be adjusting. Sean's job at Trina Turkin was a five-minute drive away, so he was able to visit every day. Jennifer saw him a few times a week and brought the children.

Dave Chapman and his wife would continue to visit him there as well. In June 2018 Chapman took a photo of a display that had Sean put together at the entrance to Timmy's unit. It included a football inscribed, "The Indiana Soldier's and Sailors Children's Home, Knightstown, IN," then "Tim Brown," "Part of Super Bowl History," and "III," with the NFL emblem at the bottom. A 1964 trading card of Timmy as an Eagle leaned against it on the left. To the right was a Los Angeles County Probation Department badge with the words "Deputy Probation Officer." On a gold plate below it were the name "Thomas A. Brown" and the dates Feb. 15, 1990, to May 28, 2000. In addition, the display contained Tim's Golden Helmet award for playing in the 1966 Pro Bowl. Chapman described the apartment as "a really nice place" and recalled that Timmy "was walking pretty well at the time." But after Timmy moved into the care facility, the Chapmans were never able again to take him out for dinner.

Then, in June, Timmy fell and broke a hip. He was taken to Eisenhower Health in Rancho Mirage for surgery. Sean worried about what would happen if he didn't make it through surgery and questioned the decision to have him at Atria. Following the surgery, Timmy was moved to Palm Springs Rehabilitation, where he stayed for months, learning to walk again.

After some time back at Atria Hacienda, he contracted a staph infection and went back to Eisenhower Health, then to Palm Springs Rehabilitation again – this time for longer. Once released, Timmy was relocated to a private care home in Palm Desert.

In September, Timmy's old Eagles teammate Tommy McDonald, who had always praised him to the skies, died. He had suffered from dementia-related illnesses for a number of years. Sean posted that "in a time when the color of my dad's skin affected almost every aspect of his life, Tommy saw past that and found a best friend and partner in crime. He encouraged others to stop looking at the world in black and white. He always stood up for my dad when others wouldn't."

Sean was moving ahead in his acting career, appearing on stage and in commercials. He started April 2019 in "Grand Hotel" at the Palm Canyon Theater, and from April 19 to 28 performed in "Asleep in the Wind" by Ellen Byron at the Pearl McManus Theater. Timmy tried to see each play in which Sean had a role.

In a story published on April 20, 2019, on the website Broadway World, Stan Jenson wrote that the play "features Sean Timothy Brown, the valley's go-to young hunk actor. This opening night was just two weeks after I saw him singing and dancing his heart out in 'Grand Hotel' at another local theatre, and he left an indelible impression earlier this season as the new professor in 'Who's Afraid of Virginia Woolf?' It's easy to see why he is so in demand, and his performance here is consistent with his earlier work." Later that year, he would take the leading role of John Proctor in Arthur Miller's "The Crucible" at Palm Canyon, again directed by Mallett. With experience in sports, music, and acting,

Sean's life was paralleling his father's, though with different outcomes.

In late July 2019, Sean, Jennifer, Ella, Leo, and Sean's half-sister Alex, now in her early 20s, went to Kauai, Hawaii, for a six-day vacation. Jennifer remembered, "I was over the moon to go, thinking it would be a trip that could help heal our relationship and be a much-deserved break from all the stress we'd been under." Sean recalled that he felt guilty going, worried that something might happen to Timmy while he was away. "For the last four years," he said, "I had rarely gone more than three days without seeing him." Jennifer said "Sean's anxiety was through the roof almost immediately after arriving, and it spoiled most of the trip, causing arguments between us. We tried to make the most out of it, but there was a tension in the air."

Nonetheless, they found some time to enjoy the vacation. Jennifer and Alex went on a hike, and as a group they "went to a few amazing beaches."

"On our last night there," she said, "I was determined for Sean and I to have some sort of moment together, so I booked an 'experience' for us with a guide named Luan (a friend to this day), who took us paddleboarding at the most incredible private beach. It was at sunset and the paddleboards were lit up so you could see the coral reef below. It was the most magical part of the trip." Sean agreed, as noted in a July 30 Facebook video post of him and Jennifer on paddleboards in the water off Anini Beach: "I'm not good on boards.... That being said this was an amazing end to an amazing trip and I only fell twice! Shortly after this the sunset and we got to watch the universe light the sky like I've never seen before, while floating in the middle of the ocean!!!!!!!"

Back in California, the private home in Palm Desert had worked out for Timmy at first. There was a caregiver who was very attentive to his needs. But when the Chapmans visited him there in June 2019, the last time they saw him, they thought that "the place was not a very good place." Ownership of the home changed. Sean remembered that the caregiver "wasn't getting much time off, [then] got three days off in a row." During the caregiver's absence, Sean said, Timmy was "not given water, food, medications, care."

Sean posted on Jan. 19 that Timmy was again hospitalized after being found "severely dehydrated and malnourished," and having been "essentially left alone to die." Once again he was taken to Eisenhower Health and then Palm Springs Rehabilitation.

In February, Timmy was moved to Aloha Home Care in Cathedral City, which Sean felt was a good fit. Jennifer recalled that Timmy seemed to do well there. "They nursed him back to health. He was happy. Brighter. He laughed. He would hum or sing to music while the children danced around.... The staff was incredible," she added. "The main caretaker would have happy hour for him in the late afternoon." Lee noted that after Sean chose a place for Timmy, she would visit, "make sure he had food, was being taken care of right, and get to know the nurses. Sean and I would collaborate on what we thought about things."

Sean said his father never forgot who he was, except on one occasion when he thought Sean was Buddy. Quickly, Sean joked, "John was 5-4 and Black, and I'm 6-2 and white and tattooed," to which, Timmy replied, "Oh, yeah. You're Sean. I remember." He rarely forgot who Jennifer was, but when he did, he thought she was "just this babe" coming in to check on him, an old girlfriend. "That was cute and fun," Sean said. "Jennifer would lean into it a little to lighten up his day." Sean said he was heartbroken that Timmy had forgotten who Henderson was. There were other light moments. On occasion, Lee brought Timmy a hamburger and milkshake, which he loved. "Sometimes," she laughed, "Sean would show up at the same time with a hamburger and milkshake, not knowing they were going to be there at the same time." At one of the care facilities, Lee and Timmy were seated at a table with residents and started singing "Pennies From Heaven." As they ended the first verse, everyone started singing with them. "It was a beautiful moment," Lee remembered. "Everyone was so happy."

And then COVID-19 hit. On Jan. 25, 2020, the first case was reported in California, an Orange County man who had been in Wuhan, China. The first coronavirus-related death was reported on Feb. 6 in Santa Clara. On March 4, Gov. Gavin Newsom declared a state of emergency. By then, 842 cases had been reported, with four deaths. Eight days later, 3,039 cases were reported with nine deaths. The next day President Donald Trump declared a national emergency. This coincided with the closure of California's K-12 schools, affecting more than 5.7 million students. A play in which Sean was to appear – ironically named "How to Survive an Apocalypse" – was canceled the day before its scheduled March 13 opening. On March 15, Newsom restricted senior home visits to end-of-life matters. It was at this time that Timmy developed pneumonia.

No longer able to visit Timmy because of the COVID shutdowns, Sean, Jennifer, and others were relegated to phone calls and talking on FaceTime. In either case, the nurse held the phone for him. Sean posted on March 30 that Timmy's disease was not COVID-related but was "life-threatening, nonetheless." He said, "It's simply his conditions catching up with his age. Honestly, I'm uncertain as to how or if he will recover." A few weeks later, when they were finally able to see Timmy again, they were told he would need to be put in hospice. His face was sunken and he was dehydrated. Despite this, Lee still saw in him an Adonis, "tight skin, chiseled, and handsome."

"He was pretty far gone by then," Sean said, recalling a phone call he got while playing with Ella and Leo at the Mesquite Golf Course. He was told, "He's not speaking anymore." Immediately, he said, he thought, "The last time I spoke to him was the last time we would ever have a conversation." Two days earlier, he remembered, he had purchased a couple of non-alcoholic beers and shared one with Timmy. Timmy was "over the moon about it," saying, "Oh, amber beer. Just what I love."

Timmy was taken back to Eisenhower Health, where he was examined and treated. While he was being hydrated, he got to the point that he couldn't swallow. A doctor said the only way to keep him alive was through feeding tubes. Timmy had indicated that he did not want to be put on life support. Doctors gave him four to 14 hours to live. But after two days, they were told he could no longer stay at the hospital, because he had lived longer than they could keep him. Sean reflected, "When it got ugly and bad, I didn't look away, knowing he would do the same for me."

He was returned to Aloha, and lived a few more days. Either Sean or Lee was with him for the entire time. The last few nights, Lee slept in his room and told Sean he should be with Jennifer and their children. Buggs came to spend time with him. Vest was there on April 1 and 2. According to Sean, "some people shied away because they didn't want to see him that way. But anyone who could get to see him got to see him." On and off in the last days, Lee said, Timmy would open his eyes, especially when she would play the Gladys Knight and the Pips video "Love Overboard," (in which Timmy had acted as her love interest), and other songs with which he was familiar. "We would always sing with him. We had wonderful moments," Lee recalled. "It was a sad reunion, but we were happy that we could say goodbye to him."

On the evening of April 4, Lee noticed that Timmy didn't seem to be breathing. She touched his chest and knew that he had died. She called Sean, then contacted the staff at the home. Sean came immediately. Word spread among those who knew him. Checker said he found out on April 7 in a text from a friend. Warwick said, "It was kind of a joke to hear of his passing. It can't be happening yet. But he lived a good life."

Through his charismatic personality, his physical gifts, and his unflagging determination to be true to himself, Timmy Brown had gone from small-town Indiana to sunny Southern California. As a young child, he knew family and neighborhood boys; as an adult, he had friendships and love affairs with some of the world's most famous people. He left the anonymous regimen of a state-run home to find stardom on the football field and roles in major films. His confidence gave him enormous strengths in connecting with people, but his past fettered him in romantic relationships. Life gave him great fame and brought him low again. At 10 p.m. Saturday, April 4, 2020, his life ended in the suburbs of Palm Springs, Calif., not a bad place to die if you could choose. Thomas Allen Brown, age 82, was survived by his former wife; his son; his two grandchildren and their mother; his only living sibling, Buggs; and the memories of hundreds of thousands of football fans. As Sean said a month after his death, Timmy had "loved his life. He had lived it to the fullest. He felt very proud about what he had done."

Author's Note

By Roy Weaver

If you've finished this book, you've learned a number of things about Timmy Brown, one of them being that he was intensely loyal. He kept friends for life, and he remembered where he had come from. One of those places was Ball State University. On Feb. 23, 2008, a Teachers College alumni reception was hosted by Gary Kinley – MAE in early childhood education and elementary education, 1976, and EDD in early childhood education, 1986 – and Roger Christensen at their home in Palm Springs, Calif. As dean of the college, I worked with Karen Staley, its director of development, in organizing the event and having invitations sent to alumni in Southern California. When I got the list of alumni, I noticed the name of Tim Brown, and wondered if he was the football player whom I watched make history against the Dallas Cowboys by running back two kickoffs for touchdowns on Nov. 6, 1966 – the first player to return two kickoffs for scores in a single game in NFL history. I called his home and told him how excited I had been when I saw the game on TV while I was a sophomore at Ball State. We talked about our time at school, and then I asked if he could come to the reception. He said he already had it on his calendar, but had a cold and wasn't sure he would feel up to it.

Timmy did come to the event, cold and all. He was stylishly dressed, polite, friendly, and outgoing. He stood out on arrival. He listened to others with interest. But he quickly became the center of attention as he responded to questions about his life. He mesmerized his fellow alums, including me. During the event, I asked him if he had ever worked with anyone on a biography. He had not. As I was planning to move from the dean's position to a faculty role in a few months, I asked if he would work with me. That was how this book got started. I thought it would take three or four years. It took 14.

Although I later learned that Timmy had already been showing some signs of memory loss, they weren't apparent in our initial talks, which began on Nov. 5, 2008. He had a clear vision for the book. He didn't want it to be an academic work, full of footnotes and obscure citations. He wanted it to be honest, authentic, and full of anecdotes and examples of what he had faced and done. Timmy was a great storyteller who loved to charm people, and he wanted the story of his life to reflect his personality. But he also knew he had not simply run from one success to another. There had been dark parts in his childhood. His entertainment career had not lived up to his dreams, in part through his poor choices. His marriage had ended in divorce. These things he wanted told honestly as well.

I began interviewing Timmy that November. As the years passed, I met his then-partner, Mary Lee Henderson; his sister Della Mitchell, known in the family as Buggs; his son, Sean; Timmy's ex-wife, Lee Hartley; and Sean's partner, Jennifer VanCamp. I realized their stories would have to be part of the book as well. And the more he talked about his life, the wider the scope of the work grew, as I discovered that I would have to speak to his family, friends, and colleagues to tell a story that was not just about one man, but the times in which he lived -- the role his race played in his upbringing and career, and the society of world-famous people in sports and entertainment in which he moved. As I found out more about his career in entertainment, I realized this biography would need someone more knowledgeable in that area than I was.

Shawn Sriver, a colleague in Teachers College, had heard about the project, and when we chatted, I realized that he had enthusiasm and expertise about music, movies, and television, and was already aware of

Timmy's involvement with "M*A*S*H." Shawn met with Timmy in 2010 when he visited Ball State campus and conducted about five hours of recorded interviews with Timmy over two days. Shawn had two other short telephone interviews with Timmy over the next few years.

We started writing the book. Then, at an April 13, 2011, Department of Journalism awards luncheon, I met David Sullivan, who had received the Outstanding Alumnus award. I told him that Shawn and I were working on the biography, and asked if he might be interested in helping. As an assistant managing editor for the Philadelphia Inquirer at the time, he said he would be willing to assist with copy editing, but had no time for more than that.

As Shawn and I continued work on the book, the prospect of finishing seemed improbable. Shawn was able to write most of what would need to be integrated into the book related to Timmy's acting, singing, and modeling. And most of the interviews and research needed for writing about Timmy's NFL career had been collected. The information stood before us as an insurmountable mountain. In late 2020, I learned that David had retired from the Inquirer. I called and mentioned the frustration and discouragement we felt, and asked if he could now help. David, who had once worked in the Inquirer's sports department, asked me to send him the information on Timmy's NFL career and said he would work on it. In just a few weeks, he had finished a draft covering his pro football career. His commitment to being a co-author, in addition to the copy editor, served as the turning point on the book.

Among the three of us, we have tried to show the life of a remarkable person. Timmy wasn't just a great athlete who tried his hand at singing and/or acting; that story could be told about many, some of whom appear in this book. He was someone who never stopped trying to find where he belonged, to whom he belonged, who he really was. On the gridiron, he could run fast, but Timmy the star never overtook Timmy the man. He never turned into his public persona. We have tried to do him justice.

Source Notes

In honoring Timmy's wishes that this book be easily readable and not full of footnotes and obscure citations, yet aware of the need for credibility and transparency about how we gathered the material, the authors have taken this approach to referencing.

The primary source of information, of course, was Timmy Brown. Between Nov. 5, 2008, and Oct. 16, 2010, he was interviewed 22 times, resulting in more than 200 pages of transcription that cover his early childhood in Richmond, time at the Indiana Soldiers' and Sailors' Children's Home, days as a student-athlete at what is now Ball State University, career in the National Football League, work as a singer and actor, career in the Los Angeles County Probation Department, marriage and divorce, the birth of his son, and his friendships with the Butler family, Chubby Checker, Jim Brown, Dionne Warwick, Diana Ross, and others. Most of these interviews were conducted by Roy Weaver. Some were done by Shawn Sriver; Marilyn Weaver, Roy's wife and chairperson emerita of the Department of Journalism at Ball State; and Lori Demo, a former Ball State journalism faculty member.

The effect of Alzheimer's disease on Timmy was apparent in the later 2010 interviews. While his recollections of his activities and emotions remained consistent, his ability to find the right word, or to recall specific names or the time order of events, showed a decline. By the time he met with David Sullivan in 2016 in Philadelphia, the disease had taken a further toll. Nevertheless, he was still able at that time to converse with full knowledge of whom he was talking to and where he was, and to recall, as he always had, the lyrics to any song he had sung or, in many cases, only heard.

Numerous documents and photos came from the boxes of materials kept in Timmy's storage unit in California. Early in the process of interviewing him, he permitted a review of materials there, and allowed Roy to move any that he wanted to his home office in Indiana. Roy took ones that related to the early chapters of the book. Much later, Sean Brown enabled further review of the storage unit contents as well as boxes found in Timmy's condo at Mesquite Country Club, and these materials then were moved to Muncie for use. These collectively are referred to below as "the Brown files."

In addition, information provided by many other people was used in the preparation of more than one chapter. Over the period of 14 years, some information was lost. On occasion, the date of an interview is missing and, as a result, n.d. appears, indicating "no date." Those people were:

Bell, Bobby. Apr. 28, 2022.

Brown, Sean. Sept. 7, 2016; Sept. 5, March 13, 2022.

Brown, Timmy. Nov. 5, 18, 2008; Jan. 22, 2009; Feb. 2, 3, 7, 8, 9, 10, 12, 19, 21, 22, Oct. 1, 2, 3, 4, 12, 13, 14, 15, 16, 2010.

Butler, Ernie. May 12, 13, 17, 2013; July 21, 2021.

Chapman, Dave. Sept. 27, 28, 2022.

Gerrard, Jeff. Jan. 8, 2021; Aug. 15, 2022.

Davis, Paul. Aug. 21, 2021.

Hartley, Lee. Apr. 18, May 8, July 25, Sept. 5, Oct. 10, 2021; Apr. 5, July 13, Aug. 23, 2022.

Hart, Jim. Feb. 12, 2012.

Hart, Sandy. July 2, 2021.

Jones, Harold. Sept. 26, 2022

Kayat, Eddie. Aug. 7, 2021.

Kilroy, Gene. March 20, 2009; March 30, 2022.

Lambert, Earl. [n.d.]

Linson, Robert. Aug. 14, 2009.

McDonald, Tommy. Sept. 14, 2010.
Mitchell, Della Brown. Oct. 27, 2013.
Shadd, Grayce Butler. Oct. 13, 2014; July 21, 2021.
Sharp, Dee Dee. July 14, 2021.
Tunney, Jim. Apr. 22, 2010.
VanCamp, Jennifer. April 22, May 18, Aug. 22, 2022.
Vest, Hollie. March 31, June 22, July 11, 2022.
Walker, George. Apr. 16, 2012; Oct. 7, 2022.
Warwick, Dionne. Sept. 20, 2022.
Whitfield, Rick. Aug. 30, 2021.

Follow-up text messages, phone calls, and emails helped clarify and verify information after the interviews. In some instances, rough drafts of text were shared for review and feedback.

Other interviews provided information relevant only to specific chapters, and are shown below with the respective chapter.

In addition, the authors are familiar with most of the areas where Timmy spent his life. Roy Weaver attended Ball State as an undergraduate and graduate student, and was a faculty member there from 1980 to 2020. He lives in Muncie, and also he lived for five years in the Los Angeles area. Shawn Sriver is a Ball State professional staff member. David Sullivan also attended Ball State, and has lived in the Philadelphia-South Jersey area since 1983; he also lived in Richmond for two years. Many items of location and general history, such as the first pages of Chapter Five, come from the authors' firsthand knowledge or professional experience in those areas.

Timmy's athletic career was well documented in college and the pros. Information on games, statistics, and interviews by journalists in the 1950s and 1960s were obtained by reading the files of the Ball State News, the Muncie Star, the Muncie Evening Press, the Green Bay Press-Gazette, the Philadelphia Inquirer, the Philadelphia Daily News, the Philadelphia Evening Bulletin, the New York Times, and the Baltimore Sun. Also used was the Pro Football Reference website.

Four magazine stories provided much valuable information on Timmy's childhood in Richmond, including his life with the Bennetts; time at Ball State; brief career with the Packers and relationship with Vince Lombardi; friendships on the Eagles including life with the Grices; views on race; relationship with Ernie Butler; and aspirations for football and entertainment. They were consulted throughout the writing of the book. One story was in the July 1964 issue of Sport magazine, "Timmy Brown: Super-Sensitive Super-Star," by Berry Stainback. Another, without an author credit, was in the August 1973 issue of Black Sports magazine, "Rap With Timmy Brown on Football-Acting." Black Sports was published in New York City from 1971 to 1978. The third, "Timmy Brown: From an Indiana Orphanage to the NFL," by Norman Jones, appeared in the spring 2010 issue of Traces of Indiana and Midwestern History, published by the Indiana Historical Society. A draft copy of the article was also provided by Jones. The fourth, "Brown Went from Home to Stardom," by Daniel Cecil, appeared in "The Home Revisited: An Abbreviated History of the Indiana Soldiers' and Sailors' Children's Home," published as a supplement to The Knightstown Banner on April 21, 2004.

Citations specific to chapters follow.

Chapter 1: The Birth of Tiny Tim

Timmy visited Indiana on two occasions, Nov. 22 to 26, 2008, and Oct. 8 to 17, 2010, to work on the book. At that time, he went to the Richmond hospital where he was born; homes where he had lived or sites where a house once stood; the Bethel A.M.E. Church; and schools he had attended.

Documents from the Brown files included his birth certificate, his parents' marriage license, the court record of his parents' divorce, and family photos. The Indiana Department of Child Services office in Richmond was consulted in regard to the dispensation of the children after John and Juanita divorced. The various names that Timmy used throughout life came from the Black Sports interview.

The Lilly Library at Earlham College and the Morrisson-Reeves Library, both in Richmond, and the Indiana State Archives supplied historical background related to the Indiana Ku Klux Klan, the Underground Railroad, the Starr Piano Co. and Gennett Records, and the city of Richmond. Tom Hamm of the Earlham College Friends Collection and College Archives provided assistance. George Blakey, owner of The Old Book Shop, was consulted regarding the history of Richmond.

The National Personnel Records Center of the National Archives provided details on John Floyd Brown's military service and separation. The Wayne County Health Department and the Wayne County Recorder's Office documented where Timmy lived and the schools that he attended, among other information.

Interviews:

Blose, Max. March 27, 28, 2022. He was with Timmy when they heard a shot on the morning Freddie Starks died.

Flood, Kenneth. Nov. 11, 2010.

Flood, Mary Jo. Nov. 12, 2022 verification of earlier interview.

Flood, Richard. Nov. 12, 2010.

Knipp, Kay, [n.d.] She was a classmate at Pershing Elementary School.

Sourbeer, Carl. [n.d.]

Winburn, Martel. Oct. 12, 2022, verification of interview many years before. He was a pastor at a number of A.M.E. churches in Indiana. The church in which he grew up was in Richmond, and he was two years younger than Timmy.

In addition, during early research, a meeting was held at Bethel A.M.E. Church in Richmond. It was set up by Mary Jo Flood, who was the church secretary at the time. The date has been lost, but in a 2022 phone conversation she recalled the meeting, at which some parishioners who had known Timmy were present.

Publications:

The (Richmond) Palladium-Item, April 25, 26, 28, 29, May 1, 2, coverage of the Starks shooting, and Nov. 12, 1976, on Bethel A.M.E. Church.

Books:

Dahan, Charles B., and Linda Gennett Irmscher, "Gennett Records and Starr Piano" (Charleston, S.C.: Arcadia Publishing, 2016).

Lutholz, M. William, "Grand Dragon: D.C. Stephenson and the Ku Klux Klan of Indiana" (West Lafayette, Ind.: Purdue University Press, 1993).

Chapter 2: A New Home at the Home

Timmy and Della provided much information about life at the Indiana Soldiers' and Sailors' Children's Home and the Brown family. Information on the history of the Home, layout of buildings and property, roster of admitted students, subjects studied, activities ranging from sports to plays, and more came from the Indiana State Archives, the Morton Memorial Retrospect Yearbook, and the files of the Knightstown Banner, as well as a visit to the site of the home and a letter from Earl Lambert.

Information in the Brown files included a scrapbook and notes, such as the one outlining his assignment by Almeda Garriott. The Indiana State Archives' Oversight Committee on Public Records provided documentation of his attendance, coursework, grades, total credits earned, class rank, aptitude and ability test records, citizenship and character rating, honors, and guidance information and recommendations. A record of admissions for the Home lists the name, age, date of birth, father's name, mother's name, company and regiment in which father enlisted, rank, date of admission, and city, and provides a space for remarks. All information was hand-written. In the column for remarks, any non-white student has the word "colored" in parentheses.

Book:

Butler, William D., "One Sports Fan Left Behind: Foul Me Out of the Ball Game" (Bloomington, Ind.: Author House, 2011). In his book, half biography and half an argument against modern-day sports, Bill Butler tells of attending Senior Day with Timmy and their meeting at a skating rink in Rushville.

Chapter 3: Having a Ball with the Ball at Ball State

The 1955 to 1959 issues of the Ball State News, the Orient yearbook, the College Bulletin, the 1959 Commencement Program, and other university information, such as hours and fees, were reviewed in the Ball State University Libraries Digital Media Repository. Copies of the B-Book (a student directory that included addresses, year in school, and home city), as well as Timmy's work schedule, were accessed in the Ball State Archives and Special Collections at the Bracken Library. Athletic events and accomplishments were detailed in a file on Timmy provided by the Ball State Athletic Department; by issues of the Muncie Star, Muncie Evening Press, and Ball State News; and by official game programs. An official transcript showing credits, courses, grades, major, and testing record was obtained by Timmy on his first visit to campus, and was shared with the writing team.

Interviews:

Baird, William. Apr. 23, 2013.
Campbell, Dean. Oct. 17, 2019.
Campbell, Larry. Aug.7, 2022, verification of earlier interview.
Campbell, Wayne. Aug. 7, 2022, verification of earlier interview.
Floyd, A.B. Oct. 27, 2021.
Hannaford, Beck. Aug. 13, 2022.
Hutson, Dick. Oct. 7, 2014.
Mikesell, Don. March 12, 2018.
O'Neal, William. [n.d.]
Snyder, Paul. Oct. 18. 2014.
Thompkins, Aaron. Apr. 15, 2013.
Warren, Anne. Apr. 7, 2013.

Papers:

Goodall, Hurley, "Desegregation of Tuhey Swimming Pool" (unpublished manuscript, 1993).

Preston, Bryan, "'These Covenants Are to Run With the Land': The Hidden History of Housing Segregation in Muncie, Indiana" (published on Medium, 2017).

Books:

Edmonds, Anthony O., and E. Bruce Geelhoed, "Ball State University: An Interpretive History" (Bloomington, Ind.: Indiana University Press, 2001).

McCabe, Larry, "'Lar'-on-the-Air'" (New York: Goldtouch Press LLC, 2022).

Chapter 4: Playing Isn't Everything

Information from the Brown files included contracts and letters.

The information on Timmy's initial contact with Jack Vainisi came from a telegram from Vainisi to Ball State, provided by the Ball State athletics office.

Much of the information on Timmy's brief career with the Green Bay Packers came from the Green Bay Press-Gazette, including a special football preview issue published on Sept. 25, 1960. The Press-Gazette's daily coverage included many anecdotes, such as the call for local entertainers to play at the kickoff dinner because the Packers' band charged too much money.

Stories in the Muncie Star, Muncie Evening Press, and Ball State News for the period were also consulted, as were those in the Bangor Daily News covering the only NFL game ever played in Maine.

Vince Lombardi talked about his decision to cut Timmy in an article published in the Sept. 19, 1967, issue of Look magazine, "Secrets of Winning Football," co-written with W.C. Heinz, and republished in "Lombardi: A Dynasty Remembered" by Mike Bynum (Green Bay: Athlon Sports, 1994).

Interview:

Skaletski, Roger, Dec. 13, 2021. The longtime Green Bay resident shared information on where Black players on the team lived in 1959, the haircut incident with Timmy, the training camp at St. Norbert, and the nature of the Green Bay community at that time.

Books:

Christl, Cliff, "A Championship Team: The Packers and St. Norbert College in the Lombardi Years" (De Pere, Wis: St. Norbert College Press, 2010).

Eisenberg, John, "That First Season: How Vince Lombardi Took the Worst Team in the NFL and Set It on the Path to Glory (Boston: Houghton Mifflin Harcourt, 2009). Eisenberg spoke to Timmy in 2009, and included information from that interview. Throughout his life, Timmy gave a number of versions of his first conversation with Lombardi; the chapter uses the one he gave to Eisenberg.

Maraniss, David, "When Pride Still Mattered: A Life of Vince Lombardi" (New York: Simon & Schuster, 1999).

Swain, Glenn, "Packers vs. Bears: The Story of Pro Football's Oldest Rivalry" (Los Angeles: Charles Publishing, 1966).

Wagner, Len, "Launching the Glory Years: The 1959 Packers" (Green Bay: Coach's Books L.L.C.).

Chapter 5: The City of Brotherly Football and Music

Information from the Brown files included letters from the Eagles to Timmy and his air travel information from 1961, his contract with Mercury Records, a program for the Bucks County Playhouse production of "A Thurber Carnival," his mail conversation with Cleveland students, and a copy of the December 1963 Home Journal detailing the visit that Timmy and Ted Dean made to Knightstown on Dec. 20.

Information on Ember Records is from an entry, "Al Silver," on the website "TIMS This Is My Story," described as "collected by Dik de Heer for [Shakin All_Over]."

Information on the United Football League came from Wikipedia. The league is not to be confused with the 2009-12 United Football League, or the United Football League that is to launch as a spring league in 2023.

Information on Georgia Malick's career came from the website of the Hagley Museum and Library and the website liquisearch.com's list of Miss New Jersey winners.

Information on Timmy's 1960s recordings came from the website Discogs.

Publications:

Timmy's career with the Philadelphia Eagles was covered extensively in the sports sections of the three Philadelphia dailies at that time, the Inquirer, the Daily News, and the Evening Bulletin. Clippings from those newspapers (and others) from 1961 through 1969 concerning Timmy were examined at what was then the library (or, in newspaper slang, morgue) of the Inquirer and Daily News. After the newspapers were sold and their physical space downsized, the files were donated to Temple University to be added to its Urban Archive, where they may be viewed today. Online databases – philadelphiaeagles.com, pro-football-reference.com, and profootballacrhives.com – also were consulted.

A Daily News column of Sept. 22, 1972, contained an anecdote about Timmy and Diana Ross, and the mention of Hy Lit in an article by Time's Richard Corliss was cited in a Feb. 9, 2014, article by Inquirer columnist Clark DeLeon.

Much of the information on record names and chart history came from the files of Billboard magazine. In addition, the July 4, 1964, issue reviewed a live performance by Timmy.

An ESPN/NFL video on "Renaissance Men of the NFL," in which Timmy was featured because of his success on the gridiron, singing, acting, and modeling, was given to the writing team by him.

In addition:

The Indianapolis Star, Dec. 28, 1960, and a Nov. 11, 1964, sports cartoon, "The Eagle Sings."

Sports Illustrated, Jan. 9, 1961. Also, Nov. 25, 2013, "And the Games Went On," by Tim Layden, which discusses Pete Rozelle's decision to play football games after the assassination of John F. Kennedy and the turmoil in the Eagles locker room that weekend.

The Evansville Courier, Dec. 8, 1961.

The New York Times, Nov. 26, 28, 1962; Oct. 5, 6, 14, 1964.

The Sporting News, Dec. 8, 1962, and Oct. 15, 1966.

(Wilmington) Evening Journal, Jan. 7, 1963.

New York World-Telegram, Aug. 16, 1963.

The Washington Post, Oct. 10, 1963, and Oct. 29, 1965, columns by Shirley Povich.

(Camden) Courier-Post, April 13, 1964. This story states that Timmy was an usher at Chubby Checker's wedding, not best man, as Timmy and Checker have stated.

The Indianapolis News, Oct. 6 and 13, 1964.

Jet Magazine, Oct. 5, 1967.

Playboy, February 1968 issue.

The (Cleveland) Plain Dealer, May 27, 2010.

The Bradenton Herald, Dec. 10, 2015.

Books:

Brown, Jim, with Steve Delsohn, "From Out of Bounds" (New York, Citadel Press Books, Kensington Publishing Corp., 1989).

Butler's "One Sports Fan Left Behind."

Daughen, Joseph R., and Peter Binzen, "The Wreck of the Penn Central" (New York: Beard Books, 1999)

Didinger, Ray, and Robert S. Lyons, "The Eagles Encyclopedia" (Philadelphia: Temple University Press, 2005).

Gordon, Bob, "The 1960 Philadelphia Eagles: The Team That They Said Had Nothing But a Championship" (Champaign, Ill.: Sports Publishing L.L.C., 2000)

Maxymuk, John, "Eagles by the Numbers: Jersey Numbers and the Players Who Wore Them (Philadelphia: Camino Books Inc., 2006)

Maxymuk, John, "Eagles Facts and Trivia: Puzzlers for the Bird-Brained (Philadelphia: Camino Books Inc., 2007)

Ribowsky, Mark, "The Supremes: A Saga of Motown Dreams, Success and Betrayal" (Cambridge, Mass.: Da Capo Press, 2010).

Chapter 6: Fly, Timmy, Fly

Information from the Brown files included letters from the Robert F. Kennedy presidential campaign to Timmy; a scrapbook showing his apartment at Society Hill Towers, dated April 23, 1967, titled "Welcome to My Housewarming, 'EL,'" referring to his use of "El Cid" as a nickname; copies of Jantzen ads showing Timmy with other pro athletes; and a copy of a Nov. 19, 1965, Department of the Army notice to report to reserve training, a May 24, 1966, "Discharge from United States Army Reserve," and an Honorable Discharge certificate dated May 30, 1966. Information on John Brown Jr.'s role with the RFK campaign came from the textual archives of the John F. Kennedy Presidential Library and Museum.

Copies of letters from Ball State committees, administrators, and others that enabled Timmy to obtain his bachelor's degree were obtained from Bracken Library Archives.

Interviews:

Lewis, Robert, and Mallas, Dave, August 2022. Lewis, sports information specialist at Pasadena City College, and Mallas, athletic director at Los Angeles Valley Community College, provided information on Rick Whitfield's college athletic career.

Publications:

In addition to the newspapers cited for Chapter 5, the online files of the Baltimore Sun were consulted for coverage of every Colts game in 1969-70.

(Philadelphia) Catholic Standard & Times, July 9, 1965.

Sports Illustrated, Sept. 13, 1965, and Sept. 12, 1966, pro football preview issues, articles on the Eagles. Nov. 10, 1966, article by Mark Kram about Baltimore. May 7, 1968, George Kiseda's track dash against Diana Ross.

The Indianapolis News, Nov. 8, 1965, and Oct. 28, 1990

The New York Times, Oct. 15, 19, Dec. 2, 22, 1965; Jan. 27, Aug. 20, Oct. 24, Nov. 7, Dec. 12, 1966; July 23, Aug. 11, 20, 21, 1967; March 7, 1968. The Oct. 15 story by William N. Wallace describes how the Eagles set up a four-pass-receiver formation to isolate Timmy against a single linebacker, and also expresses amazement that anyone would buy his recordings. Timmy's work with Seth Riggs is covered in the Aug. 20 story.

New York Herald Tribune, Paris Edition, Nov. 8, 1966, "Timmy Brown: The Loneliness of the NFL Runner," by Phil Pepe.

Sport Magazine, December 1967, "Dressed Right for Sport: Timmy Brown."

The (Baltimore) Evening Sun, Aug. 20, 1968. In this column, writer Doug Brown named the three coaches who had told Timmy that the Giants had offered nine players for him as Allie Sherman, Ken Kavanaugh, and Em Tunnell.

The Indianapolis Star, Oct. 10, 1968.

New York Daily News, Nov. 5, 1968.

A 1968 column by Leonard Lewin in the New York Post, "The Senator and the Big O," provided information on athletes supporting Sen. Robert F. Kennedy's presidential campaign.

Ball State Daily News, Dec. 4 and 5, 1969, "Ex Card Tim Brown quits pro ball" and "NFL will remember Tim Brown," by Paul Berebitsky.

The (Richmond) Palladium-Item, April 26, 1984.

A story by Melissa Isaacson of the Orlando Sentinel, published in the Muncie Evening Press of June 27. 1987, contained information about his knee injury and treatment beginning in the 1960s.

Atlantic City Press, Sept. 27, 1992.

Obituaries for Timmy with information on his career included ones on April 7, 2020, in the Inquirer and Daily News, by Les Bowen; in The Philadelphia Tribune, by Daryl Bell; on PhiladelphiaEagles.com, by Ray Didinger; and on April 8, in the (Delaware County) Daily Times, by Bob Grotz.

Books:

Didinger and Lyons, "The Eagles Encyclopedia."

Ford, Mark L., "A History of NFL Preseason and Exhibition Games 1960 to 1965" (Lanham, Md.: Rowman & Littlefield, 2014).

Frank, Reuben, and Mark Eckel, "Game Changers: The Greatest Plays in Philadelphia Eagles Football History" (Chicago: Triumph Books, 2009).

Gordon, Robert, "Game of My Life: Philadelphia Eagles: Memorable Stories of Eagles Football" (Champaign, Ill.: Sports Publishing L.L.C., 2007).

Maxymuk, "Eagles by the Numbers" and "Eagles Facts and Trivia."

Chapter 7: A Star Rises, and then Falls

Information from the Brown files included note cards from the Estelle Harman Actors Workshop classes; documentation of his charitable activities and career with the Los Angeles County Probation Department, including his medical benefit election form, resume, the posting of the position by the department; commendatory letters from the department, two school districts, and an AIDS charity; and correspondence regarding Timmy's lawsuit against the Eagles and Colts.

Information on specific movies and TV shows such as release dates, cast, and crew came from the website IMDb. One of the authors reviewed every episode of a TV program in which Timmy appeared that could be found online, such as his guest-starring roles on "Mission: Impossible" and "The Mary Tyler Moore Show."

Comments by Jamie Farr, Ring Lardner Jr., and Gene Reynolds came from interviews available on the website "Television Academy Foundation: The Interviews."

Information on Jerry Ragovoy's rediscovery of Howard Tate came from the NPR program "Fresh Air" on Oct. 27, 2003.

Publications:

Philadelphia Daily News, Sept. 22, 1972, and Sept. 10, 2003.

The Philadelphia Tribune, Sept. 27 and Oct. 3, 1972.

Ladies' Home Journal, December 1972 issue.

Los Angeles Times, April 25, 1973.

The Philadelphia Inquirer, June 17, 1973.

The New York Times, July 1, 1973, and June 12, 1975.

Burlington County Times, Aug. 9, 1975.

Newsweek, June 30, 1975.

Ebony, November 2005 issue, "Lights, Camera & the Black Role in Movies," by Melvin Van Peebles.

Cinema Journal, Summer 2011 issue, "From Exhibition to Genre: The Case of Grind-House Films," by David Church.

Books:

Brown's "Out of Bounds" contains anecdotes about Timmy, Jim Brown, and Fred Williamson clubbing, and includes the reference to "secondary women."

Hooker, Richard. "M*A*S*H" (Mattituck, N.Y.: Rivercity Press, a division of American Reprint Co., 1976). In the foreword of this reprint, Hornberger says he based Hawkeye Pierce on himself. The forewords in some earlier versions do not state that. The book was originally published by William Morrow.

Kalter, Suzy, "The Complete Book of M*A*S*H" (New York: Harry N. Abrams Inc., 1988).

Lawrence, Novotny, "Blaxploitation Films of the 1970s: Blackness and

Genre" (New York: Routledge, 2008).
Stuart, Jan, "The Nashville Chronicles: The Making of Robert Altman's Masterpiece" (New York: Limelight Editions, 2003).
Whitburn, Joel, "Joel Whitburn Presents Top Pop Singles," 17th edition, Volume 1: 1955-1989 (Menomonee Falls, Wis: Record Research Inc., 2021).

Chapter 8: Friends and Family

Information from the Brown files included contracts and travel documents for Lee Hartley's job in Japan; the music and words for the promotional jingle for Bobby Bell's Barbecue restaurants that Timmy sang; the program for the 1987 Volunteer of the Year event of the Probation Department; a list of graduates at the Juvenile Counselor Core Graduation Ceremony; appointment date and employee information for the Probation Department job; correspondence, contracts, and thank-you notes for Timmy's work with Goals for Youth, Goals for Life, and other consulting and volunteer work; a copy of the divorce papers for Timmy and Lee; and a video of the Nov. 25, 1990, Eagles Honor Roll ceremony.

Information regarding people attending Gene Kilroy's birthday party, in addition to his interview, came from online sources, including the New-York Historical Society description of the exhibit "Muhammad Ali, LeRoy Neiman, and the Art of Boxing."

Information on John Brown Jr.'s career came from the Northwestern University Library; The Sacramento Bee, Aug. 13, 1980; and "A History of Policies and Forces Shaping California Teacher Credentialing" (Sacramento, Calif.: California Commission on Teacher Credentialing, 2011).

A video of the 1990 Hall of Fame induction was given by Timmy to the writing team.

Publications:

The Kansas City Star, March 3, 1987, and April 7, 1991.

Philadelphia Daily News, Sept. 27 and Nov. 26, 1990.
Los Angeles Times, Sept. 17, 1992, and Jan. 29, 1996.
The Philadelphia Inquirer, March 22, 2022. This is the column by Mike Sielski in which Sean discusses his father's decline.

Chapter 9: Reeling in the Years

Information from the Brown files included the lease agreement for the Mesquite condo in Palm Springs and the letter from Earl Lambert regarding the 50th anniversary of the Morton Memorial Class of 1955 from Brown files.

Description of the Northridge earthquake came from a City of Los Angeles webpage posted Jan. 17, 1994.

Chapter 10: All We Will Remember

Information from the Brown files included a letter from the office of the Riverside County Asssessor-County Clerk-Recorder indicating location, date of purchase, and assessment for the Palm Springs Tennis Club timeshare; a copy of letters concerning the NFL Hall of Fame; an Aug. 22, 2007 letter from Eagles chairman/CEO Jeffrey Lurie to Timmy informing him that he had been selected as a member of the 75th Anniversary Team and would be recognized on Sept. 23 at the 1 p.m. home game against the Detroit Lions; a copy of Plan 88; cards describing the cruises that Timmy and Henderson took (along with photos); the Alzheimer's pamphlet; and a program for Chubby Checker's March 2014 Sun City performance.

The date of death of Mary Lee Henderson came from a post by Sean Brown. Of Timmy's family members, dates of death were obtained from: Juanita and Norma, from the Brown files; Anita, from Ancestry.com; Betty and John Sr., from research by Jane Beers of the Clay Township Historical Society; John Jr., from the Northwestern University Archives. Beers also confirmed the dates for all except Anita and John Jr.

A video of Timmy's presentation "Race, Sports, and Society" was taken during his visit to Ball State and a copy given to the writing team.

Information on the 2010 recognition of 1960 Eagles team came from a philadelphiaeagles.com post March 3, 2010, and a copy of the video "A Championship Season: The Philadelphia Eagles," that Timmy gave to the writing team.

Roy Weaver and David Sullivan attended the Philadelphia Sports Hall of Fame induction event in 2016 and obtained the programs there.

Information about Desert Ensemble Theater Company plays in which Sean performed came from online programs and reviews. He performed at the Palm Springs Cultural Center, the Palm Canyon Theatre, and the Pearl McManus Theatre. A review of his performance by Stan Jenson was posted on the Broadway World website on April 20, 2019.

Publications:

Philadelphia Daily News, April 7, 2006.

Ball State Alumnus, November 2006 issue, "A Reunion of Friends," by Laura Ford.

Ball State Daily News, Nov. 8, 2010.

The (Palm Springs) Desert Sun, Feb. 26, 2012, describes the BookPALS program and Timmy's role in it.

The Philadelphia Inquirer, May 17, 2020.

Books:

Fainaru-Wada, Mark, and Steve Fainaru, "League of Denial: The NFL, Concussions and the Battle for Truth" (New York: Three Rivers Press, 2013).

Jacobs, Gil, and Joe Agro, "The Singer's Drummer" (Bloomington, Ind.: Author House, 2013).

Acknowledgements

This book would not have been possible without the extraordinary support of Lee Hartley, Sean Brown, Jennifer Van Camp, Ernie Butler, Jeff Gerrard and Desirée Boschetti, Gene Kilroy, Grayce Shadd, Hollie Vest, and Rick Whitfield in providing details of Timmy's life. Again and again in the uncertain times after the arrival of COVID-19, while Timmy's death was still near in their hearts and minds, they were contacted to answer questions raised in the writing or editing of the manuscript with specific dates, activities, and comments, or provide written or photographic documentation. In addition, Lee and Sean made available without restriction box after box full of papers, photos, and memorabilia that Timmy had kept, in some cases doing so without having any clear idea what would be found in them. Like Timmy, they wanted the true story of his life told, whatever that story turned out to be.

The support of the following people from Ball State University was instrumental in developing and completing this book:

Julie Eiser, for transcription of taped interviews and other support. Joey Narramore, for transcription of most of the taped interviews. Master's graduate assistants Kasey Middleton (2017-18, 2018-19) and Carly Yoder (2017-18), and doctoral assistant Alberta Morgan (2010-11), for research support.

Becky Marangelli, archives specialist, Alexander M. Bracken Library.

Krista Stith, director of the Teachers College Center for Gifted

Studies Talent Development, author of "How to Keep an Owl Dry in the Rain," and co-author of "Leadership in Integrative STEM Education: Collaborative Strategies for Facilitating an Experiential and Student-Centered Culture," who provided guidance for all aspects of the self-publishing process.

Matthew Stuve, associate professor of educational psychology, and senior Kalyn Melham, studying English and professional writing, who helped brainstorm strategies for promoting the biography and engaging readers through website development and social media.

In addition:

Jayne Beilke, former chair of the Department of Educational Studies, for faculty research support providing assigned time to work on this biography; Emma Crunley, associate director of athletics and director of athletics development; Jim Duckham, director of public safety; Chris Flook, senior lecturer of media and local historian; E. Bruce Geelhoed, professor of history; Greg Graham, director of facilities planning, and Susan Johnson, staff architect; Joe Hernandez, retired associate athletics director for sports and alumni relations; Edward Krzemienski, associate teaching professor of history; Deborah Linegar, senior director of special events and foundation board relations; Don Park, former vice president of university advancement, and a classmate of Timmy's; Charlotte Shepperd, former director of alumni communications; and Michael Szajewski, former assistant dean for digital scholarship and special collections; and Donald Williams, copyright and scholarly communications manager, Bracken Library.

Also aiding the cause:

Jayne Beers, president of the Clay Township Historical and Preservation Society in Indiana, who provided contacts for some interviews and research, as well as the dates of John Brown Sr.'s death.

Bonita Brewer, widow of Home basketball coach Bill Brewer, and Home administrators who met with Timmy and Roy during their tour of the Home.

Stacey Chandler, archivist, John F. Kennedy Presidential Library and Museum, Boston, Mass.

Sally Childs-Helton, head, Special Collections, Rare Books, and University Archives, and Evan Miller, archives associate, Irwin Library, Butler University, Indianapolis.

Cliff Christl, historian, and Brent Hensel, Hall of Fame curator, Green Bay Packers, for providing a photo of Vince Lombardi and his wife, Marie, arriving at the airport in Green Bay in 1959.

Dave Cox, president, Meeks Mortuary, Muncie.

William C. Daw, associate curator, Curtis Theatre Collection, Hillman Library, University of Pittsburgh.

Martin George, owner of The Cup coffee shop, Muncie.

Mary Jane Herber, local historian and special collections manager, Brown County Library, Green Bay, who gave hours of support in finding books and Press-Gazette articles covering the time Timmy was with the Packers.

Catie Huggins, public services coordinator, Charles Deering McCormick Library of Special Collections and Archives, Northwestern University Libraries, Evanston, Ill.

Mandee Huenzle, senior marketing and communications manager, Bucks County Playhouse, New Hope, Pa.

Steve Liebowitz, speaker and host, Creative Rhythm, Owings Mills, Md.

Matthew Lutts of AP Images, New York, who assisted in obtaining a photo of Timmy taking a voice lesson from Carmine Gagliardi at his New York studio in October 1965.

John and Juli Metzger, The JMetzger Group, Muncie, who scanned and digitized photos used for the biography. In addition, they provided guidance for creating a website and using social media to drive interest and traffic in advance of and after its publication.

Michael Panzer, then-director of news research at the Inquirer and Daily News, who helped sort through the paper's clip files of the three

Philadelphia dailies plus New York newspapers.

Amy Proulx, Getty Images, Seattle, who assisted in obtaining a cover photo of Timmy Brown wearing No. 22 in Eagles green from the 1967 season, his last with the team.

Michael P. Smith, a Ball State graduate, former faculty member at Northwestern University, longtime friend of Roy and Marilyn, and former classmate of David, who obtained the date of death for John Brown Jr., which had eluded the authors for months. He also met with Gene Kilroy and Hollie Vest in Las Vegas.

James R. Williams, Esq., of DeFur Voran, Muncie, who offered legal counsel, interest in the biography, and encouragement.

Additional thanks are due to John D. Wilson, president of the Rush County Historical Society; Suellen Reed, former Indiana state superintendent for public instruction and a long-time Rush County resident; Jim and J.P. Lutz of the Bucks County Baseball Co. in Bristol, Pa.; and all those mentioned above as having been interviewed.

After the book was completed, the next problem was to publish it. Amy Junod, a former page designer and graphic artist at the Inquirer, provided her expertise in layout, typography, and picture presentation in creating the actual book. She also gave much-needed help in deciding on photo credits and captions, as well as photo selection.

Amy, who had been down the book publishing road before, also recommended that we obtain endorsements to go on the cover. For this, we turned to Kilroy, a former casino and Eagles executive, and business manager for Muhammad Ali; Ray Didinger, longtime Eagles beat writer for the Daily News; and Dee Dee Sharp, the legendary R&B singer. We thank them for their words of support.

And then, we needed a foreword. No one could be better for this than Merrill Reese, a Philadelphia native and legend, who has called the play-by-play on radio for the Eagles since 1977 and is the longest-tenured announcer in the NFL. Merrill has followed the Eagles since he was a child in the 1950s and remembers well the thrill of seeing Timmy taking off on a downfield run. Thanks also are due to Lloyd Zane Remick, Esq., and Stephen Vanyo, Esq., of the Law Offices of Lloyd Z. Remick in Philadelphia.

From inception to completion, work on this book covered 14 years, with a few years in the middle of that period when not as much was done. Over that length of time, notes can be lost, and memories fade. To anyone else who aided in the development of this book and who is not mentioned, we apologize for the omission.

Finally, with us over those 14 years, putting up with our obsessions, phone calls, and distractions, were our wives, Marilyn Weaver, Tanya Sriver, and Betsy Anderson. As noted earlier, Marilyn, a longtime journalism educator, participated in part of the interview process and proofread the entire manuscript. Betsy, a former newspaper reporter and communications director for nonprofits, honed many rough edges off Chapters 8 through 10. And Tanya, who has enjoyed a long career as a data analyst in the student loan industry, enjoyed, or at least loyally appeared to, hearing the many stories about Timmy. Their forbearance is appreciated more than they can ever know, although of course they will think of ways we can make it up to them.

About the Authors

Timmy with Roy and Marilyn Weaver at one of Timmy's favorite restaurants in Palm Desert, Calif., on Sept. 6, 2016.

Roy Weaver retired in 2020 as interim dean of Teachers College, Ball State University, after completing a third consecutive year as interim. He spent a significant part of his life at the university. Upon completing a teaching degree there in English in 1968, he taught for a year at Kettering East High School in Kettering, Ohio, then returned to teach for four years at Muncie Central High School while completing a master's degree in curriculum at Ball State. Then he spent two years at Indiana University, where he completed a doctorate in curriculum. From 1975 to 1980, he taught at the University of Southern California. He then returned to Ball State. He first served as a faculty member in the Center for Lifelong Education, then for a decade was associate dean of Teachers College, followed by 16 years as dean, returning to faculty in 2009. His academic research and writing focused on long-range planning, school choice, curriculum innovation, and technology. For his leadership and service to the university, in 2021 he received the Teachers College Career Achievement Award and the Ball State University Alumni Association's Distinguished Alumni Award. Key attributes for working on this biography included, like Timmy, being an impulsive Gemini, dreamer, jokester, teacher, football and music fan, father, and movie and popcorn lover. He and his wife, Marilyn, live in Muncie, Ind.

David Sullivan with Timmy at the Philadelphia Sports Hall of Fame induction ceremony on Nov. 12, 2015.

David Sullivan retired in 2020 as assistant managing editor, editing and standards for The Philadelphia Inquirer, a position he had held since 2012. He started at the paper as a copy editor on the Metro desk in 1983 and worked on the Sports, Features, Neighbors, and Metro desks until becoming assistant managing editor, copy desks, in 2001. Before working at the Inquirer, he had been a reporter and editor at The Palladium-Item in Richmond, Ind., and two newspapers in Michigan, The Ypsilanti Press and The Flint Journal. While working for the Inquirer, he led workshops on better editing and headline writing at newspapers in Georgia, Illinois, Indiana, North Carolina, Ontario, and Pennsylvania. He served as president of the Greater Philadelphia Pro Chapter, Society of Professional Journalists, and as a board member, secretary, and vice president of ACES: The Society for Editing, a national organization with nearly 5,000 members. A native of Indianapolis, he is a 1975 graduate of Ball State University, of which he was named outstanding journalism alumnus in 2011. He also is a historian of department stores, and wrote the entry on that subject in the Encyclopedia of Greater Philadelphia. Until working on this book, he never paid much attention to pro football; now, he bleeds Eagles green. He and his wife, Betsy Anderson, live in Moorestown, N.J.

Shawn Sriver with Timmy for an interview
at Teachers College, Ball State University, on Oct. 2, 2010.

Shawn Sriver is the accreditation and assessment coordinator of Teachers College, Ball State University. A proud 1979 Rochester (Ind.) High School graduate, Shawn earned his associate's degree at Vincennes University in 1981 and bachelor's degree at Indiana University in 1985. He earned a master's degree in secondary education at Indiana University-Purdue University at Indianapolis in 1991. He taught English at Bremen (Ind.) High School, where he was named Teacher of the Year in 1989, and was invited by the 1989 senior class to give the keynote speech at their commencement. He then taught English and journalism at Hamilton Southeastern High School in Fishers, Ind. He worked for 17 years at the Indiana Department of Education, spending the last four years as director of the Division of Professional Standards, which dealt with the licensing and testing of educators for the State of Indiana. In 2009, he was named accreditation and assessment coordinator for Ball State. Shawn is a historian of the golden age of rock, soul, and country music (1950-99), as well as television and film. He is also an NFL fanatic. He and his wife, Tanya, live in Fishers, Ind.

Made in the USA
Columbia, SC
13 January 2023

91a4ed11-14c8-48da-bda0-36c319760876R03